C0-APO-995

ADVANCES IN INDUSTRIAL AND LABOR RELATIONS

Volume 4 · 1987

ADVANCES IN INDUSTRIAL AND LABOR RELATIONS

A Research Annual

Editors: DAVID LEWIN
Graduate School of Business
Columbia University

DAVID B. LIPSKY
New York State School of
Industrial and Labor Relations
Cornell University

DONNA SOCKELL
Graduate School of Business
Columbia University

VOLUME 4 · 1987

Greenwich, Connecticut *London, England*

55 Old Post Road, No. 2
Greenwich, Connecticut 06836

JAI PRESS LTD.
3 Henrietta Street
London WC2E 8LU
England

ISBN: 0-89232-909-2

Manufactured in the United States of America

CONTENTS

LIST OF CONTRIBUTORS

Deborah Gladstein Ancona	Alfred P. Sloan School of Management Massachusetts Institute of Technology
Julian Barling	Department of Psychology Queen's University Canada
Ann P. Bartel	Graduate School of Business Columbia University
David E. Caldwell	Leavey School of Business and Administration Santa Clara University
Daniel B. Cornfield	Department of Sociology and Anthropology Vanderbilt University
Jack Fiorito	Department of Industrial Relations and Human Resources The University of Iowa
Clive Fullagar	Department of Psychology The University of Witwatersrand South Africa
Wallace E. Hendricks	Institute of Labor and Industrial Relations The University of Illinois

David C. Jacobs	Kogod College of Business Administration The American University
Marianne Koch	Graduate School of Business Columbia University
David Lewin	Graduate School of Business Columbia University
Frank R. Lichtenberg	Graduate School of Business Columbia University
Marick F. Masters	Graduate School of Business The University of Pittsburgh
Mark R. Peterson	Graduate School of Business Administration The University of Washington
Richard B. Peterson	Graduate School of Business Administration The University of Washington
Donna Sockell	Graduate School of Business Columbia University
Asghar Zardkoohi	College of Business Administration Texas A & M University

PREFACE

Like the previous volumes in this series, Volume 4 well demonstrates that the field of industrial relations embraces a wide variety of issues, scholarly disciplines, and research methodologies. This volume contains studies of unions as institutions, dispute resolution procedures, the distribution of human capital in selected industries, the organization of work, and the unionization and collective bargaining processes. The authors are labor economists, sociologists, psychologists, and institutionalists; the methodologies they have employed vary in techniques for gathering data—including field research, examination of secondary data, and literature reviews—and in the type of analysis, including qualitative and quantitative, descriptive and predictive treatments.

The first four chapters in this volume deal with aspects of the union as an institution. In the first chapter, "The Characteristics of National Unions," Jack Fiorito and Wallace E. Hendricks attempt to identify the key characteristics that distinguish unions from one another. To do this, the authors have amassed a most interesting and unusual data set on the characteristics of more than 150 unions. Those data, on more than 50 diverse characteristics of unions, were pieced together from previous research, government documents and other publications, and union constitutions. In addition, to consolidate those characteristics into a smaller, more manageable set, Fiorito and Hendricks conduct a factor analysis. Their findings represent perhaps the most comprehensive cross-sectional information yet gathered on individual unions. Therefore, they are likely to be of great interest to scholars who seek to explain a variety of unionization and collective bargaining phenomena.

The next chapter is a study by Clive Fullager and Julian Barling entitled "Toward a Model of Union Commitment." Here, by reviewing and synthesizing previous research on commitment, the authors construct a conceptual framework comprising the antecedents and consequences of union commitment. This study may encourage other organizational psychologists to use their special expertise to study industrial relations questions of interest to both scholars and practitioners. Indeed, unions themselves may find this research useful as they attempt to develop approaches to retain members and reverse the tide of recent representation election losses.

The following two chapters focus on aspects of unions in the United States that have periodically been neglected in the literature. Preoccupied with the characteristics of true "business unionism," many scholars have overlooked two important facts: many U.S. unions have long been involved in politics, and some unions have devoted considerable resources to addressing social issues which affect all workers, not just union members. Recently, a few scholars have turned their attention to describing and explaining the political activities of unions. "Labor Unions and the U.S. Congress: PAC Allocations and Legislative Voting," by Marick F. Masters and Asghar Zardkoohi, is a comprehensive review and extension of that emerging research. The authors document the recent rise in the number of political action committees (PACs), contributions to PACs, and lobbying staffs of unions. Moreover, they attempt to find systematic explanations for variation in PAC allocations across congressional representatives elected in 1982 and across votes cast by members of the House of Representatives on specific legislation.

Dovetailing nicely with Masters and Zardkoohi's study is "The UAW and the Committee for National Health Insurance: The Contours of Social Unionism," by David C. Jacobs. Here the author explores the United Automobile Workers' campaign for national health insurance and its participation in the Committee for National Health Insurance, which the UAW founded. Although this descriptive study does not suggest or demonstrate that unions frequently employ strategies that unite the interests of all trade unionists, workers, and the poor (which Jacobs defines as "operational social unionism"), it does indicate that not all unions conform to the rigid behavioral and ideological attributes of business unionism.

In the next chapter, the focus of the volume shifts. In "Toward a Systematic Understanding of the Labor Mediation Process," Richard B. Peterson and Mark R. Peterson review the research on mediation to provide a better understanding of the role of mediation in labor negotiations. Because, as their review indicates, there is much we do not know, or agree upon, about the mediation process, this chapter should encourage and help guide much-needed research on mediation.

The last four chapters in this volume are products of a one-day conference entitled "Employment Problems in the Information Age," held at Columbia University on June 12, 1985. Sponsored and funded by the university's Research Project in Telecommunications, which is under the direction of Professor Eli Noam, the conference was conceived of as an interdisciplinary effort to examine employment issues encountered by firms and industries that use and develop microprocessing technology—a subset of the high-technology sector. In the first chapter from that conference, "The Skill Distribution and the Competitive Trade Advantage of High-Technology Industries," Ann P. Bartel and Frank R. Lichtenberg seek to address several critical questions about high-technology industries, including what determines whether an industry is part of the high-technology sector; what are the characteristics of industries in that sector; and finally, what do we know about the employees in high-technology firms. The authors also discuss which high-technology sectors are particularly important to international trade. To address these questions, they have pulled together unusual data from a variety of sources.

In the next chapter Daniel B. Cornfield examines the potential for unionization among female clerical workers in the insurance industry—an industry that has been a pioneer in office automation. In "Women in the Automated Office: Computers, Work, and Prospects for Unionization," Cornfield seeks to identify the forces that will likely motivate, facilitate, and inhibit unionization of this group of white-collar workers. This paper offers some useful insights into the potential for unionization among other classes of workers in industries using or developing microprocessing technology.

Work and organization design and the management of work are critical to how a high-technology firm operates and how successful it is. In "Management Issues Facing New-Product Teams in High-Technology Companies," Deborah Gladstein Ancona and David F. Caldwell examine a key issue of organizational behavior in the high-technology sector, namely, managing the effectiveness of new-product teams. The authors' basic premise is that boundary management critically affects product team performance. Their more than 135 hours of interviews with managers and team participants at seven high-technology firms serve as the data base for investigating that relationship.

The last of the conference papers, and the final chapter in this volume, is a study of bargaining structure by Marianne Koch, David Lewin, and Donna Sockell. In "The Determinants of Bargaining Structure: A Case Study of AT&T," the authors review the existing literature on bargaining structure to guide them through an explanation of historical developments in the structure of bargaining between the Communications Workers of America (and its predecessor union) and AT&T. In addition, and with information from a number of interviews with key negotiators, Koch, Lewin, and Sockell attempt to predict what the likely structures of bargaining will be at AT&T in the postdivestiture era.

ACKNOWLEDGMENTS

The editors wish to thank the following individuals who served as referees for these and other manuscripts considered for this volume:

Ellen Auster
Morton Bahr
Joel Brockner
James R. Chelius
John Thomas Delaney
Diane J. Gherson
Tove Helland Hammer
T. S. Hoffman
Casey Ichniowski
James W. Kuhn
Charles O'Reilly
Eli Noam
Eric Rambusch
Sharon Smith
Seymour Spilerman
Michael Tushman

We also wish to thank Wendy L. Campbell of Research Findings in Print, who edited the manuscripts and ably consulted with the authors on matters of both form and substance.

David Lewin
David B. Lipsky
Donna Sockell
Co-Editors

ADVANCES IN INDUSTRIAL AND LABOR RELATIONS

ANNOUNCEMENT

Editorial Board and Submissions

We are pleased to announce that we have established an Editorial Board for *Advances in Industrial and Labor Relations (AILR)*, to begin refereeing papers for Volume 5 (1988) of the series. Although all papers submitted to *AILR* in the past were reviewed by scholars, the large volume of papers we now receive demands that we formalize that process. The following scholars, leading researchers in industrial relations, have kindly agreed to serve on the Editorial Board for the purpose of ensuring the continuing quality of the contributions in the annual volume.

Wendy L. Campbell will continue to serve as manuscript editor and consultant.

We hope that this knowledgeable, interdisciplinary Editorial Board will serve to encourage scholars who study any aspect of industrial relations to submit their manuscripts for publication to *AILR*. Scholars interested in submitting papers for publication should send three copies of their manuscript, entirely double-spaced, to:

Ms. Drew Claxton
Industrial Relations Research Center
710 Uris Hall
Graduate School of Business
Columbia University
New York, New York 10027

Finally, with this fourth volume Professor Donna Sockell of Columbia University becomes co-editor of *Advances in Industrial and Labor Relations*. Professors Lewin and Lipsky are delighted she has agreed to accept this post.

THE CHARACTERISTICS OF NATIONAL UNIONS

Jack Fiorito and Wallace E. Hendricks

Although the disciplines of economics and business administration have a long history of research into the structure and strategy of firms (see, for example, Berle and Means 1932 or Williamson 1967), empirical research in industrial relations has historically neglected the study of a major participant in the field—the national union. Indeed, many hypotheses commonly tested by industrial relations researchers can be traced to theories of the firm but only rarely to theories of union behavior. Many studies include measures of the percentage of workers organized or similar explanatory variables, yet very few go beyond this superficial level to examine the effects of union characteristics per se, such as unions' structure, strategy, internal distribution of authority, democracy, or similar constructs. As Anderson (1979b, 266), noted, "In fact, no published research has examined the impact of union characteristics (such as union structure, leadership, or democracy) on the union's ability to obtain favorable wages and working conditions for its membership." Although we can now note a few exceptions to this generalization (Anderson 1979a; Olson 1982; Roomkin 1976; Walker and Lawler 1979), the neglect is still great, despite the fact that industrial relations theory—from Dunlop (1958) to Shirom (1985)—suggests an important role for many such characteristics. Barbash (1969), for example, developed the concept

Advances in Industrial and Labor Relations, Volume 4, pages 1-42.

ISBN: 0-89232-909-2

of rationalization (structuring and carrying out activities in a "businesslike manner") in unions and suggested that this construct has major effects on industrial relations systems.

The lack of empirical work on union characteristics also extends to the causes of variation in these characteristics. Thus, although there is a rich historical tradition in this area (for example, Perlman 1928, Commons 1913, or Hoxie 1917), no one has made any systematic attempt to test the hypotheses put forth. For purposes of empirical research it is unfortunate that most research in this tradition is impressionistic, qualitative, or based on an examination of only one or two *local* unions. We do not mean to disparage the value of this type of research, but it offers little aid to researchers requiring quantitative measures of the constructs used in empirical analyses. As empirical research in the discipline moves increasingly to the micro level of analysis, while retaining the desire to generalize beyond specific micro units, the void of quantitative information on comparative characteristics of unions becomes increasingly problematic.

In essence the issue of research on union characteristics can be divided into three parts. First, why do unions differ? Second, how do they differ in their key characteristics (if at all)? Third, how influential are these differences in determining collective bargaining outcomes? The purpose of this paper is to begin to address the dearth of quantitative information on the second question: *how* unions differ. It is our contention that better measurement of union characteristics will provide the starting point for more rigorous inquiry into the other two questions.

We begin our analysis with a brief review of the literature on the causes and effects of union characteristics. This provides a conceptual framework for a more extensive review of the literature on union characteristics per se. Accordingly, in the next section of the paper we review that literature to identify the key characteristics of unions as organizations. In light of this review a following section examines the data on unions available from national union constitutions and other sources. We then employ factor analysis to identify the underlying dimensions of union characteristics as shown by the data. The discussion of these results compares and contrasts the empirical dimensions with the theoretical dimensions outlined in the literature. Finally, we offer conclusions and some suggestions for further research.

UNION CHARACTERISTICS: CAUSES AND EFFECTS

Unions in the United States are primarily economic institutions organized to improve the wages and working conditions of their members. As such, differences in their characteristics might be largely explainable by differences in the environments in which they must operate.[1] These environmental differences include:

1. product market differences (such as the degree of competition, the scope of the market, the degree of growth);

2. labor market differences (such as barriers to entry, the skills required, unemployment);
3. differences in the characteristics of workers (such as education, age, and alternative opportunities);
4. differences in the characteristics of jobs; and
5. legal differences (such as the right to strike).

Once union characteristics are quantified, researchers can use these environmental characteristics to explain variations in union characteristics at a given time or over time. To date, the empirical literature has tended to focus on a single union characteristic: the percentage unionized as a function of various environmental changes. The theoretical literature, on the other hand, has tended to place particular emphasis on a single environmental factor as shaping a number of union characteristics. For example, Commons (1913) emphasized the expansion of product markets as a key element in the growth of the national union. This example brings up an important point. Since we are largely concerned with factors that explain differences in characteristics of unions within the United States, environmental influences that shape the labor movement, but that do not affect individual unions differently, are missed. Thus, if all unions in the United States have nearly identical ideologies, we cannot address questions in the manner of Perlman (1928), who attempted to explain why U.S. unionism deviated philosophically from its predecessors here and in other countries.

The environmental explanation of different union characteristics might be termed a technological model, in the sense that it presupposes an optimal strategy for the union to react to its environment to obtain its goals. If there is only one such optimal strategy (or technology) to achieve unions' goals in a given environment, and if all unions know this strategy (or if market pressures eliminate those unions that adopt inferior strategies), and if all unions have identical goals, we can expect to explain different outcomes for different unions by noting different environmental influences.

These assumptions will not always hold, however, for several reasons. First, the legal system sets up barriers to competition among unions. Although a union that adopts inferior strategies may ultimately be replaced, these barriers may allow significant inefficiencies in the short run. The inefficiencies would be similar to the "X-inefficiency" proposed by Leibenstein (1966) to characterize firms that are similarly protected from competition. Second, even if all unions are forced to be efficient, there may be numerous strategies equally effective in achieving this efficiency. Competition requires equal bottom lines, not equal strategies. Third, unions may have different goals. Unlike firms that must maximize profits to stay in business in a competitive market, unions need not maximize wages or the wage bill. An equilibrium can exist with different unions providing different packages to their members.

These considerations suggest that union characteristics themselves may exert an independent influence on a host of phenomena *above and beyond the influence of environmental characteristics*. This influence could occur because certain union characteristics are associated with more efficient behavior in obtaining better bargaining outcomes or because certain union characteristics are associated with different bargaining goals. For example, suppose we observed that the more democratic unions secure lower wages for their members in bargaining. On the one hand, we might conclude that democracy weakens unions' bargaining ability and thus makes unions less efficient in dealing with management. Thus, we would associate union democracy with inefficiency. On the other hand, lower wages may mean higher employment or higher nonwage benefits. We therefore might conclude that democratic unions may pursue goals different from those of the less democratic unions (that is, the goals of their members rather than those of the leaders). Thus, we would not judge union democracy inefficient in obtaining union goals.

Beyond the direct impact of union characteristics on bargaining outcomes there may also be an indirect effect. For example, the degree of national union control over locals' strike activity may indirectly influence bargaining outcomes to the extent that strike postures influence outcomes. Whether union characteristics have a significant effect on what Kochan (1980), for example, might call the "primary dependent variables of interest" is an empirical question. That is, do characteristics such as centralization and rationalization have an impact on traditional points of interest in industrial relations, such as bargaining outcomes or strikes?

Since Hoxie's time virtually no attempt has been made to empirically describe union characteristics as a function of environmental features, although works such as Perlman's can be viewed as limited exceptions to this generalization. There have been efforts to assess the independent causal role of union characteristics, but the research on this issue, in either speculative or empirical form, is quite limited. Although unions, as a major actor in the framework of industrial relations systems, have long been viewed as a major influence on the system's output (such as work rules), research examining specific union characteristics in relation to even single system outcomes is almost nonexistent. Several speculative or impressionistic theses have been advanced, however. Kochan (1980), for example, provided an interesting review and interpretation of the centralization-democracy effect on bargaining effectiveness; Bok and Dunlop (1970), Hardman (1972), and Strauss (1977) also offered interesting views on this issue.

From a slightly different perspective Lahne (1970) addressed the potential impact of provisions in national union constitutions on bargaining outcomes. While his primary purpose was to describe selected constitutional provisions, he also took on the almost inevitable question whether those formal provisions have any practical impact. Although noting several examples of instances where the provisions are flagrantly ignored, and recognizing that provisions on certain matters may be consciously omitted for the sake of flexibility, Lahne (1970, 191) argued that it is *strategy*, not procedures, that yields bargaining strength through flexibility:

> Thus there is no reason, in terms of flexibility of strategy, for the unions to avoid specifying in their constitutions the procedures for formulating demands, for selection of negotiating personnel, for contract ratification, and so forth.

Further, Lahne concurred with Rideout (1967) on the importance of formal procedural provisions. Rideout (1967, 76–77) stated, ''No rules are proof against . . . men. Procedural rules, however, do condition the thinking of those who operate them.'' These views found further support from Strauss (1977), who argued that formal provisions are probably more important at the national union level, whereas informal norms of behavior may be more critical at the local level. Lahne went on to note that astute bargainers will familiarize themselves with the constraints or opportunities for their opponents that these formal provisions may create. We should observe that on this point Lahne is supported by most collective bargaining texts (for example, Mills 1986, 239).

In general, union characteristics may have a great many different influences on bargaining or other outcomes. For example, given that unions seek to take wages out of competition as a primary goal, one must ask whether particular strategies, structures, or tactics are especially conducive to this goal. To the extent that the secular rise in union decertifications reflects workers' concerns with union effectiveness, the importance of union characteristics that influence effectiveness is underscored. The recent issues of concessionary bargaining and union-management cooperation also raise important questions about such union characteristics as local versus national control. Once again, the systems (or similar) framework(s) of industrial relations suggests a central role for union characteristics, but researchers investigating ''middle range'' hypotheses have generally failed to consider the impact of these characteristics in their theory building. A consideration of these characteristics is unlikely to dramatically alter the conventional wisdom on bargaining outcomes, but it may serve to expand the conventional wisdom substantially—or from an empiricist's point of view, reduce the unexplained variation in outcomes.

The empirical research on union characteristics (formal or informal) and their impact on outcomes is even more limited than the speculative or conceptual literatures reviewed above. The typical study of bargaining outcomes, such as Kochan and Wheeler (1975), Kochan and Block (1977) or Feuille, Hendricks, and Kahn (1981) cites a theoretical role for union characteristics, yet the measures used, such as the percentage organized, the number of unions in the industry, or the percentage of employees organized by the predominant union, can hardly be said to speak to the potential effects of differing union characteristics. At best, those studies offer indirect evidence on the potential effects of union characteristics via their findings of significant impacts for certain employer characteristics.

A few studies do offer direct, empirical examinations of the effects of union characteristics. Roomkin (1976) examined the effect of selected specific measures on the strike propensities of different national unions, while noting: "Clearly the number of variables one could study in this connection [capturing or embodying the internal union distribution of power over negotiations] is staggering" (p. 201). Roomkin included in his analysis variables reflecting the national union's requirement that it approve local contracts and locals' decisions to strike; a proxy for product market structure; the existence of an intermediate union body; national convention frequency; and union membership size. He hypothesized that centralized control, as reflected in these measures, reduces strike propensity. His multivariate results were broadly consistent with the hypothesis, though the coefficients for several of the specific measures were not significant, and the author noted several methodological limitations of his exploratory study. The two most obvious weaknesses were that the unit of analysis, the national union, does not correspond to the negotiation unit where strikes are conducted and that no controls for other factors such as economic conditions or employer characteristics were included.

A second study (Anderson 1979a) closely followed the work of Warner (1975) with respect to measuring union characteristics, but it also included measures of internal union processes (leader competence and democracy) and union tactics (militance, political activity, and public relations). Anderson examined the effects of these characteristics on wage and nonwage outcomes indexed from public sector contracts. For his Warneresque variables Anderson, drawing support from Bok and Dunlop (1970) and Barbash (1969), hypothesized that higher levels of rationalization and centralization would "enhance union effectiveness in collective bargaining," but his results were "generally disappointing" (p. 136). Also disappointing were his results for the other measures of union characteristics, although several showed a strong bivariate relationship to alternate outcome measures and a few evidenced marginal significance in multivariate specifications. Anderson proposed that one reason for his results might have been that "the measures of union structure, process and tactics [were not] designed with a specific enough reference to collective bargaining, weakening the results" (p. 142).

Unlike Anderson, who pointed to the literature's ambiguity on the impact of union democracy on effectiveness, Olson (1982) argued for an unambiguous positive impact, asserting "democratic" unions achieve "better outcomes" (p. 12) because the alternative—centralization—generates member apathy, a lack of member solidarity and militance, and the supremacy of institutional needs. She compiled an array of 14 measures of constitutional provisions, many of which measures were similar or identical to Roomkin's (1976) measures, and compared these with data on wages and other bargaining outcomes at the bargaining unit level (five separate contract score indexes). In bivariate analyses Olson found general support for her hypothesis across the range of bargaining outcome measures. She noted, however, that in many instances the hypothesis was not supported by the comparisons of specific measures of democracy and centralization with specific measures of outcomes. Finally, as Olson observed, the bivariate analyses failed to reflect the influence of factors other than union constitutional provisions on bargaining outcomes—a major limitation of the study.

Also noteworthy are the studies of union certification elections by Cooke (1983) and Dickens (1983). Both studies reported significant effects for dichotomous union identifier variables as predictors of election outcomes. Unfortunately, their dichotomous specifications tell us only that the union involved matters, but not which characteristics of unions matter.

Walker and Lawler (1979) explicitly considered the possibility that selected characteristics of unions may influence workers' individual decision to unionize. In a study of professors' attitudes, they investigated whether there is a "qualitative difference between *aggressive* and *protective* unions based on the priority of political versus economic objectives" (p. 33, emphasis in original). Their results generally supported this hypothesis, as well as the broader proposition that union characteristics do affect the traditionally examined industrial relations outcomes, such as unionization decisions. This proposition is hardly startling; in fact, our colleagues in marketing would no doubt find it remarkable that industrial relations researchers have not generally considered union characteristics as *prime* determinants of workers' decision to join unions.

Heneman and Sandver (1986) offered a further exploration in this vein. Using the national union as the unit of analysis, they examined the effect of three basic sets of union characteristics on union success in representation elections. First, several measures reflected the types of elections in which unions engage, encompassing unit size, region, consent elections, and the proportion of elections within the union's traditional jurisdiction. These measures are not union characteristics per se but do reflect the union's organizing strategy; for instance, a high proportion of white-collar elections in a union would indicate an organizing strategy that targets white-collar workers. The second set of measures assessed the union's organizing resources, reflecting their functional specialization and staff size. Finally, the authors also examined two financial characteristics: organizing expenditures and net assets. Their results were generally disappointing: No union characteristic exhibited any persistent effect in their analysis. Using the election as the unit of analysis and different measures of union characteristics, Maranto and Fiorito (1987) found that union characteristics have a highly significant impact on union success, however. We will say more about these results in the concluding section.

Leonard's (1985) study of work force demographics also touched on the issue of union characteristics. Specifically, he linked qualitative differences in unions' discrimination policies to changes in work force composition. Although he reported no direct measures of union discrimination policies, his analysis, like Dickens' and Cooke's studies of certification elections, implied that particular union characteristics have an effect on the employment of protected groups.

In summary, study of the impact of union characteristics on dependent variables traditionally examined in industrial relations is still in its infancy. The empirical studies by Roomkin, Anderson, and Olson were, on the whole, inconclusive. Each found at least some evidence of significant effects, yet none offered any overwhelming evidence, perhaps in part because of methodological deficiencies in each study. It is interesting and important to note that these contributions did not agree on an appropriate set of measures of union characteristics, or even on which types of characteristics to emphasize. The first disagreement is explained by Roomkin's observation that there are a multitude of potential measures. The second, most obvious in the contrast between Anderson's emphasis on rationalization and centralization as forces enhancing bargaining effectiveness and Olson's exclusive emphasis on democracy (in her view, as *opposed* to centralization) as enhancing effectiveness, is theoretically more significant. It underscores the haziness surrounding many key concepts such as centralization and democracy in unions.

Together, these disagreements illuminate the need to specify union characteristics more precisely, in both practical (empirical) and conceptual terms. As Aldenderfer and Blashfield (1984) have stated, classification is a fundamental step in the development of science: "All sciences are built upon classifications that structure their domains of inquiry" (p. 8). A necessary preliminary step in classification is the development of criteria for classification. Boulding (1953, xvi–xvii) observed, "We cannot get far in the study of organizations or of anything else unless we have some kind of theoretical 'model' as a guide to perceiving what is essential in the midst of the immense mass of subordinate detail. It is important, therefore, to ask right at the outset whether there are any features of form or structure which most organizations have in common." The next section attempts to take this basic, preliminary step by examining the theoretical literature on the characteristics of unions as organizations.

THE LITERATURE ON UNION CHARACTERISTICS

We might have taken any of a number of possible slices of the literature on union characteristics. A chronological approach tracing the history of thought on the topic might be interesting, for example. Instead, however, we have chosen to organize our review along the lines of the major concepts, or, loosely speaking, the variables examined, in the study of unions as organizations. The value of this approach is that it allows us to compare different writers' views on specific issues and thus serves as a basis for assessing the state of our knowledge of these issues. A chief disadvantage of this approach is that it prevents us from presenting any one scholar's overall view or the overall coherence of that view. Moreover, this approach requires that we take liberties in reducing the diverse terminologies used by various writers to a common denominator. We hope to minimize the losses resulting from our translations, but we ask that the reader keep these cautions in mind and consult the original works for further details.

One way the various constructs in the literature may be characterized is by key words, or terms that are representative of the diversity of constructs in the literature. The key words in the literature on unions as organizations are *size*, *centralization* (of decision making and control), *rationalization*, *democracy*, *oligarchy*, *structure*, *ideology*, and *bureaucracy*. To varying degrees the constructs underlying these terms are analytically distinct, but obviously in some instances even the analytical distinction between terms may consist only of the distinction between two ends of a continuum. Democracy and oligarchy, for example, are generally conceived of as distinct points on a single scale. More subtle but no less extensive overlap exists between some of the other pairs of terms. For example, size is antithetical to some concepts of participatory democracy. Moreover, even the analytically distinct concepts reflected in the above terms are often empirically inseparable. For example, democracy and centralization may be independ concepts in theory but inseparable phenomena in practice. Nonetheless, to maintain a close link between our discussion and the literature, we consider the key words listed above as discrete concepts, while noting as we proceed the ways in which they overlap.

Size

National unions (as well as locals) vary considerably in size, from memberships of fewer than two dozen to those of close to two million. Membership, however, is only one possible measure of size; reasonable alternatives include assets, revenues, and the number of locals, among others. For purposes of collective bargaining (as distinct from political activity), the number of members may not be terribly important.[2] Taft (1973) recognized that there is little to be gained in workplace improvements by calling a huge strike of diversified members; he argued that any advantages of size lie in stability, staff, and resources. The potential advantages of staff size are particularly noteworthy, for larger staffs permit greater specialization. This point links the size concept to Barbash's (1969) rationalization concept, to Bok and Dunlop's similar observations on union administration, and to Warner's (1975) work on bureaucracy. Warner reported, for example, that staff size correlates to varying degrees with both centralization and the "structuring of activities." In applying his analysis to unions Warner found that the "main relationships were related to the differences in numbers of employees (paid and full-time) that these organizations had" (p. 49). Lipset, Trow, and Coleman (1956) also made a linkage between large scale and bureaucratic structures.

Size has also been closely linked with efficiency through the concept of economies of scale (Barbash 1969). Bok and Dunlop (1970) cited economies of scale as a major problem, especially for small local unions, which may be too small for specialized staff and effective coordination and supervision: "The result may be ineffective performance even in such important functions as bargaining . . . while other tasks may be neglected altogether" (p. 154).

Size is associated with democracy and oligarchy as well. Taft (1973, 7) observed, "To the extent that the perfect democracy is a town meeting, any growth in size either diminishes the democratic spirit or practice.'' Taft's remarks warn, however, that the relationship between size and democracy may depend to a large degree on the definition of democracy employed. Hardman (1972, 65) referred to democracy as an ''elastic term'' but nonetheless questioned whether it is ''at all possible for 'big' unionism to function democratically in dealing with 'big' industry and expanding 'big' government'' (p. 62).

Democracy and Oligarchy

The terms *democracy* and *oligarchy* are so closely related conceptually and in the literature on unions as to warrant their joint discussion here. The literature has reached no consensus on the best way to measure democracy or oligarchy, but as Hardman (1972) suggested, the consensus may be that there are several valid measures, each of which is limited in its usefulness.

Lipset, Trow, and Coleman's (1956) classic study of the International Typographical Union raised the issue of the degree of viable political opposition to the union's leadership. The ITU is a very exceptional case, however, and may be in the process of losing its exceptionalism.[3] Moreover, Bok and Dunlop (1970) cited several flaws in viewing the ITU as a ''perfect type,'' including its unnecessary politicization of many issues and its greater suppression of minority groups than are true of more autocratic unions (see especially their pp. 84–90).

Strauss (1977) suggested two alternative routes to studying union democracy. The first is an informal approach that emphasizes the existence of an occupational community and member activism within the union, while the second focuses on the union's structural features, such as formal arrangements that encourage the forming of power bases independent of the incumbent leaders. While concluding that the informal approach is less valuable at the national level or in large subunits, he also granted that ''the two approaches may be less inconsistent than they seem at first'' (p.241), since both require a ''middle mass,'' or intervening power base, though at different levels.

Because the informal approach, with its emphasis on member activism, can be investigated with behavioral measures such as member participation, voting in elections, and officer turnover, this approach receives the most attention in the empirical literature, which has tended to examine one or a few local unions. Rogow (1967) conducted an insightful case study of a large local unit in which high participation was accompanied by a very high degree of centralization. Applebaum and Blaine (1975) criticized using measures of union officer turnover as measures of democracy, claiming that they fail to account for ''in-group'' succession. They seemed to concur with Michels's (1959, 418) ''Iron Law'' of oligarchy:

> The formation of oligarchies within the various forms of democracy is the outcome of organic necessity, and consequently affects every organization. . . . Who says organization says oligarchy.

Studies of national unions tend to be more qualitative, often based on examination of a single union. Among the few researchers providing comparative analyses, Strauss (1977) and Lahne (1970) emphasized formal structure measures, such as the provisions of union constitutions. Gamm (1979, 295) argued that the election base of national union executive boards (at-large versus a district basis), "more than any other single factor, determines the representative character of the organization. . . . The election base is of utmost importance in establishing the presence or absence of genuine political life inside the national union." Her argument rests on the premise that district-based elections can provide challengers of incumbents with a secure power base. Warner (1975, 55) also allowed an important role for executive boards in linking centralization to democracy: "It seems . . . that Centralization is the institutional manifestation of the democratic and political ethos of [unions] on a 'national' basis of organization."

Olson (1982) and Roomkin, (1976) both used measures of formal structural characteristics of national unions, although neither focused on the study of union democracy. Olson used quantitative measures of features in union constitutions in examining the effect of democracy on bargaining outcomes, while Roomkin used some of the same measures to predict strike activity. Both authors, like Lahne (1970), viewed these formal measures—such as the frequency of national conventions, provisions for national approval of local contracts, and local ratification—as reflecting the internal distribution of control, which in turn may be considered a measure of democracy.

These studies by Olson and Roomkin, which employed measures of variables having some connection to democracy, obviously involve the separate question whether internal democracy matters—does it have an impact on other variables? While Hochner, Koziara, and Schmidt (1980) were able to identify six theoretical perspectives that make internal union democracy an important issue, others including Lipset (1960) argued that even dictatorial unions are better than no union, for worker interests and political democracy, provided the union is not an instrument of the employer or the state. Bok and Dunlop (1970, 90), among others, believed that democracy had received a disproportionate amount of scholarly attention at the expense of union governance, terming this tendency "curious, for members have doubtless suffered far more from inefficient and unimaginative administration than they have ever lost through corruption and undemocratic practices." Others such as Derber (1969), however, might counter that unions' primary contributions to U.S. society stem from their democratizing influence and that internal union democracy is a key prerequisite for that influence.

One conclusion that emerges from this brief review of the literature on union democracy and oligarchy is the extent to which various concepts of internal democracy are intertwined with other constructs, including size, centralization, bureaucratization, and rationalization. These intertwinings do exist, but their precise nature is not well understood. Barbash (1969, 158) noted, for example, that his concept of rationalization may conflict with the society's prevailing ideology, including norms of democracy, yet he also stated, "Rationalization in the union is not inherently incompatible with democracy.'' In this regard we should also recall Warner's (1975) view on the relationship between centralization and democracy.

Structure

To the extent that union structure can be analytically distinguished from bureaucracy and other key variables in the study of unions, it can be said to comprise three or four noteworthy aspects. First and perhaps most obvious of these is the classic distinction drawn between craft and industrial unions—no doubt one of the first distinguishing features of unions to which students of industrial relations are introduced. With the craft-industrial distinction are associated a great variety of distinguishing features, including industry, skill levels, local officials' functions, ethnicity, control of job access, apprenticeship, and product market structure (Holley and Jennings 1983). The basic distinction very closely parallels some of the distinctions drawn by Roomkin (1976) in his analysis of the effects of union characteristics on strike propensities.

A possibly distinct but closely related aspect of structure is its evolutionary nature. As in Perlman's view, the craft-industrial distinction is seen as transitory, with craft unionism ultimately yielding to the industrial form:

> Job territory will sooner or later be taken over by an *industrial* union . . . Nor need a job conscious unionism . . . arrest the growth of its solidarity, short of the boundaries of the wage earning class as a whole (Perlman 1928, 276; emphasis in original).

These first two structural concepts easily tie into a third, the concept of the occupational and industrial scope of a union. At the same time, however, the concept of scope is distinct because a union can retain craft and industrial subunits within a more general scope at the national level (such as the International Brotherhood of Electrical Workers and the Knights of Labor). And yet the occupational scope is also evolutionary, for as Seeber (1984) noted, national union jurisdictions tend to be ever expanding, so that ever more nationals may aptly be referred to as ''general'' unions.

Finally, the literature frequently distinguishes between ''simple'' and ''complex'' union structures. Complex structures are those specifying an intermediate body between the national and local bodies. There is some controversy about the role played by those intermediate bodies. Cook (1963) proposed they act to increase local autonomy by shielding locals from national power, but she also noted that this effect may be offset by the intermediate's body's assumption of collective bargaining duties. In addition, Strauss (1977) noted that intermediate bodies represent a potential power base from which to mount challenges to incumbent national leadership, in a sense anticipating, in rough form, Gamm's (1979) arguments regarding the election bases of unions' executive boards.

As with the other key concepts, structure is obviously interrelated with the other concepts. Researchers have linked the craft-industrial distinction with union democracy constructs (such as participation) through the concept of occupational community and its antecedents (Strauss 1977). Centralization is clearly bound up with the question of the roles played by intermediate bodies in national-local relations. On the other hand, Warner (1975) found the classic craft-industrial distinction of little or no significance in analyzing unions as organizations. Similarly, Hoxie (1917, 55) viewed ''structural form'' (such as the craft-industrial distinction) as ''altogether secondary,'' although his approach was very different from Warner's. Bok and Dunlop (1970), however, connected the issue of union structure specifically to centralization, and to the issues of economies of scale we discussed earlier, in the section on size.

Bureaucracy, Rationalization, and Centralization

The literature almost inextricably yokes the concepts of bureaucracy, rationalization, and centralization in its articulations of unions as organizations. We must ask just how many truly distinct dimensions subsume the various terms and concepts used to describe decision-making and administrative structures in organizations. We have already noted the considerable overlap in these terms.

In his framework for the study of union organizations, Warner (1975) specified—analytically and empirically—five ''primary structural variables,'' ''administrative features,'' or ''constituents of bureaucracy.'' These may be summarized as follows:

1. *specialization*, the division of labor and distribution of official duties within the organization;
2. *standardization*, the extent to which there are procedures, their specificity, and their standardization; the existence of techniques of rationalization (see below);
3. *formalization*, the extent of written communication or documentation;
4. *centralization*, the vertical distribution of decision making; and
5. *configuration*, the ''shape'' of role structures, as measured by various indices, particularly organizational size and vertical span of control.

Warner viewed these five constructs as analytically distinct but recognized the important empirical question ''how far bureaucracy is in fact *unitary*'' (p. 47, emphasis in the original). He reported:

> Research on a large sample of organizations has now established that these analytically independent dimensions in fact fall into two clusters: the first which has been labelled ''Structuring of Activities'' and which comprises Specialization, Standardization, Formalization, and Vertical Span, all positively correlated, either moderately or highly, and a second cluster mainly comprises Centralization and has a *negative* correlation with the first cluster, of varying magnitude (p. 47, emphasis in the original).

Barbash's (1969) use of the term *rationalization*, which emphasizes decision making through rules, formal organization, and a reliance on expertise, is often couched in terms of its opposition to *ideology*.[4] Rationalization is clearly correlated with several of Warner's "constituents of bureaucracy." In addition, Warner's configuration variable is explicitly linked to size (number of employees) and structure (levels of hierarchy). Numerous authors (for example, Kochan 1980) have discussed bureaucracy, rationalization, and similar constructs as opposites of, or at least to some extent in conflict with, union democracy. Kochan suggested that the degree of opposition between democracy and centralization depends on the issue and the time horizon under consideration. On the classic debate over centralization, democracy, and union effectiveness, he considered the possibility that both sides are correct:

> The essence of the dilemma, therefore, is that while centralization may be needed to perform effectively in bargaining . . . *at any given point in time*, the longer centralization is maintained in the absence of an effective political process, the more union effectiveness is likely to decline (Kochan 1980, 157–58, emphasis in the original).

Similar concerns involving rationalization or other aspects of bureaucracy and democracy are common, although Kochan offered one of the few explicit treatments of these issues, one that distinguishes between short-run and long-run effects.

Although noting some differences between unions and other types of organizations, Warner (1975, 48) asserted that his study of union organizations indicated they are "directly comparable" with other types of organizations, including businesses, on the basis of his five constructs. In comparison to business organizations unions tend to exhibit less standardization, rationalization, and functional specialization, and more formalization, centralization, and responsiveness to "lay committees" (executive boards, in the union case). As in other organizations, Warner reported, the critical factor in determining the character of the union appears to be organizational size, as opposed to, say, ideology or the craft-industrial distinction.[5]

In light of Warner's exposition Barbash's concept of rationalization appears to align rather closely with Warner's "structuring of activities." This parallel is reinforced by both authors' references to business organizations: Barbash (1969, 157–58) cited as a source of many problems in union democracy and administration the union leaders' ideological view of their union, "instead of what it is and what it needs to be, in large part at least—a businesslike organization which can carry out its representative function only by operating like a business organization."

Barbash, however, did not appear to draw the distinction between rationalization and structuring of activities, on the one hand, and centralization, on the other, that Warner did. Barbash specifically named the ascendancy of national unions as a manifestation of rationalization, since this trend reflected economies of scale and broadening product markets. Similarly, he tended to view the displacement of local collective bargaining functions by intermediate bodies as probably reflecting rationalization. Both of these tendencies could be viewed, in Warner's terms, as centralization tendencies without necessarily connoting rationalization. In fact, Warner's empirical results seem to raise the possibility that centralization and rationalization may be substitutes to some extent. That is, rationalization or structuring of activities may accomplish in some instances what is accomplished in other instances through centralization. Bargaining may be effectively coordinated through alternative mechanisms, for example.

Thus, although Barbash and Warner may have differed in some respects, they definitely concurred in others, including the appropriateness of comparisons between businesses and unions. Both seemed to believe that unions were lagging behind their business counterparts in developing administrative procedures. Barbash cited the political nature of unions (particularly with regard to their staffing decisions) and environmental factors (such as markets and the employers dealt with) as obstacles inhibiting rationalization. Donaldson and Warner (1974) found that electoral control of officials, an aspect of democracy, was negatively associated with structuring of activities. Bok and Dunlop (1970, 186), as well, concluded, "Judged by contemporary standards of administration, the typical international union leaves much to be desired." They also argued (p. 140) that "administrative methods have been more highly developed by business executives . . . largely because the stresses of the marketplace have put pressure on them to operate efficiently." Similar pressures seem to be having an impact on unions themselves recently.[6]

Barbash, Bok and Dunlop, and Warner all cited specific aspects of administration in which unions are deficient, and they also suggested improvements. Further, they all argued that those improvements need not come at the expense of internal union democracy, perhaps underscoring the centralization-rationalization distinction.[7] At the same time, however, Bok and Dunlop also criticized the attention researchers and others pay to democracy, as noted earlier, and further stated,

> In every case, the question should be not whether any given change will make the union more democratic, but whether it will serve the ends of the modern union—to respond to the interests of the membership, to promote them effectively, to deal fairly with individuals and minorities within its ranks, and to exhibit a due regard for legitimate interests of those beyond its walls (1970, 90–91).

Strauss (1977) raised a similar criticism, though more cautiously. He posed the question whether internal democracy is critical to union performance as a countervailing force to management.

In sum, in viewing decision-making and administrative structures in union organizations, two constructs—centralization and rationalization (or the structuring of activities)—appear to be most crucial and at least somewhat distinct analytically and empirically. The distinction between centralization and rationalization is also somewhat arbitrary, however, in part because of the possibilities of substitution between the two. Both of these constructs have been linked to other union characteristics, including size, structure, ideology, and, in particular, democracy. The literature contains much discussion of the relationships between each of these two constructs and democracy, yielding a consensus on rationalization—that it need not conflict with democracy—but no consensus on centralization and democracy. Several authors concede the possibility of conflict between rationalization and democracy, but some question whether democracy deserves the status of sacred cow they believe it has attained in the literature on unions as organizations. Finally we should note that much of the literature on decision making and administration in unions is abstract, and it tends to pay scant attention to the questions of how centralization, in particular, is manifested in unions and how it relates to key union functions such as bargaining. In light of Anderson's disappointing results, noted earlier, for rationalization and centralization as aids to union effectiveness, future researchers need to develop measures of decision-making and administrative constructs that relate directly to the bargaining process and strikes, and to questions of national versus local control of issues facing unions.

Ideology

Ideology is something of a weak link in industrial relations thought in this country. U.S. unions are often characterized as nonideological. As Hoxie (1917, 34) averred, "If the history of unionism [in the United States] seems to admit of any positive generalizations, they are that unionists have been prone to act first and formulate theories afterward." Hoxie then proceeded to identify several distinct "functional types" of unionism (and some variations within types): *business* unionism (practiced by, for example, the AFL craft unions), *friendly* or *uplift* unionism (the Knights of Labor), *revolutionary* unionism (the Industrial Workers of the World), and *predatory* unionism, the distinguishing characteristic of which is its "ruthless pursuit of the thing in hand by whatever means seem most appropriate at the time, regardless of ethical or legal codes, or effect upon those outside its own membership" (Hoxie 1917, 50). Thus, ideological contrasts were definitely a key element, if not the central element, in Hoxie's "functional types." Since Hoxie's time business unionism has emerged as the indisputably dominant form of U.S. unionism, and interunion ideological contrasts are therefore more subtle now, or at least they seem less significant. Still, meaningful differences among contemporary unions do exist, for example, in their degrees of "social-mindedness" or "political-mindedness." Indeed, the term *ideology*, by its very nature, suggests a host of possible dimensions for comparison. Fortunately, this review need only consider selected aspects of the subject.

A working definition of ideology is in order, which necessarily takes us in tow to the heart of the matter. Perlman (1928), for one, had little patience with the terminological quandaries evoked by this concept. He used the terms *philosophy*, *mentality*, and *ideology* interchangeably. In Perlman's view union ideology in the United States was simply job control, or the collective control of job opportunities, and "scarcity consciousness." In its most elementary terms the Perlmanian concept of ideology can be called "Tom, Dick, and Harry idealism" (Perlman 1928, 274). The essence of this ideology is that wage earners are willing to communize opportunity or work through a collective only to the extent that they can see relatively short-run, tangible benefits through such means. Individuals accept union "bosses" only for the resulting economic liberty on the job resulting from their acceptance.

Implicit for the most part in Perlman's concept of ideology is the notion of equality or egalitarianism, as in the egalitarian administration of scarce job opportunities through their collective administration by the union. It is probably this aspect of ideology that relates most directly to the subject at hand. Specifically, the notion of a bureaucratic structure with varying degrees of authority accorded to different positions (and thereby individuals) conflicts to some degree with the notion of egalitarianism. Further, the concept of differential rewards, structured to achieve specific bureaucratic objectives such as inducing qualified applicants to compete for positions of authority, also seems at odds with egalitarianism. On a broader level the conflict that Barbash (1969) identified between ideology and rationalization is a conflict that pits the rank-and-file as a democratic decision-making body against the specialized authority of the bureaucrat.

Yet the ideological conflict involves more than simply democracy versus bureaucracy. Returning to the issue of rewards, Strauss (1977, 238) suggested, "For some research purposes, officer salaries may serve as a meaningful proxy for ideological commitment." Underlying this proposition is the idea that tastes for egalitarianism lead some unions to pay their officers low salaries. Thus, salary structures in such organizations could hardly represent the rational structuring of rewards that bureaucratic theory would suggest is necessary to attract the best candidates for positions in the union.[8] As a test of rationalization in unions French, Hayashi, and Gray (1983) examined the salaries of national union presidents and reported some evidence of rational compensation practices, but also that ideological considerations seemed to exert a strong influence on the salaries.

On the whole the interrelations and conflicts between ideology and rationalization or other union characteristics seem to overlap considerably with similar notions of conflicts involving democracy. Thus, in many instances in the literature on union characteristics, ideology is practically synonymous with democracy, as in the conflict identified by Barbash, above.

Nonetheless, other aspects of union ideology, aside from democracy, are important in the study of union characteristics. For example, craft unionism, or more generally union structure, may in a sense be an ideology, and a distinguishing characteristic of unions. Dues levels and dues schedules relative to earnings may also indicate some aspects of unions' philosophies. Unions' political and organizing activities may reflect more about their ideologies than do their views on democracy, and so on. Walker and Lawler's (1979) distinction between aggressive and protective unions to some extent paralleled Scoville's (1973) analysis of international labor movements according to economic and political means and ends. Unfortunately, many of the features of unions that might be considered indicative of their ideologies—such as membership solidarity or consciousness of scarcity—are not easily measured. Thus, our ability to differentiate among unions systematically on the basis of ideology is quite limited, despite the intriguing nature of the entire subject.

The Key Words: A Summary

In the discussion to this point we have reviewed the literature on unions as organizations for the purpose of identifying the critical or distinguishing characteristics of national unions. Problems of varying terminology and of the interrelatedness of many of the terms have made this a less than straightforward task. At the very least the key constructs in the literature appear to be size, democracy-oligarchy, structure, centralization, rationalization (or the structure of activities), and ideology. Analytically, some of the concepts overlap with one another somewhat; empirically, they do so to an even greater extent. Moreover, many of these concepts are multifaceted, and our measurement of the overall concepts lags far behind our conceptualizations of their various facets. To this point we have made little reference to what measures are available and how the available measures compare with the concepts described above. It is to these issues we now turn.

DATA ON NATIONAL UNIONS

Unlike for many other topics in industrial relations no single major source of data on national unions exists. At first glance the *Directory of National Unions and Employee Associations* series, published by the U.S. Department of Labor and discontinued in 1982, and its replacement, the *Directory of U.S. Labor Organizations* series (Gifford 1982, 1984, 1986), published by the Bureau of National Affairs, would appear to constitute such a source. Those familiar with these series are well aware, however, that beyond their regular features on names and addresses of officers and membership counts, and irregular special features on selected issues, they have little to offer in comparing characteristics of different unions.

Consequently, data on union characteristics must be pieced together from a variety of sources. Just such an undertaking resulted in the measures reported in Table 1. Though hardly exhaustive this table reflects a fairly extensive effort to assemble comparative data on national unions in recent years. As indicated in the source notes to the table, we relied on five main sources among a variety we consulted. First were the irregular special studies reported in the two *Directory* series. The second was an analysis of provisions in union constitutions conducted by Olson (1982), following Lahne's (1970) methodology. Third, we took data on the bases of union executive boards from Gamm (1979) and data on union jurisdictions from Seeber (1984). Financial data are from *Union Financial*

Table 1. Selected Measures of National Union Characteristics

Variable	*Definition*	*Mean*
MEMBERS[a]	Number of members, 1975–76	167,329
LOCALS[a]	Number of locals as of 1976	586
ESCALE[a]	Number of members per local	701
COMPLEX[b]	1 = complex organizational structure; 0 = simple structure (no intermediate body)	.52
NATPROH[b]	1 = national prohibits certain contract clauses; 0 = no prohibitions	.10
LOCRATN[b]	1 = local ratification of contract required; 0 = not required	.22
NATAPVL[b]	1 = national approval of contract required; 0 = not required	.48
YEARSC[b]	Number of years between national conventions	3.44
YEARSNE[b]	Number of years between national elections	3.68
YEARSLE[b]	Number of years between local elections	3.02
GJUR55[c]	General jurisdiction as of 1955 (1 = union had general membership jurisdiction; 0 = craft, industrial, or other specific jurisdiction)	.13
GJUR82[c]	General jurisdiction as of 1982 (1 = union had general membership jurisdiction; 0 = craft, industrial, or other specific jurisdiction)	.55
NUMEXP[c]	Number of jurisdictional expansions, 1955–82	1.71
ELOFF[a]	1 = national officers elected by convention; 0 = elected by referendum	.83
EBATL[d]	1 = executive board elected at-large; 0 = elected by district	.68
EBFTE[d]	1 = executive board members full-time employees; 0 = not full-time employees.	.75
STRADMN[a]	Strike fund administration in 1972 (1 = local administration of strike fund, 17%; 3 = national and local administration, 46%; 5 = national administration, 37%)	3.41
BENAUTH[a]	1 = informal authority for strike benefits; 0 = constitutional authority (1972)	.17
BENSOUR[a]	1 = general fund source for strike benefits; 0 = special assessment (1972)	.22
BRIGHT[a]	1 = strike benefit eligibility based on right; 0 = based on need only (1972). (Responses of ''both'' occurred)	.63

(continued)

Table 1. (Continued)

Variable	*Definition*	*Mean*
BNEED[a]	1 = strike benefit eligibility based on need; 0 = based on right only (1972). (Responses of "both" occurred)	.41
BENWAIT[a]	Waiting period for strike benefits, in weeks (1972)	1.60
NATBBODY[a]	1 = national body authorized strike benefits; 0 = local body authorized (1972)	.89
BENLEV[a]	Dollar amount of weekly strike benefits (1972)	$28.82
SAL77[e]	Salary of chief executive officer (1977)	$68,760
TOTSAL77[e]	Salary of chief executive officer plus expenses (1977)	$85,151
AFFLINT[b]	Affiliation to intermediate body (0 = not applicable, no intermediate body, 48%; 3 = voluntary, 10%; 5 = mandatory, 42%)	2.40
FTE[a]	Number of full-time employees of national (1970)	106
FTECAP[a]	Number of full-time employees per member	.00150
MACAP[a]	Number of full-time managerial and administrative employees per member	.00030
PROFCAP[a]	Number of full-time professional employees per member	.00009
CSCAP[a]	Number of full-time clerical and secretarial employees per member	.00065
ORCAP[a]	Number of full-time organizing and field representative employees per member	.00045
BLSCORE[b,f]	Index of "nationalness" of bargaining level	2.33
FDSCORE[b,f]	Index of "nationalness" of bargaining demand formulation	1.69
NPSCORE[b,f]	Index of "nationalness" of negotiating personnel	1.69
DSSCORE[b,f]	Index of "nationalness" of decision to strike	2.55
DTSCORE[b,f]	Index of "nationalness" of decision to terminate strikes	1.80
APPLOCD[b]	National approval of local contract demands required (1 = not required, 74%; 5 = required, 26%)	2.04
ASSETS[g]	Total assets of national, in thousands of dollars (1976)	$20,571
RECEIPTS[g]	Total receipts of national, in thousands of dollars (1976)	$30,936
GBDCAP[a]	Number of governing board members per member (1978)	.00191

Table 1. (Continued)

Variable	*Definition*	*Mean*
OFFCAP[a]	Number of national officers per member (1978)	.00058
ICONC[a]	Percentage of membership in primary industry jurisdiction (1978)	83.80%
WOSHR[a]	Percentage of membership who are women (1978)	26.14%
PTSHR[a]	Percentage of membership in professional or technical occupations (1978)	18.89%
CLERKSHR[a]	Percentage of membership in clerical occupations (1978)	4.46%
SALESHR[a]	Percentage of membership in sales occupations (1978)	3.10%
BCSHR[a]	Percentage of membership in blue-collar occupations (1978)	72.77%
DEMSHARE[h]	Percentage of all federal election campaign contributions by political action committees (PACs) affiliated with national unions that went to Democratic party candidates (1978)	92.49%
CONTRCAP[h,a]	Total dollar contributions by affiliated PACs to federal election campaigns, per member (1978)	$.77
DUESRATE[i]	A proxy for members' dues payments to the national as a percentage of a member's wage rate (1976)	1.00%
ORGZNG[j]	A proxy for organizing activity in NLRB certification elections, per member, 1972–80; measured as number of persons for whom representation rights were sought divided by number of members	.19
TLOBCAP[k]	Number of federal lobbyists paid by the national, per member, 1978	.00004
CRAFT[l]	1 = craft union; 0 = other	.20

Notes:

[a]*Source*: U.S. Department of Labor, Bureau of Labor Statistics (various editions).

[b]*Source*: Olson (1982). These measures are based on Olson's analysis of union constitutions but are not necessarily identical to her measures.

[c]*Source*: Seeber (1984).

[d]*Source*: Gamm (1979).

[e]*Source*: *Business Week* (1978) reports these data, based on LMSA reports.

[f]For each of these indices, provisions were scored on a five-point scale from "localness" to "nationalness," as illustrated below:

1 = Local specified or no provision
2 = Local and intermediate body specified
3 = Intermediate or national and local specified
4 = Intermediate and national specified
5 = National specified

[g]*Source*: U.S. Department of Labor, Labor Management Services Administration (1980)

[h]*Source*: U.S. Federal Election Commission (1980). Membership figures based on U.S. Department of Labor, Bureau of Labor Statistics (1979).

(*continued*)

Table 1. (Continued)

[i]*Source*: The dues rate proxy is estimated as:

1000 × (*RECEIPTS* − .10 × *ASSETS*)/*MEMBERS*/2000/*W*,

where *W* is a union-specific estimate of wage rates for janitor or labor grades in 1976 based on rates stated in major collective bargaining agreements. See Feuille, Hendricks, and Kahn (1981) for further information on these wage data.

[j]*Source*: A computer tape containing data on NLRB elections held from 1972 to 1980 was used to construct measures of the average election unit size (*UNITSZ*) and the number of elections (*NELECTS*) each union participated in. *ORGZNG* is then defined as:

(*UNITSZ* × *NELECTS*) / *MEMBERS*

Cooke's (1983) article gives further information on these data, which were provided to us by Cheryl Maranto.

[k]*Source*: These data combine lobbyists, legislative representatives, and counselors and were provided to us by John Thomas Delaney and Marick F. Masters. See Masters and Delaney (1985) for further details.

[l]Based on authors' judgments. Craft unions are those organized on the basis of relatively narrowly defined occupation skills, such as carpenters, plumbers, and bricklayers.

Statistics 1976 (U.S. Department of Labor 1980).[9] Finally, we took data on political contributions from the Federal Election Commission's (1980) "Table B." Where indicated, the various dates for specific variables reflect the irregular basis of special studies in the first *Directory* series and of several of the other sources. The other data are based on the most recent national union constitution available for the years 1972–77. In the interest of finding comparable data we focused on the mid-1970s, years for which the most data were available.

Because we had to rely on secondary sources, our sample is obviously one of convenience. In particular, because the authors of the sources we used often purposely omitted public sector unions and employee associations from their analyses, our sample is less representative of public sector than it is of private sector organizations. Data availability varies across the measures in Table 1, but in general the data represent most of the large national or "international" U.S. unions. In total more than 150 unions are represented to varying degrees in the measures in Table 1, but for many specific measures, the number of cases with valid data is 50 or fewer.

Obviously these data are far from ideal, in terms of both standards for measurement and completeness. Nonetheless, as the most extensive collection of data on union characteristics yet compiled, these data are worthy of serious attention for at least exploratory purposes.

With these cautions in mind, we can make several general observations about the data presented in Table 1. First, and not surprisingly, the available data do not correspond closely to the analytical dimensions of union characteristics reviewed earlier. At the same time, however, the potential of these measures as proxies is apparent at an intuitive level and based on previous research. For example, several of the measures based on union constitutions provide some information on centralization, or national versus local control, as suggested by Roomkin (1976). As another example, we can use the data on the election bases of union executive boards to address the question of democracy, as suggested by

Gamm (1979). Second, at the extensive margin, the data in Table 1 provide information on a broad range of important issues, including strike benefits, authority for bargaining process and content, elections, membership, union staffing, and so on. Thus, the variables listed, though not ideal measures of the analytical constructs discussed earlier, do picture a wide range of important union characteristics. Finally, many of these measures involve empirical if not conceptual overlap. For example, it is unlikely that constitutional provisions regarding the decision to strike (*DSSCORE*) are independent of the negotiating level specified in the constitution (*BLSCORE*).

The average union in our sample is large (167,329 members and 586 locals), is made up primarily of blue-collar workers (almost 73 percent), and draws its members primarily from a single industry (almost 84 percent). Just over half of the unions have a complex structure, and considerable variation exists in national control over bargaining activities. For example, almost 90 percent of the unions give the national body control over strike benefits, but only 10 percent of these same unions prohibit certain clauses in locally negotiated contracts.

Several of the statistics suggest that unions' structures are considerably different than the structures of the firms with which they bargain. For example, the average chief executive officer salary in 1977 was $68,760,[10] a figure that would pale beside an average for firms of the same average size. In addition, the size of the union bureaucracy (as measured by the number of employees or employees per member) is quite small. These statistics suggest that national unions might more profitably be compared to industry *associations* as opposed to firms themselves.

The data also reveal a strong ideological commitment of union members to the Democratic party (which received 92 percent of all national unions' campaign contributions in 1978), although the actual monetary support for federal campaigns was very small (less than one dollar per member). Other ideological constructs are more difficult to identify. For example, there is considerable variation in whether strike benefits are based on members' need or on members' rights to these benefits.

THE UNDERLYING DIMENSIONS OF UNION CHARACTERISTICS

Although national unions might be well characterized by the few characteristics we summarized above, there are obviously many possible candidates for measurement. As Roomkin (1976) noted in his study of union strike propensities, the number of potential measures of centralization alone is "staggering." In fact, we have purposely collected data on a wider range of union features. Many of the measures we judged a priori to be of lesser importance are not shown in Table 1. Even after winnowing our list, there is still a likelihood of redundancy (multiple measures of the same underlying theoretical construct), and the number of remaining measures is still large. Practically speaking, however, our ability to digest the information contained in this many variables, as well as our ability to use the variables in subsequent analysis, is rather limited.

An alternative to describing unions by reporting results for all characteristics individually, or for only a selected subset of these characteristics, is to attempt to reduce the measured characteristics to a considerably smaller number of underlying dimensions. The appropriate technique for such a purpose is factor analysis. As long as the underlying dimensions found in this analysis can be logically labeled, this parsimonious representation of the underlying data can have significant benefits for both theory development and theory testing.

We have conducted a series of factor analyses,[11] first grouping variables on an a priori basis and then using the factor analysis procedure to help identify underlying dimensions within each group. Obviously, the criterion for the a priori groupings is critical. The criterion we used is a blend of conceptual guidance based on the analytical constructs of union characteristics (from the literature reviewed above) and pragmatism in applying this guidance to the measures available.[12] One piece of guidance from the conceptual literature is that a given measure may have multiple implications—for both democracy and centralization, for example—since the earlier review indicated that even at an analytical level the key concepts are at least somewhat interrelated. As a result several of the variables in Table 1 are used in more than one a priori grouping.

Table 2 outlines a comparison of the nine groups of descriptors we have used and our original theoretical "characteristics" of unions. An *x* in the table indicates our belief that there is some correspondence between the empirical data available and the theoretical dimension in question. For example, the centralization dimension seems to be well represented by the variables we have been able to gather. A question mark in the table indicates that the empirical data might also provide information on the theoretical dimension. For example, information on membership characteristics might provide information on the ideology of the

Table 2. Empirical Descriptors and Theoretical Dimensions

	Theoretical Dimensions:				
Empirical Descriptors	*Size*	*Democracy and Oligarchy*	*Structure*	*Bureaucracy, Rationalization, Centralization*	*Ideology*
Strike Benefits				x	?
Size	x				
Staffing			x	x	
Structure			x	x	
Centralization			x	x	?
Democracy		x			
Staffing Mix			x	x	
Membership			x		?
Ideology		?			x

union. Finally, there are multiple entries for several groupings of empirical descriptors, suggesting that their interpretations are not always clear-cut. The entries in the table indicate that we have at least some empirical proxies for all the theoretical dimensions we discussed earlier, although some measures may be much better than others.

RESULTS

We now present our results for a series of nine factor analyses and for the factor scores for the various national unions. For each analysis we present rotated factor patterns, which indicate the extent to which each variable "loads on" or is associated with the underlying factors identified; final communality estimates, which indicate the proportion of the variance in each variable that is "explained" by the factors presented; and summary information indicating the strength of the underlying factors (eigen values) and the percentage of the total variance among the variable accounted for by the factors.

Factor Analyses

Strike-Benefit Variables

The eight strike-benefits variables[13] yield two dominant factors or underlying dimensions, as indicated in Table 3, which together account for 52 percent of the total variation (cumulative percentage of variance). The first factor, which we label the "informal plan," includes informal authorization for benefits, general funding sources for benefits, benefits based on need rather than right, and a relatively long waiting period. That is, relatively high loadings on this factor occur for the variables just noted (*BENAUTH, BENSOUR, BNEED,* and *BENWAIT*). The second factor, "strategic national administration," includes a high benefit level, high- (national) level administration, and benefit eligibility based on rights. The contrast between the factors, as reflected in their labeling, seems to reflect different aspects of strike-benefit plans, but it should be kept in mind that the factors are uncorrelated (by definition) and that a given union may score high or low on both factors. The final communality estimates indicate that these two factors best capture authorization, the need versus right basis, national versus local administration, and waiting periods, among the measures considered. Conversely, the low communality values for *BENSOUR* (.40) and *BENLEV* (.37) indicate that much of the variance in these two variables is not accounted for by the two factors described.

Size Variables

As shown in Table 4, the six size variables yield two dominant factors, reflecting the size of the national—the number of members, employees, and locals, as well as assets and receipts—and the average membership size of locals.

Table 3. Factor Analysis Results for Strike-Benefit Variables

	Rotated Factor Pattern		
Variable	*Factor 1: "Informal Plan"*	*Factor 2: "Strategic National Administration"*	*Final Communality*
BENAUTH	.79	−.10	.65
BENSOUR	.63	−.07	.40
BNEED	.57	−.53	.61
BENWAIT	.70	.17	.52
BENLEV	−.02	.61	.37
STRADMN	−.04	.75	.57
Eigen value	1.97	1.14	
Percentage of variance	33	19	
Cumulative percentage of variance	33	52	

N = 41 national unions

Notes: *BENAUTH* = informal authority for strike benefits; *BENSOUR* = general fund source for strike benefits; *BNEED* = strike benefit eligibility based on need; *BENWAIT* = waiting period for strike benefits, in weeks; *BENLEV* = dollar amount of weekly strike benefits; *STRADMN* = index of "nationalness" in strike fund administration. Further information on these variables and the data sources for them appears in Table 1.

Thus, while the literature emphasizes staff counts as a key analytical component of union size, within national unions, staff counts and numbers of members are empirically almost indistinguishable. In addition, the results in Table 4 suggest that these two factors—national and local size—account for the major share of variation in all of the variables except the number of locals.

Table 4. Factor Analysis Results for Size Variables

	Rotated Factor Pattern		
Variable	*Factor 1: "National Size"*	*Factor 2: "Local Size"*	*Final Communality*
MEMBERS	.91	−.11	.85
LOCALS	.61	−.36	.50
ESCALE	.03	.95	.90
FTE	.95	.00	.90
ASSETS	.84	.04	.71
RECEIPTS	.84	.06	.71
Eigen value	3.53	1.04	
Percentage of variance	59	17	
Cumulative percentage of variance	59	76	

N = 59 national unions

Notes: *MEMBERS* = number of union members; *LOCALS* = number of union locals; *ESCALE* = number of members per local; *FTE* = number of full-time employees of the national union; *ASSETS* = total assets of the national union, in thousands of dollars; *RECEIPTS* = total receipts of the national union, in thousands of dollars. See also Table 1.

Staffing Variables

The factor analysis for the nine staffing variables yields three underlying factors, as shown in Table 5. The first of these, "support intensity" indicates that staffing mixes are relatively even, that is, that the various staff occupations tend to go together. This factor also seems to emphasize, however, larger support than administrative staffs. The second factor, conversely, tends to emphasize greater administrative staffing intensity. The ambiguous role (support versus function) of managerial and administrative employees seems consistent with these interpretations. Finally, the third factor emphasizes the overall staffing level, as reflected in the number of full-time employees and paid executive board members, and is thereby closely related to the "national size" factor from Table 4.

The fact that many of the per-member staffing variables load slightly negatively on the "staff level" factor weakly suggests some economies of scale in staffing. The communality estimates indicate that only the employment status of executive board members is not well accounted for by these three factors.

Structure Variables

Two underlying dimensions are apparent in the results for the structure variables shown in Table 6. First, the dominant factor, "complex structure," distin-

Table 5. Factor Analysis Results for Staffing Variables

	Rotated Factor Pattern			
Variable	*Factor 1: "Support Intensity"*	*Factor 2: "Functional Intensity"*	*Factor 3: "Staffing Level"*	*Final Communality*
FTE	.13	−.16	.84	.75
FTECAP	.93	.30	.05	.96
PROFCAP	.94	−.11	−.07	.91
MACAP	.81	.48	−.08	.89
CSCAP	.93	−.02	.02	.88
ORCAP	.10	.86	.23	.81
EBFTE	−.20	.21	.55	.39
GBDCAP	.74	.49	−.24	.85
OFFCAP	.16	.93	−.14	.91
Eigen value	4.47	1.74	1.14	
Percentage of variance	50	19	13	
Cumulative percentage of variance	50	69	82	

N = 59 national unions

Notes: *FTE* = number of full-time employees of the national union; *FTECAP* = number of full-time employees of the national union, per member; *PROFCAP* = number of full-time professional employees per member; *MACAP* = number of full-time managerial and administrative employees per member; *CSCAP* = number of full-time clerical and secretarial employees per member; *ORCAP* = number of full-time organizing and field representative employees per member; *EBFTE* = executive board members full-time employees; *GBDCAP* = number of governing board members per member; *OFFCAP* = number of national officers per member. See also Table 1.

guishes those nationals having intermediate bodies from those that do not. Moreover, this factor indicates that the existence of intermediate bodies is strongly associated with mandatory affiliation to those bodies by locals. The moderate loading for the *CRAFT* variable seems to indicate that complex structures tend to be somewhat more common in craft than in industrial and other unions. The second factor, "rational diversification" indicates that large locals tend to be found in unions that have industrially diverse jurisdictions. This result seems to suggest a "rational diversification" concept. The moderately negative loading for the *CRAFT* variable here implies that large locals and industrial diversity are not typical features of craft unions.

The final communality estimates indicate that all five variables are reasonably well accounted for by these two factors, which together account for 71 percent of the common variance. Given the ambiguity of the structure concept, it should be noted that these factors are relatively robust with respect to the inclusion of additional measures of structure. Specifically, in alternative analyses (not shown here) including membership-occupation and gender-mix measures and Seeber's (1984) jurisdiction measures, the two underlying factors shown in Table 6 were also apparent.[14]

Centralization Variables

The factor analysis of the nine centralization variables, all based on union constitutions, yields three underlying dimensions, as shown in Table 7. The dominant factor is the national union's control over contract content, with heavy loadings on national approval of local contract demands (*APPLOCD*) and of local

Table 6. Factor Analysis Results for Structure Variables

	Rotated Factor Pattern		
Variable	*Factor 1: "Complex Structure"*	*Factor 2: "Rational Diversification"*	*Final Communality*
COMPLEX	.94	.16	.91
AFFLINT	.95	.15	.93
ESCALE	−.03	.84	.71
ICONC	−.21	−.73	.58
CRAFT	.51	−.40	.42
Eigen value	2.15	1.39	
Percentage of variance	43	28	
Cumulative percentage of variance	43	71	

N = 44 national unions

Notes: *COMPLEX* = complex organizational structure (including intermediate body); *AFFLINT* = affiliation to intermediate body mandatory; *ESCALE* = number of members per union local; *ICONC* = percent of members in primary jurisdiction; *CRAFT* = craft union. See also Table 1.

contracts (*NATAPVL*), national prohibition of certain contract clauses (*NATPROH*), and the "nationalness" of bargaining demand formulation (*FDSCORE*). All these variables pertain to the content of bargaining and resultant agreements. The second factor, "national process control," deals more with the process or conduct of negotiations. The strong loadings for the "nationalness" of negotiating personnel (*NPSCORE*), the "nationalness" of the strike decision (*DSSCORE*), the "nationalness" of the bargaining level (*BLSCORE*), and local ratification of the contract (*LOCRATN*) all indicate strong national control of the bargaining process. The final factor in this group, "checks and balances" is enigmatic. It seems to reflect varying degrees of national and local control in the subdimensions represented by the nine variables, and thus overall a sort of balancing. For example, the *FDSCORE* loading mildly suggests national control of bargaining content, but this is balanced by local control of the final agreement's content, as reflected in the *LOCRATN* loading. The strong loading for the "nationalness" of the decision to terminate strikes (*DTSCORE*) measure is consistent with this theme in that it reflects the *technical* right of the national to maintain a strike despite local ratification. As a practical matter, a local (or its membership) retains control of the decision to terminate a strike on a local level regardless of the national constitution. These complications, in conjunction with

Table 7. Factor Analysis Results for Centralization Variables

	Rotated Factor Pattern			
Variables	*Factor 1: "National Content Control"*	*Factor 2: "National Process Control"*	*Factor 3: "Checks and Balances"*	*Final Communality*
NATPROH	.58	−.31	−.21	.48
LOCRATN	.21	−.48	.49	.51
NATAPVL	.77	.16	.14	.63
BLSCORE	.23	.63	.04	.45
FDSCORE	.49	−.02	.39	.39
NPSCORE	.04	.65	−.23	.48
DSSCORE	−.15	.64	.35	.55
DTSCORE	.05	.04	.81	.65
APPLOCD	.79	.11	.08	.64
Eigen value	2.05	1.60	1.15	
Percentage of variance	23	18	13	
Cumulative percentage of variance	23	41	53	

N = 50 national unions

Notes: *NATPROH* = national union prohibits certain contract clauses; *LOCRATN* = local ratification of contracts required; *NATAPVL* = national approval of contracts required; *BLSCORE* = index of "nationalness" of bargaining level; *FDSCORE* = index of "nationalness" of bargaining demand formulation; *NPSCORE* = index of "nationalness" of negotiating personnel; *DSSCORE* = index of "nationalness" of decision to strike; *DTSCORE* = index of "nationalness" of decision to terminate strikes; *APPLOCD* = national approval of local contract demands required. See also Table 1.

the literature's noting of outright contradictions in union constitutions, may illuminate this factor's meaning. These three factors are moderately successful in accounting for the variation in each of the individual variables, as indicated by the communality estimates.

Democracy Variables

Three underlying dimensions are apparent from the factor analysis of the eight democracy variables, as shown in Table 8. The dominant factor, "national autocracy" tends to support Gamm's (1979) contentions; the unions that elect their executive board on an at-large basis (*EBATL*) tend to have the longest intervals between both national elections (*YEARSNE*) and national conventions (*YEARSC*). To a lesser extent the unions with high scores on *EBATL* also do not provide for local ratification of agreements, (*LOCRATN*). The second dimension, "local autocracy" tends to parallel the first, but at a local level. Nationals with large locals (*ESCALE*) holding infrequent local elections (*YEARSLE*) score highest on this factor. In addition, the loading for the *COMPLEX* variable mildly suggests that intermediate bodies do tend to inhibit national control, but in doing so they may end up suppressing democracy at the local level. Nevertheless, the generally low loadings for *COMPLEX* across all three factors may reflect the variable's ambiguous implications, as suggested in the literature. Finally, the last

Table 8. Factor Analysis Results for Democracy Variables

	Rotated Factor Pattern			
Variable	*Factor 1: "National Autocracy"*	*Factor 2: "Local Autocracy"*	*Factor 3: "Representative Democracy"*	*Final Communality*
EBATL	.67	.02	−.10	.47
ELOFF	.27	−.05	.81	.72
YEARSC	.85	−.05	.10	.73
YEARSNE	.84	−.20	.12	.77
YEARSLE	−.14	.75	−.26	.64
COMPLEX	.18	−.42	.33	.32
ESCALE	.10	.86	.27	.82
LOCRATN	−.35	−.04	.67	.58
Eigen value	2.34	1.47	1.25	
Percentage of variance	29	18	16	
Cumulative percentage of variance	29	48	63	

N = 44 national unions

Notes: *EBATL* = executive board elected at-large (as opposed to by district); *ELOFF* = national officers elected by convention (as opposed to by referendum); *YEARSC* = number of years between national conventions; *YEARSNE* = number of years between national elections; *YEARSLE* = number of years between local elections; *COMPLEX* = complex organizational structure (including an intermediate body); *ESCALE* = number of members per local; *LOCRATN* = local ratification of contract required. See also Table 1.

factor in Table 8, "representative democracy" shows heavy loadings on national elections by convention (*ELOFF*) and on local ratification of contracts (*LOCRATN*). That these two variables both load fairly strongly indicates that the convention basis for national officer elections may yield more effective local control (and thus greater democracy within the national as a whole) than the referendum basis for national elections, a possibility suggested by Bok and Dunlop (1970). The final communality estimates are generally high, indicating these three factors account for substantial variance in most of the variables.

Staffing-Mix Variables

This factor analysis examines a subset of the staffing variables considered earlier. Here, only those variables reflecting the mix of occupations are considered. The analysis yields two underlying factors, "office staffing intensity" versus "field staffing intensity." Although the occupational breakdowns on which this analysis is based do not indicate a true field-versus-office dichotomy, this dichotomy, which tends to parallel the support-versus-administrative distinction noted earlier, is at least suggested by the factor patterns in Table 9. The strongest loadings for the primary factor occur for the clerical (*CSCAP*) and professional (*PROFCAP*) staffing level variables, while the heaviest loading for the second factor occurs for the organizer and field representative staffing intensity variable (*ORCAP*). The loadings for the remaining three staffing intensity variables are relatively weak for this second factor. Since these categories can be fairly closely associated with an office-versus-field distinction, this interpretation of the factor pattern appears justified. The ambiguity of the managerial-admini-

Table 9. Factor Analysis Results for Staffing-Mix Variables

	Rotated Factor Pattern		
Variable	*Factor 1: "Office Staff Intensity"*	*Factor 2: "Field Staff Intensity"*	*Final Communality*
MACAP	.48	.02	.23
PROFCAP	.83	−.14	.70
CSCAP	.81	.41	.82
ORCAP	−.01	.97	.95
Eigen value	1.66	1.04	
Percentage of variance	42	26	
Cumulative percentage of variance	42	68	

N = 104 national unions

Notes: *MACAP* = number of full-time managerial and administrative employees per member; *PROFCAP* = number of full-time professional employees per member; *CSCAP* = number of full-time clerical and secretarial employees per member; *ORCAP* = number of full-time organizing and field representative employees per member. See also Table 1.

strative staffing measure noted earlier is apparent here as well, and is reflected in the low communality for this variable.

Membership Characteristics

This factor analysis of four membership-characteristic measures yields two dominant factors that which together account for 80 percent of the common variance, as shown in Table 10.[15] The first factor, "professional" distinguishes primarily between unions with traditional blue-collar memberships (*BLSHR*) and those with substantial proportions of professional and technical members (*PTSHR*). The second factor, "clerical female," provides a similar distinction, but also seems to reflect the empirical inseparability of female gender (WOSHR) and clerical occupations (*CLERKSHR*). The second factor also draws a weaker distinction vis-à-vis blue-collar workers than the first. Together these two underlying factors account for major shares of variation in all of the occupational variables, but only a moderate share of the variation in the gender variable. Both factors represent a nontraditional type of union (that is, not a blue-collar, male union), but they reflect distinct nontraditional facets.

Ideology Variables

This last factor analysis examines a rather diverse set of measures that can be linked to ideology. Four distinct factors are indicated by the results in Table 11. The first factor, "executive compensation," shows strong loadings for the two chief executive officer compensation measures (*SAL77* and *TOTSAL77*). That these measures stand so far apart from the remaining ideology measures raises questions as to just what ideological aspect this factor represents, but rationaliza-

Table 10. Factor Analysis Results for Membership-Characteristic Variables

	Rotated Factor Pattern		
Variable	*Factor 1: "Professional"*	*Factor 2: "Clerical Female"*	*Final Communality*
WOSHR	.26	.62	.46
PTSHR	.99	.01	.98
CLERKSHR	.01	.90	.81
BCSHR	−.89	−.40	.95
Eigen value	2.20	1.00	
Percentage of variance	55	25	
Cumulative percentage of variance	55	80	

N = 83 national unions

Notes: *WOSHR* = percentage of membership who are women; *PTSHR* = percentage of membership in professional or technical occupations; *CLERKSHR* = percentage of membership in clerical occupations; *BLSHR* = percentage of membership in blue-collar occupations. See also Table 1.

tion and egalitarian considerations seem pertinent. The second factor, "political activism" shows strong loadings for the two membership-adjusted measures of federal political activity: federal election campaign contributions (*CONTRCAP*) and federal lobbyists (*TLOBCAP*).

The third factor, labeled "liberal economic," loads heavily on the share of the union's political contributions going to Democratic party candidates (*DEMSHARE*) and on per-member organizing activity (*ORGZNG*). To some extent the second and third factors together seem to parallel Walker and Lawler's (1979) union typology of aggression versus protection but also the more fundamental economic-versus-political distinction drawn by Scoville (1973). The third factor may reflect attempts by unions engaged in extensive organizing to obtain a more favorable legal climate for union organizing. The last factor, "relative dues," reflects a single item, dues levels relative to wages (*DUESRATE*). This factor could be viewed as ideological in the sense that it reflects a decision by unions and their members to use their resources collectively rather than individually, which could be linked to Perlman's (1928) "union mentality" notion. The final communality estimates indicate that these factors account for the majority of variation in each of the constituent measures. Finally, these four factors account for 90 percent of the total variation in these seven measures.

Because of the small sample size (N = 21) in this factor analysis, we should

Table 11. Factor Analysis Results for Ideology Variables

	Rotated Factor Pattern				
Variable	*Factor 1: "Executive Compensation"*	*Factor 2: "Policical Activism"*	*Factor 3: "Liberal Economic"*	*Factor 4: "Relative Dues"*	*Final Communality*
SAL77	.97	.14	.04	−.07	.97
TOTSAL77	.97	.12	−.06	−.01	.97
CONTRCAP	.18	.96	.08	.04	.97
DEMSHARE	.05	−.01	.83	.26	.75
DUESRATE	−.07	−.06	.01	.96	.91
TLOBCAP	.09	.97	.04	−.14	.98
ORGZNG	−.07	.13	.79	−.28	.73
Eigen value	2.50	1.54	1.22	1.02	
Percentage of variance	36	22	17	15	
Cumulative percentage of variance	36	58	75	90	

N = 21 national unions

Notes: *SAL77* = salary of chief executive officer of national union; *TOTSAL77* = salary of chief executive officer plus expenses; *CONTRCAP* = total dollar contributions by national unions' PACs to federal election campaigns, per member; *DEMSHARE* = percentage of all contributions by national unions' PACs to federal election campaigns that went to Democratic party candidates; *DUESRATE* = a proxy for members' dues payments to the national as a percentage of a member's wage rate; *TLOBCAP* = number of federal lobbyists paid by the national, per member; *ORGZNG* = a proxy for organizing activity per member. See also Table 1.

Table 12. Factor Scores For Selected Unions

Factor	Lowest Score	Highest Score	Union(s) with Lowest Score(s)	Union(s) with Highest Scores	Teamsters	Auto Workers	ITU	Air Line Pilots	Laborers	Retail, Wholesale	Service Employees	Office Employees	Steel workers
1. Informal plan	−1.1	5.0	Newspaper Guild	Leather Workers	−.1	−.5		1.1				−.3	
2. Strategic national administration	−2.4	2.9	Allied Industrial Workers	Air Line Pilots	.6	.7		2.9				−.6	
3. National size	−.6	5.0	Numerous unions	Auto Workers		5.0	−.1	−.2	.5	−.4	.0	−.5	3.7
4. Local size	−1.6	7.1	Letter Carriers (AFL-CIO)	Maritime		.9	−.1	.1	−.1	.0	.2	−.0	−1.1
5. Support staff intensity	−.5	7.1	Numerous unions	Air Line Pilots		.2	.9	7.1	−.4	−.3	−.5	−.3	.1
6. Administrative staff intensity	−.8	6.9	Numerous unions	Leather Workers		−.4	−.2	−.8	−.3	−.5	−.5	−.1	−.3
7. Staffing level	−1.8	4.0	Flint Glass Workers	Auto Workers		4.0	.6	−.8	.5	−1.2	−.2	−.1	3.3
8. Complex structure	−1.2	1.2	Meat Cutters	Firemen and Oilers		−1.1	−1.0		.8	.6	.6		−.9
9. Rational diversification	−1.4	2.6	Coopers	Service Employees		1.4	−1.1		.5	1.3	2.6		.5
10. National content control	−1.3	2.3	Boot and Shoe Workers	Leather Goods, Plastic and Novelty Workers		.3	1.8		−.6	−.7	−.8		−.3
11. National process control	−2.0	1.8	Plumbing and Pipe Fitting	Textile Workers		.3	−.9		.6	−.7	1.4		.2
12. Checks and balances	−1.4	2.1	Leather Goods, Plastic and Novelty Workers	Brick and Clay Workers		1.7	−1.3		−.3	.5	−.9		.2

13. National autocracy	−2.1	1.5	Electrical Workers (UE)	Laborers		−1.2	−1.3		1.5	−.5	1.0		−1.0
14. Local autocracy	−1.3	3.9	Cement Workers	Seafarers		.6	.6		.1	−.5	2.2		−.4
15. Representative democracy	−2.5	1.7	Typographical (ITU)	Retail, Wholesale, and Department Store		1.3	−2.5		.3	1.7	.5		−1.9
16. Office staff intensity	−.6	6.1	Brick and Clay Workers	Air Line Pilots		−.4	.2	6.1	−.4	−.4	−.4	−.4	−.2
17. Field staff intensity	−1.1	8.5	Air Line Pilots; Broadcast Employees	Tool Craftsmen		.2	−.0	−1.1	−.3	−.3	−.5	−.3	−.0
18. Professional	−.6	2.2	Numerous unions	Numerous unions				2.0	−.6	−.1		−.5	
19. Clerical female	−1.0	5.0	Masters, Mates and Pilots; Flight Engineers; Railway and Airline Supervisors	Office Employees				−.6	−.6	.6		5.0	
20. Executive compensation	−1.4	3.1	Electronic Workers (IUE)	Teamsters	3.1	−.5			1.1	−.8			.0
21. Political activity	−.9	4.2	Teamsters	Seafarers	−.9	.1			−.3	−.3			−.1
22. Liberal economic	−3.5	1.5	Painters	Retail, Wholesale, and Department Store	1.2	.4			−.4	1.5			.2
23. Relative dues	−1.1	3.3	Retail, Wholesale, and Department Store; Painters	Auto Workers	−.6	3.3			−.2	−1.1			1.1

note that the factors identified are fairly robust to specification. That is, in experiments in which we omitted variables alternately to augment the sample size (decrease the case-wise deletions), the resulting factor patterns tended to parallel closely those reported in Table 11.[16]

Factor Scores for Selected Unions

One way to assess the meaningfulness of the preceding factor analyses is to examine factor scores[17] for specific unions. This process permits a comparison between the rather abstract, quantitative information from the factor analyses with qualitative information on particular unions, in short, a test of the conventional wisdom on these unions. Toward this end Table 12 presents the lowest and highest scores for each factor and identifies the union(s) obtaining these extremes. In addition, since missing data might eliminate consideration of some leading candidates that exhibit particular dimensions, Table 12 also presents factor scores for a selected group of relatively well-known unions.

In numerous instances these data lend credibility to our results. As an obvious example the United Automobile Workers score highest on the "national size" factor, followed closely by the United Steelworkers. (The Teamsters cannot be scored here because of missing data.) More subtle examples also tend to confirm the validity of our analyses, however. For example, the Laborers score highest on the "national autocracy" factor, while the Electrical Workers (UE) score lowest—neither inconsistent with the conventional wisdom. Likewise, the Service Employees score highest and the Coopers score lowest on the "rational diversification" factor.

The Typographical Union (ITU) serves as an interesting case, especially in light of its prominence in the literature. The ITU scores lowest on the "representative democracy" factor, an apparently counterintuitive result. But this score reflects the heavy weight this factor gives to officer election by convention (rather than by referendum) and to local ratification of contracts. The ITU constitution provides for election by referendum and includes no local ratification requirement. More in line with what we know of the ITU, the union scores very low on "national autocracy." In general, therefore, the data in Table 12 tend to verify the meaningfulness of the factor scores as measures of union characteristics.[18]

DISCUSSION

Perhaps the best way to view our work on union characteristics is to look at it as an outline of the available descriptors of these characteristics. The major headings of this outline are our a priori groupings of variables—the "empirical descriptors"—such as strike benefits and size (see Table 2). The subheadings under these are the underlying factors such as "national size" and "local size" (Tables 3–11). Finally, listed under each subheading are the individual variables that load highly in these factors (the variables listed in Tables 3–11).

Some of the empirical descriptors presented in Table 2, such as size, structure, and centralization, are reasonably straightforward and seem to be well captured by the factor analyses. Rationalization and ideology, however, are two descriptors about which the results seem to say little, at least in a direct manner. In the case of rationalization, this defect may be more apparent than real, since rationalization is linked to centralization to some extent and to several of the other factors and variables outlined because of its multifaceted nature. The variable *FTECAP* (full-time union employees per member) and the factor "strategic national administration" would seem to have connections to rationalization, to name just two examples.

On the other hand, the ideology construct is indeed troublesome. Although ideology is certainly related to a number of the variables and factors described above, the relationships are tenuous. In part these tenuous links are due to the construct's haziness, but they are more attributable to the lack of plausible measures of ideology. It may be, however, that the range of ideological variation among U.S. national unions is, quite simply, limited. For example, the percentage of unions' contributions to federal election campaigns that went to Democratic party candidates (*DEMSHARE*) in this sample averaged over 92 percent, with a standard deviation of only 13 percent. There is simply not a great deal of variation in this aspect of ideology among U.S. national unions. (This generalization may apply to certain nonideological issues as well.) More meaningful ideological differentiation within this context may require collection of data on more subtle facets of the construct ideology.

In another light the results may be viewed more optimistically. As noted earlier, Anderson (1979a) found disappointing results for his measures of union characteristics as predictors of bargaining outcomes and suggested that the reason might have been that his measures were too far removed from the bargaining process. In this regard the empirically based factors yielded from our factor analyses may be very promising. Many of the factors, such as those involving national versus local control of contract negotiations and content, are clearly linked to bargaining. Once again, while the study of union characteristics is worthy of interest for its own sake, the importance of the study lies in the possibility of empirically assessing the impact of these characteristics on industrial relations outcomes. Of course, not all of the factors identified in our analyses are equally relevant to all outcomes, and in some instances the specific variables may be more appropriate than the composite factors. Future research will have to consider these issues in more detail.

CONCLUSIONS AND FUTURE DIRECTIONS

This exploratory study has taken a step toward filling a significant gap in industrial relations research. Specifically, the discussion and results above suggest some potentially fruitful avenues of inquiry for improving the understanding of union effects on industrial relations system outcomes. The composite factors we have identified will, we hope, be useful as a menu of union characteristics for consideration in conducting such inquiries.

Several recently completed empirical studies suggest that the factors are, in fact, useful in explaining variation in bargaining outcomes (Fiorito and Hendricks 1987), in single union certification election outcomes (Maranto and Fiorito 1987), and in union political activities, such as political action committee (PAC) spending and lobbying (Delaney, Fiorito, and Masters, in press). In general terms these studies have followed the conceptual scheme for defining union characteristics outlined in this paper—with encouraging results. In each study the union characteristics measures used demonstrated bivariate correlations with the dependent variables of about the same magnitude as more traditional market-based variables, such as the degree of unionization. And in each case the set of union characteristics employed explained a significant percentage of the variation in the dependent variables. The results have also suggested further avenues of inquiry. For example, the Fiorito and Hendricks paper found a negative relationship between political spending and bargaining outcomes. This suggests reverse causation: a poor showing in bargaining causes unions to devote more resources to activities beyond the bargaining arena. Nonetheless, no systematic attempts have yet been made to empirically investigate why union characteristics vary (that is, what causes them). This remains an important topic of inquiry.

In any event this paper demonstrates that a substantial amount of information on national union characteristics is already available, and that a great deal of this information bears directly on the critical analytical dimensions of union characteristics previously identified in the literature. Still, an original, comprehensive survey of national unions would be a valuable contribution to industrial relations research. The survey design should, of course, be guided by analytical conceptualizations of union characteristics rather than by data availability. Although many union characteristics, such as leadership style and personality will remain unmeasurable, we expect that any such survey will tap many of the same factors as those identified in our analyses here.

ACKNOWLEDGMENTS

We wish to acknowledge the assistance of Sid Camp, Anne C. Gray, and Kathryn J. Ready in preparing the data used for this study. William N. Cooke, John Thomas Delaney, Cynthia L. Gramm, Cheryl L. Maranto, and Marick F. Masters provided helpful comments on an earlier draft.

NOTES

1. The concept of unions (and other organizations) as social organisms occupying particular niches in the social ecosystem is developed at length in Boulding (1953). Boulding drew several interesting analogies between social systems and biological systems by employing concepts of adaptation, exchange, and control mechanisms. Hoxie (1917), interestingly, also drew from the biological

sciences in his analysis, referring to his study of union functional types as a ''genetic'' approach (p. xxv).

2. Roomkin (1976), however, viewed membership size as a proxy for internal control because of the diversity of interests among a large membership and the consequent need for centralized control. Membership size may be a plausible proxy for other concepts as well, including staff size, political power, or financial resources.

3. Recently, the ITU has been in the process of affiliating with the Communications Workers of America.

4. For example: ''In most direct encounters between ideology and rationalization, the former has invariably given ground in the United States'' (Barbash 1969, 157). Ideology is defined in the following section.

5. Barbash would appear to join Warner on this latter point insofar as he suggested that industrial unionism itself reflects rationalization through accommodation to modern industry structures.

6. Gray (1981) described in some detail the increasing tendency of unions to adopt ''managerial'' techniques. See also Craft, Abboushi, and Labovitz (1985).

7. Recall, too, that Kochan specifically posed the conflict in terms of *centralization* versus democracy.

8. A limitation on this potential proxy is suggested by the fact that empirical studies of union leader salaries tend to find that traditional (nonideological) approaches to pay determination are generally applicable.

9. Although the Labor Management Services Administration (LMSA) has collected extensive data from unions since its establishment in 1963, the only published comparative data are the selected data for 1976 published in this volume. At the time of this writing the LMSA is revising its information system to make more extensive information available on a timely basis and in a more accessible form in the near future (telephone conversation with Earl List of the LMSA, October 1984).

10. The salary figure is based on salaries of presidents of large unions, and no doubt overstates typical union president salaries.

11. The factor analyses followed principal-components and varimax-rotation methods. Since factor analysis is somewhat uncommon in industrial relations, we offer the following, nontechnical description of the technique. Factor analysis is a numerical procedure for identifying underlying dimensions that lead to common variance in measures. Rotated factor patterns indicate, through ''loadings,'' or values (which range from -1 to $+1$), on specific measures, the extent to which the variance in a particular measure is due to its association with the underlying factor. In other words, the factor can be viewed as a weighted combination of the measures analyzed, and the rotated factor pattern loadings indicate the relative weights of the measures making up the factor. Final communalities indicate the extent to which variations in specific measures are accounted for by variations in the underlying factor; these communalities range from 0 to 1. Eigen values are directly proportional to the amount of common variance among the variables accounted for by each factor; and the cumulative percentage accounted for by the factors is presented in each table (Tables 3–11) showing factor analysis results. Also presented are rotated factor patterns (loadings) and final communality estimates. Further information on factor analysis can be found in many statistics texts, such as Green and Tull (1978).

12. Upon presenting his ''functional types'' of unionism, Hoxie (1917, 52 n. 14) noted, ''The writer is also fully alive to the fact that no first attempt at functional analysis of unionism can be regarded as final, and will welcome any and all criticism and cooperation that may lead to greater accuracy in this respect.'' Similarly, our analysis of national union characteristics is but a first attempt, and we offer no claims of a monopoly on theory or good judgment. As in the more familiar regression methodology, factor analysis raises concerns of robustness and replicability. We cannot assert that others will agree with our judgments, but we have attempted to detail our measures and procedures so that future researchers will be able to determine how we arrived at our results and conclusions and may thereby correct any errors arising from our analysis.

13. Two variables, *NATBBODY* and *BRIGHT*, were dropped because after casewise deletions for missing values these measures were constant or linear combinations of other variables.

14. Seeber's (1984) measures (*GJUR55* and *GJUR82*, here) help to distinguish between recent and historical general jurisdictions; and member characteristics together identify a traditional/nontraditional dimension (where *traditional* means a narrow jurisdiction of blue-collar, male workers). Nonetheless, because of the small samples that resulted when including all of these measures, we preferred using instead the analysis in Table 6. A separate factor analysis reported below provides further information on member characteristics.

15. The *SALESHR* variable was omitted from this analysis because it is a linear combination of the other membership-characteristic variables.

16. In addition, when we considered a measure of union-specific strike probabilities (based on contract data provided to us by Cynthia Gramm; see Gramm 1987), this strike measure loaded strongly on the "liberal economic" factor, lending support to its interpretation as reflecting economic rather than political activity. We decided, however, that the strike measure is more appropriately termed an outcome than a union characteristic, and we therefore omitted it from the factor analysis of the ideology variables. In general, we found the results for this and the other factor analyses to be relatively insensitive to the inclusion or omission of specific variables or cases with extreme values.

17. In essence a factor score is an index that weights each variable in a given factor analysis in proportion to its rotated factor pattern loadings. Hence, the factor scores may be considered "synthetic" variables or indexes for the respective underlying dimensions.

18. There are, of course, some anomalies other than that in the ITU case already noted. For example, the relatively high "liberal economic" score for the Teamsters may puzzle some readers. Recall from Table 11 the two dominant loadings for this factor are for the *DEMSHARE* and the *ORGZNG* variables. The Teamster values for these variables exceed the sample means for both variables (94.06 versus 92.49 for *DEMSHARE* and .37 versus .19 for *ORGZNG*). As with the ITU illustration in the text, this example illustrates that labeling the factors is more art than science, and that some apparent anomalies may stem from limitations of factor labels and the particular variables used as the basis for the factor analysis.

REFERENCES

Aldenderfer, Mark S., and Roger K. Blashfield. 1984. Cluster Analysis, Sage University Paper Series on Quantitative Applications in the Social Sciences, 007-44, Beverly Hills, CA: Sage Publications.

Anderson, John C. 1979a. Bargaining Outcomes: An IR System Approach. *Industrial Relations* 18 (Spring):127–43.

_________. 1979b. Determinants of Bargaining Outcomes in the Federal Government of Canada. *Industrial and Labor Relations Review* 32 (January):224–41.

Applebaum, Leon, and Harry R. Blaine. 1975. The "Iron Law" Revisited: Oligarchy in Trade Union Locals. *Labor Law Journal* (September):597–600.

Barbash, Jack. 1969. Rationalization in the American Union. In *Essays in Industrial Relations Theory*, ed. Gerald G. Somers, 147–62. Ames: Iowa State University Press.

Berle, A. A., Jr., and Gardner C. Means. 1932. *The Modern Corporation and Private Property*. New York: Commerce Clearing House.

Bok, Derek C., and John T. Dunlop. 1970. *Labor and the American Community*. New York: Simon & Schuster.

Boulding, Kenneth E. 1953. *The Organizational Revolution*. New York: Harper and Brothers.

Business Week. 1978. Where Tradition and Politics Rule. 15 May, 94ff.

Commons, John R. 1913. American Shoemakers, 1648–1895, in *Labor and Administration*, New York: Macmillan; reprinted in *Readings in Labor Economics and Labor Relations*, ed. Richard L. Rowan. Homewood, IL: Richard D. Irwin, 1980.

Cook, Alice H. 1963. *Union Democracy: Practice and Ideal*, Ithaca, NY: New York State School of Industrial and Labor Relations, Cornell University.

Cooke, William N. 1983. Determinants of the Outcomes of Union Certification Elections. *Industrial and Labor Relations Review* 36 (April):402–14.

Craft, James A., Suhail Abboushi, and Trudy Labovitz. 1985. Concession Bargaining and Unions: Impact and Implications, *Journal of Labor Research* 6 (Spring):167–80.

Delaney, John Thomas, Jack Fiorito, and Marick F. Masters. In press. The Effect of Union Organizational and Environmental Characteristics on Union Political Action. *American Journal of Political Science*.

Derber, Milton. 1969. "Industrial Democracy" as an Organizing Concept for a Theory of Industrial Relations. In *Essays in Industrial Relations Theory*, ed. Gerald G. Somers, 177–90. Ames: Iowa State University Press.

Dickens, William T. 1983. The Effect of Company Campaigns on Certification Elections: *Law and Reality* Once Again. *Industrial and Labor Relations Review* 36 (July):560–75.

Donaldson, Lex, and Malcolm Warner. 1974. Bureaucratic and electoral Control in Occupational Interest Associations. *Sociology* 8 (January):47–57.

Dunlop, John T. 1958. *Industrial Relations Systems*. New York: Holt.

Feuille, Peter, Wallace E. Hendricks, and Lawrence M. Kahn. 1981. Wage and Nonwage Outcomes in Collective Bargaining: Determinants and Tradeoffs. *Journal of Labor Research* 2 (Spring):39–53.

Fiorito, Jack, and Wallace E. Hendricks. 1987. Union Characteristics and Bargaining Outcomes. *Industrial and Labor Relations Review* 40 (July):569–84.

French, J. Lawrence, Paul Hayashi, and David A. Gray. 1983. The Compensation of National Union Presidents: Moderating Effects of Union Size. *Journal of Labor Research* 4 (Summer):225–37.

Gamm, Sara. 1979. The Election Base of National Union Executive Boards. *Industrial and Labor Relations Review* 32 (April):295–311.

Gifford, Courtney. 1982; 1984; 1986. *Directory of U.S. Labor Organizations* (three editions: 1982–83, 1984–85, and 1985–87). Washington, DC: Bureau of National Affairs.

Gramm, Cynthia L. 1987. New Measures of the Propensity to Strike During Contract Negotiations. *Industrial and Labor Relations Review* 40 (April):406–17.

Gray, Lois S. 1981. Unions Implementing Managerial Techniques. *Monthly Labor Review* 104 (June):3–13.

Green, Paul E., and Donald S. Tull. 1978. *Research for Marketing Decisions*, 4th ed. Englewood Cliffs, NJ: Prentice-Hall.

Hardman, J. B. S. 1972. *Labor at the Rubicon*. New York: New York University Press.

Heneman, Herbert G., III, and Marcus H. Sandver. 1986. Union Characteristics and Organizing Success, photocopy. Madison, WI: Graduate School of Business, University of Wisconsin.

Hochner, Arthur, Karen Koziara, and Stuart Schmidt. 1980. Thinking About Democracy and Participation in Unions. In *Proceedings of the Thirty-Second Annual Meeting, 28–30 December 1979, Atlanta*, Barbara D. Dennis, (ed.) 12–19. Madison, WI: Industrial Relations Research Association.

Holley, William H., and Kenneth M. Jennings. 1983. *The Labor Relations Process*, 2d ed. Hinsdale, IL: Dryden Press.

Hoxie, Robert F. 1917. *Trade Unionism in the United States*. New York: D. Appleton.

Kochan, Thomas A. 1980. *Collective Bargaining and Industrial Relations: From Theory to Policy and Practice*. Homewood, IL: Richard D. Irwin.

Kochan, Thomas A., and Richard N. Block. 1977. An Interindustry Analysis of Bargaining Outcomes: Preliminary Evidence from Two-Digit Industries. *Quarterly Journal of Economics* 91(August):431–52.

Kochan, Thomas A., and Hoyt N. Wheeler. 1975. Municipal Collective Bargaining: A Model and Analysis of Bargaining Outcomes. *Industrial and Labor Relations Review* 29(October):46–66.

Lahne, Herbert J. 1970. Union Constitutions and Collective Bargaining Procedures. In *Trade Union Government and Collective Bargaining*, ed. Joel Seidman, 167–95. New York: Praeger.

Leibenstein, Harvey. 1966. Allocative Efficiency v. "X-Efficiency." *American Economic Review* 56 (June):392–415.

Leonard, Jonathan S. 1985. The Effect of Unions on the Employment of Blacks, Hispanics, and Women. *Industrial and Labor Relations Review* 39 (October):115–32.

Lipset, Seymour Martin. 1960. *Political Man*. New York: Doubleday.

Lipset, Seymour Martin, Martin Trow, and James Coleman. 1956. *Union Democracy*. Glencoe, IL: Free Press.

Maranto, Cheryl L., and Jack Fiorito. 1987. The Effect of Union Characteristics on the Outcome of NLRB Certification Elections. *Industrial and Labor Relations Review* 40 (January):225–40.

Masters, Marick F., and John Thomas Delaney. 1985. The Causes of Union Political Involvement: A Longitudinal Analysis. *Journal of Labor Research* 6 (Fall):341–62.

Michels, Robert. 1959. *Political Parties*. Glencoe, IL: Free Press.

Mills, Daniel Quinn. 1986. *Labor-Management Relations*, 3d ed. New York: McGraw-Hill.

Olson, Anne. 1982. Union Organizational Characteristics and Bargaining Outcomes, M.A. tutorial. Champaign: University of Illinois.

Perlman, Selig. 1928. *A Theory of the Labor Movement*. Philadelphia: Porcupine Press (1979, first published in 1928).

Rideout, R. W. 1967. Responsible Self-Government in British Trade Unions. *British Journal of Industrial Relations* 5 (March):74–86.

Rogow, Robert. 1967. Membership Participation and Centralized Control. *Industrial Relations* 7 (February):132–45.

Roomkin, Myron. 1976. Union Structure, Internal Control, and Strike Activity. *Industrial and Labor Relations Review* 29 (January):198–217.

Scoville, James G. 1973. Some Determinants of the Structure of Labor Movements. In *The International Labor Movement in Transition*, Adolf Sturmthal and James G. Scoville, 58–78. Urbana, IL: University of Illinois Press.

Seeber, Ronald L. 1984. The Expansion of National Union Jurisdictions, 1955–1982, photocopy. Ithaca, NY: New York State School of Industrial and Labor Relations, Cornell University.

Shirom, Arie. 1985. The Labor Relations System: A Proposed Conceptual Framework. *Relations Industrielles/Industrial Relations* 40 (2):303–23.

Strauss, George. 1977. Union Government in the U.S.: Research Past and Future. *Industrial Relations* 16 (May):215–42.

Taft, Philip. 1973. Internal Union Structure and Functions. In *The Next Twenty-Five Years of Industrial Relations*, ed. Gerald G. Somers. Madison, WI: Industrial Relations Research Association.

U.S. Department of Labor, Bureau of Labor Statistics. Various biennial editions. *Directory of National Unions and Employee Associations*. Washington, DC: GPO.

U.S. Department of Labor, Labor Management Services Administration. 1980. *Union Financial Statistics 1976*, Washington, DC: GPO.

U.S. Federal Election Commission. 1980. *FEC Reports on Financial Activity 1977–78*, Final Report, Party and Non-Party Political Committees, vol. III—Non-Party Detailed Tables (Corporate and Labor). Washington, DC: Federal Election Commission, April.

Walker, J. Malcolm, and John J. Lawler. 1979. Dual Unions and Political Processes in Organizations. *Industrial Relations* 18 (Winter):32–43.

Warner, Malcolm. 1975. Unions as Complex Organizations. *Relations Industrielles/Industrial Relations* 30(April):43–59.

Williamson, Oliver E. 1967. *The Economics of Discretionary Behavior: Managerial Objectives in a Theory of the Firm*. Chicago: Markham.

TOWARD A MODEL OF UNION COMMITMENT

Clive Fullagar and Julian Barling

Organizational psychology has passed through a dark age of research on organized labor (Gordon and Burt 1981; Gordon and Nurick 1981; Huszczo, Wiggins, and Currie 1984). Since the 1950s, a decade Strauss (1977, 240) referred to as the "Golden Age of research and discussion on union democracy," theorizing and research in psychology has largely avoided the topic of labor and trade unions. Indeed, it has been estimated that no more than one percent of research conducted by industrial and organizational psychologists focuses on labor and trade union issues (Campbell, Daft, and Hulin 1982). This neglect can be attributed to a number of causes. First, as a result of organizational psychologists' traditional identification with management, their theory and methods are often perceived as preventing the consolidation of unions (Gordon and Burt 1981; Huszczo, Wiggins, and Currie 1984; Walker 1979). Second, organizational psychologists have been concerned with serving mainly those organizations capable of sponsoring research. Third, organizational psychologists' inadequate conceptualization of industrial conflict, stemming from the philosophies of scientific management and human relations (Fullager 1983; Gordon and Burt 1981; Kornhauser 1961; Strauss 1977), precludes an adequate focus on industrial relations issues. As a result, organizational psychologists remain largely ignorant about the psychology of unions, while unionists remain skeptical and suspicious

Advances in Industrial and Labor Relations, Volume 4, pages 43-78.

ISBN: 0-89232-909-2

about research in organizational psychology. As Huszczo, Wiggins, and Currie (1984, 432) pointed out, unionists perceive "the contributions of psychologists, at best, to be unrelated to their needs, at worst to be antithetical to their interests."

This situation is surprising, since many industrial relations theorists acknowledge the important contribution of organizational psychology to the understanding of labor-management relationships. Nevertheless, it is only since the late 1970s that organizational psychologists have undertaken research focusing on organized labor (Gordon and Burt 1981; Huszczo, Wiggins, and Currie 1984; Srinivas 1981; Stagner 1981). This renewed interest among psychologists is evidenced in the formation of various committees within the American Psychological Association, special editions of the *International Review of Applied Psychology* (1981) and the *Journal of Occupational Psychology* (1986), a special section of the *American Psychologist* (1984), and, as we will discuss, a growing body of empirical research—all specifically addressing the topic of psychology's relationship with, and contribution to, labor.

One aspect of organizational theory of particular relevance is the concept of member commitment to unions. Research on union commitment represents an attempt to clarify the relationships between union psychological, behavioral, and attitudinal variables, on the one hand, and union participation, on the other. The central role of union commitment in labor organizations is evident in Gordon and his colleagues' (1980, 480) observation:

> Since the ability of union locals to attain their goals is generally based on the members' loyalty, belief in the objectives of organized labor, and willingness to perform services voluntarily, commitment is part of the very fabric of unions.

Gordon and Nurick (1981) judged that union commitment is a major variable in any applied psychological approach aimed an understanding unions. Investigating commitment in labor organizations should enhance our understanding of the psychological processes involved in unionization; provide unions with research of some practical efficacy; and test the generality of current models of commitment (for example, Mowday, Porter, and Steers 1982) in a different social institution, namely, the not-for-profit labor organization. In short, union commitment is a crucial topic for investigation.

In trying to understand the causes and consequences of members' attachment to their unions, previous research has focused almost exclusively on the union membership itself (for example, Brett 1980; Freeman and Medoff 1984). Yet many people who belong to unions do not necessarily do so willingly (as, for example, in organizations with strong union security agreements); and many who do not have the opportunity to join a union would choose to if they could. Focusing exclusively on union members to understand union psychology thus creates a false dichotomy, ignoring the diversity of attitudes, beliefs, and behaviors of union members and nonmembers alike. In the following review of the literature we will address this problem in more detail.

COMMITMENT AND LABOR ORGANIZATIONS

Although unions have much in common with commercial organizations, they retain unique properties (Strauss 1977). The extent to which the goals of labor organizations differ from those of their commercial counterparts likely affects the nature of membership commitment.

Democracy is one primary objective of many unions (Stein 1972; Strauss and Warner 1977). Union democracy has been defined as the extent of rank-and-file participation in union activities (Seidman et al. 1958). To achieve a democratic ethos and provide grassroots support to its collective actions, the union must maintain not only a political structure that is accessible to control by all members, but also a level of commitment that facilitates participation.

Commitment, therefore, is a crucial facet of organized labor because it can help determine the success and effectiveness of the union in imposing sanctions against the employer and in consolidating its bargaining power. Kanter (1968) has distinguished three types of commitment. First is "continuance commitment," the individual's commitment to participate in the organization and remain a member. This form of commitment reduces organizational turnover. Second, "cohesion commitment" is the individual's commitment to group solidarity, which in turn makes the organization more resistant to external threats. Finally, "control commitment" is the individual's commitment to the ideology of the organization, a commitment that ensures conformity to organizational norms. The success of the union's political economy depends on the extent to which the organization can secure all three types of commitment from its members. One common index of the extent of members' commitment to the union is their involvement in union elections and meetings. Child, Loveridge, and Warner (1973) noted that an understanding of commitment to unions becomes important to unions when they are confronted, for example, by declining attendance at union meetings and elections:

> The general lack of appreciation of member orientations, of the processes leading to their emergence and the way they are acted out through behavior in the union, have been serious omissions, not just of trade union studies, but much of organizational theory in general (p. 75).

TOWARD A DEFINITION OF UNION COMMITMENT

Despite the relevance of commitment to an understanding of union psychology, it was only in 1980 that a serious attempt was made to formalize a definition of union commitment based on data already obtained on organizational commitment. Previous research in the 1950s had investigated allegiance and loyalty to the union (Purcell 1954; Stagner 1954, 1956), but only in the context of members' dual allegiance to both the union and the employer. Furthermore, the definitions of this concept of allegiance were anecdotal and subjective. Purcell (1954, 49), for instance, defined allegiance as "an attitude of favorability towards the . . . union . . . or general approval of [its] over-all policies." Stagner (1954) described the concept in more general terms as the acceptance of membership within a group and the expression of favorable feelings toward the group. He noted that allegiance "has less connotation of depth and intensity" than commitment, but "is more intense than passive membership" (p. 42). Rosen and Rosen (1955) suggested that allegiance is a static phenomenon with little relationship to situational variables.

Other research on labor organizations tended to adopt a distinction between the reasons individuals become members of unions and the development of union loyalty. Stagner (1956), for example, saw involvement in unions as the result of feelings of frustration on the job and the perception of the union as a means for expressing aggression against management.

Commitment to the union, then, was viewed as the outcome of a calculative involvement with the union and a desire for better economic and working conditions, control over benefits, and self-expression and communication with higher management (Sayles and Strauss 1953). None of these early references to union allegiance, however, constituted a systematic exploration and operationalization of the concept of union commitment.

More recently, attempts have been made to apply psychological models and typologies to phenomena related to commitment. For example, an expectancy-value model has been used to explain union support (Allen and Keaveny 1983) and participation (Klandermans 1984). This model suggests commitment is dependent on three types of perceptions: the perceived valence of the outcomes of collective action, such as higher wages, fairer treatment, better working conditions and quality of working life, pickets and strikes, and union dues; the extent of members' expectancy that changes in their effort or participation in union activities will lead to changes in union performance; and the perceived instrumentality of unions in achieving valued outcomes. The model predicts that the higher the positive value attached to outcomes and the stronger the expectancy and instrumentality beliefs associated with having a union, the greater the motivation to support or participate in the union. Although expectancy-value theory has not been directly applied to union commitment, DeCotiis and LeLouarn (1981) have found it to be applicable to the decision to unionize; Laliberte and Barling (1986) have shown that perceived union instrumentality predicts nonunion workers' attitudes toward unions; and Klandermans (1984) has validated the expectancy-value model in studying the willingness to participate in social movements.

Child, Loveridge, and Warner (1973) suggested a schema for understanding membership attachment to labor organizations. Their typology consists of two dimensions: the extent of the member's active involvement in union affairs, and the degree of congruence between member expectations and the policies of the union. Although this conceptualization of attachment has heuristic value as an explanatory framework within which changes in commitment or attachment can be monitored and analyzed, no empirical research has validated the typology. Nevertheless, the two dimensions are strongly analogous to components of more recent definitions of union commitment.

In 1980 Gordon et al. constructed a measure of union commitment, drawing on more general research into organizational commitment. Theirs constituted the first systematic attempt by organizational psychologists to analyze union commitment. The basis of their conceptual approach was to define commitment as the binding of the individual to the organization, be it union or employer. Their measure of union commitment reflected many of the components identified in previous definitions of organizational commitment (for example, Buchanan 1974; Porter and Smith 1970). It also underscored the importance of the exchange relationship between member and union (defined below; Steers 1977) in the development of commitment. The Gordon et al. definition of union commitment is an attitudinal one because it conceptualizes attitudes of commitment as leading to committed behaviors rather than vice versa. We discuss the distinction between attitudinal and behavioral approaches to commitment in more detail later.

The research by Gordon and his colleagues precipitated three studies that attempted to establish the concurrent and construct validity of their measure of union commitment (Fullager 1986a; Gordon, Beauvais, and Ladd 1984; Ladd et al. 1982). The results of those studies suggest that union commitment subsumes four major constructs, which have been distilled from factor analyses:

1. an attitude of loyalty to the union,
2. a feeling of responsibility to the union,
3. a willingness to exert strong effort on behalf of the union, and
4. a belief in the goals of unionism.

Union loyalty denotes a sense of pride in the union and reflects the exchange relationship highlighted by previous research on organizational commitment (for example, Steers 1977). The union member, in exchange for the gratification of various needs and the provision of benefits, develops attitudes of loyalty to the union. Not surprisingly, union loyalty correlates highly with general satisfaction with the union (Gordon et al. 1980). Thus, to some extent, loyalty indicates a "calculative involvement" (Etzioni 1961; Kidron 1978) in labor organizations (Gordon et al. 1980; Ladd et al. 1982) based on members' perceptions of the union's instrumentality. Finally, loyalty to the union implies a desire to retain union membership. This would support a priori definitions of organizational commitment that emphasize the desire to remain a member of the organization (Porter and Smith 1970).

Responsibility to the union and willingness to exert effort for the union again reflect Porter and Smith's (1970) notion of organizational commitment, whereby the individual member is prepared to exert a great deal of effort on behalf of the organization and to provide a service to the organization, in this case, the union. Schneider (1985) proposed that the willingness to exert effort beyond that normally required for membership in an organization is the hallmark of commitment. According to Katz's (1964) typology this effort not only involves the fulfillment of dependable role behaviors, but also includes behavior beyond prescribed roles. Responsibility to the union and willingness to exert effort have been found to correlate significantly with behavioral indices of participation in union activities. Specifically, the greater these commitment components, the more likely the individual is to fulfill those routine responsibilities of membership that are necessary for the effectiveness of the union. These responsibilities include making sure that the collective bargaining agreement is upheld; ensuring that shop stewards perform their jobs correctly; making use of the grievance procedure; and so forth (Gordon et al. 1980). In addition, these constructs of union commitment are associated with behavioral participation over and above the required activities. Extra effort thus means helping new members learn about aspects of the agreement that affect them; talking about the union with friends; promoting the values and objectives of the union; and teaching new members how to use the grievance procedure.

Finally, belief in the values and goals of the unions reflects Kanter's (1968) concept of ideological conformity and support. It also reflects Porter and Smith's (1970) definition of commitment as a belief in the values and objectives of the organization.

These four constructs of union commitment—loyalty, responsibility, effort, and belief in union goals—appear to be generalizable across various samples of workers. Both Ladd et al. (1982) and Gordon, Beauvais, and Ladd (1984) have demonstrated the validity of these constructs in samples of engineers, technicians, and nonprofessional workers who were members of white-collar unions. Fullager (1986a) has also shown their stability and generalizability in a sample of blue-collar workers of differing occupational status. Together these three studies support the contention by Gordon et al. (1980) that union commitment is a pervasive attitude that is normally distributed throughout the labor force.

Thus, the relevant research conducted on union commitment has generated a definition of union commitment that is stable, valid, generalizable, and operational. This definition also reflects many of the core characteristics associated with more general concepts of organizational commitment, especially those suggested by Porter and Smith (1970). A reasonable definition of union commitment, therefore, would consist of the following adaptation of Porter and Smith's (1970, 2) description of organizational commitment:

1. a strong loyalty to the union and a desire to remain a member of the union,

2. a feeling of responsibility to the union and a willingness to exert strong effort on behalf of the union, and
3. a belief in and acceptance of the values and goals of both the individual union and organized labor as a whole.

It is insufficient, however, merely to outline an attitudinal definition of union commitment and then investigate the extent and level of these attitudes. It may be that the constructs of union commitment are stable, but the causes and consequences of union commitment vary for different segments of the labor force and for union members of differing occupational status. For instance, pro-union attitudes have been shown to vary with position in the organizational hierarchy as well as with related variables such as the availability of information and effective influence mechanisms (Maxey and Mohrman 1980). Moreover, just because the constructs of commitment are stable across unions and organizations does not mean that the causes and consequences of organizational and union commitment cannot differ. For example, whereas job satisfaction and organizational commitment are positively related (Mowday, Porter, and Steers 1982), job satisfaction is negatively related to the desire to join a union (Brett 1980). Consequently, it is necessary to develop a model that identifies both the antecedents and outcomes of union commitment across heterogeneous samples of workers.

A MODEL OF UNION COMMITMENT

Before outlining our model of commitment to the union, we must offer a cautionary note. The processes of commitment described below are based mainly on correlational data derived from cross-sectional research in several areas of investigation. First, the research on unionization has established the correlates of various nominal measures of involvement in unions, such as membership levels, voting intention, voting behavior, and attitudes. Union commitment can be viewed as related to these, yet, as noted earlier, we need a broader approach than to focus on union members alone, especially in light of the prevalence of closed-shop agreements in Canada and union-shop agreements in the United States. Second is the research on organizational commitment. Although in this line of research the causal inferences made about antecedents and outcome are largely speculative, the research does serve as a valuable empirical base for the development of a model of union commitment (Fukami and Larson 1984). Finally, there is a considerable amount of psychological and industrial relations research that can provide a theoretical basis for a psychological model of union commitment. Not only has this research demonstrated the relevance and applicability of behavioral science concepts to the field of industrial relations, but also we hope that it will prove another step in redressing the historical neglect by psychologists of labor issues. A model of union commitment is presented in Figure 1.

Figure 1. A Hypothetical Model of Commitment to Labor Organizations

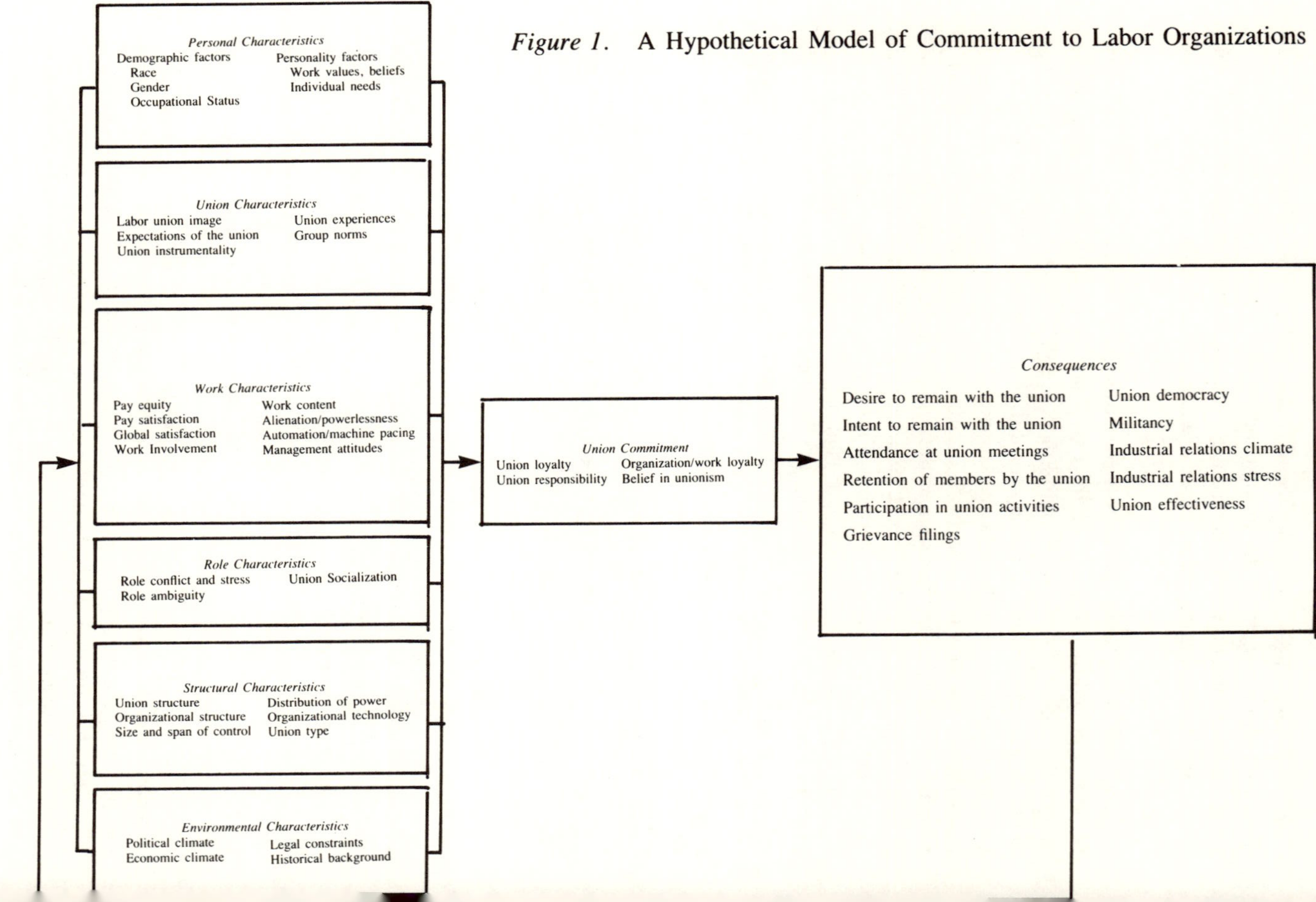

Personal Characteristics
Demographic factors
Race
Gender
Occupational Status
Personality factors
Work values, beliefs
Individual needs
Union Characteristics
Labor union image
Expectations of the union
Union instrumentality
Union experiences
Group norms
Work Characteristics
Pay equity
Pay satisfaction
Global satisfaction
Work Involvement
Work content
Alienation/powerlessness
Automation/machine pacing
Management attitudes
Role Characteristics
Role conflict and stress
Role ambiguity
Union Socialization
Structural Characteristics
Union structure
Organizational structure
Size and span of control
Distribution of power
Organizational technology
Union type
Environmental Characteristics
Political climate
Economic climate
Legal constraints
Historical background
Union Commitment
Union loyalty
Union responsibility
Organization/work loyalty
Belief in unionism
Consequences
Desire to remain with the union
Intent to remain with the union
Attendance at union meetings
Retention of members by the union
Participation in union activities
Grievance filings
Union democracy
Militancy
Industrial relations climate
Industrial relations stress
Union effectiveness

Antecedents of Union Commitment

Personal Characteristics

Numerous studies have found personal characteristics to be related to commitment to organizations. Most evidence suggests that organizational commitment is positively related to age and tenure with the organization (Angle and Perry 1981; Hrebiniak 1975; Morris and Sherman 1981) and inversely related to education (Angle and Perry 1981; Morris and Sherman 1981; Morris and Steers 1980; Steers 1977). Moreover, men exhibit higher levels of organizational commitment than women (Angle and Perry 1981; Hrebiniak and Alutto 1972). A few studies have shown positive relationships between organizational commitment and such personal attitudes and motivations as a work ethic (Buchanan 1974; Kidron 1978; Rabinowitz and Hall 1977), work-oriented central life interest (Dubin, Champoux, and Porter 1975), and achievement motivation and higher order need strength (Morris and Sherman 1981; Steers and Spencer 1977). It would appear, then, that personal characteristics must be accounted for in the development of a model of union commitment.

Various studies have attempted to relate the demographic characteristics of union members to several measures of unionization including membership levels, voting intention, voting behavior, and member attitudes toward the union. In particular, variables such as gender, age, tenure, number of dependents, occupational level, income, and urbanization are weakly associated with these measures of unionization (Bigoness 1978; Blinder 1972; Getman, Goldberg, and Herman 1976; Kochan 1978; Uphoff and Dunnette 1956). Most studies, however, suggest that there is little evidence to support the idea of a "union type" (Fullagar 1986b; Gordon et al. 1980).

The only demographic variables that have been found associated with union commitment are members' gender (Gordon et al. 1980) and members' race (Fullagar 1986b). Gordon et al. (1980) also found that female members' expression of union loyalty was more positive than that of male workers. Yet men participate more in union activities than women do. This phenomenon is attributed not to gender per se, but rather diverse causes, such as women's greater experience of gender-role conflict (Chusmir 1982). Family commitments may interfere with full participation in union affairs by women, who experience greater levels and forms (simultaneous rather than sequential) of interrole conflicts than their male counterparts (Hall 1972). This example indicates that a lack of active participation in the union does not preclude strong feelings of attachment to the organization; it also brings into focus the distinction between attitudinal and behavioral commitment and the possibility that each may have different causes, correlates, and consequences.

As to race, unorganized black workers have been shown to be more willing to join unions than their white counterparts (Kochan 1980, 147). This finding was explained by Buchholz (1978b), who found that black workers had stronger perceptions of oppression and discrimination, fewer opportunities to obtain alternative employment, and fewer opportunities to express higher order needs than white workers. The discrepancy, therefore, is not because of race per se, but because of the racist practices and attitudes that still prevail among employers. Race can be construed as a "marker" variable that denotes the existence of important underlying influences.

In Fullagar's (1986b) research subjects were drawn from a South African, blue-collar labor sample, heterogeneous in terms of race. The author found that race influenced the relationship between loyalty to the union and work and union experiences. Race therefore denoted differences in privilege, job security, wages, union protection, and access to political, organizational, and social institutions for the satisfaction of both lower and higher order needs. Thus, although the four union commitment constructs are stable across professional, nonprofessional, and technical categories of workers (Gordon, Beauvais, and Ladd 1984), and also across black and white workers in skilled, semiskilled, and unskilled occupations (Fullagar 1986a), the antecedents of commitment are moderated by race. The different causes of commitment are a reflection of the varying needs of a divided labor force (such as the one that exists in South Africa).

In formulating a model of union commitment, we must distinguish between demographic variables and personality characteristics as antecedents to union commitment. As noted above, even where demographic variables (such as race) predict commitment, these demographic variables are "marker" variables, merely denoting the existence of important underlying influences. In contrast, personality variables *are* underlying psychological influences. Separating the personal, demographic antecedents from the personality antecedents allows us to consider reciprocal relationships between personality antecedents and union commitment. Obviously, demographic characteristics cannot have a reciprocal relationship with union commitment; for example, while age might influence commitment, it is impossible for commitment to affect age. On the other hand, it is possible that psychological conservatism influences and is in turn influenced by union commitment.

Mowday, Porter, and Steers (1982) noted the importance of individual values and beliefs in determining initial levels of commitment to the organization. Studies suggest that employees with a strong belief in the value of work and who perceive work as a central life interest are more likely than others to develop high levels of commitment to the employing organization and to identify with the goals and values of the organization (Dubin, Champoux, and Porter 1975; Hall and Schneider 1972; Kidron 1978; Rabinowitz and Hall 1977). Similarly, the literature asserts that union members' beliefs must be compatible with the process of unionization for the members to become involved in the union. Employees with a strong work ethic are more highly committed to their work organizations (Buchanan 1974; Card 1978; Goodale 1973; Hall, Schneider, and Nygren 1970; Hall and Schneider 1972; Hulin and Blood 1968; Kidron 1978). The work ethic is only one of many belief systems (Buchholz, 1978b), however; and others such as the Marxist belief system may be related to union commitment, particularly since the Marxist work belief has been shown to predict union attitudes (Laliberte and Barling 1986). Commitment, then, is probably related to the beliefs of the individual, which in turn are a product of both the culture of the organization and the culture of the society to which the individual belongs.

The relationship between work values and union commitment is moderated by race (Fullagar 1986b). The work ethic is a more important determinant of union commitment among affluent white workers than among alienated black workers. Among disenfranchised black workers, however, Marxian work beliefs are stronger predictors of union commitment than among privileged white workers. The indication here is that greater perceptions of alienation and exploitation, and a well-developed class consciousness, cause greater loyalty to the union among the less privileged sectors of the blue-collar labor force.

New members entering labor organizations bring with them different goals and needs that they seek to satisfy through trade union membership. As with organizational commitment, the initial levels of union commitment may be associated with members' perceptions of the congruence between their own goals and those of the union and their perceptions of the union as instrumental in the attainment of those goals. For example, in the case of the work organization the higher the need for achievement, the higher the initial levels of organizational commitment (Mowday and McDade 1980). It is likewise possible that power and affiliation needs influence commitment to the union. Glick, Mirvis, and Harder (1977) contended that a complex relationship exists between union satisfaction and participation. Satisfaction is positively correlated with participation among members who express great needs for "decision making, accomplishment, and growth," whereas among union members only weakly holding these needs participation may indicate dissatisfaction with the union. Further research is required to clarify the nature and direction of the relationship between the perceived instrumentality of the union in satisfying member needs and union members' initial levels of commitment. Not only may individual needs have a direct influence on initial commitment, but they may also moderate the relationship between early experiences with the union and union commitment.

Union Characteristics and Perceptions

Several studies have shown that new members of organizations who have realistic expectations of the benefits offered by the organization are less likely to leave voluntarily than those who hold unrealistic beliefs (Wanous 1980). Other research evidence suggests that the extent to which the expectations of new members are met has a direct, albeit limited, influence on commitment (Grusky 1966; Steer 1977). This research parallels research on unions that has indicated a significant and strong relationship between workers' perceptions of the union's effectiveness in improving work conditions and their decision to vote for or against unionization (Beutell and Biggs 1984; Bigoness and Tosi 1984; Brett 1980; DeCotiis and LeLouarn 1981; Kochan 1979; Youngblood et al. 1984), and between these perceptions and union attitudes in general (Laliberte and Barling 1986). Indeed, union instrumentality is more predictive of union support among both white-collar and blue-collar workers than either intrinsic or extrinsic job satisfaction (Kochan 1979). Kochan (1979) also found that perceptions of union instrumentality were significantly more predictive of voting behavior than the general image workers had of organized labor. Recent research, using path analysis to ascertain causality, has found union instrumentality to be a strong predictor of both attitudes of commitment to the union and behavioral participation in union activities in a sample of unionized, blue-collar workers (Fullagar 1986b).

The initial level of commitment upon joining a union is related to both perceived union instrumentality and union commitment. It is probable that workers who join unions with initially high levels of commitment are more likely than other new members to participate in union activities, such as attending meetings, voting in elections, finding out about union contracts, and engaging in behaviors beyond those expected by the union. These behaviors in themselves may engender commitment and, in turn, further reinforce the new members' commitment attitudes and behaviors. As Mowday, Porter, and Steers (1982, 57) commented,

> The likelihood of developing a self-reinforcing cycle of commitment . . . is largely dependent on the opportunity to engage in behaviors that are committing. In other words, the opportunities to provide to new [members] are crucial in determining whether initially high levels of commitment are translated into more stable attachments.

Job Characteristics

From the research conducted on unionization it would appear that there are several job characteristics that might engender union commitment. A prevalent explanation of the process of unionization is that workers join unions because of perceived deprivations and various dissatisfactions with the conditions of their employment (Bigoness 1978; Dubin 1973; Farber and Saks 1980; Fiorito, Gallagher, and Greer 1986; Getman, Goldberg, and Herman 1976; Kochan 1978; Schriesheim 1978; Walker and Lawler 1979; Zalesny 1985). Most of these approaches make the distinction between extrinsic, economic and intrinsic, noneconomic job conditions and satisfaction. For example, LeLouarn (1979) and Schriesheim (1978) reported significant associations between satisfaction with extrinsic factors such as wages and working conditions and union voting behavior. Duncan and Stafford (1980), on the other hand, investigated intrinsic variables such as the degree of autonomy, skill utilization, and machine pacing on the job and found that these factors facilitated unionization. The available evidence suggests that overall job satisfaction is negatively associated with the perceived need for a union (Allen and Keaveny 1983) and that dissatisfaction with extrinsic factors is a more important influence on unionization than dissatisfaction with intrinsic factors. For example, dissatisfaction with wages and job security is strongly associated with union voting behavior (Getman, Goldberg, and Herman 1976). Schriesheim (1978) also found that pro-union voting was more strongly related to satisfaction with extrinsic factors—such as pay, working conditions, job security, and company policy—than to intrinsic factors, such as independence and the opportunity to satisfy higher order needs.

The literature suggests, therefore, that unions cannot, and should not, deal with noneconomic, quality-of-working-life issues (Beer and Driscoll 1977; Kochan, Lipsky, and Dyer 1974; Strauss 1977). The literature are not unequivocal, however. Schriesheim (1978) showed that most of the studies outlined above used measures that questioned only workers' satisfaction with specific extrinsic job characteristics and working conditions. By excluding measures of a sufficient number of noneconomic satisfaction factors, the studies may have caused the economic factors to seem particularly potent and to carry more weight.

Studies examining some intrinsic factors, such as work content and the desire for more influence, have found that these are as important predictors of unionism as extrinsic factors (for example, Bigoness 1978; Garbarino 1975, 1980; Herman 1973; Ladd and Lipset 1973; Walker and Lawler 1979). Specifically, intrinsic aspects of the job such as degree of worker autonomy, skill utilization, machine pacing, worker distrust in decision making, and worker powerlessness are associated with unionization (Duncan and Stafford 1980; Hammer and Berman 1981). Hammer and Berman, for example, showed that worker powerlessness and distrust in managerial decision making are important noneconomic factors in union voting. Interestingly, whereas most studies emphasize a deprivation and dissatisfaction model of unionization, Hammer and Berman view a lack of power as the underlying source of distrust and dissatisfaction with job content, which in turn leads to unionization.

From the studies reviewed above, we can conclude that unionization is related to workers' dissatisfaction with both intrinsic and extrinsic factors of their jobs. The lower the motivating potential of a job and the greater the dissatisfaction with the work environment, the greater the union commitment of workers. Kochan (1979) found that among blue-collar workers dissatisfaction with extrinsic factors was more strongly related to union support than dissatisfaction with intrinsic factors. Nevertheless, he also found dissatisfaction with intrinsic factors such as the nature of work was more strongly associated with the inclination to support a union among white-collar workers than among blue-collar workers. It is possible the unions that organize white-collar workers focus more on improving the intrinsic conditions of work than do unions that organize predominantly blue-collar workers. Thus, white-collar workers who are dissatisfied with intrinsic factors are more likely to support a union in an effort to improve the intrinsic aspects of their work than they are to do so to improve the extrinsic aspects.

Among unionized workers Gordon et al. (1980) found negative or nonsignificant associations between (1) satisfaction of lower and higher order needs and (2) feelings of responsibility to the union, an expressed willingness to work for the union, and a general belief in unionism. The pattern of correlations here suggested that white-collar workers who were dissatisfied with the extrinsic aspects of their job were more willing than other white-collar workers to be actively involved in the union. Similarly, a belief in the goals of organized labor were stronger among those workers who stated that their extrinsic needs were not being satisfied. The satisfaction of intrinsic needs was not associated with either beliefs in organized labor or a willingness to work for the union. This conforms with previous findings (Kochan, Lipsky, and Dyer 1974) that workers do not perceive unions as instrumental in providing jobs with greater challenge, responsibility, or autonomy—in other words, in improving the intrinsic factors of jobs. In addition, the relationship between facets of union commitment and extrinsic or intrinsic job satisfaction does not seem to be moderated by only a simple blue-collar/white-collar distinction. Several factors, such as the nature of the membership and the type of union under investigation, also appear to influence the relationship. For example, Gordon, Beauvais, and Ladd (1984) found that although union loyalty was significantly associated with extrinsic and intrinsic satisfaction in a sample of technicians, a similar association did not exist for engineers.

The positive relationship between union loyalty and extrinsic and intrinsic job satisfaction in Gordon et al.'s study (1980) gives rise to two suggestions. First, given the instrumental nature of union loyalty and the *positive* correlation between this factor and satisfaction of both higher and lower order needs, Gordon et al. suggested that white-collar workers "regard union membership and the actions of their bargaining units as important influences on all . . . facets of their employment." Nevertheless, dissatisfaction with extrinsic factors was more strongly associated with "willingness to work for the union" and "belief in unionism" than was dissatisfaction with intrinsic factors. Second, some of the subjects in the Gordon et al. study were involved in a cooperative effort with management aimed at investigating noneconomic issues at the workplace. This effort may have inflated their expectations concerning the satisfaction of intrinsic needs and made the results somewhat atypical.

Recent empirical research has confirmed that dissatisfaction with extrinsic job characteristics predicts union commitment among both black and white union members, and especially among affluent workers (Fullagar 1986b). Among black union members who were more alienated from their jobs, however, dissatisfaction with intrinsic factors was a more significant cause of attitudes of commitment than was dissatisfaction with extrinsic factors. These findings corroborate the perspective in industrial relations that attachment to unions is a consequence of both dissatisfaction *and* perceived deprivation (Begin 1979; Kemerer and Baldridge 1975; Walker and Lawler 1979).

Further differences in the causes of commitment between different segments of blue-collar workers are such factors as differing decision making processes, compensation, and supervision (Fullagar 1986b). Maxey and Mohrman (1980) found that influence deprivation and job environment, as well as economic variables, were associated with pro-union attitudes among white-collar employees and that these attitudes were moderated by hierarchical position in the work organization.

Kochan (1979) proposed that dissatisfaction with extrinsic job factors may be due to several factors: workers' viewing working conditions as inadequately administered; their viewing absolute levels of working conditions as below some acceptable standard or level (such as the minimum wage); and their judging that inequities exist between their own wages and physical working conditions and those of similar others. Perceptions of equity correlate negatively with the propensity to unionize (Kochan 1979); and measures of wage inequity, such as perceived underpayment or wage differentials between unionized and nonunionized employees, are consistently associated with pro-union attitudes and union membership (Duncan and Stafford 1980; Farber and Saks 1980; Maxey and Mohrman 1980). Although pay inequity per se is unrelated to union commitment (Fukami and Larson 1984), the relationships between these two variables may differ across different levels of occupational status and different types of jobs. For example, perceived inequity in wages is positively and significantly related to the willingness to unionize among white-collar but not blue-collar workers (Kochan 1979). This difference exists despite the fact that dissatisfaction with wages is significantly related to support of the union in both groups (Kochan 1979).

The strong link between intrinsic job satisfaction and union commitment among the South African workers in Fullagar's sample may be the result of those workers' stronger desire to influence the content (the noneconomic factors) of their jobs, particularly since black employees in that country are unable to influence the noneconomic aspects of their working environment through other means, be they more informal, individualistic, or employer-initiated. Using Hirschman's (1970) framework of exit, voice, and loyalty, we could restate this possibility as: Affluent white workers have greater access to the exit-and-entry mechanism than do black workers because the former have greater freedom to choose jobs and move between jobs in the South African context. For the majority of black workers, on the other hand, union "voice" is perhaps the only channel of participation in a democratic process they have.

The inability of the organization or task to satisfy the salient needs of the individual worker, together with inadequacies in organizational structure, are major determinants of alienation (Seeman 1959). Kanungo (1979) believes that alienation and its resultant cognitive states of powerlessness, meaninglessness, normlessness, isolation, and self-estrangement emanate from the inability of the organization or the work to satisfy the salient needs of the individual. Workers might be more predisposed to become committed to labor organizations if they are in alienating work situations, which can be defined as: providing the worker with no power or control because the pace of work is controlled and mechanized (powerlessness); breaking down and simplifying the work process (meaninglessness); providing insufficient information for the worker to plan and predict his work environment (normlessness); offering the worker little or no potential to satisfy his social needs (isolation); and providing the worker little or no opportunity to self-actualize (self-estrangement). The effects of both job dissatisfaction and alienation are probably moderated, however, by worker perceptions of the union's instrumentality in improving conditions of work to which the organization has been unresponsive (Brett 1980; DeCotiis and LeLouarn 1981; Kochan 1980, 145–46).

A few sociological studies have associated alienation with the process of unionism. Tannenbaum (1952), for example, viewed trade unionism as a response to the worker's sense of alienation from both the job and the larger society. In his view the union provides workers with a collectivity in which they can relate to employers, fellow workers, and their jobs. Unions increase workers' power and control and reduce their feelings of normlessness, isolation, and self-estrangement. To Tannenbaum, therefore, the union was not merely an economic organization but also a social and ethical system that provided a means for the worker to reestablish the values through which he had found dignity. Blauner (1964) also saw the union as a reform movement that could counteract worker powerlessness. These are yet further examples of union concommitants that are more anecdotal than empirical.

Only two studies have empirically investigated the relationship between job involvement, alienation, or unionization. In the first Pestonjee, Singh, and Singh (1981) found a significant negative correlation between job involvement and attitudes toward unions ($r = -0.58$) in a sample of 200 blue-collar textile workers in Northern India. They concluded that,

> pro-union employees are more involved in union activities and are not in a position to devote much of their time to the job. . . . Alternatively, workers who are frustrated or annoyed by jobs with which they feel no involvement may respond with high union involvement (p. 213).

In the second study, of a sample of blue-collar workers in South Africa, Fullagar (1986b) found the relationship between job involvement and unionization is moderated by the marker variable race, denoting level of privilege. Affluent white union members who were loyal to the union indicated higher levels of job involvement than did black workers whose job involvement scores suggested far greater alienation. The white union members showed no particularly strong sense of alienation from organizational political processes, not surprisingly, since they have traditionally been more integrated into organizational decision-making processes. This finding suggests that the more privileged workers who have greater access to organizational decision making will function similarly as union members and as employees, that is, as is described by the concept of dual allegiance (Martin 1981; Purcell 1960; Stagner 1956). In other words, workers who express positive attitudes toward their job will also tend to have positive attitudes toward their union (Purcell 1960).

Fukami and Larson (1984) examined dual loyalty with parallel models of union and organizational commitment by using the same antecedent conditions. Although they found that the predictors of organizational commitment did not predict union commitment, organizational commitment was positively and significantly correlated with union commitment. Attempts to ascertain the construct validity and stability of the union commitment concept amongst blue-collar workers have isolated an "organizational/work loyalty" factor that is independent of union loyalty (Fullagar 1986a). The meaning of this factor is that workers view loyalty to work rather than to the union as instrumental to their individual success. This would suggest that the concept of dual allegiance is not inevitable but may instead be moderated by occupational status. Recent research indicates that job involvement is positively related to attitudes of union commitment among affluent white workers, whereas among black union members the two concepts are negatively related (Fullagar 1986b).

Martin (1981) suggested that dual allegiance is moderated by the type of union. Using Walker and Lawler's (1979) distinction between "protective" and "aggressive" unions, Martin speculated that dual allegiance is more characteristic of protective unions consisting of privileged workers than it is of aggressive unions, whose memberships consist of more alienated and economically deprived individuals.

Tannenbaum and Kahn (1958) posited that dual allegiance is also explicable on the assumption that union workers perceive the primary function of their union to be that of protecting their interests on the job. Dual allegiance may be uncommon at the lower, more alienated levels of the organizational hierarchy because there is less opportunity for organizational involvement and the satisfaction of higher order needs (Barling 1983). Thus, dual allegiance may be related to a motivational framework in which organizational and union commitment covary among intrinsically motivated workers but not among extrinsically motivated individuals. Finally, dual loyalty generally exists in workplaces where the labor-management relationship is cooperative and supportive (Bigoness and Tosi 1984; Fukami and Larson 1984).

Role Characteristics

Individual socialization into an organization and the nature and quality of experiences during membership are important correlates of organizational commitment. Most of the research investigating these antecedents has focused on organizational rather than union commitment. Recently, however, Fukami and Larson (1984) identified work experiences as the only significant predictors of *both* organizational and union commitment. Certain individual experiences in the initial stages of organizational socialization may therefore be generalizable to labor organizations and may contribute to the development of a model of union commitment.

The socialization processes that organizations establish for their new members may influence the development of attitudes of commitment (Gordon et al. 1980; Mowday, Porter, and Steers 1982). The development of organizational commitment is hypothesized to be dependent on the extent to which the organization inducts the newcomer and transmits important values and norms about behavior through various planned socialization experiences. Despite the theoretical importance of socialization practices in organizations, little research has been conducted to investigate how specific socialization experiences influence individual commitment. Van Maanen and Schein (1979) identified several socialization tactics that influence the degree to which the new member accepts his organizational role, but these relationships have not been tested empirically in the union context.

Although anticipatory socialization experiences (that is, socialization that takes place before the individual has become a member of the organization) have been found to influence attitudes (Feldman 1976; Porter, Lawler, and Hackman 1975; Van Maanen 1977), the more important influence may derive from early socialization experiences once organizational membership starts (Stagner 1956). Early commitment predicts the development of greater organizational commitment (Mowday and McDade 1980). The literature on attitude formation (for example, Kelman 1974; Salancik 1977) also suggests that if employees perform well initially in the roles designated to them by the organization, the employees will develop greater attitudinal commitment. They do so because employees tend to develop attitudes consistent with their behavior.

Early socialization experiences in the organization are consistently and positively correlated with all aspects of commitment to the union (Fullagar 1986b; Gordon et al. 1980). Members who reported that they had positive socialization experiences in their first year were those who expressed the greatest loyalty and sense of responsibility to the union, the greatest willingness to work for the union, and the strongest belief in unionism of all the members surveyed.

Personal interactions with established union and organizational members are the primary avenues whereby new members internalize the implicit mores of the organizational climate and refine their initial expectations concerning the organization and their roles (Van Maanen and Schein 1979). It may be that a process of socialization that involves the new member in role behaviors beyond those usually required by the organization generates greater feelings of attachment through cognitive consonance, whereby attitudes become congruent with behaviors (Salancik 1977; Stagner 1956). Nevertheless, whatever the direction of the attitude-behavior relationship, social involvement and the extent and nature of initial socialization experiences are important correlates of members' attachment to unions (Fukami and Larson 1984; Gordon et al. 1980).

A few studies have highlighted the relationship between commitment and the degree to which initial experiences fulfill expectations concerning the organization (Grusky 1966; Steers 1977). The greater the perceived dependability of the organization in attending to its members' interests, the greater their commitment (Buchanan 1974; Steers 1977). This finding is important in the light of results that suggest a high level of calculative involvement in unions. We already noted that the perceived instrumentality of unions in acquiring benefits, better working conditions, pay, and so forth is an important aspect of the concept of members' commitment to labor organizations.

Role conflict is inversely related to organizational commitment, but the relationship between role ambiguity and commitment remains equivocal (Morris and Koch 1979; Morris and Sherman 1981). In constructing a model of commitment common to both union and employer organizations, Fukami and Larson (1984) found that job scope and stress predicted commitment to the employer, but not to the union. This finding may have resulted from Fukami and Larson's sole concentration on job characteristics pertaining to their subjects' roles in the work organization rather than on the scope, stresses, conflicts, and ambiguities associated with their roles as union members. For example, the conflicting demands placed on workers in their role as a union member or official and in their role as an employee may affect both their union and their work organization commitment. Furthermore, the irregular scheduling of union meetings may introduce conflict between union and family roles that in turn influence union commitment (compare Bluen and Barling 1985; Gullahorn 1956; Nicholson 1976).

Structural Characteristics

Stagner (1962) noted that structural variables may be more important than personal characteristics in influencing such labor issues as union members' participation in managerial decision making. A number of structural characteristics are associated with commitment to organizations in general. These include size, span of control (the number of people reporting to a supervisor), the formalization of rules and procedures, functional dependence, and the decentralization of the organization (Steers 1977; Stevens, Beyer, and Trice 1978). For example, both worker ownership and worker participation in managerial decision making are positively related to organizational commitment (Rhodes and Steers 1981). This parallels Tannenbaum and Kahn's (1958) finding of a positive correlation between the participation of the rank-and-file in union activity and member control over the union. Certain structural characteristics of the union have been shown to influence the extent of union democracy and participation, including not only factors such as size and the span of control, but also the degree of openness in the admission policy, the extent of decentralization in collective bargaining, and the rank-and-file's access to participation in union politics. The structure of the labor organization likely facilitates member participation and commitment to the extent that the union possesses structures that encourage democracy.

So far we have viewed commitment as a consequence of various deprivations and dissatisfactions experienced by the worker. An alternative approach would be to view union attachment as a response to the unequal distribution of power and control between the workers, or the union, and the employer. Again using Walker and Lawler's (1979) aggressive-protective typology, we can hypothesize that the two categories of union differ in terms of their emphasis on resolving the power imbalance. Aggressive unions represent workers who feel alienated from the political processes of the organization and who seek to rectify the imbalance between management and employees in the authority structure. Protective unions, on the other hand, represent relatively privileged, skilled workers who have greater access to decision-making structures within the work organization and consequently who are less concerned with the distribution of power. It is quite feasible that these different types of union, which reflect differing needs and interests within the labor force, will have members who exhibit varying levels and manifestations of commitment.

Turner (1962) proposed that different types of unions are associated with different styles of government. These differing styles in turn result in varying levels of member participation. For example, high participation levels would be found in "closed" occupational unions, those with rigid membership controls. Within more general, "open" unions that cover a wide range of occupations, a lower level of membership participation would prevail. Again, no data exist on the relationship between union type and commitment, and thus the predicted effects outlined above are merely speculative.

So far our focus has been on the structure of the union and how it impinges on union democracy and membership participation and commitment. The structure of the employing organization also has effects on labor relations (Bacharach and Mitchell 1983). As organizations grow they shift away from direct and personal styles of management to those that are more formalized, standardized, and impersonal. As organizational complexity increases, so does the possibility of union-management conflict (Marginson 1984). When union-management relations are conflictual, there is greater membership loyalty and participation in such union activities as attending meetings, picketing, and other behaviors over and above those required for routine union membership (Barling 1985; Stagner and Eflal 1982).

Studies have indicated that small firms tend to exhibit better labor-management relations because they are less bureaucratic, encourage greater interaction between levels of the organizational hierarchy, and engender more involvement in the organization (Ingham 1970). Not only does the size of the employing organization influence the extent of impersonal supervision and the provision of employee benefits, but it also has an effect on union success. Kochan (1979) has shown that intermediate-size organizations are more prone to unionization than large or small ones. Moreover, the size of the organization is associated with both employee dissatisfaction (Berger and Cummings 1979; Porter and Lawler 1965) and strike activity (Brett and Goldberg 1979; Britt and Galle 1974; Shorter and Tilly 1974). Bureaucracy, however, does not have a uniform relationship with size (Marginson 1984); large organizations are not necessarily more bureaucratic or centralized. Often an increase in size brings with it greater decentralization and flexibility and fewer bureaucratic properties. Nor is size necessarily related to conflict. Although the incidence of strike activity increases with the size of the organization, quitting and absenteeism (regarded as alternative symptoms of conflict and correlated with commitment) often have a negative or equivocal relationship with size (Ingham 1970).

The effects of the size of employing organization may be exacerbated by technological factors. Nonroutine technologies are associated with higher job variability and greater worker participation. By contrast, routine technologies are characterized by standardized roles, strict supervision, one-way communication, and an overall organizational climate that is not conducive to worker participation. The restrictions imposed within routine technological organizations make organized action through the union the only effective means for workers in these organizations to influence the work process, thereby increasing the likelihood of their commitment to the union.

Another structural characteristic of the organization that may influence commitment is workers' freedom to associate with the union of their choice or with no union. The level and nature of union commitment may differ between companies that have two or more competing labor organizations and companies governed by a single union shop agreement. Research on job choice in organizations has shown that chosen jobs are rated as more attractive, and valued more highly, than jobs for which no choice is offered (Lawler et al. 1975; Vroom and Deci 1971). Similarly, using cognitive dissonance theory (Festinger 1957), one would predict that selecting one out of a number of unions would influence new members' attitudes toward the union. As mentioned previously, one of the important characteristics of behaviors that make them committing is that they must be freely engaged in (Salancik 1977). The presence of a number of unions in any one plant or industry increases the individual worker's freedom of choice. Salancik (1977) avowed that, given a number of alternatives from which to choose, a worker will become behaviorally committed to his final decision in an effort to justify having joined a particular labor organization.

Environmental Characteristics

Market context and sociopolitical variables may also influence members' commitment to labor organizations. Economic downturns, inflation, the extent of unemployment, and changes in employment and wage rates probably influence commitment levels. Economic recessions are said to produce labor unrest because of employer retrenchments and a climate that facilitates exploitation of labor market conditions. Consequently, a swing in favor of unionization may occur during recessions (Adams and Krislov 1974; Ashenfelter and Pencavel 1969; Moore and Pearce 1976). Unions thrive during periods of low unemployment or rapid employment growth (Ashenfelter and Pencavel 1969; Bain and Elsheikh 1976; Roomkin and Juris 1978). Although several authors' findings contradict these (compare Anderson, O'Reilly, and Busman 1980; Fiorito 1982; Mancke 1971; Moore and Pearce 1976; Sheflin, Troy, and Koeller 1981), they do suggest the probable role of labor market influences in union commitment. To date, however, commitment studies have not focused on these macroeconomic determinants.

The Consequences of Union Commitment

The literature has identified several consequences of organizational commitment: increased tenure (Mowday, Steers, and Porter 1979; Steers 1977); a moderate (but equivocal) decline in attendance and absenteeism (Angle and Perry 1981); a significant reduction in turnover (Angle and Perry 1981; Koch and Steers 1977); a decrease in tardiness (Angle and Perry 1981; Koch and Steers 1978; Porter et al. 1974; Steers 1977); and a weak increase in job performance and effort (Porter, Crampon, and Smith 1976; Steers 1977). Although many of these consequences are not directly relevant to labor organizations, they are still relevant to the concept of union commitment. To formulate a causal model of commitment to labor organizations, it is necessary to ascertain the causal nature of the relationship between commitment attitudes and commitment behaviors.

Mowday, Porter, and Steers (1982) distinguished between behavioral (or social psychological) and attitudinal (or organizational behavioral) approaches to the study of organizational commitment. The behavioral approaches conceptualize attitudes of commitment as the outcome of behaviors enacted by the individual that bind him to the organization (Becker 1960; Salancik 1977; Staw 1977). In other words, committed behaviors determine subsequent attitudes (Salancik and Pfeffer 1977). Much research has supported the hypothesis that commitment behaviors facilitate consonant attitudes (see Salancik 1977, for a review). For example, organizational commitment has been associated with various work behaviors, such as participation in decision making (Rhodes and Steers 1981), supervisor ability or behavior (Michaels and Spector 1982; Morris and Sherman 1981), and role clarity and freedom from conflict (Jamal 1984; Morris and Koch 1979; Welsh and LaVan 1981).

The attitudinal approaches, in direct opposition, view attitudes of commitment as leading to committed behaviors. Here organizational commitment is defined as a combination of both attitudes and behavioral intentions (Angle and Perry 1981; Buchanan 1974; Ferris and Aranya 1983; Mowday, Porter, and Steers 1982; Porter and Smith 1970). Research conducted within this approach has attempted to ascertain the various behavioral outcomes of commitment. For example, organizational commitment has been variously related to attendance and absenteeism (Koch and Steers 1978; Larson and Fukami 1985; Mowday, Steers, and Porter 1979; Steers 1977); tardiness (Angle and Perry 1981); turnover (Angle and Perry 1981; Hom, Katerberg, and Hulin 1979; Koch and Steers 1978; Larson and Fukami 1985; Mowday, Steers, and Porter 1979; Porter, Crampon, and Smith 1976; Porter et al. 1974; Steers 1977); involvement (Hall and Schneider 1972; Hrebiniak and Alutto 1972; Porter et al. 1974; Stevens, Beyer, and Trice 1978); and performance (Larson and Fukami 1985; Van Maanen 1975). The association found between commitment and job performance, however, has been positive and weak (Mowday, Porter, and Steers 1982; Steers 1977). Mowday, Porter, and Steers (1982, 36) explained these findings thus:

> Performance is influenced by motivation level, role clarity, and ability. . . . Attitudes like commitment would only be expected to influence one aspect of actual job performance. Hence, we would not expect a strong commitment-performance relationship.

The problem with research in both the behavioral and the attitudinal traditions is that it assumes, without empirical support, the antecedent and consequent nature of the behavioral variables found to be associated with organizational commitment (Bateman and Strasser 1984). The cross-sectional designs and correlational analyses employed in these studies shed little light on the causal relationships that exist between commitment attitudes and behaviors.

Three decades ago Stagner (1956) postulated participation in union activities as causing individual attachment to the union. Since then, however, very little research has investigated the behavioral correlates of union commitment. Gordon et al. (1980) found all the factors of their concept of union commitment to correlate very significantly with participation in such union activities as serving in an elected office, voting, attending general membership meetings, knowing the terms of the union contract, and filing grievances. All four of their union commitment factors also correlated positively with recent participation in activities that were supportive of the union. These findings have been corroborated in subsequent research, in which the four commitment constructs correlated significantly and in the appropriate direction with participation in both formal, essential activities and informal, more peripheral behaviors (Fullagar 1986a). Nevertheless, both these studies used cross-sectional designs that only provide indications of the relationship between union commitment attitudes and behavioral participation in union affairs.

Previous research, therefore, on both organizational and union commitment, has hypothesized causal relationships with behavioral variables on the basis of either theory or intuition. Most of the studies have viewed behavior as a consequence rather than an antecedent of commitment. Mowday, Porter, and Steers (1982) suggested that the relationship between commitment attitudes and behaviors is most parsimoniously viewed as being reciprocal:

> It is equally reasonable to assume that (a) commitment attitudes lead to committing behaviors that subsequently reinforce and strengthen attitudes, and (b) committing behaviors lead to commitment attitudes and subsequent committing behaviors. The important issue is not whether the commitment process begins with either attitudes or behaviors. Rather what is important is to recognize that the development of commitment may involve the subtle interplay of attitudes and behaviors over time (p. 47).

Recent research has investigated the causal nature of the relationship between commitment attitudes and behavioral participation in such formal union activities as attending union meetings, voting in union elections, knowing the terms of the labor agreement, and filing grievances. To examine the causal effects of union loyalty (a primary dimension of union commitment) on behavioral participation in the union, Fullagar (1986b) computed cross-lagged regression analyses using longitudinal data. These analyses consistently demonstrated the causal effects of attitudes of loyalty to the union on subsequent participation in union affairs. The findings are consistent with the prediction that affective commitment contributes to the development of behavioral indices of commitment; they also support the theoretical causal presumptions about attitudinal commitment (Angle and Perry 1983; Buchanan 1974; Ferris and Aranya 1983; Mowday, Porter, and Steers 1982). More specifically, the results indicate the causal direction leads from commitment to the union to union participation (Gordon et al. 1980). Nonetheless, although union loyalty is the major dimension of union commitment and is stable across different unions and workplaces (Barling 1985; Gordon et al. 1980; Ladd et al. 1982), the direction and nature of the relationship between other dimensions of commitment and behavioral participation may be different.

Previous research has indicated that measures of formal union participation (specifically, use of the grievance procedure) are the most effective measures to differentiate between active and inactive union members (Tannenbaum and Kahn 1958). Formal participation strongly correlates with responsibility to the union and willingness to work for the union (Gordon et al. 1980). Indeed, the grievance procedure is central to the collective bargaining process (Allen and Keaveny 1985; Slichter, Healy, and Livernash 1960). Demographic, personality, and attitudinal characteristics do not seem to contribute substantially to the variance in rank-and-file grievance filings (Ash 1970; Kissler 1977; Ronan and Prien 1973; Stagner 1956, 1962; Sulkin and Pranis 1967). One finding that warrants further investigation is that the more committed shop stewards are to the union, the less likely they are to consult with potential grievants and generally engage in filing grievances (Dalton and Todor 1982). Allen and Keaveny (1985) outlined a model that differentiates the characteristics of grievants from those of nongrievants. The model includes employer and union characteristics as well as individual attributes (age, attitudes toward supervisors, the desire to participate in the grievance procedure, attitudes toward the union, and participation in the union). Attitudes toward the union were better predictors of grievance filing than the job and demographic variables. Given the strong relationship between union commitment and participation in union activities (such as grievance filing), one direction for further research would be to ascertain the influence that union commitment attitudes exert on the decision to file a grievance and satisfaction with grievance resolution.

It would appear, then, that union commitment is associated with union behaviors such as attending union meetings, filing grievances, and various other participative activities. Nevertheless, although there is a consistent relationship between organizational commitment and voluntary turnover, no research exists to indicate whether union commitment *causes* union turnover and retention of members. This is an important issue in organizations where more than one union jostles for membership and in those where workers leave one union to join another. As Katz and Kahn (1978) noted, one characteristic of a successful organization is the ability to attract and retain members. This criterion is as relevant for labor organizations as it is for commercial organizations. If union commitment is predictive of members' participation in essential activities, and if it is influential in determining voluntary performance in actions that ensure the union's attainment of its goals, commitment is a crucial determinant of union success. For example, the union's effectiveness strongly depends on its ability to impose sanctions or threaten to impose sanctions on the employer through boycotts, strikes, or slowdowns. Obviously, the union must be able to count on its members in carrying out these sanctions. Furthermore, the past history of the union's success in negotiating better wages and working conditions will influence members' perceptions of the union's instrumentality. The issue of union effectiveness and its definition need further development. Although Kochan (1980, 175) defined the concept as being guaged by members' assessment of "the substantive achievements in bargaining and the correspondence of these achievements with their personal goals and priorities," additional dimensions of effectiveness, such as the union's ability to attract and maintain a membership, the extent of union democracy, and the development of an effective leadership, warrant further consideration.

Some research has attempted to understand union militancy (attitudinal support for and active participation in organized conflict with management) in terms of the union member's position in the work organization, his social background, and the sources of his job dissatisfaction (Schutt 1982). Militancy can vary from involvement in nationwide boycotts and strikes to local work stoppages and interpersonal conflict with management. Generally, two theories of union militancy have been advanced corresponding to an extrinsic-intrinsic dichotomy: (1) Economic factors such as dissatisfaction with pay and basic working conditions are the sources of discontent which facilitate militancy; or (2) incongruence among members' desire for more control, power and participation, and the constraints of the job and organizational structure produce militancy (Schutt 1982). Regarding the influence of social background Leggett (1968) found working-class consciousness to be associated with active participation in militant activities. An overall understanding of the influences of union commitment attitudes on member behaviors should include an understanding of these attitudinal effects on militancy. So far the literature has ignored this question.

Although some studies indicate that work attitudes and experiences cause subsequent union attachment (Fullagar 1986b), others suggest the reverse—that unionization influences work attitudes. For example, if the union is instrumental in raising wages and improving working conditions, employee attitudes may well improve as a result (Allen and Keaveny 1983). Alternatively, in alerting their members to the unpleasant aspects of the work, union officials might cause a deterioration in work attitudes (Goldberg 1981). Kochan (1980, 374–76) found that union membership significantly improved workers' satisfaction and their compensation but decreased their satisfaction with job content and resource adequacy. Berger, Olson, and Boudreau (1983) argued that employees' satisfaction with the economic terms of their work will improve if they perceive the union as instrumental in securing tangible gains. At the same time, however, employees' satisfaction with the intrinsic aspects of their work will diminish as the employees become more aware of problems inherent in their work through their experiences as union members. The Berger, Olson, and Boudreau findings also highlight unions' influence in shaping work values. For example, unions generally place greater emphasis on seniority than on achievement as a criterion for advancement (Olson and Berger 1983). Moreover, employees who are consistently promoted year after year will eventually be forced to resign from the union once they come to join the supervisory or managerial ranks. Thus, the more committed the employee is to the union, the less he may value or be satisfied with promotion. An interesting task for future research, therefore, would be to assess whether attitudes of union commitment affect work values and attitudes toward the job and employing organization.

One attitudinal outcome of commitment attitudes is industrial relations climate, a derivative of organizational climate (Dastmalchian, Blyton, and Abdollahyan 1982; Nicholson, 1979). Three basic dimensions of industrial relations climate have been conceptualized: "issue climate," or workers' perceptions of the mechanisms for dealing with problems and the occurrence and satisfactory resolution of industrial relations problems (Nicholson 1979); "interpersonal climate," or workers' perceptions of interactions with members of the "other side" at all levels of the organization (Nicholson 1979); and "union support," or the extent to which workers perceive the organization as being supportive of institutionalized industrial relations (Dastmalchian, Blyton, and Abdollahyan 1982). Interpersonal climate correlates significantly with measures of absenteeism, labor turnover, and perceived union-management disharmony, whereas the issue-climate and union-support dimensions are associated with measures of organizational effectiveness. All three dimensions of industrial relations climate appear to moderate the relationship between behavioral outcomes and organizational effectiveness variables (Dastmalchian, Blyton, and Abdollahyan 1982). In developing future models of union commitment, therefore, industrial relations climate cannot be ignored as an important consequence.

Finally, until recently (Bluen and Barling 1985) the literature largely ignored the psychological consequences of involvement in industrial relations processes. Even Gordon and Nurick's (1981) agenda for future psychological research on union-management relations did not suggest investigating the potentially stressful role of individual involvement in industrial relations. Several stressors are inherent in the union leader's role (Bluen 1984). Union leaders face the dilemma, for example, of maintaining internal union democracy while simultaneously being pressured into adopting a more bureaucratic structure to meet environmental demands (Anderson 1978). Insufficient union budgets can translate into insufficient numbers of union officials, which in turn leads to role overload (Warr 1981). Nicholson (1976) identified several forms of role stress (quantitative and qualitative overload) associated with being a shop steward. Stewards reported high levels of both role ambiguity, having received no clear-cut guidelines or training, and role conflict, having had continually to interact with members of management and the rank-and-file. Union members themselves are subjected to various other sources of stress, such as management victimization, discharge for being a union member, threatened dismissal and plant closure, denial of privileges, and transfer to lower paying jobs (Bluen 1984). Finally, strikes themselves are obviously stressful (Barling and Milligan 1987; Thompson and Borglum 1973). MacBride, Lancee, and Freeman (1981) measured the psychological responses of striking air traffic controllers in Canada and found that during the dispute the subjects exhibited very high levels of psychological distress (such as feelings of worthlessness, depression, and strain) and a marked deterioration of perceived general functioning, physical health, and psychological well-being. Barling and Milligan (1987) also found psychological stress levels among union members to increase after involvement in strike activity. These various examples illustrate that stress may be yet another outcome of participation in unions. Union commitment may act as a buffer to some of these stresses or it may increase role overload (both qualitative and quantitative). Either way, any model of union commitment must consider the stressful outcomes of union involvement.

CONCLUSIONS

In this chapter we have attempted to formulate a model of union commitment based on the findings of a variety of research. One of the major problems with previous research on organizational and union commitment is that it has relied mainly on cross-sectional data. As such, distinctions between the antecedents and consequences of commitment remain speculative. The literature points to a number of relevant variables as significant concomitants of union commitment. These should provide valuable guidelines for future research in ascertaining the nature and direction of the relationship between variables in the commitment process. This research must, however, avoid an overreliance on cross-sectional designs that illuminate associational rather than causal relationships and concentrate on longitudinal approaches that will enable a process model of union commitment to be developed.

Research on union commitment has also operated under the assumption that participative behaviors are a consequence rather than an antecedent of commitment attitudes (Gordon et al. 1980). This research has relied on attitudinal measures of both commitment and participation—both of which are susceptible to autocorrelational bias. Future investigators could avoid this source of bias by using more direct observations of behavior. Such research would also be useful in assessing whether perceived behavioral outcomes of union commitment reinforce and even cause the hypothesized antecedents. For example, participation in union activities might cause an awareness of inequalities in the political structures of organizations, which in turn facilitates dissatisfaction and stronger attitudes of attachment to the union. Alternatively, greater behavioral commitment or participation in union affairs might conceivably cause greater conflict among job, family, and union roles. The process of union commitment probably consists of reinforcing feedback loops between attitudes and behaviors, and between outcomes and antecedents (see Figure 1).

Further research will also have to unravel the complexity in the interactions among the antecedent variables of commitment. For example, commitment to "protective" unions results from concerns to increase job security and prevent job dilution, whereas commitment to "aggressive" unions is more a response to a lack of power, a desire for participation, and general alienation. Kochan (1979) demonstrated that extrinsic dissatisfaction is moderated by occupational status. Future studies need not only to ascertain the exact nature of the relationship between the speculated causes of commitment and its consequences, but also to investigate the relationships among the antecedent factors themselves. Only through such research can we determine whether methodological problems limit our knowledge about the process of commitment.

Recent research emphasizes the importance of socialization in the early stages of union membership as a predictor of commitment (Fullagar 1986b; Gordon et al. 1980). Nevertheless, as Mowday, Porter, and Steers (1982) indicated, we must investigate commitment as a continuous process that develops and fluctuates with union tenure, development, success, and history. Research shows that the employees' stage in their careers influences organizational commitment (Buchanan 1974). Research on union commitment must similarly assess how negotiations, strikes and their outcomes (Barling 1985), the prevailing economic climate, and the union's previous bargaining history (for example, its success in satisfying members' needs) influence attitudes of attachment and participatory behavior. Consistent with the data on organizational commitment, a strength of the proposed model is the wealth of information on the antecedents of union commitment. At the same time, however, there is a paucity of information on the potential consequences of union commitment. Since an understanding of both the causes and consequences of union commitment is required for a comprehensive model of the concept, further research focusing on the consequences of union commitment is overdue.

Another consideration in developing or testing a model is whether the empirical support for the multidimensional nature of union commitment is consistent (Fullagar 1986b; Gordon et al. 1980; Ladd et al. 1982). It is quite possible that the different components of union commitment (which are theoretically and statistically unrelated to one another) have diverse causes and different consequences. For example, personal beliefs about work (for example, Buchholz 1978b) might be more important in predicting beliefs in unionism in general than in predicting loyalty to a specific union. On the other hand, dissatisfaction with supervision and the perceived instrumentality of the union would probably predict loyalty to a specific union more than unionism as a concept. Consequently, a comprehensive model of union commitment must still consider the multidimensional nature of union commitment. In so doing, the model will be extended, and the prediction of commitment and its consequences will be enhanced.

To conclude, this chapter has attempted to illustrate the importance of the concept of union commitment and to develop a model of its antecedents and outcomes. Commitment provides researchers and unions with a measure of member involvement and attachment to labor organizations. An understanding of commitment is important—not only for psychological research on unions, but also for labor leaders who wish to address the deteriorating levels of union participation and increase democratic involvement of rank-and-file members. Measures of commitment could be employed to judge the effectiveness of labor organizations, assess training programs for shop stewards, and ascertain the success of negotiations and the strength of the union (Gordon et al. 1980). Nonetheless, additional research of both a theoretical and an empirical nature will be required to develop a full understanding of the conditions that foster member commitment and the processes through which union commitment grows.

ACKNOWLEDGMENTS

Portions of this chapter were completed while the second author was supported by a grant from the Social Sciences and Humanities Research Council of Canada. We gratefully acknowledge Michele Laliberte for her constructive comments on previous drafts of this chapter.

REFERENCES

Adams, Avril, and Joseph Krislov. 1974. New Union Organizing: A test of the Ashenfelter-Pencavel Model of Trade Union Growth. *Quarterly Journal of Economics* 88(2):304–11.

Allen, Richard E., and Timothy J. Keaveny. 1983. *Contemporary Labor Relations*. Reading, MA: Addison-Wesley.

———. 1985. Factors Differentiating Grievants and Nongrievants. *Human Relations* 38(6):519–34.

American Psychologist. 1984. Psychology in the Public Forum. Vol. 39 (4):428–45.

Anderson, John C. 1978. A Comparative Analysis of Local Union Democracy. *Industrial Relations* 17(3):278–95.

Anderson, John C., Charles A. O'Reilly, and Gloria B. Busman. 1980. Union Decertification in the U.S.: 1974–1977. *Industrial Relations* 19(1):100–107.

Angle, Harold, and James Perry. 1981. An Emprirical Assessment of Organizational Commitment and Organizational Effectiveness. *Administrative Science Quarterly* 26(1):1–14.

Ash, Philip. 1970. The Parties of the Grievance. *Personnel Psychlogy* 23(1):13–37.

Ashenfelter, Orley, and John H. Pencavel. 1969. American Trade Union Growth: 1900–1960. *Quarterly Journal of Economics* 83(3):434–48.

Bacharach, Samuel B., and Stephen M. Mitchell. 1983. The Sources of Dissatisfaction in Educational Administration: A Role-Specific Analysis. *Educational Administration Quarterly* 19(1):101–28.

Bain, George S., and Farouk Elsheikh. 1976. *Union Growth and the Business Cycle: An Econometric Analysis*. Oxford: Basil Blackwell.

Barling, Julian. 1983. Work Motivation. In *Behaviour in Organisations: South African Perspectives*, ed. Julian Barling, 341–72. Johannesburg: McGraw-Hill.

———. 1985. *Union Commitment During a Strike*, photocopy. Kingston, Ontario: Queens University.

Barling, Julian, and Jill Milligan. 1987. Some Psychological Consequences of Striking: A Six Month Longitudinal Study. *Journal of Occupational Behavior* 8:127–38.

Bateman, Thomas S., and Stephen Strasser. 1984. A Longitudinal Analysis of the Antecedents of Organizational Commitment. *Academy of Management Journal* 27(1):95–112.

Becker, Howard S. 1960. Notes on the Conceptualization of Commitment. *American Journal of Sociology* 66(1):32–42.

Beer, Michael, and James W. Driscoll. 1977. Strategies for Change. In *Improving Life at Work: Behavioral Science Approaches to Organizational Change*, ed. J. Richard Hackman and J. Lloyd Suttle. San Fransisco: Goodyear.

Begin, J. P. 1979. Faculty Bargaining and Reward Systems. In *Academic Rewards in Higher Education*, ed. D. R. Lewis and W. E. Becker. Cambridge, MA: Ballinger.

Berger, Chris J., and L. L. Cummings. 1979. Organizational Structure Attitudes and Behaviors. In *Research in Organizational Behavior, vol. 1*, ed. Barry M. Staw, 169–208. Greenwich, CT: JAI Press.

Berger, Chris J., Craig A. Olson, and John W. Boudreau. 1983. Effects of Unions on Job Satisfaction: The Role of Work-Related Values and Perceived Rewards. *Organizational Behavior and Human Performance* 32(3):289–324.

Beutell, Nicholas J., and David L. Biggs. 1984. Behavioral Intentions to Join a Union: Instrumentality, Valence, Locus of Control, and Strike Attitudes. *Psychological Reports* 55:215–22.

Bigoness, William J. 1978. Correlates of Faculty Attitudes towards Collective Bargaining. *Journal of Applied Psychology* 63(2):228–33.

Bigoness, William J., and Henry L. Tosi. 1984. Correlates of Voting Behavior in a Union Decertification Election. *Academy of Management Journal* 27(3):654–59.

Blauner, Robert. 1964. *Alienation and Freedom*. Chicago: University of Chicago Press.

Blinder, Alan S. 1972. *Who Joins Unions?* Working paper no. 36. Princeton: Industrial Relations Section, Princeton University.

Bluen, Stephen D. 1984. *Psychological Stressors and Strains Associated with the Practice of Industrial Relations*, paper presented at the Second National Congress of the Psychological Association of South Africa, Stellenbosch, October.

Bluen, Stephen D., and Julian Barling. 1985. *Development and Validation of the Industrial Relations Event Scale*, paper presented at the Canadian Psychological Association Annual Congress, Halifax, Nova Scotia, June.

Brett, Jeanne M. 1980. Behavioral Research on Unions and Union Management Systems. In *Research in Organizational Behavior, vol. 2*, ed. Barry M. Staw and Larry L. Cummings, 177–214. Greenwich, CT: JAI Press.

Brett, Jeanne M., and Stephen B. Goldberg. 1979. Wildcat Strikes in Bitumous Coal Mining. *Industrial and Labor Relations Review* 32(4):465–83.

Britt, David, and Omer Galle. 1974. Structural Antecedents of the Shape of Strikes: A Comparative Analysis. *American Sociological Review* 39(5):642–51.

Buchanan, Bruce. 1974. Building Organizational Commitment: The Socialization of Managers in Work Organizations. *Administrative Science Quarterly* 19(4):533–46.

Buchholz, Rogene. 1978a. The Work Ethic Reconsidered. *Industrial and Labor Relations Review* 31(4):450–59.

————. 1978b. An Empirical Study of Contemporary Beliefs about Work in American Society. *Journal of Applied Psychology* 63(2):219–27.

Campbell, John P., Richard L. Daft, and Charles L. Hulin. 1982. *What to Study: Generating and Developing Research Questions*. Beverly Hills, CA: Sage.

Card, Josephina J. 1978. Differences in Demographic and Sociopsychological Profiles of ROTC vs. Non-ROTC Students. *Journal of Vocational Behavior* 11(2):196–215.

Child, John, Andrew Loveridge, and Malcolm Warner. 1973. Towards an Organizational Study of Trade Unions. *Sociology* 7(1):71–91.

Chusmir, Leonard H. 1982. Job Commitment and Organizational Woman. *Academy of Management Review* 7(4):595–602.

Dalton, Dan R., and William D. Todor. 1982. Antecedents of Grievance Filing Behavior: Attitude/Behavior Consistency and the Union Steward. *Academy of Management Journal* 25(1):158–69.

Dastmalchian, A., F. Blyton, and M. R. Abdollahyan. 1982. Industrial Relations Climate and Company Effectiveness. *Personnel Review* 11:35–39.

DeCotiis, Thomas A. and Jean-Yves LeLouarn. 1981. A Predictive Study of Voting Behavior in a Representation Election Using Union Instrumentality and Work Perceptions. *Organizational Behavior and Human Performance* 27(1):103–10.

Dubin, Robert. 1973. Work and Non-Work: Institutional Perspectives. In *Work and Non-Work in the Year 2001*, ed. Marvin D. Dunnette, 53–68. Monterey, CA: Brooks/Cole.

Dubin, Robert, Joseph E. Champoux, and Lyman W. Porter. 1975. Central Life Interests and Organizational Commitment of Blue-Collar and Clerical Workers. *Administrative Science Quarterly* 20(3):411–21.

Duncan, Greg J., and Frank P. Stafford. 1980. Do Union Members Receive Compensating Wage Differentials? *American Economic Review* 70(3):355–71.

Etzioni, Amitai. 1961. *A Comparative Analysis of Complex Organizations*. New York: Free Press.

Farber, Henry S., and David H. Saks. 1980. Why Workers Want Unions: The Role of Relative Wages and Job Characteristics. *Journal of Political Economy* 88(2):349–69.

Feldman, Daniel C. 1976. A Contingency Theory of Socialization. *Administrative Science Quarterly* 21(3):433–52.

Ferris, Kenneth R., and Nissim Aranya. 1983. A Comparison of Two Organizational Commitment Scales. *Personnel Psychology* 36(1):87–98.

Festinger, Leon. 1957. *A Theory of Cognitive Dissonance*. Evanston, IL: Row, Peterson.

Fiorito, Jack. 1982. Models of Union Growth: A Test of the Bain-Elsheikh Model for the U.S. *Industrial Relations* 21:123–27.

Fiorito, Jack, Daniel G. Gallagher, and Charles R. Greer. 1986. Determinants of Unionism: A Review of the Literature. In *Research in Personnel and Human Resources Management*, vol. 4, ed. K. M. Rowland and G. R. Ferris, 269–306. Greenwich, CT: JAI Press.

Freeman, Richard B., and James L. Medoff. 1984. *What Do Unions Do?* New York: Basic Books.

Fukami, Cynthia V., and Erik W. Larson. 1984. Commitment to Company and Union: Parallel Models. *Journal of Applied Psychology* 69(3):367–71.

Fullagar, Clive. 1983. Organisational Behaviour in South Africa: An Historical Overview. In *Behaviour in Organisations: South African Perspectives*, ed. Julian Barling, 3–28. Johannesburg: McGraw-Hill.

————. 1986a. A Factor Analytic Study on the Validity of a Union Commitment Scale. *Journal of Applied Psychology* 71(1):129–37.

———. 1986b. *Causes, Correlates and Outcomes of Union Commitment*, doctoral dissertation. Johannesburg: University of the Witwatersrand.

Garbarino, James W. 1975. *Faculty Bargaining, Change and Conflict*. New York: McGraw-Hill.

Getman, Julius G., Stephen B. Goldberg, and Jeanne B. Herman. 1976. *Union Representation Elections: Law and Reality*. New York: Sage.

Glick, William, Philip Mirvis, and Diane Harder. 1977. Union Satisfaction and Participation. *Industrial Relations* 16(2):145–51.

Goldberg, M. 1981. Formulating Worker Consciousness. *Social Dynamics* 7(1):32–41.

Goodale, James G. 1973. Effects of Personal Background and Training on Work Values of the Hard-Core Unemployed. *Journal of Applied Psychology* 57(1):1–9.

Gordon, Michael E., Laura L. Beauvais, and Robert T. Ladd. 1984. The Job Satisfaction and Union Commitment of Unionized Engineers. *Industrial and Labor Relations Review* 37(3):359–70.

Gordon, Michael E., and Robert E. Burt. 1981. A History of Industrial Psychology's Relationship with American Unions: Lessons from the Past and Directions for the Future. *International Review of Applied Psychology* 30(2):137–56.

Gordon, Michael E., and Aaron Nurick. 1981. Psychological Approaches to the Study of Unions and Union-Management Relations. *Psychological Bulletin* 90(2):292–307.

Gordon, Michael E., John W. Philpot, Robert E. Burt, Cynthia A. Thompson, and William E. Spiller. 1980. Commitment to the Union: Development of a Measure and an Examination of its Correlates. *Journal of Applied Psychology* 65:479–99.

Grusky, Oscar. 1966. Career Mobility and Organizational Commitment. *Administrative Science Quarterly* 10(4):488–503.

Gullahorn, John T. 1956. Measuring Role-Conflict. *American Journal of Sociology* 61(4):299–303.

Hall, Douglas T. 1972. A Model of Coping with Role Conflict: The Role Behavior of College Educated Women. *Administrative Science Quarterly* 17(4):471–86.

Hall, Douglas T., and Benjamin Schneider. 1972. Correlates of Organizational Identification as a Function of Career Pattern and Organizational Type. *Administrative Science Quarterly* 17(3):340–51.

Hall, Douglas T., Benjamin Schneider, and Harold T. Nygren. 1970. Personal Factors in Organizational Identification. *Administrative Science Quarterly* 15(2):176–90.

Hammer, Tove H., and Michael Berman. 1981. The Role of Noneconomic Factors in Faculty Union Voting. *Journal of Applied Psychology* 66(4):415–21.

Herman, Jeanne B. 1973. Are Situational Contingencies Limiting Job Attitude-Job Performance Relationships? *Organizational Behavior and Human Performance* 10(2):208–24.

Hirschman, Albert O. 1970. *Exit, Voice, and Loyalty*. Cambridge: Harvard University Press.

Hom, Peter W., Ralph Katerberg, and Charles L. Hulin. 1979. Comparative Examination of Three Approaches to the Prediction of Turnover. *Journal of Applied Psychology* 64(3):280–90.

Hrebiniak, Lawrence G. 1975. Effects of Job Level and Participation on Employee Attitudes and Perceptions of Influence. *Academy of Management Journal* 17(4):649–62.

Hrebiniak, Lawrence G., and Joseph A. Alutto. 1972. Personal and Role-Related Factors in the Development of Organizational Commitment. *Administrative Science Quarterly* 17(4):555–72.

Hulin, Charles L., and Milton I. Blood. 1968. Job Enlargement, Individual Differences, and Worker Responses. *Psychological Bulletin* 69(1):41–45.

Huszczo, Gregory E., Jack S. Wiggins, and John S. Currie. 1984. The Relationship Between Psychology and Organized Labor. *American Psychologist* 39(4):432–40.

Ingham, Geoffrey K. 1970. *Size of Industrial Organisation and Worker Behaviour*. London: Cambridge University Press.

International Review of Applied Psychology. 1981. Psychologists and Unions. Vol 30 (2):127–327.

Jamal, Muhammad. 1984. Job Stress and Job Performance Controversy: An Empirical Assessment. *Organizational Behavior and Human Performance* 33(1):1–21.

Journal of Occupational Psychology. 1986. Psychology and Industrial Relations. Vol. 59 (3):161–272.

Kanter, Rosabeth M. 1968. Commitment and Social Organization: A Study of Commitment Mechanisms in Utopian Communities. *American Sociological Review* 33(4):449–517.

Kanungo, Rabindra N. 1979. The Concept of Alienation and Involvement Revisited. *Psychological Bulletin* 86(1):119–38.

Katz, Daniel. 1964. The Motivational Basis of Organizational Behavior. *Behavioral Science* 9(1):131–46.

Katz, Daniel, and Robert E. Kahn. 1978. *The Social Psychology of Organizations*, 2d ed. New York: John Wiley.

Kelman, Herbert C. 1974. Attitudes Are Alive and Well and Gainfully Employed in the Sphere of Action. *American Psychologist* 29(5):310–24.

Kemerer, Frank R., and J. Victor Baldridge. 1975. *Unions on Campus*. San Francisco: Jossey-Bass.

Kidron, Aryeh. 1978. Work Values and Organizational Commitment. *Academy of Management Journal* 21(2):239–47.

Kissler, Gary D. 1977. Grievance Activity and Union Membership: A Study of Goverment Employees. *Journal of Applied Psychology* 62(4):459–62.

Klandermans, P. G. 1984. Mobilisation and Participation in Trade Union Action: An Expectancy-Value Approach. *Journal of Occupational Psychology* 57(1):107–20.

Koch, James L., and Richard M. Steers. 1978. Job Attachment, Satisfaction, and Turnover among Public Employees. *Journal of Vocational Behavior* 12(2):119–28.

Kochan, Thomas A. 1978. *Contemporary Views of American Workers Toward Trade Unions*. Washington, DC: U.S. Department of Labor.

———. 1979. How American Workers View Labor Unions. *Monthly Labor Review* 102(1):23–31.

———. 1980. *Collective Bargaining and Industrial Relations: From Theory to Policy and Practice*. Homewood, IL: Richard D. Irwin.

Kochan, Thomas A., David B. Lipsky, and Lee Dyer. 1974. Collective Bargaining and the Quality of Work: The Views of Local Union Activists. In *Proceedings of the Twenty-Seventh Annual Winter Meeting, December 28–30, 1973*, ed. J. L. Stern and B. D. Dennis, 150–62. Madison, WI: Industrial Relations Research Association.

Kornhauser, Arthur. 1961. Observations on the Psychological Study of Labor-Management Relations. *Personnel Psychology* 14(3):241–49.

Ladd, Robert T., Michael E. Gordon, Laura L. Beauvais, and Richard L. Morgan. 1982. Union Commitment: Replication and Extension. *Journal of Applied Psychology* 67(5):640–44.

Ladd, Robert T., and Seymour M. Lipset. 1973. *Professors, Unions and American Higher Education*. Berkeley, CA: Carnegie Commission on Higher Education.

Laliberte, Michele M. and Julian Barling. 1986. *Predicting Attitudes to Unions among Non-Unionized Individuals*, photocopy. Kingston, Ontario: Queen's University.

Larson, Erik W., and Cynthia V. Fukami. 1985. Union Commitment as a Moderator of the Relationship Between Company Commitment and Worker Behaviors. Paper presented at the Academy of Management meeting, Boston.

Lawler, Edward E., Walter Kuleck, John Rhode, and James Sorenson. 1975. Job Choice and Post Decision Dissonance. *Organizational Behavior and Human Performance* 13(1):133–45.

Leggett, John C. 1968. *Class, Race and Labor*. New York: Oxford University Press.

LeLouarn, Jean-Yves. 1979. Predicting Union Votes from Worker Attitudes and Perceptions. In *Proceedings of the Thirty-Second Annual Meeting, December 28–30, 1978*, ed. Barbara D. Dennis, 72–82. Madison, WI: Industrial Relations Research Association.

MacBride, Arlene, William Lancee, and Stanley J. Freeman. 1981. The Psychosocial Impact of a Labour Dispute. *Journal of Occupational Psychology* 54(1):125–33.

Mancke, Robert B. 1971. American Trade Union Growth, 1900–1960: A Comment. *Quarterly Journal of Economics* 85(1):187–93.

Marginson, Paul M. 1984. The Distinctive Effects of Plant and Company Size on Workplace Industrial Relations. *British Journal of Industrial Relations* 22(1):1–13.

Martin, James E. 1981. Dual Allegiance in Public Sector Unionism. *International Review of Applied Psychology* 30(2):245–59.

Maxey, Charles, and Susan A. Mohrman. 1980. Worker Attitudes towards Unions: A Study Integrating Industrial Relations and Organizational Behavior Perspectives. *Proceedings of the Thirty-Third Annual Meeting, December 28–30, 1979*, ed. Barbara D. Dennis, 326–33. Madison, WI: Industrial Relations Research Association.

Michaels, Charles, and Paul Spector. 1982. Causes of Employee Turnover: A Test of the Mobley, Griffith, Hand, and Meglino Model. *Journal of Applied Psychology* 67(1):53–59.

Moore, William J., and Douglas K. Pearce. 1976. Union growth: A Test of the Ashenfelter-Pencavel Model. *Industrial Relations* 15(2):244–47.

Morris, James, and James L. Koch. 1979. Impacts of Role Perceptions on Organizational Commitment, Job Involvement and Psychosomatic Illness among Three Vocational Groupings. *Journal of Vocational Behavior* 14(1):88–101.

Morris, James, and J. David Sherman. 1981. Generalizability of Organizational Commitment Model. *Academy of Management Journal* 24(3):512–26.

Morris, James, and Richard M. Steers. 1980. Structural Influences on Organizational Commitment. *Journal of Vocational Behavior* 17(1):50–57.

Mowday, Richard T., and Terence McDade. 1980. The Development of Job Attitudes, Job Perceptions, and Withdrawal Propensities during the Early Employment Period. Paper presented at the fortieth annual meeting of the Academy of Management, Detroit.

Mowday, Richard T., Lyman W. Porter, and Richard M. Steers. 1982. *Employee-Organization Linkages: The Psychology of Commitment, Absenteeism, and Turnover*. New York: Academic Press.

Mowday, Richard T., Richard M. Steers, and Lyman W. Porter. 1979. The Measurement of Organizational Commitment. *Journal of Vocational Behavior* 14(1):43–77.

Nicholson, Nigel. 1976. The Role of the Shop Steward: An Empirical Case Study. *Industrial Relations Journal* 7(1):15–26.

Nicholson, Nigel. 1979. Industrial Relations Climate: A Case Study Approach. *Personnel Review* 8(1):20–25.

Olson, Craig A., and Chris J. Berger. 1983. The Relationship Between Seniority, Ability, and the Promotion of Union and Nonunion Workers. In *Advances in Industrial and Labor Relations*, vol. 1, ed. David B. Lipsky and Joel M. Douglas, 91–129. Greenwich, CT: JAI Press.

Pestonjee, D. M., A. P. Singh, and S. P. Singh. 1981. Attitude towards Union as Related to Morale and Job Involvement. *International Review of Applied Psychology* 30:209–16.

Porter, Lyman W., William J. Crampon, and Frank J. Smith. 1976. Organizational Commitment and Managerial Turnover: A Longitudinal Study. *Organizational Behavior and Human Performance* 15(1):87–98.

Porter, Lyman W., and Edward E. Lawler. 1965. Properties of Organization Structure in Relation to Job Attitudes and Job Behavior. *Psychological Bulletin* 64(1):23–51.

Porter, Lyman W., Edward E. Lawler, and J. Richard Hackman. 1975. *Behavior in Organizations*. New York: McGraw-Hill.

Porter, Lyman W., and Frank J. Smith. 1970. *The Etiology of Organizational Commitment*, photocopy. Irvine: University of California.

Porter, Lyman W., Richard M. Steers, Richard T. Mowday, and Paul V. Boulian. 1974. Organizational Commitment, Job Satisfaction, and Job Turnover among Psychiatric Technicians. *Journal of Applied Psychology* 59(5):603–9.

Purcell, Theodore V. 1954. *The Worker Speaks His Mind on Company and Union*. Cambridge: Harvard University Press.

————. 1960. *Blue Collar Man*. Cambridge: Harvard University Press.

Rabinowitz, Samuel, and Douglas T. Hall. 1977. Organizational Research on Job Involvement. *Psychological Bulletin* 84(2):265–88.

Rhodes, Susan R., and Richard M. Steers. 1981. Conventional vs. Worker-Owned Organizations. *Human Relations* 34(12):1013–35.

Ronan, William W., and Erich P. Prien. 1973. An Analysis of Organizational Behavior and Organizational Performance. *Organizational Behavior and Human Performance* 9(1):78–99.

Roomkin, Myron, and Hervey A. Juris. 1978. *Unions in the Traditional Sectors: The Mid-Life Passage of the Labor Movement*. In *Proceedings of the Thirty-First Annual Meeting, December 28–30, 1977*, ed. Barbara D. Dennis, 212–23. Madison, WI: Industrial Relations Research Association.

Rosen, Harold, and Ruth Rosen. 1955. *The Union Member Speaks*. New York: Prentice-Hall.

Salancik, Gerald R. 1977. Commitment and the Control of Organizational Behavior and Belief. In *New directions in organizational behavior*, ed. Barry M. Staw and Gerald R. Salancik, 1–54. Chicago: St. Clair Press.

Salancik, Gerald R., and Jeffrey A. Pfeffer. 1977. An Examination of Need Satisfaction Models of Job Attitudes. *Administrative Science Quarterly* 22(3):427–56.

Sayles, Leonard R., and George Strauss. 1953. *The Local Union*. Chicago: Harcourt, Brace and World.

Schneider, Benjamin. 1985. Organizational Behavior. *Annual Review of Psychology* 36:573–611.

Schriesheim, Chester A. 1978. Job Satisfaction, Attitudes towards Workers and Voting in a Union Representation Election. *Journal of Applied Psychology* 63(5):548–53.

Schutt, Russell K. 1982. Models of Militancy: Support for Strikes and Work Actions among Public Sector Employees. *Industrial and Labor Relations Review* 35(3):406–22.

Seeman, Melvin. 1959. On the Meaning of Alienation. *American Sociological Review* 24(6):783–91.

Seidman, Joel, John London, Bernard Karsh, and Daniel Tagliacozzo. 1958. *The Worker Views His Union*. Chicago: University of Chicago Press.

Sheflin, Neil, Leo Troy, and Timothy Koeller. 1981. Structural Stability in Models of American Trade Union Growth. *Quarterly Journal of Economics* 85(1):77–88.

Shorter, Edward, and Charles Tilly. 1974. *Strikes in France: 1830 to 1968*. Cambridge: Cambridge University Press.

Slichter, Sumner M., James J. Healy, and E. Robert Livernash. 1960. *The Impact of Collective Bargaining on Management*. Washington, DC: Brookings Institution.

Srinivas, Kalburgi M. 1981. Psychology, Labour and Worklife: New Challenges. *International Review of Applied Psychology* 30(2):261–75.

Stagner, Ross. 1954. Dual Allegiance as a Problem in Modern Society. *Personnel Psychology* 7(1):41–46.

Stagner, Ross. 1956. *Psychology of Industrial Conflict*. New York: John Wiley.

Stagner, Ross. 1962. Personality Variables in Union-Management Relations. *Journal of Applied Psychology* 46(5):350–57.

———. 1981. The Future of Union Psychology. *International Review of Applied Psychology* 30(2):321–28.

Stagner, Ross, and Boaz Eflal. 1982. Internal Union Dynamics during a Strike: A Quasi-Experimental Study. *Journal of Applied Psychology* 67(1):37–44.

Staw, Barry M. 1977. Antecedents and outcomes of organizational commitment. *Administrative Science Quarterly* 27(1):46–56.

Steers, Richard M. 1977. Antecedents and Outcomes of Organizational Commitment. *Administrative Science Quarterly* 27(1):46–56.

Steers, Richard M., and Daniel G. Spencer. 1977. The role of Achievement Motivation in Job Design. *Journal of Applied Psychology* 62(4):472–79.

Stein, E. 1972. The Dilemma of Union Democracy. In *Organizational Issues in Industrial Society*, ed. J. Shepheard. Englewood Cliffs, NJ: Prentice-Hall.

Stevens, John M., Janice M. Beyer, and Harrison M. Trice. 1978. Assessing Personal, Role, and

Organizational Predictors of Management Commitment. *Academy of Management Journal* 21(3):380–96.

Strauss, George. 1977. Union Government in the United States: Research Past and Future. *Industrial Relations* 16(2):215–42.

Strauss, George, and Malcolm Warner. 1977. Research on Union Government: Introduction. *Industrial Relations* 16(2):115–25.

Sulkin, Howard A., and R. W. Pranis. 1967. Comparison of Grievants with Non-Grievants in a Heavy Machinery Company. *Personnel Psychology* 20(1):111–19.

Tannenbaum, Arnold S., and Robert L. Kahn. 1958. *Participation in Local Unions*. Evanston, IL: Row, Peterson.

Tannenbaum, Frank. 1952. *A Philosophy of Labor*. New York: Alfred Knopf.

Thompson, Duane E., and Richard F. Borglum. 1973. A Case Study of Employee Attitudes and Labor Unrest. *Industrial and Labor Relations Review* 27(1):74–83.

Turner, Herbert A. 1962. *Trade Union Growth, Structure and Policy*. London: Allen and Unwin.

Uphoff, William H., and Marvin D. Dunnette. 1956. *Understanding the Union Member*. Minneapolis: University of Minnesota Press.

Van Maanen, John V. 1975. Police Socialization: A Longitudinal Examination of Job Attitudes in an Urban Police Department. *Administrative Science Quarterly* 20(2):207–28.

_________. 1977. Toward a Theory of the Career. In *Organizational Careers: Some New Perspectives*, ed. John V. Van Maanen, 161–79. New York: John Wiley.

Van Maanen, John V., and Edgar H. Schein. 1979. Toward a Theory of Organizational Socialization. In *Research in Organizational Behavior, vol. 1*, ed. Barry M. Staw, 209–64. Greenwich, CT: JAI Press.

Vroom, Victor, and Edward L. Deci. 1971. The Stability of Post-decisional Dissonance: A Follow-up Study of the Job Attitudes of Business School Graduates. *Organizational Behavior and Human Performance* 6(1):36–49.

Walker, J. Malcolm, and John J. Lawler. 1979. Dual Unions and Political Processes in Organizations. *Industrial Relations* 18(1):32–43.

Walker, Kenneth F. 1979. Psychology and Industrial Relations: A General Perspective. In *Industrial Relations: A Social Psychological Approach*, ed. Geoffrey M. Stephenson and Christopher J. Brotherton, 5–32. Chichester: John Wiley.

Wanous, John P. 1980. *Organizational Entry: Recruitment, Selection and Socialization of Newcomers*. Reading, MA: Addison-Wesley.

Warr, Peter. 1981. Psychological Studies of Union Management Relations in the United Kingdom. *International Review of Applied Psychology* 30(2):311–20.

Welsh, Harold P., and Helen LaVan. 1981. Inter-relationships between Organizational Commitment and Job Characteristics, Job Satisfaction, Professional Behavior and Organizational Climate. *Human Relations* 34(12):1079–89.

Youngblood, Stuart A., Angelo S. DeNisi, Julie L. Molleston, and William H. Mobley. 1984. The Impact of Work Environment, Instrumentality Beliefs, Perceived Labor Union Image, and Subjective Norms on Union Voting Intentions. *Academy of Management Journal* 27(3):576–90.

Zalesny, Mary D. 1985. Comparison of Economic and Noneconomic Factors in Predicting Faculty Vote Preferences in a Union Representation Election. *Journal of Applied Psychology* 70(2):243–56.

LABOR UNIONS AND THE U.S. CONGRESS:

PAC ALLOCATIONS AND LEGISLATIVE VOTING

Marick F. Masters and Asghar Zardkoohi

Labor unions have long recognized the practical inseparability of politics and economics. In fact, U.S. unions' record of achievement has often depended as much on what happened in Congress as at the bargaining table. Labor unions have traditionally committed themselves, therefore, to a broad plan of political action. In the 1980s in particular, evidently in response to their difficulties in securing gains in organizing and at the bargaining table, they have stepped up their political activities, especially in electoral politics.

Researchers have begun to pay more attention to labor's political role as it has expanded in recent years. Published studies on the subject fall into four principal categories. First, scholars have analyzed the environmental and organizational variables associated with differences in political "inputs" among unions, especially with respect to political action committee (PAC) contributions and lobbying personnel (Delaney, Fiorito, and Masters 1986; Masters and Delaney 1984, 1985, 1987a). Second, several studies have analyzed the determinants of unions' PAC allocations among legislators and other congressional candidates

Advances in Industrial and Labor Relations, Volume 4, pages 79-117.

ISBN: 0-89232-909-2

(Chappell 1982; Gopoian 1984; Grier and Munger 1986; Herndon 1982; Kau, Keenan, and Rubin 1982; Kau and Rubin 1981; Masters and Zardkoohi 1986a; Saltzman 1987). The third emphasis has been the impact of unionization and labor PAC money on legislators' roll-call voting (Chappell 1982; Kau, Keenan, and Rubin 1982; Kau and Rubin 1978, 1979, 1981, 1982; Masters 1986; Masters and Zardkoohi 1986b; Peltzman 1984; Saltzman 1987; Silberman and Durden 1976). Finally, researchers have also studied the legal restrictions on political activities by unions, especially in campaign financing, and the normative issues raised by the expenditure of union funds for political purposes (Epstein 1976, 1980; Cohan 1973; Rehmus and Kerner 1980).

Although insightful and broad in scope, this research has its limitations. In particular it has tended to ignore the crucial question of labor's impact on public policy. Moreover, only a few studies have examined union political activities and their effects on a disaggregate basis.

This study addresses these shortcomings. Specifically, our purposes are as follows:

1. To present evidence documenting labor's growing political involvement.
2. To offer a theoretical framework to explain labor's role in politics.
3. To analyze, on both an aggregate and a disaggregate basis, the determinants of allocations from labor PACs to legislators.
4. To analyze, again on an aggregate and a disaggregate basis, the impact of unions on legislators' votes on diverse public policy issues.
5. To present a set of questions to direct future research on this topic.

(Unless otherwise noted, the terms *union, labor*, and *labor organizations* are used interchangeably).

A caveat is worthy of note at the outset: We do not aspire to answer these questions definitively. They are too complex and multifaceted to treat fully in a chapter-length manuscript, even if enough relevant empirical evidence could be assembled. We do intend, however, to provide some insights on the subject and to provide a broad perspective on the range of labor's political activities. As the title of this chapter indicates, our emphasis is on labor's relationship with Congress, partly because of legislators' key role in the realization of labor's objectives for national labor policy and also because data on particular aspects of this relationship, especially campaign financing, are available for our scrutiny.

EVIDENCE OF UNIONS' INVOLVEMENT IN POLITICS

Labor unions invest resources in politics in many different ways. For analytical convenience their investments may be divided into two parts: electoral and lobbying. In electoral politics unions endorse candidates for public office, supply those candidates with financial and in-kind assistance, and attempt to deliver votes to office seekers on election day, among other things. The ultimate purpose of their electoral activities is to shape the ideological makeup of lawmaking bodies and thus affect public policy. Lobbying activities include testifying before congressional committees and otherwise furnishing information to lawmakers, arranging meetings between lawmakers and their constituents, and forming interest-group coalitions on an ad hoc or permanent basis. It is not by chance, therefore, that many labor organizations, including the AFL-CIO, the International Association of Machinists and Aerospace Workers, and the National Education Association, maintain their headquarters in the nation's capital.

A complete documentation of labor's investments in these forms of electoral and legislative politics is impossible, since many activities are either undisclosed or unrecorded. Federal laws require the disclosure of union PAC finances in congressional and presidential elections, but they do not mandate that unions fully report their expenditures made in other pursuits (such as political education and voter mobilization).[1] Moreover, federal laws require minimal disclosure of lobbying activities, limited mainly to the identification of union lobbyists and their direct salaries and expenses.[2]

Data are available, however, on two important avenues of union political action. As noted above, unions must disclose the money they give to federal candidates through their PACs. The Federal Election Campaign Act of 1971, as amended, prohibits unions from contributing their treasury money to federal election campaigns but allows them to establish "separate segregated funds" (or PACs) and to contribute this "voluntarily" raised money to office seekers. The law stipulates among other things that unions fully disclose these contributions to the Federal Election Commission (FEC). Second, in a series of volumes titled *Washington Representatives: Who Does What for Whom in the Nation's Capital?* Close (1979, 1981, 1983) has identified the persons who represent labor in governmental affairs in Washington, D.C. From these data we can compute the sizes of lobbying staffs and infer therefrom the extent to which unions are committed to lobbying per se. Larger staffs permit unions to engage in more governmental activities, other things being equal.

Table 1 reports descriptive statistics on the growth in overall activity by labor PACs between the 1973–74 and 1983–84 election cycles.[3] The data show that the total number of labor PACs nearly doubled over this ten-year period. Total labor PAC contributions to congressional candidates over this period rose proportionately more, to an amount almost four times greater than the amount in 1973–74.

Table 2 reports data on labor unions' lobbying staff between roughly 1978 and 1982.[4] For the period as a whole a sizable increase is evident. Little change occurred between 1980 and 1982, however, partly because some unions laid off staff as a consequence of membership losses at the time (Masters and Delaney 1987a).

Table 1. Labor PACs and Their Contributions, 1974–84

Two-Year Election Cycle	*Total Number of Labor PACs*	*Total Labor PAC Contributions to Congressional Candidates (in millions)*
1973–74	201	$ 6.3
1975–76	224	8.2
1977–78	217	10.3
1979–80	297	13.2
1981–82	380	20.3
1983–84	394	24.8

Sources: These data are from various reports and press releases issued by the Federal Election Commission.

At first blush these aggregate data appear impressive. They testify to the magnitude and growth in labor's involvement in national politics in recent years. Nevertheless, the data report on only two specific dimensions of political activity—PAC contributions and lobbying activity—and they mask the variation in these dimensions among different unions. In a detailed examination of union PAC contributions and lobbying staff sizes, Masters and Delaney (1987a) found that between 72 and 80 different labor unions made PAC contributions to congressional candidates in the 1978, 1980, and 1982 election periods. This means that the majority of the roughly 190 national labor organizations in the United States did not make PAC donations. Similarly, between 61 and 64 labor organizations employed Washington lobbyists during the same period. One should not be misled into believing, however, that organized workers are generally un-

Table 2. The Number of Union Lobbyists in Washington, D.C., 1978–82

Year	*Number of Union Lobbyists*
1978	185
1980	282
1982	287

Source: Close (1979, 1981, 1983). *Who Does What for Whom in the Nation's Capital?*

Note: Close reports the total number of lobbying personnel retained by labor organizations. He also reports the total number of law and consulting firms retained for lobbying purposes. In computing the totals reported here we added the number of lobbyists to the number of firms retained. Thus, if a union retained five lobbyists and two firms, we computed a total of seven Washington representatives. Although this computation is somewhat arbitrary, it is difficult to estimate the number of personnel and the amount of effort the law and consulting firms devote to their individual union clients.

represented in politics, since those unions that are active in politics represent the overwhelming majority of unionized workers.

Other studies have demonstrated a marked dispersion among the active organizations. Several unions have been at best only nominally active in supporting PACs. In the 1980 election cycle, for instance, 15 labor unions gave less than $10,000 in total to congressional candidates; in contrast, the PACs sponsored by 20 other unions accounted for over 80 percent of labor's total contributions (Masters and Delaney 1984). Although union size is significantly correlated with this variation in PAC contributions, it does not explain why several small unions gave relatively large amounts—in total and on a per-member basis (see Masters and Delaney 1984, 1985; Delaney, Fiorito, and Masters 1986). In the 1981–82 election period, for example, the 12,000-member National Marine Engineers' Benficial Association contributed $47.94 in PAC money per union member; all other unions with PACs contributed but $1.32 on average per union member (Delaney, Fiorito, and Masters 1986).[5]

Significant differences also exist in the sizes of unions lobbying staffs. Predictably, larger unions employ more personnel. In 1982, for instance, unions with 1,000,000 or more members retained eight lobbyists on average; unions with fewer than 50,000 members retained fewer than two lobbyists on average (Masters and Delaney 1987a). Once again, however, membership size is not the sole explanatory factor. Several other organizational and environmental factors contribute to the apparent differences in the import unions attach to lobbying (Masters and Delaney 1985, 1987a; Delaney, Fiorito, and Masters 1986). As one example, the primary industry the union has organized is correlated with the level of the union's lobbying activity, with unions located primarily in regulated industries generally employing more lobbyists, other things equal (Masters and Delaney 1985, 1987a).

These interunion differences imply several things. First, they suggest that the pressures for political action vary across labor organizations, depending upon their organizational characteristics and environmental contexts. Second, they imply that it would be a mistake to assume that labor's political interests are monolithic. Third, to the extent that political resources yield power, we may expect that political power will vary across unions. On a broader note, the differences bespeak the case for analyzing union political activities on a disaggregate as well as an aggregate basis.

THEORETICAL PERSPECTIVES

Why are unions politically active? What are the incentives for unions and their members to support political activity? To answer these questions, we turn to existing theory. Several researchers have offered alternative explanations of organizational (interest group) political participation that are relevant to our study of unions.

At least three theoretical perspectives exist to explain the origins and maintenance of labor's political involvement, which, in contemporary American politics, has mainly been in the form of interest-group activity.[6] Pluralists interpret American politics in terms of groups. Groups emerge around common interests in a fluid process that offers numerous opportunities to influence political decision making. Interestingly, James Madison provided one of the first such interpretations. Writing in the celebrated *Federalist No. 10*, he discussed—lamented!—the inevitability of political factionalism. Economic inequalities among the citizenry made factions unavoidable: "The most common and durable source of factions has been the various and unequal distribution of property. Those who hold and those who are without property have ever formed distinct interests in society" (Madison 1788, 56).

David Truman (1951) offered a more contemporary and elaborate interpretation of the pluralist viewpoint in *The Government Process*. Briefly stated, he argued that individuals joined or formed interest groups when an advantage could be gained to their common needs through collective political effort. Truman observed that groups are formed in an organic, equilibrating process, one in which individuals combine partly in response to imbalances in their extant political power.

The pluralist perspective has been attacked vigorously. Critics have questioned its most basic premise, namely, individuals participate in group activities as a rational action. Mancur Olson (1965) articulated a particularly widely cited criticism. He argued that individual participation in group activities is in the main irrational, for at least two reasons. First, the "collective" nature of public policy benefits violates the property of *exclusivity*. That is, these benefits are not available exclusively to those who participated, through group political action, in their attainment; nonparticipants as well may enjoy the harvest. Second, most people will rationally calculate that their individual contribution to group activity will have only a minimal effect on the group's chances of achieving political success.

Olson did acknowledge, however, the existence of union participation in politics. How, then, did he explain this possibly special case? He offered a provocative "by-product" theory of union political involvement, according to which a union's political activities are a by-product of labor's legal right and practical desire to negotiate union security provisions that insure a continual flow of money to the labor organization. At least part of the flow could be diverted toward political action and away from other functions, regardless of membership support for the action.

From Olson's perspective it would not be rational for employees to join unions for the purpose of engaging in politics or supporting union political activities. In the absence of coercive mechanisms, therefore, union political activities would be expected to languish. As Olson (1965, 136) stated:

> Labor unions came to play an important part in the political struggle only long after they had forsaken political action as a major goal. It is worth noting that the Wagner Act, which made organizing a union with compulsory union membership much easier, and which led to the

> greatest increase in union membership, was passed *before* labor unions came to play a really important role in politics. . . . If, then, it is true that a democratic nation would not normally want to make membership in a purely political union compulsory, and that compulsion is essential to a stable labor movement of any size, then it follows that the political power of unions is a by-product of their nonpolitical attributes.

Implicitly, then, union leaders can be expected to channel revenues coerced from members into political activities that bolster the leaders' prestige and institutional position (in other words, that shield them from unwanted challenges). As Edelman (1971, 147) commented in a related train of thought:

> Union leaders . . . win important support for their organizational positions from friendly governments and sometimes from unfriendly ones. Wide publicity is given to the fact that they are . . . consulted by the President, the political party leadership, and the Secretary of Labor. . . . In return for the aura of popular support they confer on the government, they receive an aura of high influence and statesmanship which helps them in winning a customer from the public generally and retaining a union following.

Although somewhat persuasive, given the reticence of many citizens to participate in politics, Olson's arguments fail on two counts. First, substantial amounts of political resources are raised through the voluntary contributions of union members. While one might suspect that some PAC money is less "voluntary" than other PAC money, it is unlikely that unions raised the tens of millions of PAC dollars they did over the past decade primarily through *de facto* coercion. Much of unions' political activity on all fronts is undoubtedly made possible by the voluntary actions of union members. Second, from a comparative perspective Olson's theory does not explain the political activities of unions in industrial societies that disallow union security arrangements.[7]

A review of the social science literature reveals another theoretical perspective that implicitly combines the more plausible aspects of the previous two. Exchange theory recognizes that there are many benefits, economic and noneconomic, collective and selective, that may motivate individuals to decide rationally to join in collective political action. This motivation is encouraged when the expected or real benefits of action outweigh its expected or real costs.

Several different perspectives on exchange theory appear in the literature (Salisbury 1969; Moe 1981; Lange and Ross 1982; Reshef 1986). Lange and Ross in particular developed a model specifically describing union political action, and we therefore use it here. It provides a logical and elaborate explanation of the role of labor and the state in the political economy. Lange and Ross mentioned several salient bases for reciprocation between these two parties.

Specifically, they delineated two related exchanges that determine the rationality of union political action: one between union members (current and prospective) and union leaders or organizations, and the other between unions and the state. With regard to the first exchange, unions must "be able to coerce support . . . or be able to gain consent" (Lange and Ross 1982, 220) in order to perform effectively in politics or economic affairs. Although union security arrangements, as Olson thought, might enable unions to coerce support and resources for political purposes, they do not fully supplant the union's need for members' consent. Union members may vote to decertify their union if they are dissatisfied with its representation, and nonunion members may rebuff the union organizing attempts if they are unconvinced that the union will serve their interests properly. The importance of consent imposes on union leaders the burden of justifying their political involvement, among other things. The justification, as previously suggested, is the expected or real exchange of goods between the state and labor.

Lange and Ross offered a typology of four kinds of benefits the parties may exchange. Exchanges are rational to the extent that each party reaps net benefits, or at least expects to do so. The conceptually distinct benefits are material, purposive, identity, and sociability,[8] defined by Lange and Ross (1982, 221) as follows:

> *Material*—tangible rewards: money, or things and services readily priced in monetary terms [In the case of unions this includes gains for workers in terms of hours of work, working conditions, and the like.];
>
> *Purposive*—suprapersonal goals which are constituted as the ends for which the organization is maintained, are pursued through the rules of the game and are open to compromise in order to increase the likelihood of at least partial success in the attempt to achieve them;
>
> *Identity*—the privilege to identify and be identified with the set of principles and rights as expressed by and embodied in an organizational entity which claims to seek to promote those principles and rights over the resistance of other organizations and social and political forces;
>
> *Sociability*—intangible rewards created by the act of associating and the interpersonal social bonds which come from feeling part of a relatively small and defined group.

Unions provide "some mix of [these] incentives to obtain [political and nonpolitical] resources from supporters" (Lange and Ross 1982, 221). Conventional wisdom holds that of the four, material benefits are usually the most attractive.

The logic of the second exchange, between the state and labor organizations, again lies in the benefits conferred. The state has the power to extend, directly and indirectly, benefits to unions. Theoretically, unions will seek these benefits to the extent that the real or expected costs of their attainment are not greater. Union members will presumably support—or at least be indifferent to—union political activities to the extent that they receive net benefits from these or other union services.

Since the New Deal, government has been involved in an array of socioeconomic affairs through a host of public policies and programs. These policies have varied widely in their relevance to, and impact on, unions. To simplify matters, Freeman and Medoff (1984) and Masters and Delaney (1987b) have grouped policies into three broad categories based on their closeness to labor relations law. In modified form these categories are labor relations law, general labor legislation, and law unrelated to labor. In each category, however, some policies have directly or indirectly benefited unions per se, union members, or both. For instance, the National Labor Relations Act of 1935 (in the first category) extended to employees the right to unionize and be free of managerial coercion in the process. Minimum wage laws, which fall in the second policy domain, have raised the relative cost of nonunion labor, thus making unions less unattractive to employers (Kau and Rubin 1981). Finally, various public expenditures, such as spending on education, have employed and benefited public workers, many of whom are unionized. This is why federal employee unions have focused on appropriations bills that are not technically related to labor relations or working conditions. Moreover, all unions can potentially benefit from advocating policies in this domain, such as civil rights legislation, because in so doing, they may forge important alliances with other interest groups.

But what incentives are there for lawmakers to enact labor-backed policies? In this heterogeneous democracy, noted for its individualistic thought and behavior, lawmakers are not preordained puppets of unions, nor are they constitutionally obliged to shield unions from untoward economic and social forces. In examining the benefits labor may confer on legislators, we must establish the motivation underlying much legislative behavior.

Legislators are strongly motivated to win reelection. The amount of energy and money they devote to electoral politics testifies to the force of this motivation. It follows, then, that a primary way in which unions can benefit legislators is by aiding their political campaigns. As already noted, unions offer a variety of types of campaign assistance. We do not thereby imply that labor buys lawmakers but rather that unions aid campaigns primarily to elect lawmakers who are likely to support union-backed policies in the first place. This aid serves as a continual reminder to legislators of labor's electoral support and potential.

In conclusion, exchange theory postulates that unions and lawmakers will supply each other benefits to the extent that the costs of doing so are not greater than the benefits. There is no reason, however, to believe that these benefits and costs are constant across lawmakers or unions, for they operate in distinct organizational and environmental situations that create different incentive systems (Greenstone 1977). Thus, exchange relations are more likely to occur between certain legislators and unions than others. From whom, then, do labor unions primarily seek their public policy benefits? From whom do they appear to receive the greatest support? We turn to these and related questions in the following analyses of the allocation of PAC contributions among legislators and the impact of these allocations on legislative voting.

PAC ALLOCATIONS

Labor unions invest a lot into politics. In making investments, what kinds of allocation rules do they follow? Who are the principal beneficiaries? What inferences can be made therefrom as to the general political orientation of unions? We address these questions by analyzing the determinants of labor PAC allocations to candidates who won election in 1982.[9] PAC money is one of labor's principal investments, and the manner in which it is allocated says a great deal about the political philosophy of unions. Although it would be preferable to examine other resource allocations as well, sufficient data are unavailable. Because the empirical analyses focus on candidates who *won* election in 1982 and served in the 98th Congress, we used the terms *candidate* and *legislator* interchangeably.

Allocation Model

In modeling the PAC allocation process, we borrow extensively from past research (Chappell 1982; Gopoian 1984; Herndon 1982; Kau and Rubin 1981; Kau, Keenan, and Rubin 1982; Masters and Zardkoohi 1986a; Peltzman 1984; Saltzman 1987; Wright 1985). Research suggests that PACs, labor and nonlabor alike, face a major strategic choice: whether to pursue an "electoral" or an "access" strategy. An electoral strategy is devoted to helping the campaigns of ideologically compatible office seekers. An access strategy focuses on aiding those candidates most likely to win election to avoid antagonizing probable officeholders and to insure that these elected officials will at least grant access to the sponsors of the PACs.

Two factors support the proposition that labor unions are likely to follow an electoral strategy. First, most labor unions subscribe to a liberal political doctrine, typically associated with the Democratic party.[10] Whether their policy interests are met depends largely on whether ideologically compatible legislators are elected. Shaping the makeup of Congress through electoral activities is therefore a major thrust of unions' political program.

Second, as mass organizations labor unions are well suited to influence election outcomes and help elect candidates (Kau and Rubin 1981). They may use their PAC money to complement other political activities in behalf of ideological sympathetic candidates.

Consistent with the proposition that labor follows an electoral strategy is the expectation that unions will target their PAC money to those races in which sympathetic candidates might profit most. Generally speaking, this means candidates whose election vote percentage was close to 50 percent. In other words, one expects labor PACs to prefer spending money, other things equal, on Democratic candidates who are not sure winners but rather who face stiff competition. The proposition that unions will follow an electoral strategy leads to these hypotheses:

Hypothesis 1: Labor PACs will prefer Democratic candidates over Republican candidates, other things equal.

Hypothesis 2: Labor PACs will prefer candidates involved in competitive races (races in which both parties have a reasonable chance of winning election), other things equal.

We measure electoral competition as the legislator's percentage of the vote in 1982. We expect to find an inverse relationship between vote percentage and labor PAC receipts: the lower the percentage, the greater the receipts from labor PACs.

Two other sets of factors are theoretically determinative of labor PAC allocations: legislators' position and power in Congress and their constituents' characteristics. Labor unions may prefer certain legislators who are in a better position to achieve particular goals. Unions may favor legislators who, for instance are assigned to a committee handling labor relations and related legislation because they have a stronger voice on these important matters. Legislation is typically handled first in committees, which have a major role to play in drafting statutory language and deciding on which issues are worthy of study. In this analysis, we predict that legislators seated on the Committee on Education and Labor of the House of Representatives will be preferred because of this committee's legislative jurisdiction over labor law and Department of Labor programs.

Unions may also prefer senior over junior legislators because seniority often confers power in Congress. Senior legislators are more likely to hold a committee chair, or be next in line for that position, as committee rank is generally extended on a seniority basis. In addition, senior legislators usually know their way around Congress better than junior lawmakers, having had more time to develop professional and personal contacts with other legislators, congressional staff, and lobbyists.

We therefore predict:

HYPOTHESIS 3: Legislators assigned to the House Committee on Education and Labor will receive greater sums of labor PAC money than legislators assigned to other committees, other things equal.

HYPOTHESIS 4: Labor PAC contributions will be positively correlated with legislators' seniority in Congress, other things equal.

At least four constituency characteristics arguably affect PAC allocations. First, the state of unionization in a legislator's geographical area should be positively correlated with the PAC money he or she receives. To some extent union members may influence the disbursement of PAC money. They may encourage PAC directors or managers to channel money into districts in which they are heavily represented.[11]

Second, constituents' ideological conservatism should be negatively associated with labor PAC contributions. Although unions are generally expected to help electorally vulnerable legislators who are favorably predisposed to labor, they cannot be expected to squander money on candidates engaged in hopeless contests. Thus, unions may be deterred from contributing to candidates in solidly conservative districts. We use the percentage of votes cast by a district's constituents for President Reagan in 1984 as a proxy for ideological conservatism.

Third, the percentage of minorities in a district may influence labor PAC allocations. For various reasons labor unions have historically been politically allied with numerous groups representing blacks and Hispanics, for example, the National Association for the Advancement of Colored People (NAACP). Labor may cement these alliances by supporting similarly allied candidates in districts with a relatively large minority population.

Finally, the relative affluence of constituents may affect labor's willingness to contribute to candidates. Affluent constituents may be less supportive of labor's public policy agenda and thus less likely to vote for labor-backed candidates. To some extent they may be more willing to aid the campaigns of anti-labor candidates, perhaps by contributing money. This may cause unions to give additional support to pro-labor opponents to offset the affluent community's financial advantage.

Thus, we have four main hypotheses about constituents' characteristics:

HYPOTHESIS 5: The proportion of the labor force that is unionized in a legislator's home district will be positively correlated with the legislator's contributions from labor PACs, other things equal.

HYPOTHESIS 6: The percentage of votes cast for President Reagan in a legislator's district in 1984 will be negatively correlated with his or her receipts from labor PACs, other things equal.

HYPOTHESIS 7: The percentage of minority population in a legislator's district will be positively associated with his or her receipts from labor PACs, other things equal.

HYPOTHESIS 8: The affluence of the legislator's constituents will be positively correlated with his or her receipts from labor PACs, other things equal.

Parenthetically, we use the median price of housing in a legislator's district as a proxy for constituency affluence.

Empirical Procedures

Data and Sample

As noted above, the units of observation in the empirical analyses below are the 435 candidates for the U.S. House of Representatives who won election in 1982 to the 98th Congress. Unless otherwise noted below, data on legislator and constituency characteristics are from Barone and Ujifusa (1983). Data on PAC allocations are from the FEC (1983).

Equation and Method

The PAC allocation model was tested using an ordinary-least-squares (OLS) multiple regression procedure. Parameters are estimated in the following equation:

$$\begin{aligned} PAC\ ALLOCATION = a &+ b_1\ DEMOCRAT + b_2\ COMPETITION \\ &+ b_3\ EDUCLAB + b_4\ SENIORITY + b_5\ UNION \\ &+ b_6\ REAGAN + b_7\ MINORITY + b_8\ AFFLUENCE \\ &+ e, \end{aligned}$$

where

PAC ALLOCATION = the total amount of labor PAC money received by a legislator in the 1981–82 election.
a = a constant term.
DEMOCRAT = a dummy variable equal to 1 if a legislator belonged to the Democratic party in 1981–82 and 0 if he or she was a Republican.
COMPETITION = the percentage of the election vote received by the legislator in 1982.
EDUCLAB = a dummy variable equal to 1 if a legislator served on the House Committee on Education and Labor and 0 if otherwise.
SENIORITY = the number of continuous years a legislator had held the office as of 1982.
UNION = the percentage of the nonagricultural labor force unionized in a legislator's state. Data are from the U.S. Department of Labor (1980).
REAGAN = the percentage of the election vote received by President Reagan in 1984 in a legislator's district. Data are from Barone and Ujifusa (1985). (We did not use 1980 voting data because of the congressional redistricting that occurred after 1980.)
MINORITY = the percentage of nonwhite population in a legislator's district.
AFFLUENCE = the median price of housing in a legislator's district.
e = an error team.

Results

The results of the OLS analysis are reported in Table 3. They support several of our hypotheses. The *DEMOCRAT* coefficient is statistically significant and positive, and the *COMPETITION* coefficient is negative and significant. These results indicate that labor PACs as a whole follow an electoral rather than an access strategy. The *EDUCLAB* coefficient shows that a legislator's position in Congress is a significant consideration in deciding how much PAC support to give, other things equal. The *AFFLUENCE, REAGAN*, and *UNION* results suggest that some constituency characteristics are also relevant in determining PAC allocations. The *REAGAN* vote in particular suggests that a conservative constituency for a legislator diminishes labor PAC contributions.

Extended Analyses

We selected 23 labor union PACs for our disaggregate analyses. (These organizations reflect the diversity in the labor movement, in terms of both union size and industrial-occupational composition.[12] Although these PACs by no means make up the total labor PAC population, they contributed approximately 65 percent of the labor PAC money received by the legislators in the sample. Table 4

Table 3. OLS Regression Results of the Aggregate Analysis of Labor PAC Allocations

Explanatory Variables	*Coefficients (Standard Errors)*
MINORITY	−119.60 (77.04)
EDUCLAB	8136.81* (4485.62)
AFFLUENCE	0.09* (0.05)
REAGAN	−324.06** (131.56)
UNION	41577.63*** (13016.82)
DEMOCRAT	36080.08*** (52.85)
SENIORITY	−88.11 (141.60)
COMPETITION	−719.53*** (81.18)
F	47.10 ($p < .001$)
R^2	.47
N	430

* $p < .10$ (two-tailed test).
** $p < .05$ (two-tailed test).
*** $p < .001$ (two-tailed test).

reveals the dispersion in these unions' PAC allocations. Labor PACs differ widely in the total amount they give to legislators, the number of PAC recipients, and average PAC donations per recipient. These differences suggest that it is appropriate to examine the PAC allocation model on a dissaggregate basis.

Table 4. Descriptive Analysis of Labor PAC Allocations, 1981–82

Union[a]	*Number of PAC Recipients*[b]	*Average PAC Contribution*[c]	*Total PAC Contributions*[d]
AFGE	177	$1,003.54	$177.626
AFL-CIO	132	3,228.03	426,100
AFSCME	153	1,684.25	257,690
AFT	88	1,459.73	128,456
ALPA	122	1,070.08	130,550
APWU	216	977.61	211,164
CJA	190	1,721.22	327,032
CWA	147	2,031.15	298,579
IAFF	56	3,982.14	22,300
IAM	177	4,475.40	792,148
MEBA	158	2,806.35	443,404
NAGE	6	350.00	2,100
NALC	211	1,018.26	214,853
NAPFE	14	717.86	10,050
NEA	228	3,084.63	703,297
NFFE	37	521.62	19,300
NTE	129	1,008.63	130,114
RLCA	132	638.26	84,250
SIUNA	235	2,060.92	484,317
UAW	214	4,436.14	949,335
UFCW	200	1,704.30	340,861
UMW	120	1,119.63	134,356
USA	136	2,561.63	348,382

Source: Data on disaggregate PAC allocations were obtained from the Federal Election Commission's "D Index" on nonparty PAC contributions in 1981–82.

[a]The union abbreviations listed above stand for the American Federation of Government Employees; American Federation of Labor–Congress of Industrial Organizations; American Federation of State, County and Municipal Employees; American Federation of Teachers; International Air Line Pilots Association; American Postal Workers Union; United Brotherhood of Carpenters and Joiners of America; Communications Workers of America; International Association of Fire Fighters, International Association of Machinists and Aerospace Workers; National Marine Engineers' Beneficial Association; National Association of Government Employees; National Association of Letter Carriers; National Alliance of Postal and Federal Employees; National Education Association; National Federation of Federal Employees; National Rural Letter Carriers' Association; National Treasury Employees Union; Seafarers' International Union of North America; United Automobile, Aerospace and Agricultural Implement Workers of America; United Food and Commercial Workers; United Mine Workers of America; and United Steelworkers of America.

[b]The number of recipients is the number of candidates elected in 1981–82 who received PAC money from the individual union.

[c]This figure is the total PAC contributions in the next column divided by the number of legislators who received money from the PAC in 1981–82.

[d]This figure is the total amount of PAC money the union's principal PAC gave to legislators who were elected in 1982.

Table 5. OLS Regression Results of the Disaggregate Analysis of Labor PAC Allocations Determinants

	Explanatory Variables (Standard Errors)								
Union	*Minority*	*Educlab*	*Affluence*	*Reagan*	*Union*	*Democrat*	*Seniority*	*Competition*	R^2
AFGE	2.49	490.06**	0.003	−14.94**	89.99	440.66**	2.39	−5.08	.15
	(3.15)	(183.47)	(0.002)	(5.39)	(531.52)	(96.15)	(5.79)	(3.31)	
AFL-CIO	1.57	−75.38	−0.002	−2.76	613.90	1778.52***	−41.70***	−52.83***	.27
	(6.51)	(379.81)	(0.004)	11.15	(1100.37)	(199.04)	(11.98)	(6.85)	
AFSCME	−2.6	339.94	0.002	−12.12*	1904.89**	972.27***	−18.35**	−19.47***	.22
	(4.13)	(240.93)	(0.003)	(7.07)	(698.01)	(126.26)	(7.60)	(4.35)	
AFT	−3.15	224.57	-0.001	−4.52	1054.00**	447.49***	−4.22	−9.67***	.12
	(2.71)	(157.77)	(0.002)	(4.63)	(457.08)	(82.68)	(4.98)	(2.85)	
ALPA	−3.47	−59.14	0.0003	−4.38	240.62	118.32	17.37***	−4.88*	.05
	(2.61)	(151.96)	(0.002)	(4.46)	(440.24)	(79.63)	(4.79)	(2.74)	
APWU	2.05	501.21***	0.003**	−10.52**	836.57***	623.87***	11.05**	−7.18**	.32
	(2.25)	(131.50)	(0.001)	(3.86)	(380.98)	(68.91)	(4.15)	(2.37)	
CJA	−0.36	338.99	0.006**	−0.81	1530.64**	1208.38***	1.87	−21.72***	.29
	(3.66)	(213.31)	(0.002)	(6.26)	(618.00)	(111.79)	(6.73)	(3.85)	
CWA	6.09	368.60	0.001	−4.39	338.80	1063.61***	−23.69**	−23.42***	.14
	(5.66)	(329.70)	(0.003)	(9.72)	(960.33)	(173.26)	(10.41)	(5.97)	
IAFF	−0.86	30.02	0.0008**	−1.46	9.29	76.31***	−0.77	−0.71	.08
	(0.55)	(31.99)	(0.0003)	(0.94)	(92.69)	(16.77)	(1.01)	(0.58)	
IAM	12.62	754.25	0.013**	−17.55	3688.46**	3388.98***	−50.02**	−74.46***	.37
	(9.18)	(535.17)	(0.0005)	(15.71)	(1550.45)	(280.46)	(16.88)	(9.66)	
MEBA	−19.59**	−440.81	0.019***	−35.46**	−1069.84	474.81**	31.83**	−11.43*	.10
	(6.58)	(383.50)	(0.004)	(11.26)	(1111.04)	(200.97)	(12.10)	(6.92)	
NAGE	−0.20	12.34	-0.1×10^{-5}	0.14	24.50	3.59	−0.22	0.53**	.03
	(0.19)	(11.33)	(0.1×10^{-3})	(0.33)	(32.84)	(5.94)	(0.36)	(0.20)	
NALC	−1.49	284.58**	0.003*	−6.99*	783.72**	782.81***	5.92	−13.20***	.34
	(2.21)	(128.88)	(0.001)	(3.78)	(373.37)	(67.54)	(4.06)	(2.32)	

NAPFE	1.39**	131.46**	−0.001**	−2.78	68.24	−8.89	−0.13	−0.58	.09
	(0.69)	(40.35)	(0.0004)	(1.18)	(116.91)	(21.15)	(1.27)	(0.73)	
NEA	−3.03	214.78	0.008*	−0.68	−559.73	2813.98***	−42.24**	−75.37***	.35
	(7.84)	(456.86)	(0.005)	(13.41)	(1323.59)	(239.42)	(14.41)	(8.24)	
NFFE	−1.06*	31.67	0.0005	−1.73	90.74	73.23***	0.92	−0.41	.07
	(0.62)	(36.38)	(0.0004)	(1.07)	(105.39)	(19.06)	(1.15)	(0.66)	
NTE	−0.22	475.07***	0.002*	−1.40	725.56*	467.63***	2.47	−4.40*	.17
	(2.20)	(128.40)	(0.001)	(3.77)	(371.98)	(67.29)	(4.05)	(2.31)	
RLCA	−0.36	390.25***	−0.001	2.328	103.37	212.25***	4.79*	−2.27	.10
	(1.52)	(88.80)	(0.001)	(2.607)	(257.27)	(46.54)	(2.80)	(1.60)	
SIUNA	−3.55	66.81	0.003	−10.06	2599.99**	1287.40***	10.36	−11.91*	.17
	(5.76)	(336.03)	(0.004)	(9.86)	(973.52)	(176.10)	(10.60)	(6.06)	
UAW	−14.72	633.01	.001	−33.28**	5932.02***	3489.32***	−39.66**	−56.30***	.37
	(9.39)	(547.67)	(.006)	(16.08)	(1586.68)	(287.01)	(17.27)	(9.89)	
UFCW	−1.01	207.14	0.005*	−8.46	868.95	1316.40***	−10.94*	−25.01***	.34
	(3.62)	(210.85)	(0.002)	(6.19)	(610.85)	(110.50)	(6.65)	(3.80)	
UMW	−9.12**	622.42**	−0.005**	−7.85	1078.81*	577.01***	16.76**	−9.50**	.13
	(3.87)	(225.70)	(0.002)	(6.63)	(653.88)	(118.28)	(7.12)	(4.07)	
USA	−2.05	821.60**	−0.003	−8.83	2647.58**	1346.65***	−21.03**	−26.23***	.22
	(5.51)	(321.27)	(0.003)	(9.43)	(930.77)	(168.37)	(10.13)	(5.80)	
No. of positive, significant coefficients	1	8	9	0	11	20	5	1	
No. of negative, significant coefficients	3	0	2	6	0	0	8	17	
No. of significant coefficients	4	8	11	6	11	20	13	18	

Note: The union abbreviations are spelled out in Table 4.
*p < .10 (two-tailed test).
**p < .05 (two tailed test).
***p < .001 (two-tailed test).

We therefore conducted 23 separate PAC allocation analyses, one for each of the 23 union PACs listed in Table 4. The model and statistical procedures used here are the same as those used in the aggregate analysis, but here the dependent variable is the amount of money received by a legislator from the individual PAC. Disaggregate labor PAC data were obtained from the Federal Election Commission's "D-Index" microfilm on nonparty PACs that contributed money to federal candidates in 1981–82.

Table 5 shows the statistical results for these disaggregate analyses. The two most consistently significant predictors of PAC allocations were the *DEMOCRAT* and *COMPETITION* variables. These results further support the electoral-strategy proposition; the electoral strategy is evidently pervasive in the labor movement. Legislator and constituency characteristics are decidedly less consistent predictors of PAC allocations, although the coefficients are usually in the expected direction when statistically significant. The *UNION* variable, for instance, is positive and significant in 11 of the 23 PAC equations.

Perhaps these inconclusive results are due to the fact that more particularistic factors influence individual unions' PACs. A union's specific membership size in a district, for example, may be more relevant than overall union membership in the district. Somewhat similarly, as unions' public policy interests vary, depending on their memberships' needs and their institutional situations, unions may place greater value on legislator assignments to committees other than the Education and Labor Committee. Identifying the real policy priorities and interests of unions, however, is hindered by their multifacted formal agendas and, in some cases, by the heterogeneity of their membership and leadership interests. Nevertheless, nothing suggest that labor PACs serve conflicting purposes in their allocations. The pervasiveness of the electoral strategy indicates that labor PACs are relatively homogeneous in their preferences. They prefer Democrats—period!

In summary, labor PAC allocations vary widely in total and average (per legislator) amounts, but they exhibit some consistent patterns on both aggregate and disaggregate bases. In allocating funds to legislators labor PACs follow an electoral strategy. They are ideologically committed to the Democratic party. As a whole they may also be partly influenced by certain constituency characteristics, such as unionization, ideology, and affluence.

THE IMPACT OF LABOR ON PUBLIC POLICY

As major actors in the political system, labor organizations undoubtedly have an impact on some legislation. Several factors, however, complicate measuring their effect. One is the labyrinthine nature of legislative decision-making processes. Labor is only one of many actors in the system; it competes against and collaborates with numerous groups, thereby making it difficult to grasp its particular contribution. Another complicating factor is that many of labor's political activities are unreported or unnoticed. Nonetheless, researchers have taken several approaches to this question. Some studies have meticulously documented the role of labor in singular legislative and electoral decisions, such as the passage of the Landrum-Griffin Act of 1959 (McAdams 1964; Miller and Ware 1963). Other studies have examined labor's assessments of legislators' voting records, based on so-called legislative voting guides or scoreboards periodically published by unions (Masters and Delaney 1982, 1987a, 1987b; Freeman and Medoff 1984; Pohlmann and Crisci 1982–83). Several labor organizations publish these scoreboards, which report whether legislators voted "right" (in support of the union's position) or "wrong" (against the union's position) on selected roll-call votes in Congress. From these statistics researchers have inferred the extent to which labor has had political success.

The third set of analyses has statistically estimated the impact of labor union membership rates or PAC contributions on legislators' roll-call votes on specific issues (Chappell 1982; Coughlin 1985; Kau and Rubin 1978, 1979, 1981, 1982; Kau, Keenan, and Rubin 1982; Masters 1986; Masters and Zardkoohi 1986b; Peltzman 1984; Saltzman 1987; Silberman and Durden 1976). These studies have posited and tested models of legislative voting behavior, estimating the effect of various legislator and constituency characteristics on the probability that a legislator will vote in line with labor's public policy preferences.

We will briefly review the literature on the second and third approaches in order to develop a model of legislative voting behavior. We then statistically test labor's impact on voting across different issues. We attempt to advance past research in two ways: first, by focusing on a diverse set of issues cited by labor organizations in their voting guides; and second, by examining the impact of aggregate and disaggregate labor PAC money on legislators' votes.

Legislative Records

Several studies have looked at labor organizations' voting guides during different time periods since the late 1940s. Freeman and Medoff (1984) examined AFL-CIO voting guides during the period from the late 1940s to the early 1980s. Masters and Delaney (1982, 1987a) examined AFL-CIO ratings of legislators' voting during the years 1974–84 and the ratings of legislators by eight other labor organizations during President Reagan's first term in office, 1981–84 (Masters and Delaney 1987b). Pohlmann and Crisci (1982–83) reviewed selected AFL-CIO ratings of legislators during the 89th (1965–66) and 95th (1977–78) Congresses, comparing the bases of labor's legislative support in these two Democratic-controlled bodies. Masters (1985) reviewed the legislative voting guides of three federal employee unions during the years 1977–81.

Together these studies offer a few common conclusions about the support labor has had in Congress. First, legislators' support for labor has varied widely over time. Second, the levels of their support have paralleled the Democrats' control of the House and Senate, although Democratic control does not necessarily translate perfectly into labor backing (Pohlmann and Crisci 1982–83). Third, labor's support in Congress has differed across legislative issues. Unions have lobbied for an array of public policies, ranging from civil rights to environmental protection. But analyses of voting guides have found that Congress has exhibited precious little legislative movement toward a more favorable stance vis-à-vis unions since the mid-1930s. Against unions' opposition Congress passed the Taft-Hartley Act of 1947 and the Landrum-Griffin Act of 1959. It has also refused to repeal the "right-to-work" allowance of the former act. Nor did Congress enact labor law reform in the late 1970s. Fourth, on the other hand, labor has successfully defeated many attempts to weaken or repeal protective labor laws (such as minimum wage legislation and the David-Bacon Act). Lastly, the voting guides show that different unions may have very different assessments of the extent of legislators' support for their agendas. This difference is due partly to the differences in union lobbying priorities and in the selection of issues for these guides. (In the course of interviews with numerous union lobbyists over the past several years, we have been struck by the marked variety in their public policy preferences and priorities.[13]) Some unions focus on matters more or less directly pertinent to their members' material interests (as with the Air Line Pilots Association's interest in airline safety). Others run the gamut; the UAW in particular lobbies on policies of national defense, international affairs, trade, and immigration, to name but a few (see, for example, Jacobs 1987).

In short, previous research has identified considerable variability in labor's records of support in Congress—over time, across issues, and among unions. Implicitly, then, legislators face competing political pressures which lead to these differences. An important issue for labor unions, therefore, is to identify the conditions that either aggravate or mitigate these pressures.

Legislative Voting Model

In recent years numerous published studies have appeared on the determinants of legislators' voting behavior (Chappell 1982; Coughlin 1985; Kalt and Zupan 1984; Kau and Rubin 1978, 1979, 1981, 1982; Kau, Keenan and Rubin 1982; Peltzman 1984; Saltzman 1987; Silberman and Durden 1976; Welch 1982). Although these studies have focused on different legislative votes, they have provided a common body of ideas on how to conceptualize and operationalize voting decision models. With respect to issues relevant to labor's policy impacts, the studies have examined, among other things, the correlation between labor PAC contributions or union membership rates, on the one hand, and legislator's roll-call votes, on the other. We rely on this research in particular in developing our own predictive voting model.

To an increasing degree the legislative voting process is analogous to an economic marketplace. Forces exist that affect both the *demand* for public policies and lawmakers' willingness to *supply* these policies. Typically, the sources of demand are twofold: constituency characteristics, and interest-group pressures. In theory these two may overlap or conflict. They also affect legislators' willingness to supply legislation because they affect lawmakers' electability. As already argued, legislators are implicitly rational in their behavior in the political arena, interested in securing enough votes for reelection. Toward this end they depend on interest groups for campaign money and support, and they can ill afford to alienate too many constituency groups by voting against their wishes in Congress. Thus, the same factors that generate demand for public policy enactments will affect the probability that the laws will be supplied, given that legislators are electorally minded. Independently, however, a legislator's personal ideology on certain matters may be decisive.

Three types of variables are thus theoretically relevant to predicting voting behavior: constituency characteristics, legislator characteristics, and interest-group pressure. We selected the specific variables used in the analyses reported below because of their potential relevance to identifying labor's political impact. We caution, however, that this model will not yield perfect prediction; legislators face many competing economic, political, psychological, and social pressures in making public policy decisions. Our model is intended to capture only the salient aspects of this decision-making process.

Constituency Characteristics

At least four constituency characteristics appear relevant to the potential demand for labor-backed legislation. First, the rate of unionization in a legislator's geographic area may affect the real and perceived demand for legislation. To some extent unions attempt to marshal grassroots support for public policies, and lawmakers may thus hear directly from their union constituents. Moreover, union leaders may give or withhold grassroots electoral support, depending on a legislator's voting record. Thus, legislators whose districts contain a sizable union bloc in the electorate may be loath to jeopardize this support.

HYPOTHESIS 1: The rate of unionization in a legislator's district will be positively correlated with his or her votes on labor-backed legislation, other things equal.

Second, for similar reasons, a constituency's dominant ideological preferences may encourage or discourage support for labor. In general, constituents' and legislators' preferences may be expected to parallel each other. A generally conservative congressional district will usually elect like-minded lawmakers. Given that labor's political preferences are frequently counter to conservatives', one might expect the demand for labor-backed legislation to be weaker in ideologically conservative districts. In light of apparent constituency preferences, legislators in such areas will be less willing to supply these public policies. As before, we use the percentage of votes cast for President Reagan in 1984 in legislator's district as a proxy for constituency ideology.

HYPOTHESIS 2: The percentage of votes cast for President Reagan in 1984 in a legislator's district will be negatively correlated with his or her vote on labor-backed legislation, other things equal.

Third, the proportion of minority residents in a legislator's district may create additional pressures for legislators to support labor in Congress. As noted earlier, labor and minority groups are often allied on many issues. Similarly, as part of interest-group coalitions unions frequently are major supporters of laws intended primarily to benefit these groups. Like unions, minority groups occasionally attempt to stir up grassroots support in their communities on issues jointly pursued by both types of organizations.

HYPOTHESIS 3: The percentage of minority residents in a legislator's geographical area will be positively correlated with his or her propensity to support labor's public policy positions, other things equal.

The fourth constituency characteristic is the relative affluence of citizens in a legislator's district. As a general proposition, labor advocates public policies that entail relatively greater economic burdens for the affluent. Unions favor progressive personal and corporate income taxation and a panoply of so-called welfare state programs that can be costly to government and hence taxpayers. From a cost-benefit point of view, then, the comparatively affluent may oppose labor's policies and mount political efforts against them. We must mention a caveat here, however; unions, through their collective bargaining activities, also raise the affluence of their members vis-à-vis nonunion employees (Moore and Raisian 1983). To the extent that unionized districts are thus more affluent than others and that these union members, on the whole, retain their ideological ties to union policies, affluence may signal *greater* pressure for labor-backed legislation. On balance, however, we expect a negative association.

HYPOTHESIS 4: The relative affluence of citizens in a legislator's district will be negatively correlated with his or her support for labor-backed public policies, other things equal.

Legislator Characteristics

Legislators bring their own set of personal predispositions with them when they enter Congress. Their personal references may influence their willingness to enact laws sought by unions. Political party affiliation is one indicator, albeit imperfect, of these preferences. In the main Democrats are more liberal than Republicans. Given the ideological alliance between labor and the Democratic party, lawmakers in this party are typically predisposed to support labor on numerous matters. Another reason exists for Democrats, on average, to be more supportive than Republicans. The majority leadership of the U.S. House of Representatives comes mainly from the liberal wing of the Democratic party. Using a variety of persuasive tactics, these leaders may attempt to influence Democratic lawmakers to vote according to labor's wishes. Appeals to party loyalty may on occasion be enough to sway vacillating legislators.

Hypothesis 5: Democratic legislators are more likely to support labor on roll-call votes than Republican legislators, other things equal.

Interest-Group Pressure

Interest groups compete vigorously in many legislative debates. Conventional thinking suggests that corporations usually oppose labor in major debates, and there is certainly a mountain of anecdotes testifying to such conflict. Witness the intense clash that took place over Labor Law Reform in the late 1970s. Pressure-group activity can be felt in many ways, including the allocation or refusal of PAC money.

Hypothesis 6: The amount of labor PAC money received by a legislator will be positively correlated with his or her support for labor on roll-call votes, other things equal.

Hypothesis 7: The amount of corporate PAC money received by a legislator will be negatively associated with his or her support for labor's policy preferences, other things equal.

Control Measures

We included two other variables in the following analyses to control for other factors that may affect voting. The first is a legislator's region. In general, the culture and history of the South have been relatively devoid of a significant union presence. We may therefore expect that Southern legislators will be less receptive to labor's political views than legislators from other regions of the country.

Second, a legislator's electoral vulnerability may influence his or her voting, although the direction of the impact is theoretically uncertain. Legislators who face little serious threat to their reelection may feel more comfortable in distancing themselves from their constituents' opinions on some occasions, whereas vulnerable lawmakers may be more averse to taking risks. Research suggests that a legislator's electoral percentage in a given election is often a harbinger of the opposition exhibited in the next one (Jacobson 1980). The closer the vote in one election, the greater the competition in the next. We therefore use a legislator's percentage of the electoral vote in 1982 as a proxy for expected competition.

Hypothesis 8: Legislators from the South will be less likely to support labor's public policy views, other things equal, than legislators from other regions.

Hypothesis 9: A legislator's percentage of the electoral vote in the previous election will affect his or her willingness to support labor on public policies, other things equal. (The direction of this influence is uncertain.)

Empirical Procedures

Data and Sample

The units of analysis are the votes cast by members of the U.S. House of Representatives on 34 separate roll-call votes, 33 of which were taken in the first session of the 98th Congress (1983); the remaining roll call was held in 1984. (The 1984 roll call vote was on the particularly important issue of amending the bankruptcy laws to make it more difficult for employers in bankruptcy proceedings to nullify their bargaining contracts.) These roll-call votes were published in the legislative voting guides of six labor organizations (the AFL-CIO, AFSCME, IAM, NEA, UAW, and USA). The 34 roll calls represent all the distinct issues cited by the labor organizations in their voting guides at the time.

The reader might question whether it is appropriate to examine such diverse legislation for the purpose of drawing inferences as to the bases of support for organized labor in Congress. One might argue that labor's interests are not involved in many of the votes. We believe, however, that for our purposes it is appropriate to examine diverse legislative votes. First, labor organizations themselves cited these votes as being important to the legislative agendas, important enough for the unions to want to rate members of Congress. Second, labor's legislative agenda is in fact capacious. Although that agenda may not necessarily be altruistically motivated, organized labor purports to seek social and economic programs and policies aimed at creating a more egalitarian society. Finally, as previously suggested, many public policies in the social and economic arena may directly or indirectly benefit unionism per se, even though they do not pertain specifically to labor relations law. A stimulative fiscal policy, for instance, may reduce unemployment and hence enhance labor's power at the bargaining table. More broadly, therefore, although these roll-call votes cover diverse issues, labor's position is generally one consistent with a liberal, "welfare state" philosophy. The *basic* interest-group alliances in support of this philosophy should not change much across these issues.

As Table 6 reports, the 34 roll-call votes cover a wide range of issues, including appropriations, trade, taxation, social, and civil rights legislation. Broadly speaking labor fared well on these issues, winning a majority of votes in 27 of the 34 roll calls. Yet there is variation in support across issues, testifying to the fluctuating pressures legislators face in voting on different public policies.

Table 6. Legislative Issues Selected by Six Labor Organizations in Rating Legislators' Voting Records in the 98th Congress

	Rating of Roll-Call Vote[b]		
Issue[a]	*"Right"*	*"Wrong"*	*Favorability*
1. *Social Security.* Amendment to a social security reform bill to raise the retirement age to 67. 9 March 1983.	202	228	–
2. *Budget Resolution.* Democratic substitute budget that limited defense spending and restored funding for social programs. 23 June 1983.	239	186	+
3. *Defense.* Amendment to eliminate $2.6 billion in funding for the MX missile. 20 July 1983.	207	220	–
4. *General Revenue Sharing.* Attempt to reduce general revenue sharing funds by $420 million. 2 August 1983.	248	176	+
5. *Health Care for the Unemployed.* Reagan-initiated attempt to reject a bill providing health care for the unemployed. 3 August 1983.	255	171	+
6. *Equal Rights Amendment.* Vote on the passage of the ERA amendment to the Constitution. A two-thirds majority is required to pass. 15 November 1983.	278	147	+
7. *Tax Reform.* An $8 billion tax reform package to close loopholes for large corporations. 17 November 1983.	204	214	–
8. *Taxation.* Bill to limit scheduled tax savings to $720 per taxpayer and thus save revenues. 23 June 1983.	229	191	+
9. *Budget Resolution.* Democratic budget resolution to restore social spending. 23 March 1983.	229	196	+
10. *Job Creation.* A $3.5 billion job creation package. 2 September 1983.	246	178	+
11. *Housing Aid.* A $760 million aid package of loans for jobless homeowners faced with mortgage foreclosure proceedings. Amendment was offered to defeat the loan program. 11 May 1983.	220	197	+
12. *Domestic Auto Content Legislation.* Bill to require foreign auto and truck producers to produce more of their product parts in the United States. 13 November 1983.	219	199	+
13. *Regulation.* Amendment to deny housing aid to communities that require rent control projects. 12 July 1983.	208	206	+

(*continued*)

Table 6. (continued)

Issue[a]	Rating of Roll-Call Vote[b]		
	"Right"	*"Wrong"*	*Favorability*
14. *Defense.* Amendment to give nuclear freeze and weapons reduction proposals equal weight in a resolution to freeze nuclear weapons. 11 March 1983.	215	209	+
15. *Occupational Safety and Health.* Amendment to relocate the National Institute for Occupational Safety and Health from Maryland to Washington, D.C. 17 November 1983.	186	207	−
16. *Regulation.* Amendment to eliminate a ban on the imposition of a long-distance access charge for residential telephone users. 10 November 1983.	264	142	+
17. *Labor-Management Relations.* Proposal to reject a move to attack legislation making it more difficult for firms to use bankruptcy proceedings to nullify labor-management contracts. 21 March 1984.	242	166	+
18. *Desegregation.* Legislation to reinstate federal assistance for school desegregation.	299	120	+
19. *Budget.* Proposal to reduce education and other domestic spending by $964 million. 13 September 1983.	283	124	+
20. *Budget.* Bill to increase education spending by $175 million. 22 September 1983.	302	111	+
21. *Budget.* Continuing appropriations bill containing an additional $729 million for education programs. 8 November 1983.	203	206	−
22. *Jobs.* Proposal to cut $423 million in funding for a job creation program. 3 March 1983.	256	158	+
23. *Trade.* Motion to prevent debate on a bill that would prevent the exportation of jobs to the Caribbean basin nations. 13 July 1983.	204	212	−
24. *Davis-Bacon.* Amendment to remove the Davis-Bacon provisions covering local constructing projects under the Economic Development Act. 12 July 1983.	270	148	+
25. *Unemployment Compensation.* Motion to cut the maximum time period for unemployment benefits from 16 weeks to 12 weeks. 29 September 1983.	278	141	+
26. *Federal Workers Pay.* Amendment to delay a scheduled federal workers' pay raise for three months. 25 October 1983.	176	245	−
27. *Coal Slurry Pipeline.* Bill that would grant the power of eminent domain to coal slurry pipeline firms. 27 September 1983.	235	182	+

Table 6. (continued)

Issue[a]	Rating of Roll-Call Vote[b] "Right"	"Wrong"	Favorability
28. *Domestic Auto Content.* Amendment to proposed domestic auto content bill that would weaken the bill's enforcement power. 3 November 1983.	232	178	+
29. *Martin Luther King Holiday.* Legislation to designate a national holiday commemorating the birthday of the late Dr. Martin Luther King. 2 August 1983.	338	90	+
30. *Jobs.* Antirecession jobs and assistance program. 3 March 1983.	324	95	+
31. *Social Security/Unemployment Benefits.* A bill to protect the solvency of the Social Security system and extend unemployment compensation benefits. 9 March 1983.	282	148	+
32. *Jobs.* A bill targeting defense spending to areas of light unemployment. 26 July 1983.	218	201	+
33. *Trade.* Move to recommit a trade adjustment assistance bill. 15 September 1983.	218	194	+
34. *Defense.* Resolution calling for a mutual and verifiable freeze on the production and development of nuclear weapons. 4 May 1983.	278	149	+
Overall Favorability	27+	7−	

[a]Of the 34 roll-call votes listed above, 33 represent the number of distinct roll calls selected by six labor organizations to rate members of the U.S. House of Representatives in 1983 (the first session of the 98th Congress). The remaining roll call (issue number 17) was selected because of its importance in the labor-management area. Many of these role call votes appeared in more than one of the voting guides, but the unions were consistent in their ratings. The following union voting guides (or scoreboards) were used: AFSCME, *AFSCME's Voters' Guide: 98th Congress*; USA, *Steelworkers Congressional Voting Record: 98th Congress*; NEA, *Legislative Report Card: 98th Congress*; AFL-CIO, *AFL-CIO News*, 21 January 1984; IAM, *The Machinist: 98th Congress Voting Record*, September 1984; UAW, *UAW Voting Record*, 98th Congress.

[b]The votes listed under the "right" column represent the total number of "right" votes according to the union's perspective. The "wrong" column represents the total number of "wrong" votes, again from the union's perspective.

Equation and Method

We estimated the determinants of the legislators' votes on each of these issues in the following equation:

$$\begin{aligned} VOTE_{(1\text{-}34)} = a &+ b_1\, UNION + b_2\, MINORITY + b_3\, AFFLUENCE \\ &+ b_4\, CORPAC + b_5\, LABPAC + b_6\, COMPETITION \\ &+ b_7\, DEMOCRAT + b_8\, REAGAN + b_9\, REGION \\ &+ e, \end{aligned}$$

where:

$VOTE_{(1\text{-}34)}$ = a dichotomous variable for each of the 34 roll calls, with 1 being assigned to legislators who voted "right" and 0 to legislators who voted "wrong."

a = a constant term.

UNION = the percentage of unionized nonagricultural workers in a legislator's state. Data are from the U.S. Department of Labor (1980).

MINORITY = the percentage of nonwhite population in a legislator's congressional district. Data are from Barone and Ujifusa (1983).

AFFLUENCE = the median price of housing in a "legislator's district. Data are from Barone and Ujifusa (1983).

CORPAC = the total amount of corporate PAC contributions received by a legislator in 1981–82, divided by the total campaign receipts of the legislator in 1981–82. Data are from the Federal Election Commission (1983).

LABPAC = the total amount of labor PAC contributions received by a legislator in 1981–82, divided by the total campaign receipts of the legislator in 1981–82. Data are from the Federal Election Commission (1983).

COMPETITION = the percentage of the votes received by a legislator in the 1982 congressional elections. Data are from Barone and Ujifusa (1983).

DEMOCRAT = a dichotomous variable, with 1 equal to Democrat and 0 equal to Republican. Data are from Barone and Ujifusa (1983).

REAGAN = the percentage of votes received by President Reagan in a legislator's district in the 1984 Presidential election.[14]

REGION = a dichotomous variable, with 1 assigned to legislators located in one of the 14 southern states and 0 assigned to all other legislators.[15]

e = an error term.

We estimate this equation for each of the 34 roll-call votes, yielding 34 separate statistical analyses. Because the dependent variable is dichotomous, we use a logit statistical technique. We avoid a potential simultaneity problem by using labor and corporate PAC contributions from the election *preceeding* the roll-call votes (Welch 1982). *CORPAC* and *LABPAC* are predetermined endogenous variables and thus analogous to exogenous variables. Legislators' votes in 1983–84 cannot alter PAC contributions in 1981–82, but money contributed in 1981–82 may affect subsequent legislative behavior.

Results

The results of the logit analyses are reported in Table 7. They show several interesting patterns. First, Democrats in the 98th Congress were much more likely to support labor's position, other things equal. In 33 of the 34 equations the *DEMOCRAT* coefficient is positive and statistically significant. Second, a conservative constituency ideology in the legislator's district, as measured by *REAGAN*, was negatively associated with political support for labor in that Congress. Legislators in districts where Reagan was to fare well in 1984 were less willing to vote according to labor's wishes than legislators located in areas where the President was less popular. Third, *LABPAC* (labor PAC contributions) was significant in 30 of the 34 equations, and in the expected direction. For logical reasons labor gives its PAC money to those lawmakers most likely to vote in its favor. Interestingly, however, the *CORPAC* coefficient was not statistically significant in most (25) of the equations. Arguably, corporations dilute the voting impact of their PAC donations by supporting a sizable number of Democrats. In 1981–82 almost every candidate who was elected received corporate PAC money; and Democrats received one-third of all corporate PAC allocations, despite their party's close ties to labor.

Apart from *REAGAN*, the constituency variables are statistically nonsignificant in most of the equations. Nevertheless, the unionization coefficient (*UNION*) is significant in 16 equations, and in the hypothesized direction in most of these instances.

Extended Analyses

The above results show a consistent correlation between aggregate labor PAC contributions and pro-union legislative voting. This finding is consistent with empirical evidence in several previous studies (Kau and Rubin 1981; Kau, Keenan, and Rubin 1982; Coughlin 1985). But the documented dispersion in the amount of contributions made by individual union PACs suggests that the relationship between PAC allocations and voting behavior may not be constant across unions. Along this line Chappell's (1982) research does not support a correlation between disaggregate labor PAC allocations and legislators' votes on selected issues, although this research focused on only a few unions' PAC contributions.

In a set of analyses reported below, we examine the impact of individual unions' PAC contributions on the 34 roll-call votes listed previously in Table 6. The same 23 labor PACs used in the analyses of allocation determinants (see Table 4) make up this disaggregate sample. We analyzed the effect of these unions' PAC contributions on roll-call votes, using the legislative voting model posited above, with the exception that individual union PAC contributions replace aggregate labor PAC contributions. The union PAC variable is computed by dividing the total amount of contributions a legislator received from a union's PAC in 1981–82 by his or her total campaign receipts in that election period.

Table 7. Logit Analyses of Congressional Roll Calls

Issue	Minority	Region	Affluence	Reagan	Competition	LABPAC	CORPAC	Democrat	Union	N
	Explanatory Variables									
1.	−0.008	0.236	-0.190^{10-5}	−0.067**	−0.003	9.315***	−3.377*	2.149***	6.880**	425
2.	−0.003	0.063	0.117^{10-4}	−0.113***	−0.035**	10.628***	−3.051	3.804***	−0.749	421
3.	−0.022	−3.070***	0.525^{10-5}	−0.102***	0.014	9.842***	−8.196***	2.066***	−10.839***	423
4.	−0.001	1.205**	0.295^{10-5}	−0.088***	−0.008	6.273***	−2.220	1.628***	11.935***	420
5.	0.029	−0.549	-0.141^{10-4}	−0.111**	−0.025	12.139**	−2.218	4.810***	4.548	423
6.	−0.002	−0.989**	-0.141^{*10-4}	−0.081***	0.007	9.355**	−5.306**	1.123**	−4.384*	422
7.	0.001	0.051	0.102^{10-4}	−0.051**	−0.014	3.308**	0.618	2.828***	3.074	415
8.	0.018	−0.324	-0.600^{10-6}	−0.114**	−0.011	10.707***	2.190	4.317***	−5.920	417
9.	−0.035*	0.048	0.182^{10-5}	−0.158***	−0.027	15.279***	−3.228	4.664***	−2.761	419
10.	0.031*	−1.405**	-0.208^{**10-4}	−0.152***	0.004	6.084**	1.616	3.886***	6.605**	421
11.	0.022	−1.467*	-0.934^{10-5}	−0.139***	0.005	15.109	−5.355***	3.928	−2.114	414
12.	0.021*	−0.118	-0.181^{**10-4}	−0.023	0.013	9.088**	−3.878**	1.151**	9.845	414
13.	0.021	−0.120	0.115^{10-4}	−0.088**	−0.001	6.737***	−2.829	2.801***	5.682*	411
14.	−0.024	−2.073**	0.250^{**10-4}	−0.169***	−0.003	18.729***	−6.864**	2.634***	−9.245**	417
15.	0.002	−2.153***	0.139^{*10-4}	−0.093***	−0.011	6.998***	2.787	2.485***	−1.753	392
16.	−0.046**	0.995	-0.557^{10-5}	−0.101	−0.010	8.736**	−4.433	4.386***	3.414	403
17.	−0.023	1.181	0.129^{10-4}	−0.164***	−0.026	14.845***	2.989	4.187***	7.404*	406

18.	0.012	1.558***	0.789^{10-5}	−0.110***	0.023*	3.791	−5.557*	1.998***	8.212**	415
19.	−0.061**	0.745	0.377^{10-5}	−0.152***	0.004	53.925***	−3.020	3.131***	1.020	405
20.	−0.059**	1.881**	-0.502^{10-5}	−0.170***	−0.026*	24.746**	−3.454	2.790***	7.690**	409
21.	0.016	−0.285	-0.956^{10-5}	−0.075***	−0.010	1.331	−1.769	2.382***	2.351	406
22.	0.009	0.294	-0.648^{10-5}	0.009	0.004	5.670**	1.370	3.508***	−3.325	412
23.	−0.021	−0.559	-0.419^{10-5}	0.018	−0.005	5.503**	−5.903***	1.636***	3.287	413
24.	0.007	0.410	0.738^{10-5}	−0.130	−0.013	18.594**	−3.783*	2.251***	10.706**	417
25.	−0.003	−0.847	-0.119^{10-4}	−0.146***	−0.012	15.008**	1.887	3.747***	5.297	415
26.	0.018*	0.156	0.135^{**10-4}	−0.056***	0.009	2.546*	0.574	0.775**	6.763**	419
27.	−0.010	−0.636*	$-0.224^{***10-4}$	0.003	−0.003	4.654***	0.852	0.154	1.105	419
28.	0.020	−0.762	-0.126^{10-4}	−0.027	−0.001	12.548***	−2.516	2.248***	6.081**	407
29.	0.003	0.117	0.395^{10-5}	−0.066**	−0.032**	16.122**	−1.201	2.002***	4.356*	426
30.	0.012	−0.881	-0.137^{*10-4}	−0.070**	−0.015	−28.413***	−2.769	2.134***	3.737	416
31.	−0.015*	0.989**	-0.616^{10-5}	−0.005	−0.022**	−0.560	1.726	0.772**	0.696	427
32.	0.001	−1.953***	-0.163^{**10-4}	−0.060**	−0.001	1.692	−2.174	0.955**	15.019***	417
33.	0.034**	0.141	-0.975^{10-5}	−0.099***	−0.009	9.338***	0.020	2.588***	10.823***	410
34.	−0.019	−1.801**	0.874^{10-5}	−0.128***	−0.008	16.833***	−1.777	1.225**	−2.602	425
No. of Positive, Significant Coefficients	4	4	3	0	1	30	0	33	14	
No. of Positive, Significant Coefficients	6	9	6	28	4	0	9	0	3	

Note: The numbered issues are described in Table 6.
*p < .10 (two-tailed test).
**p < .05 (two-tailed test).
***p < .001 (two-tailed test).

Table 8. Summary of the Logit Results of the Disaggregated PAC and Issue Analyses

		Explanatory Variables								
Labor Organization[a]	*Sign*[b]	*Minority*	*Region*	*Affluence*	*Reagan*	*Competition*	*PAC*[c]	*CORPAC*	*Party*	*Union*
AFGE	+	2	4	3	0	1	18	0	30	16
(30)	–	7	9	3	24	7	0	11	0	1
AFL-CIO	+	4	4	3	0	1	11	0	30	15
(31)	–	5	11	5	28	5	0	11	0	1
AFSCME	+	4	2	2	0	1	12	0	26	14
(27)		3	8	5	22	3	1	9	0	0
AFT	+	5	3	3	0	1	19	0	27	12
(27)	–	5	10	6	24	5	1	9	0	1
ALPA	+	5	3	3	0	1	15	0	34	16
(34)	–	5	13	6	29	7	0	21	0	2
APWU	+	4	1	1	0	1	5	0	16	11
(16)	–	3	6	3	12	2	1	7	0	0
CJA	+	4	4	2	1	1	28	0	33	17
(34)	–	7	9	5	30	7	1	8	0	1
CWA	+	3	4	4	0	1	17	0	31	16
(31)	–	7	10	5	28	6	0	12	0	1
IAFF	+	4	2	2	0	1	5	0	27	14
(27)	–	5	9	6	24	8	0	14	0	1
IAM	+	3	4	3	0	1	17	0	30	15
(31)	–	7	10	5	28	5	0	9	0	3
MEBA	+	1	3	3	1	1	10	0	34	18
(34)	–	8	13	6	30	8	0	20	0	1
NAGE	+	1	2	0	0	0	0	0	14	5
(14)	–	2	6	3	12	3	0	6	0	1

NALC	+	1	4	3	0	1	23	0	31	16
(32)	−	7	7	6	27	6	0	13	0	1
NAPFE	+	0	3	1	0	1	0	0	15	6
(14)	−	2	5	3	11	3	3	7	0	0
NEA	+	4	3	3	0	1	16	0	33	18
(34)	−	6	12	6	31	2	0	12	0	1
NFFE	+	4	1	3	0	1	0	0	24	13
(24)	−	3	10	5	21	6	2	13	0	1
NTE	+	4	3	3	0	1	12	0	32	17
(32)	−	5	10	6	29	6	0	15	0	1
RLCA	+	4	4	3	0	1	5	0	33	17
(34)	−	6	12	6	31	9	0	18	1	2
SIUNA	+	2	4	3	0	1	20	0	34	17
(34)	−	9	11	6	30	10	0	18	0	2
UAW	+	4	3	4	0	1	22	0	29	14
(30)	−	5	10	4	25	4	0	9	0	2
UFCW	+	2	3	3	0	1	18	0	31	17
(32)	−	6	11	4	28	5	0	12	0	1
UMW	+	3	2	3	0	1	2	0	24	11
(24)	−	3	11	4	21	2	1	13	0	1
USA	+	3	2	3	0	1	12	0	25	13
(25)	−	6	9	5	23	4	0	11	0	1

Note: The Union abbreviations are spelled out in Table 4.
[a]The numbers in parentheses in this column refer to the total number of voting equations that yield estimates of all the coefficients.
[b]This column indicates positive (+) and negative (−) signs for the coefficients.
[c]*PAC* is the total campaign contributions given by a union's PAC to a legislator, divided by the legislator's total campaign receipts.

Table 8 summarizes the results of the disaggregate PAC and issue analyses. Appendices reporting the coefficients are available upon request. Before discussing the results, we must note that in some of the logit analyses we could not use the legislative voting model to yield estimates of the PAC coefficients. This was mainly the case where union PACs contributed small amounts of money to a relatively few number of legislators and where there was little variation in legislators' votes. We eliminated from the summary table the roll-call votes where this problem occurred.

The summarized results are interesting in several respects. First, in contrast to the aggregate analyses, where labor PAC contributions were consistently correlated with pro-union voting, the individual PAC results vary across unions. Although the PAC coefficients, when significant, are in the expected direction in almost every case, they are significant and positive in a majority of the voting analyses for only 10 of the 23 labor PACs. The disaggregate PAC results suggest that there is variation in the impact of campaign contributions across unions. Yet, the aggregate effect is apparently consistent.

Second, the results for constituency characteristics are qualitatively consistent with those in the aggregate PAC-voting analysis. The results here show that the *MINORITY* and *AFFLUENCE* variables are generally nonsignificant predictors of voting, although the *AFFLUENCE* coefficients tend to be in the expected direction when significant. The *UNION* variable performs somewhat better, attaining statistical significance with the hypothesized sign in nearly 50 percent of the disaggregate analyses. As was also the case in the aggregate analysis, *REAGAN* is a consistent predictor of voting; it is negative and significant in a majority of equations.

Third, party affiliation is the most consistent and significant correlate of voting behavior. *DEMOCRAT* shows a positive relationship with pro-union voting in almost all of the analyses across union PACs. This finding further attests to the pervasiveness of alliance between the Democratic party and unions in national politics.

In sum, the disaggregate results are basically consistent with the aggregate analyses, with the exception of the PAC-voting relationship, which did not hold up as well in the individual union results. This suggests that the effect of labor PAC money is cumulative and, perhaps, synergistic. A Republican legislator who is ideologically conservative sacrifices an array of union PAC money, whereas Democrats can generally expect to take in a sizable sum from labor organizations.

CONCLUSIONS AND RESEARCH QUESTIONS

The empirical findings of our analyses prompt several conclusions. First, unions engage in various activities to generate a demand for and supply of a host of socioeconomic policies. The demand and supply forces interact in an exchange relations framework in which unions and lawmakers offer each other mutually beneficial goods. The sizable amount of PAC money unions raise from their members suggests that many rank-and-file unionists expect the benefits of PAC activity to outweigh the costs, even though the sought-after goods may be collective or public in nature.

Second, despite the variation in the degree of unions' involvement, there appears to be a common philosophical motive behind their involvement. On an aggregate and a disaggregate basis unions identify with the Democratic party, which adheres to a philosophy of government different from the Republicans'. Although policy priorities vary across unions, reflecting their different needs and environmental contexts, they appear to be generally consistent with the philosophy that sanctions government intervention in economic and social affairs when it is aimed at redistributing wealth and power or otherwise improving working conditions. The PAC allocations of unions, which unequivocally favor Democrats, testify resoundingly to this shared philosophical disposition.

Third, labor and the Republican party have little rational basis for an exchange relationship. The legislative voting analyses show that Democratic party affiliation is the most consistent predictor of support for union policy preferences in Congress. A non- or bipartisan political strategy is seemingly unworkable for labor.

Fourth, the pervasiveness of labor's attachment to, or dependence on, the Democratic party suggests that the real impact of labor on major policy disputes is likely to be seen most clearly at the aggregate rather than the disaggregate level. Unions evaluate lawmakers through a more or less common set of lenses. A few legislators may be able to oppose labor on most issues and still cultivate some official support among unions, but they are definitely the exceptions. In general a conservative ideology smoothens that possibility.

Fifth, the 1986 congressional elections may have presaged a change in labor's political fortunes. With Democrats firmly in control of both the House and the Senate, by 258–177 and 55–45 majorities, respectively, they are in a much better position to shepherd union-backed legislation through Congress. Furthermore, with a Democratic majority in both houses, the pressure is even greater now for labor to use its political clout to elect a Democrat to the White House in 1988. Obviously, if a favorable (from the unions' perspective) Democrat is elected president, labor will have a much better chance than in the Reagan years to secure the major policy changes (such as labor law reform) it has long sought.

In addition to these conclusions, this study suggests some important topics for future research. Despite the fact that unions engage in numerous political activities, we know little about their impact apart from PAC contributions. What impact do unions' political education initiatives have on union members' voting? What impact does in-kind electoral assistance have on election outcomes? Is the rate of return for this assistance greater than it is for PAC contributions? What opportunities are there for deriving economies of scale through grassroots electoral activities undertaken by a coalition of unions?

We also know little about how labor sets its political priorities. Who determines these priorities? To what extent do union members participate in these determinations? Whose interests are represented? Answers to these questions may have important implications for labor's potential effectiveness in politics. If a sizable portion of these rank-and-file feel left out or disenfranchised in these determinations, their willingness to help the union politically may wane. Previous research suggests that union leaders and members do not always agree on politics; in fact, substantial disagreement often surfaces (see Masters and Delaney 1987c), for a review of the literature on the leader-member attitudes on political questions).

In conclusion, we have learned that U.S. labor unions have made substantial investments in politics, that they have made these investments in pursuit of a more or less common philosophy, and that they apparently have had an impact on certain policy outcomes. We know little, however, about labor's activity and impact outside the PAC arena. Until we do, we will have only a restricted view of labor in American politics. We encourage additional research into these topics, especially since the 1986 elections have given unions a new breath of political fresh air.

ACKNOWLEDGMENT

A faculty research grant from the Graduate School of Business, University of Pittsburgh, partially funded the research reported here.

NOTES

1. The Federal Election Campaign Act of 1971, as amended, requires among other things that unions and other organizations disclose the amount of money their PACs raise and expend in congressional campaigns. It does not require, however, the full disclosure of all in-kind assistance unions may provide candidates, especially when these activities take place within the union itself. See Epstein (1976, 1980) and Alexander (1980) for discussions of the federal election laws.

2. Federal laws regulating lobbying require that unions' and other organizations' lobbyists register with designated offices in Congress, but they do not require the full itemization or disclosure of their lobbying budgets. Nor does the Landrum-Griffin Act.

3. The Federal Election Commission, which was established by the Federal Election Campaign Act Amendments of 1974, reports PAC finances on a two-year election cycle basis.

4. Close (1979, 1981, 1983) does not indicate the precise time period during which these data were collected. It seems reasonable to expect a lag of at least one year between the time of collection and publication; we therefore estimate the time of collection to be around 1978, 1980, and 1982.

5. The contribution per union member is computed by dividing a union's total PAC contributions to congressional candidates by the union's membership.

6. This is to say that unions, at least in the post–New Deal era, have eschewed independent labor parties. Instead, they have attempted to support and influence lawmakers through the existing major parties, principally the Democratic party.

7. In West Germany, for instance, union membership is voluntary, yet unions there are quite active politically.

8. This typology is obviously not all-inclusive. It does not explicitly recognize the role that the acquisition of personal power or prestige might play in exchange relationships. But it is inclusive enough to establish an incentive system behind exchange relationships.

9. The selection of this particular sample was not arbitrary. First, to keep the aggregate and disaggregate analyses within manageable proportions, we believed it appropriate to focus on only one election cycle. Other studies have examined the determinants of labor PAC allocations in previous elections (see, for example, Herndon 1982; Chappell 1982; Kau and Rubin 1981; Kau, Keenan, and Rubin 1982; Masters and Zardkoohi 1986a). Second, at the time this study was well under way, data on unions' ratings of legislators voting records were available only for the 98th Congress (1983–84). We therefore could not use those legislators elected in 1984 to serve in 1985–86 as a sample for the subsequent voting analyses.

10. We admit that party affiliation is an imperfect measure of legislators' ideologies. Neither party is ideologically pure, but there are powerful central tendencies in each that separate the Republican and Democratic parties philosophically. Further, the leaderships of these parties are philosophically opposed, particularly on socioeconomic matters. To the extent that party leaders can persuade other Democratic and Republican legislators to tow the party line, they reinforce the main philosophical fissures between the two.

11. It might be argued that labor PAC money could be more effectively used in districts where unions are underrepresented. In this regard PAC money would be a substitute for membership presence—or votes—on election day. On balance, however, we expect a positive relationship between union membership in the legislator's district and PAC allocations. Our previous empirical research offers limited support for this expectation (Masters and Zardkoohi 1986a).

12. The disaggregate sample includes most of the unions with large PACs. It also includes each of the labor organizations that provided the voting guides or scoreboards used in the legislative voting analyses below.

13. Since 1981 Masters has interviewed lobbyists for 13 of the unions listed in Table 5. The interviews focused on a variety of subjects, including union legislative priorities. They revealed a vast array of lobbying priorities, although few outright conflicts in policy objectives.

14. As previously noted, we are compelled to use 1984 data because of the congressional redistricting that was constitutionally mandated after the 1980 census.

15. The states are Alabama, Arkansas, Florida, Georgia, Kentucky, Louisiana, Mississippi, North Carolina, Oklahoma, South Carolina, Tennessee, Texas, Virginia, and West Virginia.

REFERENCES

Alexander, Herbert E. 1980. *Financing the 1980 Elections*. Lexington, MA: D. C. Health.

Barone, Michael, and Grant Ujifusa. 1983. *The Almanac of American Politics, 1984*. Washington, DC: Barone & Company.

———. 1985. *The Almanac of American Politics, 1986*. Washington, DC: Barone & Company.

Chappell, Henry W., Jr. 1982. Campaign Contributions and Congressional Voting: A Simultaneous Probit-Tobit Model. *Review of Economics and Statistics* 64(February):77–83.

Close, Arthur, ed. 1979, 1981, 1983. *Washington Representatives: Who Does What for Whom in the Nation's Capital*? Washington, DC: Columbia Press.

Cohan, Robert M. 1973. Of Politics, Pipefitters, and Section 610: Union Political Contributions in Modern Context. *Texas Law Review* 51:936–93.

Coughlin, Cletus C. 1985. Domestic Content Legislation: House Voting and the Economic Theory of Regulation. *Economic Inquiry* 23(July):437–48.

Delaney, John Thomas, Jack Fiorito, and Marick F. Masters. 1986. The Effects of Union Organization and Environmental Characteristics on Union Political Action, photocopy. New York: Graduate School of Business, Columbia University.

Edelman, Murray. 1971. *Politics as Symbolic Action: Mass Arousal and Quiescence*. Chicago: Markham.

Epstein, Edwin M. 1976. Labor and Federal Elections: The New Legal Framework. *Industrial Relations* 15(October):257–74.

———. 1980. Business Poltical Activity: Research Approaches and Analytical Issues. In *Research in Corporate Social Performance and Policy*, vol. 2, ed. Lee E. Preston, 1–55. Greenwich, CT: JAI Press.

Federal Election Commission. 1983. *FEC Reports on Financial Activity, 1981–1982; U.S. Senate and House Campaigns*. Washington, DC: Federal Election Commission.

Freeman, Richard B., and James L. Medoff. 1984. *What Do Unions Do*? New York: Basic Books.

Gopoian, J. David. 1984. What Makes PACs Tick? An Analysis of the Allocation Patterns of Economic Interest Groups. *American Journal of Political Science* 28(May):259–81.

Greenstone, J. David. 1977. *Labor in American Politics*. Chicago: University of Chicago Press.

Grier, Kevin, and Michael C. Munger. 1986. The Impact of Legislator Attributes on Interest-Group Campaign Contributions. *Journal of Labor Research* 6(Fall):349–61.

Herndon, James F. 1982. Access, Record, and Competition as Influences on Interest Group Contributions to Congressional Campaigns. *Journal of Politics* 44(November):996–1020.

Jacobs, David C. 1987. The UAW and the Committee for National Health Insurance: The Contours of Social Unionism. In *Advances in Industrial and Labor Relations*, vol. 4, ed. David Lewin, David B. Lipsky, and Donna Sockell, 000–00. Greenwich, CT: JAI Press.

Kalt, Joseph P., and M. A. Zupan. 1984. Capture and Ideology in the Economic Theory of Politics. *American Economic Review* 74(June):279–300.

Kau, James B., Donald Keenan, and Paul H. Rubin. 1982. A General Equilibrium Model of Congressional Voting. *Quarterly Journal of Economics* 97(May):271–94.

Kau, James B., and Paul H. Rubin. 1978. Voting on Minimum Wages: A Time Series Analysis. *Journal of Political Economy* 86(April):337–42.

———. 1979. Self-interest, Ideology and Logrolling in Congressional Voting. *Journal of Law and Economics* 22(October):365–84.

———. 1981. The Impact of Labor Unions on the Passage of Economic Legislation. *Journal of Law and Economics* 2(Spring):133–46.

———. 1982. *Congressmen, Constituents, and Contributors*. Boston: Martinus Nijhoff.

Lange, Peter, and George Ross. 1982. Conclusions: French and Italian Union Development in Comparative Perspective. In *Unions, Change and Crisis: French and Italian Union Strategy and the Political Economy, 1945–1980*, ed. Peter Lange and Maurizio Vannicelli. London: Allen & Unwin.

Madison, James. 1788. The Federalist No. 10. Reprinted in *The Federalist Papers*. New York: Modern Library, 1937.

Masters, Marick F. 1985. Federal-Employee Unions and Political Action. *Industrial and Labor Relations Review* 38(July):612–28.

———. 1986. The Politics of Comparable Worth: A Case Study, photocopy. Pittsburgh: Graduate School of Business, University of Pittsburgh.

Masters, Marick F., and John Thomas Delaney. 1982. The AFL-CIO's Political Record, 1974–1980. In *Proceedings of the Thirty-Fourth Annual Meeting, December 28–30, 1981*, ed. Barbara D. Dennis, 351–59. Madison, WI: Industrial Relations Research Association.

———. 1984. Interunion Variation in Congressional Campaign Support. *Industrial Relations* 23(Fall):410–16.

———. 1985. The Causes of Union Political Involvement: A Longitudinal Analysis. *Journal of Labor Research* 6(Fall):341–62.

———. 1987a. Contemporary Labor Political Investments and Performance. *Labor Studies Journal* 11(Winter).

———. 1987b. "Union Legislative Records During President Reagan's First Term." *Journal of Labor Research* 8(Winter).

———. 1987c. Union Political Activities: A Review of the Empirical Literature. *Industrial and Labor Relations Review* 40(April):336–53.

Masters, Marick F., and Asghar Zardkoohi. 1986a. The Determinants of Labor PAC Allocations to Legislators. *Industrial Relations* 25(Fall):328–38.

———. 1986b. The Impact of Corporate PAC Contributions on Legislators' Union Voting Records, photocopy. Pittsburgh: Graduate School of Business, University of Pittsburgh.

McAdams, Alan K. 1964. *Power and Politics in Labor Legislation*. New York: Alfred A. Knopf.

Miller, Glenn, and Stephen Ware. 1963. Organized Labor in the Political Process: A Case Study of the Right-to-Work Campaign in Ohio. *Labor History* 4(Winter):51–67.

Moe, Terry M. 1981. Toward a Broader View of Interest Groups. *Journal of Politics* 43(May): 531–43.

Moore, William J., and John Raisian. 1983. The Level and Growth of Union/Nonunion Relative Wage Effects, 1967–79. *Journal of Labor Research* 4(Winter):65–79.

Olson, Marcur. 1965. *The Logic of Collective Action*. Cambridge, MA: Harvard University Press.

Peltzman, Sam. 1984. Constituent Interest and Congressional Voting. *Journal of Law and Economics* 27(April):181–210.

Pohlman, Marcus, and George S. Crisci. 1982–83. Support for Organized Labor in the House of Representatives: The 89th and 95th Congresses. *Political Science Quarterly* 97(Winter): 639–52.

Rehmus, Charles M. 1984. Labor and Politics in the 1980s. *Annals of the American Academy of Political and Social Science* 473(May):40–51.

Rehmus, Charles M., and Benjamin A. Kerner. 1980. The Agency Shop After *Abood*: No Free Ride, But What's the Fare? *Industrial and Labor Relations Review* 34(October):90–100.

Reshef, Yonatan. 1986. Political Exchange in Israel: Histadrut-State Relations. *Industrial Relations* 25(Fall):303–19.

Salisbury, Robert H. 1969. An Exchange Theory of Interest Groups. *Midwest Journal of Political Science* 13:1–32.

Saltzman, Gregory M. 1987. Congressional Voting on Labor Issues: The Role of PACs. *Industrial and Labor Relations Review* 40(January):163–79.

Silberman, Jonathan J., and Gary C. Durden. 1976. Determining Legislative Preferences for the Minimum Wage: An Economic Approach. *Journal of Political Economy* 84(April):317–29.

Truman, David B. 1951. *The Government Process*. New York: Alfred A. Knopf.

U.S. Department of Labor, Bureau of Labor Statistics. 1980. *Directory of National Unions and Employee Associations, 1979*, BLS Bulletin 2079. Washington, DC: GPO.

Welch, William P. 1982. Campaign Contributions and Dairy Price Supports. *Western Political Quarterly* 25:478–95.

Wright, John R. 1985. PACs, Contributions and Roll Calls: An Organizational Perspective. *American Political Science Review* 79:400–414.

THE UAW AND THE COMMITTEE FOR NATIONAL HEALTH INSURANCE:

THE CONTOURS OF SOCIAL UNIONISM

David C. Jacobs

Many unions in the United States have long been committed to fundamental reform of the nation's health care system. The United Automobile, Aerospace and Agricultural Implement Workers of America (UAW) in particular has demonstrated its commitment to such reform, as founder and continuing sponsor of the Committee for National Health Insurance (CNHI). CNHI is a citizens' research, educational, and lobbying organization that seeks enactment of a compulsory national system of health insurance under social security.

The UAW's commitment to health care reform is worthy of attention as an example of union concerns that transcend individual workplaces and bargaining relationships. In the past industrial relations theorists have discounted social unionism—union concern for social issues beyond the immediate workplace—as one of the roles played by unions in the United States. Through an investigation of the UAW's twofold strategy of bargaining on health care issues and supporting CNHI activities, I hope to demonstrate the error in that perspective. To further illuminate union ideology, I will contrast it with business perspectives on health care issues.

Advances in Industrial and Labor Relations, Volume 4, pages 119-140.

ISBN: 0-89232-909-2

BARGAINING APPROACHES

Primary responsibility for addressing health care issues within the UAW has traditionally fallen to the union's Social Security Department. A staff division of the international union, created in 1948, the department has as its principal charge to report to the UAW president on matters of pensions, health benefits, life and disability insurance, supplementary unemployment benefits, social security, and related legislative issues. It is the center of strategic planning for the union on private and public benefits. In pursuing its charge the department has followed a "two way" approach to social security reform: the simultaneous employment of bargaining and legislative strategies.[1] As an early Social Security Department staffer argued (Bloch 1951, 175):

> The outside observer who reviews the negotiated workers' security programs spearheaded by the UAW-CIO may approach the subject with the preconceived opinion that this is a militant union making every effort to secure for its membership privileges over and above the standards enjoyed by the general population. But the two-way approach to the problem of long-range security has already won improvements in social security legislation, from which millions of persons far beyond the union's reach are deriving benefits. When the concept of the two-way approach fully develops in the field of medical care as well, an even larger number of persons will benefit from it. The union has stated its policy of reducing the emphasis on negotiated workers' security programs as legislation progresses.

The staff of the UAW Social Security Department has consciously and consistently sought substantial reorganization of the health care industry, through both collective bargaining and lobbying for national health insurance legislation. A review of UAW Social Security Department activities suggests that at the heart of the Department's approach to health care bargaining and national health insurance are these principles:[2]

1. All citizens have a right to adequate health care.
2. An equal standard of health care should apply to all citizens.
3. Consumers of health care should participate in the administration of the nation's health insurance programs.
4. The health services provided should be comprehensive, to guard against a variety of possible misfortunes. (Departures from comprehensive coverage like coinsurance, deductibles, and "catastrophic" benefits employ price as a rationing device and are opposed by the Social Security Department.)
5. The health care system should provide incentives to develop organized medical teams that can efficiently provide comprehensive health care, including preventive care.
6. The financing of health services should be regulated so as to control costs; health care providers should not be permitted to set costs unilaterally.

7. The health care system should be designed to encourage further reform consistent with these principles.

Social insurance experts within the UAW view the U.S. health care industry as archaically organized, in effect, a cottage industry distorted by the profit motivations of doctors and insurance companies. They attribute the recent rising costs of health care, uneven quality of care, inequality of access to care, physician shortages, and the like to the organization of the health system. The principles listed above represent their proposed remedies for these problems. whether pursued in a limited fashion through a collectively bargained health plan or more fully through national health insurance (Jacobs 1983, 31–42).

Department staff reject the market, or the notion of competition among health plans, as a means to provide consumers with influence over the plans. In Hirschman's terms (1970) the staff prefer "voice" to "exit" as an instrument for communicating consumer preferences. Union participation in health plan administration is an obvious example of consumer voice. But one important feature of the health care economy in the United States is the partial management of consumer demand by providers. In rendering a diagnosis, doctors determine the scope, and ultimately the expense, of treatment. Although consumers may determine when they visit physicians, the visits in themselves determine costs far less than do the treatments doctors prescribe. This fact, combined with the extreme imbalance in medical knowledge prevailing between doctor and patient, ensures that the health care industry violates the crucial assumption of perfect information in neoclassical economic analysis. The Social Security Department therefore proposes regulatory initiatives (or direct bargaining with insurance companies) rather than measures based on "free choice" in the marketplace.

A close examination of the UAW's negotiated health plans demonstrates that the union has sought to apply the seven principles of health care reform identified above. The UAW has endeavored to win through bargaining an equal standard of health care for all members. In other words the union has sought to improve and standardize health benefits for workers in a wide variety of plants and firms (U.S. Department of Labor 1973, 1978; Munts 1967, 74–78; Jacobs 1983, 31–42).

In particular, the union has promoted health maintenance organizations (HMOs) (or group health plans) as a means to provide comprehensive care, including preventive services, to members. HMOs are structured to permit consumers' participation in the administration of health care services. The UAW has consistently advocated community participation in the HMOs it has helped organize. And through group health organizations unionists have attempted to make a measure of health security available to nonmembers as well (Munts 1967, 74–78).

The UAW has also urged the auto companies to cooperate in pressuring private insurance carriers to improve benefits for union members and nonmembers.

In fact, the union has won representation, along with the auto companies, on the governing boards of some Blue Cross plans (Munts 1967, 74–78).

In addition, the union has consistently resisted deductibles and copayments in negotiated health plans. In recent years newly negotiated plans have replaced these mechanisms with full financing by the employer. Only in the case of prescription drugs has the deductible been increased.

The health plans for employees of UAW-organized firms have been expanded repeatedly over the course of bargaining rounds to cover new categories of health maintenance. Prenatal and postnatal care, dental, vision, and psychiatric care, prescription drugs, and rehabilitation programs are among the most recently added benefits in UAW contracts. To my knowledge the health plans negotiated by the UAW are unmatched in their comprehensiveness.

The UAW has not instituted these reforms without management resistance. As a Ford representative[3] remarked in 1961:

> I think we [the UAW and Ford] differ . . . on the role that collective bargaining should play in shaping hospital and medical practice as such, and in solving broad community problems. The UAW quite regularly seeks, through bargaining pressure, to force out aid in implementing its social or community objectives. We, on the other hand, have a deep conviction that the collective bargaining arena, designed to resolve labor-management differences over conditions of employment, is one of the most ill-suited places for resolving these other kinds of problems.

In fact, these comments from management serve to confirm the reformist thrust of UAW health care bargaining.

The Social Security Department of the UAW has been, in effect, an agency of planning for health care reform. The union's initiatives in health care bargaining, as guided by the department, have been designed to promote reorganization of the health care industry, and these efforts have been consistent with the seven principles identified earlier.

UAW political activities on behalf of health care reform (through national health insurance) have also been coordinated with the work of the Social Security Department. Since the late 1960s these activities have been channeled through the Committee for National Health Insurance.

THE COMMITTEE FOR NATIONAL HEALTH INSURANCE

Links Between the UAW and CNHI

During the 1940s national health insurance received the attention of the U.S. labor movement in the form of the Wagner-Murray-Dingell bill, which never succeeded in passing the U.S. House of Representatives. The advocates of national health insurance, led by I.S. Falk, a public health specialist and dean of the health care reformers at the time, therefore retreated in 1950 to the more politically expedient notion of health insurance for the elderly under social security. After passage of the medicare amendments to the Social Security Act in 1965 (for which the UAW had lobbied extensively), national health insurance reemerged as a public issue. The UAW Social Security Department played a substantial role in this development (Falk 1977).

Earlier, in 1963, Melvin Glasser, a professor of social work and dean at Brandeis University, was appointed director of the UAW Social Security Department. He had agreed to take the position only on UAW president Walter Reuther's assurances that the resources of the union would soon be committed to a new campaign for national health insurance. In 1965 Glasser convened an informal working group of 20 health and social insurance experts to consider the merits of national health insurance legislation. Falk was a leading member of this group. The original charge was to formulate a national health insurance plan that would rely on the private insurance industry, but the group soon rejected that strategy, viewing private carriers as obstructive to cost-control and other objectives. The product of these deliberations was the Committee for National Health Insurance, launched in 1968 with $75,000 from the UAW. In the years since then CNHI has pursued three primary goals: to develop proposals for national health insurance, to educate the public on the issue, and to lobby.[4]

CNHI is a citizens' group comprising trade unionists, liberal activists, and dissident physicians; Table 1 lists the members of the CNHI board of directors in 1987. As shown in the table, the CNHI board (formerly called the Executive Committee) is dominated by labor representatives: 14 of its 21 members are union officials; and the board chair has always been the current or former UAW president. Interestingly, it is primarily the "mass" institutions of unionism (Barbash 1965)—the industrial unions and AFL-CIO departments, rather than the craft unions—that support the committee. Also providing support is the CNHI Committee of One Hundred, an advisory group of prominent individuals in labor and health care.

The Health Security Action Council (HSAC) is the political arm of CNHI, responsible for the group's lobbying activities. HSAC also has a board of directors. As shown in Table 2, 13 of the 21 HSAC board members directly or indirectly represent unions. The representation of functional departments of the AFL-CIO—namely, its legislation, social security, and industrial union departments—allows these top-level staff to advise the council on national questions of strategy and programming. The AFL-CIO's Director of Legislation obviously can contribute a great deal to lobbying efforts on national health insurance.

The UAW has consistently contributed about one-fourth of CNHI's annual revenues since the committee's founding. The UAW's annual contribution peaked at $190,000 during the late 1970s when the union's leaders hoped to finally succeed in enacting national health insurance with assistance from the Carter administration. Nonetheless, although the UAW's financial support for

Table 1. Members of the CNHI Board of Directors, 1987

Union Officials	
Douglas A. Fraser Chair, CNHI Former president, UAW	Jay Mazur President, International Ladies' Garment Workers' Union
Owen F. Bieber President, UAW	Howard D. Samuel President, Industrial Union Department, AFL-CIO
Don Cameron Executive Director, National Education Association	Lynn Williams President, United Steelworkers of America
Patrick J. Campbell President, United Brotherhood of Carpenters and Joiners of America	William H. Wynn President, United Food and Commercial Workers
Jacob Clayman President, National Council of Senior Citizens (labor-founded and funded), and former president, Industrial Union Department, AFL-CIO	*Others*
Thomas R. Donahue Secretary-Treasurer, AFL-CIO	Dr. Rashi Fein (ex officio) Professor, Department of Social Medicine and Policy, Harvard Medical School
Robert A. Georgine President, Building and Construction Trades Department, AFL-CIO	Mitchell I. Ginsberg Professor of Social Work, Columbia University
Melvin Glasser Executive director, CNHI, and former director, UAW Social Security Department	John Jacob President, National Urban League
William Hoffman Director, UAW Social Security Department	Vernon Jordan Attorney, Akin, Gump, Strauss, Hauer and Feld
Raymond Majerus Secretary-Treasurer, UAW	Coretta King President, Martin Luther King Center for Nonviolent Social Change
	Mrs. Albert Lasker President, Albert and Mary Lasker Foundation
	Philip R. Lee Director, Institute for Health Policy Studies, University of California, San Francisco

Source: Interview with Melvin Glasser, executive director, CNHI, 16 February 1987, Washington, D.C.

CNHI has been significant and consistent, its monetary assistance is an incomplete measure of the union's commitment to lobbying for national health insurance.[5] The UAW Social Security Department and the UAW's own lobbyists have worked closely with the committee, for example. In fact, CNHI depends in large part for its existence on in-kind services provided by sympathetic organizations.

The other major contributors to CNHI are the Amalgamated Clothing and Textile Workers Union; the AFL-CIO; the American Federation of State, County and Municipal Employees; the International Association of Machinists and Aero-

Table 2. Members of the HSAC Board of Directors, 1987

Union Officials and Staff

Douglas A. Fraser
Chair, HSAC; Chair, CNHI; and former president, UAW

Owen F. Bieber
President, UAW

Jacob Clayman
President, National Council of Senior Citizens (labor-founded and funded) and former president, Industrial Union Department, AFL-CIO

Thomas R. Donahue
Secretary-Treasurer, AFL-CIO

Murray H. Finley
President, Amalgamated Clothing and Textile Workers Union

Melvin Glasser
Executive director, HSAC; executive director, CNHI; and former director, UAW Social Security Department

William Hoffman
Director, UAW Social Security Department

Leonard Lesser
General counsel, Center for Community Change, and former counsel, UAW and Industrial Union Department, AFL-CIO

Robert McGlotten
Director, Department of Legislation, AFL-CIO

Lenore Miller
President, Retail, Wholesale and Department Store Union

Howard D. Samuel
President, Industrial Union Department, AFL-CIO

Bert Seidman
Director, Department of Occupational Safety, Health, and Social Security, AFL-CIO

John J. Sweeney
President, Service Employees' International Union

Others

Mark Battle
Executive Director, National Association of Social Workers

Mary Dublin-Keyserling
Conference on Economic Progress

Arthur S. Flemming
Former Secretary, U.S. Department of Health, Education and Welfare

Vernon Jordan
Attorney, Akin, Gump, Strauss, Hauer and Feld

Ruth Kobell
Legislative Assistant, National Farmers Union

Mrs. Albert Lasker
President, Albert and Mary Lasker Foundation

Philip R. Lee
Director, Institute for Health Policy Studies, University of California, San Francisco

Howard Newman
Attorney, Powell, Goldstein, Frazer and Murphy

Source: Interview with Melvin Glasser, executive director, CNHI, 16 February 1987, Washington, D.C.

space Workers; the National Education Association; the United Food and Commercial Workers; and the United Steelworkers of America. Mrs. Albert Lasker, a philanthropist, has also provided funds for the committee, but the UAW and other unions pay almost all the costs.

The Technical Committee of CNHI is responsible for drafting legislative proposals. Those proposals it has issued—to guarantee all citizens a right to an equal and adequate standard of health care, to institute comprehensive health services, provided in such a way as to control costs, to promote group practice, and to involve consumers in administration—closely correspond with the seven principles of health care reform listed in the previous section. Three stipulations further define CNHI objectives. First, national health insurance should be an integral part of the U.S. social security system, with financing from employer and employee contributions[6] and from general tax revenues. Second, health care should be provided through a pluralistic system of delivery organizations, privately owned for the most part but publicly regulated. (This proposal precludes the need for a massive restructuring of the existing health care system prior to enactment and also thwarts charges of "socialized medicine.") Third, the overall program must require detailed prospective budgeting, with annual ceilings on health care expenditures, hospital budgets, and negotiated fee schedules for doctors. Thus are health care costs to be contained under the CNHI plan.

All told, therefore, the ties between the UAW and CNHI have been financial, political, organizational, and philosophical. Through its participation in CNHI the UAW has found expression for its longstanding commitment to major health care reform.

Legislative Initiatives

The first bill endorsed by CNHI was drafted in 1970 by its Technical Committee in cooperation with Senator Edward Kennedy's staff. According to current CNHI director Melvin Glasser, Kennedy was interested in succeeding Lister Hill as "Mr. Health" in the Senate. Representative James Corman (Democrat, California) was the chief sponsor in the House. The Kennedy-Corman bill conformed to CNHI guidelines and relied upon public, rather than private, insurance, as the UAW working group had recommended in the mid-1960s. The bill met with little success, never reaching the floor of either body.

In 1970 as well the AFL-CIO introduced its own national health insurance bill under the sponsorship of Representative Martha Griffiths (Democrat, Michigan), following the lead of CNHI. It differed in no important features from Kennedy-Corman, which remained in committee. At the urging of Melvin Glasser, then director of the UAW Social Security Department, UAW president Leonard Woodcock met with AFL-CIO president George Meany in June 1970 to coordinate their efforts on behalf of the legislation. The two men agreed to permit joint action by the UAW and the AFL-CIO through CNHI. Lane Kirkland, then secretary-treasurer of the AFL-CIO, became secretary of the committee, and the UAW and AFL-CIO jointly endorsed the Kennedy-Griffiths-Corman bill. This joint endorsement secured a broad base of support for CNHI throughout the U.S. labor movement.

Kennedy-Griffiths-Corman, as introduced yearly in the early 1970s, called for the following reforms of health care in the United States, all of which met the goals of CNHI (Feder, Holahan, and Marmor 1980, 686–705):

1. federal administration of national health insurance under the U.S. Department of Health, Education and Welfare (HEW);
2. financing by a payroll tax increase, a tax on unearned income, and general revenues;
3. universal coverage of all U.S. citizens;
4. extensive benefits without cost-sharing by the patient;
5. establishment of a national health budget with funds allocated to regions and local areas and with regulation of the costs of health care services; and
6. national health planning under HEW in cooperation with preexisting state planning agencies, with funds for improved health care delivery including assistance for the development of HMOs.

CNHI activities during the 1970s and 1980s might be divided into three critical periods. The first was the committee's campaign for national health insurance during the Nixon administration years. The 1970s witnessed a swelling public interest in national health legislation. President Nixon, the American Medical Association, and the insurance industry had all proffered proposals for limited health care reforms to counter the growing call for genuine national health insurance. Representative Wilbur Mills, as chairman of the House Ways and Means Committee, was able to block consideration of the CNHI measure on the House floor. To resolve the impasse, Senator Kennedy sought to fashion a compromise with Mills, and the Kennedy-Mills bill was introduced in 1974.

The new bill was a form of catastrophic insurance and thus failed to meet CNHI's criteria of comprehensiveness and uniform treatment of patients of all income levels. The Kennedy-Mills bill required, for example, deductibles and coinsurance for hospital care and most medical services. (For the lowest income families general revenues would support cost sharing.) Private insurers would administer benefits. The CNHI leadership responded to Kennedy's calls for compromise with private deliberations concerning the possibility of modifying Kennedy-Mills, and they looked for new sponsors for the CNHI initiative in the Senate. Walter Mondale was interested in assuming such a role, but it appears that Kennedy was not eager to lose his special relationship to the committee. The bill was soon abandoned, and Kennedy retained his leadership role in the CNHI campaign.[7]

During the second critical period in CNHI's legislative initiatives, the committee threw itself into a strenuous effort to win President Carter's endorsement of its proposals. CNHI leaders were hopeful that support from the President would be sufficient to radically alter the balance of political forces in Congress. Carter had assured Leonard Woodcock of his commitment to national health insurance in the 1976 presidential campaign, ostensibly to win the Autoworkers' votes in the Michigan Democratic primary. In a campaign speech before the Student National Medical Association, Carter had promised a "universal and mandatory" national health insurance plan. Members of CNHI expected the plan would be among the first issues addressed by the Carter administration (Califano 1981, 88–135).

Carter had not specifically endorsed Kennedy-Corman, however. In fact, as a fiscal conservative, uncomfortable with the social programs of the liberal-labor agenda, Carter was in no hurry to push Kennedy-Corman. Piore (1983, 38–39) has written of Carter that his "neo-classical economic philosophy made it impossible to see social programs and institutions (at least those which like unions abridged market mechanisms) as anything more than pay-offs to the special interest constituencies which had been responsible for the President's election." The administration established an Advisory Committee to consider the legislative alternatives, a committee that became an arena for intraadministration lobbying for genuine national health insurance. Carter appointed Karen Davis, formerly of Rice University and the Brookings Institution, Deputy Assistant Secretary for Planning and Evaluation at HEW and Richard Warden, of UAW headquarters, HEW's Assistant Secretary for Legislation. Davis, her staff, and Warden were the HEW officers most sympathetic to national health insurance, while Carter's economic and budget advisors, Charles Schultz, Robert Strauss, James McIntyre, and Michael Blumenthal represented the conservative, budget-conscious opposition. CNHI, the UAW, and other labor unions acquired representation on the Advisory Committee, worked with Davis, and struggled, in vain, to counter the internal lobbying of these much more powerful advisors within the Carter administration.[8]

It became clear to the proponents that Carter was particularly concerned to ensure that national health insurance legislation (1) rely primarily on private carriers and (2) have minimal impact on the federal budget. The CNHI leadership therefore worried that Carter's commitment to national health insurance was so qualified as to endanger their program.

The differences between Carter and Kennedy were already apparent at the 1977 UAW convention, at which both spoke. Kennedy warned, "Health reform is in danger of becoming the missing promise" of the Carter administration, citing its procrastination on the issue. The Autoworkers' delegates cheered Kennedy. Carter seemingly had no choice but to promise action on national health insurance, which he did in his speech to the UAW convention. The President expressed his preference for a "phased-in" program and implied that all was contingent on adequate economic growth (Califano 1981).

CNHI backed a related bill Carter had proposed for hospital cost containment and was prepared to compromise with the President on the inclusion of private insurance carriers in national health insurance, but the committee ultimately came to the conclusion that a final agreement with the administration was impossible. In mid-1978 Carter prepared to announce his approach to national health insurance: a series of bills, to be introduced one at a time as the economy permitted, beginning with reform of medicare and medicaid and catastrophic insurance for citizens not covered by those programs. Kennedy and CNHI then broke with the administration and in May 1979 unveiled the Kennedy-Waxman bill.

Kennedy-Waxman differed from Kennedy-Corman most importantly in its stipulation that private carriers be heavily regulated. Carter's plan ultimately included complete financing of prenatal, delivery, and first-year infant care and all medical expenses over $1,250 in a given year. There was no doubt that passage of this plan would reduce somewhat the cost burden of negotiated health plans on employers and unions. Nonetheless, the plan did not meet the CNHI criterion of comprehensiveness and therefore could not gain CNHI support.

With the election of Ronald Reagan as President, CNHI entered a third period, characterized by less ambitious goals. During the 1980s the committee has chosen to concentrate on support for health care cost containment through governmental regulation (the Kennedy-Gephardt bill), protection of medicare and medicaid from funding cutbacks, and legislation to guarantee health care to the unemployed (Health Security Action Council n.d.). The Reagan administration has inspired this course in two ways. First, the prospects for enactment of national health insurance have been poor under the Reagan administration's conservative, "free market" policies—despite evidence of substantial public support.[9] Second, the administration favors taxation of health insurance premiums, further reductions in medicaid and medicare funding, and other measures that limit health protection under public and private plans (Starr, 1983)—proposals antithetical to the original CNHI principles.

It must be noted, however, that one member of the Reagan administration, Secretary of Health and Human Services Otis Bowen, has proposed a modest expansion of medicare to serve medicare recipients who require long-term care. This recommendation has met the opposition of Reagan's Domestic Council. But even if the administration ultimately fails to push Bowen's plan, it will thereby have provided some impetus to the debate over national health insurance.

Two other factors may lead to improved prospects for health care reform. First, the reinstatement of a Democratic majority in the Senate after the 1986 elections has shifted Congress in a slightly more liberal direction. Second, the objective need for reform of the health care system has actually increased. Over the past decade—with a smaller share of the labor force unionized, a decline in high-wage manufacturing employment, and further growth in health care costs—the private health insurance system has been serving a smaller and smaller proportion of U.S. citizens. Nonunion and service sector workers often have few or no health benefits. Melvin Glasser estimates that since 1980 there has been a 42 percent decline in the number of people protected by private insurance. This distressing news has led some members of Congress to propose mandating employer-provided health benefits. Although this approach would fall far short of national health insurance, the positive reception it has elicited may indicate a promising shift in congressional sentiment.

BUSINESS PERSPECTIVES

The significance of the UAW's campaign for national health insurance and support for CNHI may be clarified through a brief review of business perspectives on health care issues. No prominent business executive has been publicly identified with national health insurance. One might expect, however, that corporations that provide substantial health benefits might be willing to examine the arguments in favor of this reform simply because of the potential savings on insurance premiums they could reap.

Evidence of business perspectives on health care is available from two organizations in which UAW-organized firms have participated: the Labor-Management Group and the Washington Business Group on Health.

John Dunlop, of Harvard University, convened the Labor-Management Group, a governmental advisory group of leaders of labor and major corporations, in 1975. As Secretary of Labor under the Ford administration Dunlop chaired the group, which attempted to establish a consensus on national labor policy. After he resigned from the administration in protest of President Gerald Ford's veto of common situs picketing legislation, the Labor-Management Group reassembled on a private basis. The group dissolved in 1979 after the defeat of labor law reform bills in 1977 and 1978 had spawned renewed labor-management tensions. Douglas Fraser, then president of the UAW, was the first to leave the panel, charging:

> I believe leaders of the business community, with few exceptions, have chosen to wage a one-sided class war today in this country—a war against working people, the unemployed, the poor, the minorities, the very young and the very old, and even many in the middle class of our society (Herling 1978).

(The Labor-Management Group was resurrected in 1981 and has since devoted its energies to the problem of "reindustrialization.")

In 1978 the Labor-Management Group released a report prepared by its Staff Health Care Task Force, chaired by Bert Seidman of the AFL-CIO and W. Gordon Binns, Jr., of General Motors Corporation. Patrick Killeen of the UAW social security department was also a member of the task force. Four of the nineteen participants in the task force represented General Motors Corporation. Table 3 lists the complete membership of the task force.

This position paper by the task force addressed rising health care costs and recommended the following possible remedies (Labor-Management Group 1978):

1. prospective reimbursement of medical expenses by third-party payors;
2. extension of the health maintenance organization concept;
3. improved state and local planning of hospital facilities through Health System Agencies;[10]

Table 3. Members of the Staff Health Care Task Force of the Labor-Management Group, 1978

Co-Chairmen	Willis B. Goldbeck Washington Business Group on Health
Bert Seidman AFL-CIO	George Hanshaw U.S. Steel
W. Gordon Binns, Jr. General Motors	Susan C. Karp General Motors Corporation
Members	
John M. Batisell Mobil Oil Corporation	Patrick F. Killeen UAW
Paul Connelley United Brotherhood of Carpenters and Joiners of America	Barbara P. Pomeroy General Electric Company
Walter L. Davis Retail Clerks International Union	James R. Robinson E. I. du Pont de Nemours & Co.
D. A. Deshaw General Motors Corporation	Richard E. Shoemaker AFL-CIO
Diana K. Dragan Mobil Oil Corporation	C. Stephen Tsorvas General Electric Company
Richard D. Dugan General Motors Corporation	Robert B. Vaney Seafarers' International Union of North America
Cramer Gilmore International Brotherhood of Teamsters	Stanley Wisniewski Service Employees' International Union

Source: Labor-Management Group (1978).

4. hospital preadmission testing programs on a pilot basis for collectively bargained health benefits and insurance contracts;
5. prospective surgical review to discourage unnecessary surgery;
6. hospital services utilization review for collectively bargained health plans and insurance contracts;
7. expansion of alternatives to inpatient hospital treatment;
8. increased reliance on nurse practitioners and physicians' assistants;
9. cost-effective use of new medical technology in hospitals;
10. improved peer review programs for physicians, improved information for patients, and voluntary arbitration to reduce expenses deriving from malpractice claims; and
11. increased attention to health education, including educational programs for employees served by collectively bargained health plans.

The report did not recommend national health insurance as a means to achieve health care cost containment. The foreword to the report indicated that members of the Labor-Management Group disagreed on the advisability of national health insurance, for which reason the issue was not considered in the body of the paper. When Fraser resigned from the group, he identified national health insurance as an issue against which "the business elite" was obstructionist (Herling 1978).

In other words major unions, including the UAW, and major corporations, including General Motors, together confronted the problem of rising health care costs, particularly in collectively bargained health plans. The two parties were able to agree on a list of limited remedies, mostly private and administrative in nature. The primary issue engendering complete disagreement was national health insurance.

The second group offering an insight into business perspectives is the Washington Business Group on Health, a lobbying organization of about 200 large corporations (including the major automakers) that cooperate in formulating national health policy. Member firms are concerned with the improved administration of their private employee health plans. Willis Goldbeck, the group's current executive director, was a member of the Labor-Management Group's Staff Health Care Task Force. The staff of the Washington Business Group on Health double as staff for the Business Roundtable's Task Force on Health.[11]

According to Goldbeck the Business Group is sympathetic to some market-oriented approaches to health care cost containment, in which the federal government would encourage employers to provide employees with multiple choices among competing plans. The group's members generally prefer a free market for insurance carriers to direct government regulation. They also support efforts to exercise joint union-management leverage over specific carriers. They recognize that a large sum of money invested in premiums for a single carrier can lend the insured a great deal of influence over the quality of the benefits provided.

The practical reason why employers would support either private administrative remedies or public policies that would grant employees a choice among competing carriers is that each remedy allows the individual firm to continue to reap the employment and public relations benefits of a generous private health plan. Employers know that generous plans enhance employees' loyalty to the firm. More specifically, employee turnover and health-related absenteeism, which are potentially very costly to employers, are reduced under such plans. Simply put, a governmental program of health insurance would deprive the employer of these residual benefits of private health care plans (Allen 1969).

The ideological justification for conservative, market-oriented remedies for rising health care costs is based in neoclassical economics. According to the neoclassical model only the market-based approaches can introduce discipline into demand to prevent "overinsurance" and force competition among providers and carriers for cost-conscious consumers. On the other hand, national health insurance necessarily involves "overinsurance" because healthy individuals receive more comprehensive and expensive coverage than they might rationally choose. A national program would effectively redistribute health care resources and promote an equality that is offensive to conservatives (Pauly 1980). It also obviously means more government not less—another ideological goal of conservatives.

Auto company executives do not necessarily worry about overinsurance in the abstract because they derive the aforementioned residual benefits from generous private health plans. They do worry, however, about rising insurance premiums, and they accept the neoclassical conclusion that consumers (employees) must be cost-conscious (share in costs). Moreover, auto executives are perhaps wary of governmental programs like national health insurance that contribute to the esteem in which the federal government is held and restrict the power of the private sector.

The Business Group, of course, favors the private administrative remedies recommended in the 1978 report of the Labor-Management Group. In addition, the group supports experimentation with employer self-insurance. Self-insurance is fully consistent with employers' preference for private administrative remedies.

The Washington Business Group on Health might be regarded as the corporate analog to CNHI, although Willis Goldbeck denies this. One of its primary functions is to identify common elements in major corporations' varied perspectives on employee health plans. Corporate members of the group are educated as to this corporate consensus on health policy, and Congress learns of corporate views.

Since 1976 the UAW and the Big Three automakers—General Motors, Ford, and Chrysler—have together promoted health maintenance organization, "preferred provider" organizations, legislation to reduce excess hospital bed capacity in Michigan, and similar, limited schemes to contain costs. Through the Michigan Cost-Containment Coalition, the union and the auto companies have coordinated their efforts at cost-containment with Blue Cross and Blue Shield. The Washington Business Group on Health supports measures such as these. But in all these efforts to address health care issues the employers have stopped short of considering national health insurance as an alternative—despite UAW pressure to do so and despite the possibility that national health insurance would cost the auto companies less (considering payroll taxes) than their existing private plans.[12]

As long as employers choose to or are obliged to finance health plans, they will be willing to consider most union schemes to control health costs—except national health insurance. In the face of this opposition the UAW's continuing preference for a national program as a strategy of cost-containment must derive from the fact that it is the only measure that also promotes equality of access to health care in the interest of all workers. The private administrative strategies upon which the UAW and management can agree cannot, in the end, satisfy the UAW's goal of fundamental health care reform.

OPERATIONAL SOCIAL UNIONISM

The UAW's stance toward health issues represents a substantial departure from traditional business unionism. Labor unions' concern for issues beyond wages, benefits, and workplace conditions has often been termed "social unionism."

A good deal has been written about social unionism, but seldom with the detail and precision that characterize the classical models of business unionism (for example, Perlman 1949). Daniel Bell (1960, 208–21) wrote that some unions have the flavor of a social movement and are involved in campaigns for the extension of the welfare state. J. David Greenstone (1977, 8–18) argued that unions are active on behalf of welfare state reforms and other liberal initiatives largely to satisfy their allied constituencies within the Democratic party and improve party fortunes. Jack Barbash (1965, 491–96) distinguished between the "programmatic," welfare-state orientation of the industrial unions and the narrow, "pressure group" behavior of the craft unions. Although these writers and others have contributed to our understanding of the social concerns of unions, I believe the concept of "operational social unionism" (OSU) better describes the UAW's commitment to health care reform.

Under operational social unionism the leaders of a labor union confront a problem within the workplace or otherwise of concern to members by choosing from among a variety of possible responses the one strategy that unites (1) the interests of members as workers and citizens, (2) the interests of all trade unionists, and (3) the interests of the poor and unorganized. In this context the labor organization pursues reforms that receive union members' support and that satisfy the members' needs as unionists and citizens. The UAW's support for national health insurance constitutes operational social unionism because this reform would serve all workers, including the unorganized, while also lifting a burden, in this case, the increasing cost of negotiated health benefits, from collective bargaining in general.

Operational social unionism does not contradict a union's particular interests in specific bargaining relationships. Obviously it would ask too much of social unionism to require that it injure the union's immediate and pragmatic interests. Nevertheless, the union can pursue a variety of strategies beyond collective bargaining that at the same time protect its collective bargaining interests. Operational social unionism links the solution of union problems to the needs of the working class as a whole. It serves the bargaining interests of the organized and the class interests of the unorganized.

OSU is therefore expressed, by definition, through political institutions parallel to the institutions of collective bargaining. Since, today, less than a fifth of the labor force is organized into unions, and since social unionism involves campaigns on behalf of broad union and nonunion constituencies, these parallel institutions provide for the representation and mobilization of diverse constituencies. I will term these "institutions of social unionism." CNHI is a fitting exemplar of an institution of social unionism.

Institutions of social unionism might be regarded as alternate forms of labor organization in society. Most industrial relations scholars accept the current form of trade unionism in the United States as inevitable, even immutable. In doing so, they dismiss such early U.S. labor organizations as the Knights of Labor and the National Labor Union, each of which combined both social reform affiliates and collective bargaining affiliates, as misguided and unworkable. These observers err in the assumption that "business unionism"—unionism preoccupied with wages, benefits, and working conditions—is the ideal form of unionism and labor's end state in this country. In particular, they overlook the significance of these parallel institutions.

Operational social unionism is likely to engender political conflict between labor and employer groups. Since OSU, by definition, represents a broad working-class interest, it meets the opposition of management on ideological or practical grounds. Individual employers are more inclined to collaborate with individual unions on issues of narrow self-interest than on broad issues of social policy. Operational social unionism does not offer such opportunities for collaboration.

The fundamental issue in examining operational social unionism is to define the self-interest that governs union behavior. OSU is not a disinterested altruism, which would be untenable as union policy. Rather, as I have said, it is a way of defining self-interest so as to incorporate the concerns of unorganized workers.

A citizens' group with the following characteristics might be judged to be an institution of social unionism, a significant part of the broader labor movement:

1. The membership or constituency served must be working class or otherwise exclude executives and top management.
2. The leadership must be drawn from the official labor movement.
3. The political program of the organization must be consistent with, although not necessarily identical to, that of official unions.
4. A substantial portion of the group's resources should come from organized labor.

A consumer or citizens' group that satisfies these criteria is not merely allied with labor; it is, in my judgment, a part of the labor movement.

By examining the UAW's role in health care reform and by advancing a theory of operational social unionism and institutions of social unionism, I hope to encourage more careful and systematic analysis of union activities that transcend individual workplaces and bargaining relationships.

OTHER INSTITUTIONS OF SOCIAL UNIONISM SPONSORED BY THE UAW

Beyond its efforts on behalf of CNHI the UAW has founded a variety of other institutions of social unionism over the years.[13] Although these institutions have pursued very diverse goals, they all have served to organize key constituencies for UAW political campaigns on issues of significance to working people in general.

Americans for Democratic Action (ADA), the Citizens Crusade Against Poverty, the Progressive Alliance, and the Committee for National Health Insurance were all established with substantial support from the UAW. ADA was formed in 1948 as a left-wing (but anti-Communist) pressure group within the Democratic party. Walter Reuther, then the newly elected president of the Autoworkers, was a founding member of ADA, along with several other trade union leaders. Neither Reuther nor his fellow labor leaders dominated ADA, which also represented nonlabor constituencies in the arts and professions.

The ADA activists nonetheless viewed the labor movement, particularly the CIO, as an anchor of liberalism in the United States. The UAW and other CIO unions provided a substantial share of ADA's funds. Although ADA and organized labor grew estranged as Eugene McCarthy and Hubert Humphrey contested the Democratic presidential nomination in 1968, they repaired their relations in the 1970s. Over most of ADA's history, its leadership has included trade unionists. (For example, Reuther's assistant Jack Conway chaired the ADA executive committee in the 1960s, and former UAW counsel Joseph Rauh, Jr., has been active in ADA since its founding.)

In light of the financial, programmatic, and other ties between the ADA and official trade unions, one might regard ADA as a surrogate for a labor party. Indeed, in the absence of disciplined parties and a parliamentary system in the United States, the political activity of labor consists of its collaboration with the bloc of pro-labor Democrats in Congress on individual issues. ADA's lobbying on behalf of a liberal-labor agenda serves an important purpose in this context. Labor and allied liberals cannot rely upon a party mechanism to discipline members of Congress. Instead, they scrutinize the congressional voting record and strive to increase the number of representatives and senators with congenial views.

In the 1960s Reuther founded the Citizens Crusade Against Poverty to unite liberal labor leaders, civil rights leaders, and others in a campaign to extend President Lyndon Johnson's War on Poverty. The UAW provided funds to support the organization. The union also financed experimentation with "community unions," residential associations of the poor equipped to bargain collectively with landlords and private and public agencies.

In 1978 Douglas Fraser, who was then president of the UAW, formed the Progressive Alliance, a coalition of unions, public interest groups, and such organizations as ADA, the Democratic Socialist Organizing Committee, and the National Association of Social Workers. For about two years, the Progressive Alliance was active in addressing such issues as reform of the Democratic party, plant closing legislation, and other liberal-left initiatives. Fraser's decision to create the Progressive Alliance was, in part, a result of the defeat of labor law reform by Senate conservatives in 1978 and related tensions within the Labor-Management Group chaired by John Dunlop. The almost immediate organization of the Alliance after the Labor-Management Group disintegrated suggests the two institutions embodied separate but related strategies for the pursuit of labor's ends. The Labor-Management Group represented an effort to moderate labor-management conflict and achieve detente between the major unions and employers so that their constituencies might reap limited economic gains. The Progressive Alliance represented an effort by the UAW and other unions to broaden conflict with employers to include political issues on which organized workers, the poor, and the unorganized could coalesce.

In 1980 the Progressive Alliance was weakened by internal disagreements over the merits of President Carter versus his rival in the Democratic primaries, Senator Edward Kennedy. The Alliance abandoned its other concerns to promote labor unity on behalf of Carter after the Democratic convention. With Ronald Reagan's election the organization soon dissolved.

THE SIGNIFICANCE OF OSU

Although it is difficult to argue that the UAW and other unions have no interests outside of collective bargaining, it is not easy to pinpoint the significance of these interests and the importance of institutions of social unionism. The UAW's commitment to health care reform and support for the Committee for National Health Insurance may or may not represent evidence that business unionism fails to describe a portion of the labor movement. This problem raises the following basic questions for further research on U.S. unionism:

1. To what degree do other unions share the UAW's apparent operational social unionism? Are craft unions less likely to practice OSU than industrial and public sector unions because of their narrow constituencies and potent pressure group role in the local politics of public works?
2. How will the burgeoning international competition in the auto industry affect the priority the UAW accords to a goal like national health insurance? Will the union become increasingly preoccupied with defending its position in a volatile economy at the expense of the campaign for health care reform?

I am not persuaded that the UAW will abandon its interest in health care reform within the threatening context of international competition. Since health care costs are likely to continue rising, cost containment should remain a serious issue for UAW leaders. The officers and staff of this and other unions have for many years favored national health insurance as a remedy for health care cost inflation. I see no evidence that the UAW has reconsidered this position. The problem of foreign competition, if anything, justifies increased union attention to means to socialize that portion of labor costs derived from health benefits. If the UAW and even CNHI have recently deemphasized national health insurance in their lobbying, it is because prospects for congressional enactment of this program are dim indeed under the Reagan administration.

In the current political environment any new social program faces tremendous opposition, on both budgetary and ideological grounds. Within the Democratic party "neoliberals" like Gary Hart and Bill Bradley have contributed to the political resistance to government programs by stressing "entrepreneurial" solutions to social problems. The international crises of trade and productivity have commonly been defined to direct attention to entrepreneurial solutions, to relief for business from high labor costs and governmental regulation rather than protection of international labor standards. Unions have the difficult task of fostering a political climate that will even allow discussion of the alternatives to these accepted bromides.

I believe that further testing of the descriptive power of operational social unionism as a concept will be particularly important in examining the deliberations of the AFL-CIO's Committee on the Evolution of Work. In its report entitled "The Changing Situation of Workers and Their Unions" (1985), the committee recommended that unions experiment with new approaches to represent workers' interest. If increased attention to legislative remedies for workers' problems becomes one response to these recommendations, scholars in industrial relations will want to consider more carefully than they have the varied political institutions of the U.S. labor movement.

ACKNOWLEDGMENTS

I would like to thank the following people, whose insights proved helpful in developing the concept of operational social unionism: Melvin Glasser, Willis Goldbeck, John Herling, Thomas R. Knight, David B. Lipsky, Theodore Lowi, Cathy Schoen, the late Nelson Cruikshank, and the late Nat Weinberg.

NOTES

1. The UAW's "two-way" approach recalls Sidney and Beatrice Webb's (1897, 559) characterization of organied labor's threefold strategy for the pursuit of workers' interests: mutual insurance, collective bargaining, and legislative enactment.

2. This description of the views of UAW social insurance specialists is based on interviews with Melvin Glasser, executive director of CNHI, on 6 November 1981 and 16 February 1987, and with the late Nelson Cruikshank, former AFL-CIO social security director, on 25 January 1982, all in Washington, D.C.

3. R. L. Jacobus, manager, Insurance Department of Ford Motor Company, cited in Series II, Box 8, UAW Social Security Department Collection, Walter P. Reuther Labor History Archives, Detroit, Michigan. Although Garbarino (1960) described the commitment of various unions to health care reforms, he does not anticipate the UAW's role in helping lead the campaign for national health insurance.

4. Much of this chronology is based on interviews with Melvin Glasser (see note 2 above).

5. For an analysis of labor's varied forms of political involvement, see Masters and Zardkoohi (1987, 79–117).

6. In the 1970s the UAW won contractual commitments from the auto companies to pay any employee contributions that might be required under any future national health insurance system (U.S. Department of Labor 1978).

7. Minutes of Technical Committee Meeting, 29 May 1974, Box 60, Committee for National Health Insurance Collection, Walter P. Reuther Labor History Archives, Detroit, Michigan.

8. Interview with Cathy Schoen, health care specialist for the Service Employees' International Union, 28 January 1982, Washington, D.C.

9. A *Newsweek-Gallup* poll released on 8 February 1982 reported that 55 percent of the registered voters surveyed would be more likely to vote for a congressional candidate who favored an "all-inclusive government sponsored national health insurance program" than for other candidates (Alpern 1982).

10. Unions were among the early supporters of the 1974 federal health planning law, but enlightened employers in the Labor-Management Group and the Washington Business Group on Health later supported this form of government intervention in the health care economy. This is the major exception I have found to employers' preference for private, as opposed to public, remedies for rising health care costs (Demkovich 1982).

11. Telephone interview with Willis Goldbeck, executive director, Washington Business Group on Health, 22 May 1982.

12. Of the Big Three Firms only Chrysler has been governed by international contract, covering autoworkers in the United States and Canada. The Canadian system of national health insurance results in one-third to one-half lower health care costs per employee for Chrysler-Canada than for Chrysler's U.S. operations, including employer taxes for the Canadian program (Demkovich 1982).

13. Interview with Leon Shull, national director, Americans for Democratic Action, 24 September 1980, Washington, D.C.

REFERENCES

American Federation of Labor-Congress of Industrial Organizations (AFL-CIO), Committee on the Evolution of Work. 1985. The Changing Situation of Workers and Their Unions. Washington, DC: AFL-CIO.

Allen, Donna. 1969. *Fringe Benefits: Wages or Social Obligation*. Ithaca, NY: New York State School of Industrial and Labor Relations, Cornell University.

Alpern, David M. Polarizing the Nation? *Newsweek*, 8 February 1982, 34.

Barbash, Jack. 1965. The Structure of Union Political Action: A Trial Analytic Framework. *Proceedings of the 1965 Spring Meeting of the Industrial Relations Research Association*. Buffalo: IRRA.

Bell, Daniel. 1960. *The End of Ideology: On the Exhaustion of Political Ideas in the Fifties*. Glencoe, IL: Free Press.

Bloch, Max. 1951. Negotiated Social Security Plans for North American Automobile Workers. *International Labor Review* 64(August-September):175–206.

Califano, Joseph A., Jr. 1981. *Governing America: An Insider's Report from the White House and the Cabinet*. New York: Simon and Schuster.

Demkovich, Linda E. 1982. When It Goes to the Bargaining Table, Labor Looks to Control Health Costs. *National Journal*, 7 February 1982, p. 230.

Falk, I.S. 1977. Proposals for National Health Insurance in the USA: Origins and Evolution, and Some Perceptions for the Future. *Milbank Memorial Fund Quarterly: Health and Society* (Spring):101–91.

Feder, Judith, John Holahan, and Theodore Marmor. 1980. *National Health Insurance: Conflicting Goals and Policy Choices*. Washington, DC: Urban Institute.

Garbarino, Joseph W. 1960. *Health Plans and Collective Bargaining*. Berkeley: University of California Press.

Greenstone, J. David. 1977. *Labor in American Politics*. Chicago: University of Chicago Press.

Health Security Action Council. N.d. Health Security Action Council Program, 1985–86, brochure in the author's possession. Washington, DC: HSAC, Committee for National Health Insurance.

Herling, John. 1978. Warning Shot Across the Bow. *John Herling's Labor Letter*, 22 July, p. 1.

Hirschman, Albert O. 1970. *Exit, Voice, and Loyalty: Responses to Decline in Firms, Organizations, and States*. Cambridge: Harvard University Press.

Jacobs, David C. 1983. The United Auto Workers and the Campaign for National Health Insurance: A Case Study of Labor in Politics, Ph.D. dissertation. Ithaca, NY: Cornell University.

Labor-Management Group. 1978. *Position Papers on Health Care Costs*. Washington, DC: Labor-Management Group.

Masters, Marick F., and Asghar Zardkoohi. 1987. Labor Unions and the U.S. Congress: PAC Allocations and Legislative Voting. In *Advances in Industrial and Labor Relations*, vol. 4, ed. David Lewin, David B. Lipsky, and Donna Sockell, 79–117. Greenwich, CT: JAI Press.

Munts, Raymond. 1967. *Bargaining for Health: Labor Unions, Health Insurance, and Medical Care*. Madison: University of Wisconsin Press.

Pauly, Mark V. 1980. Overinsurance: The Conceptual Issues. In *National Health Insurance: What Now, What Later, What Never?* ed. Mark V. Pauly, 201–19. Washington, DC: American Enterprise Institute.

Perlman, Selig. 1949. *The Theory of the Labor Movement*. New York: Augustus M. Kelley.

Piore, Michael J. 1983. Can the American Labor Movement Survive ReGomperization? *Proceedings of the Thirty-Fifth Annual Meeting, December 28–30, 1982, New York City*, ed. Barbara D. Dennis, 30–39. Madison, WI: Industrial Relations Research Association.

Starr, Paul. 1983. The Laissez-Faire Elixir. *New Republic*, 18 April, pp. 19–23.

U.S. Department of Labor, Bureau of Labor Statistics. 1973. Wage Chronology: Ford Motor Co. and the Auto Workers, Vol I, 1941–1973, bulletin 1787. Washington, DC: GPO.

_________. 1978. Wage Chronology: Ford Motor Co. and the Auto Workers, Vol. II, 1973–1979, bulletin 1994. Washington, DC: GPO.

Webb, Sidney and Beatrice Webb. 1897. *Industrial Democracy*. London: Longmans.

TOWARD A SYSTEMATIC UNDERSTANDING OF THE LABOR MEDIATION PROCESS

Richard B. Peterson and Mark R. Peterson

Labor mediation remains an ill-defined process even though a fair number of books and articles have dealt with it. For the purpose of this paper we follow Cooley's (1986, 209) definition of labor mediation: "a process in which an impartial intervenor assists the disputants to reach a voluntary settlement of their differences through an agreement that defines their future behavior." Mediation is a more active form of third-party intervention than factfinding because the mediator can use more persuasive tactics than the factfinder; it is less active than arbitration because, unlike an arbitrator, the mediator does not render a final and binding decision.

All mediator proposals are just that—proposals. They must be accepted by the parties to be put into force. Indeed, the mediator's assistance in resolving disputes is not meant to supplant the negotiations process, but instead to reinforce the supremacy of the two parties in achieving a settlement (Simkin 1971).

Theodore Kheel, a well-known mediator, has argued that in the study of labor-management relations "there has to be a recognition of the mutuality of interests, but there also has to be a recognition of basic conflicts of interest" (Lawrence and Miller 1979, 35). Mediation can thus be understood as a means of resolving

Advances in Industrial and Labor Relations, Volume 4, pages 141-160.

ISBN: 0-89232-909-2

conflict that at the same time upholds basic precepts concerning the parties' long-term relationship. The mediator, in contrast to the arbitrator, is more interested in helping the parties find a compromise than in rendering a decision per se. Mediators can also prove helpful in resolving disputes over labor grievances (Bierman and Youngblood 1985; Brett and Goldberg 1983).

This paper addresses several important issues of labor mediation. First is the question whether mediation is an art or a science—a subject of much of the literature on mediation. If mediation is an art, little can be gained in trying to model the process for predictive purposes. On the other hand, if mediation has elements of a science, such modeling is a worthwhile endeavor. We take the position that the labor mediation process does exhibit systematic characteristics worthy of study.

Second, we review the mediation literature to identify those factors that are common to mediation in diverse kinds of labor disputes. Finally, we discuss some broad conclusions about the labor mediation process. Throughout we hope to provide a better understanding of the labor mediation process.

MEDIATION: ART OR SCIENCE?

Writers on labor mediation usually take one side or the other in the ongoing debate over whether mediation is an art or a science. Here we will briefly review the arguments advanced by both sides as support for their case.

Mediation as an Art

With rare exception scholars describe the mediation process as an art (Simkin 1971; Maggiolo 1971). Many practicing mediators take the same viewpoint. The term *art* as it is used in the debate over mediation can be defined as "a specific skill . . . conceived as requiring the exercise of intuitive faculties that cannot be learned solely by study" (American Heritage Dictionary, s.v. *art*). This concept, applied to the mediator's role as a third party, suggests that the mediator reacts to each individual conflict with a different set of tactics. Although we accept the individuality of every mediator and recognize the variety of actions at his or her disposal, it is our belief that describing mediation simply as an art obscures the nature of the process. If this view is taken to an extreme, the mediator is simply a *reactor* to the situation at hand, not an *initiator* of strategies and tactics.

Maggiolo (1971) described the United States as a political system firmly based on a "meeting of the minds," a country that functions on the principle of compromise. The labor-management relationship is a microcosm of this societal endorsement of compromise. As a result, in Maggiolo's view, the mediator is expected to bring a new approach to every case. The mediator should therefore be knowledgeable about the numerous tactics and strategies that might be applicable to the given situation. In this sense the mediator is an artist in using his or her skills to fashion a unique strategy for resolving the specific labor-management dispute.

Mediation as a Science

Not everyone agrees that mediation is an art. Some scholars and practitioners believe there are certain characteristics of mediation that transcend a mediator's intervention in any labor-management dispute. In fact, some of them believe that the traditional view of mediation as an art has stifled the study of third-party intervention.

As Kochan and Jick (1978, 209) noted, "There is a void of empirical research and statistical analysis on mediation." They attributed that void to two main factors: the lack of a widely accepted, systematic theory of mediation, and the widely held view that mediation is an art. These two points are inextricably related; no systematic theory can be accepted as long as the majority of scholars and practitioners reject the application of scientific, or at least systematic, methods to the study of the topic in question. Fortunately, over the last decade or so the industrial relations community has begun to consider some systematic elements in the mediation process (Kolb 1981, 1983b; Pruitt and Johnson 1972; Kochan and Jick 1978).

Stevens (1967) presented the first model of the mediation process to replace the multifaceted strategies of the mediator with generalized ones. Rather than concentrating on the unique elements of each mediation process, he created a systems model, one that emphasized inputs and outputs. Stevens's assumption was that the mediator is a highly rational individual who employs certain tactics as a consequence of environmental signals or influences.

This line of reasoning was pursued by Brett, Drieghe, and Shapiro (1986), who pointed to the systematic link between mediator styles and roles and the negotiations environment. The authors wrote that "while mediators' styles vary, and many mediators vary their style on a case-by-case basis, that variance is due to mediators' perceptions of their role, their assessment of the likely outcome of the case, and their beliefs about what techniques are most effective in bringing about each type of outcome" (p. 283).

Suggesting that the process of mediation has a scientific base usually leads to misinterpretation of the exact meaning of *science*. Perhaps it is clearer if we define the systematic elements of mediation as those that suggest a "purposeful regularity," or mediation strategies and tactics that can be identified in a broad range of mediation cases. Although these consistently applied tactics and strategies do not guarantee a predetermined outcome, they do suggest general parameters of mediation goals and actions that, once identified, can provide a better understanding of the mediation process.

The generalizations that have dominated the literature on mediation for decades have defined the art-science debate in a strict manner. Both of these viewpoints have merit, but the extremity of the generalizations does an injustice to the central question evoked in this discussion: Are there *replicable* elements to the mediation process? Stevens argued in the affirmative, and yet his theory disregards the personal basis of mediation. Maggiolo, though correct in recognizing the individual characteristics of the mediation process, failed to consider sufficiently the systematic elements that both characterize the process and influence the outcome of mediation.

We firmly believe, therefore, that there is little to be gained in continuing the debate over whether labor mediation is an art or a science. It is doubtful whether either position can be defended in its pure form. Practitioners, for the most part, will favor the artistic properties of the process. On the other hand, researchers in general will be more at home with the position that labor mediation can be studied in a systematic manner.

It is our position that labor mediation represents a systematic process in which mediators choose a particular "theory" of the case based upon their assessment of the situation, the parties involved, and their own definition of the role of the mediator. We now turn our attention to the literature on labor mediation to identify key characteristics that have been associated with the mediation process.

INSIGHTS FROM THE LITERATURE

Here we focus on several major themes in the study of mediators and mediation effectiveness. We begin by discussing the roles that mediators choose to take on. Then we look at the various functions of the mediator in the different stages of bargaining. We also discuss the literature on mediator strategy and tactics, the influence of time pressures, and personal characteristics of the mediator. Finally, we address the issue of mediation and mediator effectiveness and several innovations in the field.

Mediator Roles

Our literature review revealed no one dominant role of mediators in labor-management disputes. Instead, each mediator chooses a given role to play. The role chosen has an impact upon the structure and character of the mediation effort.

A mediator's intervention into the labor-management negotiations process is infused with important issues regarding the limits of mediator authority. The art-science arguments discussed earlier are examples of extreme positions; somewhere between these poles the mediator must conceive a role that is (1) sufficiently appropriate to the dispute as to allow an opportunity for compromise; and (2) acceptable to the parties involved.

Kolb (1981, 1983a, 1983b) took the position that the mediator's role is a crucial variable in the dispute process:

> Role is central to any understanding and explanation of practice. How a mediator defines himself in the process influences how he will structure a case, the nature of the interactions he has with the parties, and, particularly, the nature and the use of strategies he will employ (1983b, 6).

The concept of role encompasses two general components. The way in which a mediator conceives of his or her relationship with the central parties dictates both (1) the content and process of the negotiations and (2) the strategies and tactics to be exercised during the mediation process.

It appears that mediators have some choice in the role they will play in any given negotiations. First, they can take an active or a passive role in the bargaining process. Second, they can focus on content or process. Finally, they can choose to accept the differences in bargaining power between the parties or strive for an equitable settlement.

In a recent ethnographic study comparing and contrasting mediator roles in state and federal agencies, Kolb (1981, 1983a) discovered wide differences in role conceptions between the two branches. She concluded that whereas the state mediators "emphasize their personal contribution to the substantive development of the final package, the federal mediators . . . attend more to the process by which the parties are able to reach agreement" (1981, 7).

In broad terms Kolb found that the state mediators took a more activist approach, entered negotiations at an earlier stage, and tended to focus on manipulating the content of the negotiations. She characterizes these mediators as "deal makers." The federal mediators, in contrast, perceived their role as improving the structural context of negotiations. Through facilitating clearer communication and a deeper understanding of the issues in conflict, these mediators served as "orchestrators," according to Kolb.

Helburn (1984) and Rehmus (1984) criticized Kolb's conclusions. They contended that the intensity of the dispute, not the mediator's affiliation with a state or federal agency, determines whether the mediator will be a deal maker or an orchestrator. Rodgers (1986), in a study of public sector disputes where strikes took place, found that the more intense the dispute, the more likely the mediator was to play an active and content-oriented role.

The last major choice of role facing a labor mediator concerns the ultimate goal or outcome of the negotiations. Should the mediator take the role of helping the parties strive towards a "fair" bargain? Or should the mediator accept the likelihood that the party with the most bargaining power will gain the most in negotiations?

Although a number of scholars and mediators have examined the power balance in negotiations between labor and management, few agree on or even discuss the degree of manipulative force the mediator should exercise (Simkin 1971; Maggiolo 1971; Kolb 1981). Bargaining power can be understood as the complete range of outcomes that each party can impose on the opponent. The major question of role in this context is whether the mediator should attempt to control, or manipulate, the power relationship between the parties.

The majority of writers on this subject at least tacitly accept several fundamental norms of behavior. One subsumes the concepts of fairness and impartiality (Simkin 1971; Kolb 1981). Some writers argue that the major responsibility of the mediator is that of assisting the two parties in achieving a settlement based *only* on the present bargaining strength of the parties. This viewpoint is an essentially conservative attitude; it assumes that labor relations works most efficiently and effectively if the mediator accepts the existing bargaining power of the two parties.

There are two fundamental problems with this viewpoint. First, it is difficult to imagine how a third party could participate in the negotiation process without suggesting, consciously or otherwise, that the parties pursue a compromise settlement. In essence, a subjective attitude of what constitutes a "fair deal" is part and parcel of the concept of compromise. In examining a series of disputes, Deutsch and Kraus (1962) concluded that the mediator, as a third source of opinion, was "doing more than simply suggesting the content of communication. He was, in effect, establishing a social norm of 'fairness' or 'equality' " (p. 57). Compromise does not necessarily entail, however, splitting the difference evenly between the positions of the two parties.

A second problem with the status quo viewpoint is that grossly imbalanced settlements can have serious consequences for the future labor-management relationship. If the mediator concerns himself with a compromise based only on the relative economic, social, and political strengths of the two parties, the eventual settlement is likely to reinforce any existing power imbalance and lead to the development of a more antagonistic relationship in the future. Ultimately, the perpetuation of a power discrepancy could reduce or end one party's interest in continuing the relationship or, instead, could result in the weaker party continuing to acquiesce in the demands of the stronger party. In the latter case the interparty relationship may stabilize on the very base of the power imbalance. Unfortunately, the existing evidence on this important question is inconclusive.

Countering the status quo viewpoint is the contention the mediator should consider means of narrowing the power differences. The theoretical basis for this view is the proposition that power inequality in a bargaining environment exacerbates negotiating problems (Borah 1963; Baranowski and Summers 1972). Rubin (1979), writing on third-party interventions within a more general context, argued that the mediator, by "favoring the weaker party [can provide] the underdog with a greater counterpower" (p. 12).

Also supporting this countervailing view is the proposition that an "equitable" compromise is more stable and contributes to the long-term bargaining relationship between labor and management. Although a settlement based on equal concessions by the two parties may contribute to an improved environment for negotiations, the standards by which the mediator manipulates both the process and the content of negotiations may be unacceptable to the parties. In pursuing such an approach, the mediator compromises the positions of the bargaining teams, removes the parties' responsibility for the negotiations, and hampers their development of bargaining skills. Obviously, the mediator also asserts a primacy in the process not intended when mediation was conceived as an alternative through which labor and management could settle outstanding issues more efficiently and with less conflict. Thus, a consistent domination of the process by the mediator engenders a very real danger, encouraging a lack of responsibility among representatives of the parties and possibly subverting the labor relations process. Evidence of this danger is found in research on the ''chilling'' and ''narcotic'' effects of interest arbitration in the public sector.

Nonetheless, in studies on attitudes toward mediation both labor and management have stated their unwillingness to surrender their ''collective negotiating power'' to normative standards of fairness (Krislov, Mead, and Goodman, 1975). Byrnes (1978) found that both parties view the role of the mediator as one of assisting, not directing, labor and management toward a settlement. It seems likely that any mediator who openly attempts to manipulate the interplay of bargaining power will encounter serious resistance, or dismissal, from the negotiators.

Mediator Functions

Numerous authors have attempted to identify the various functions mediators perform at various stages in the intervention. Although they have observed a wide variety of functions, we can classify them into five basic categories central to most disputes:

1. providing information;
2. clarifying the issues under dispute;
3. manipulating the structuring of issues;
4. applying pressure tactics to increase the parties' motivation and incentive to compromise;
5. initiating proposals the labor or management representatives are unwilling to put forth themselves for strategic reasons.

Providing Information

In providing information, the mediator uses tactics that are aimed at improving the process of negotiation as well as modifying the social context in which the parties are bargaining. Manipulating the channels of communication (of both information and feelings) is a crucial tactical tool of the mediator; with experience, the mediator should be able to choose from among a constellation of approaches.

Negotiations stalled by negotiator intransigence, for example, can be shifted to caucuses in which the mediator meets with the parties separately. Maggiolo (1971) commented, "In the mediation process, the most effective reconciliation of differences occurs during the separate meetings or caucuses of the parties with the mediator" (p. 52).

As we will further elaborate in our discussion of pressure tactics, control of communication channels provides the mediator with an opportunity to press for a settlement by emphasizing only some of the information being released by the parties. Especially as a consequence of independent caucuses, the mediator has significant control over the content of information available to the negotiating teams as well as the expressions of feelings held by both sides.

Finally, the structural way in which the mediator develops the communicative relationship between the parties can improve his own understanding of the key issues in dispute. Each party may be more willing to share information privately with the mediator than in any joint forum. The mediator's access to information is critical in differentiating between the high- and low-priority issues being negotiated.

Clarifying the Issues

In clarifying the issues of importance to the parties, the mediator is actually accomplishing two related functions. In addition to establishing the priority each party attaches to the individual issues at hand, this process provides the mediator with a clearer perception of the tactics that will be necessary to achieve a settlement. In other words, by clarifying the issues the mediator can both help the parties articulate their interests and begin to develop an idea of where there is room for compromise (Simkin 1971).

Kheel (Lawrence and Miller 1979) has argued that one of the most important functions of the mediator is that of acting as a sounding board through which the parties' can pin down their interests and goals. This process is necessary because the parties' perceptions of each other's intent and commitment are often unclear and unstable. In fact, these misperceptions have been noted as a major source of misinformation that leads to inappropriate views of the other party's interests and, in turn, to continued conflict (Jervis 1976). Although not an absolute guarantee of settlement, an increased flow of information between the negotiating parties contributes to more realistic expectations concerning the final nature of the agreement.

Structuring the Issues

Distinguishing between the relatively unimportant issues and the substantive issues is required of mediators in nearly all cases. Rarely does a conflict between the two parties emerge out of disagreement on a single position. Although the parties may attach their highest priorities to wage and seniority clauses, agreement on the secondary issues is often crucial to priming the parties for an overall settlement. Where the representatives have presented apparently irreconcilable demands on the key issues, their ability to accept concessions on the more peripheral issues may begin to satisfy the parties that they can reach an overall agreement.

In pursuing agreement on the secondary issues, the mediator may develop a "total package" that sets up the secondary issues as trade-offs between the conflicting proposals of the central parties (Meyer 1960; Grigsby and Bigoness 1982). By broadening the parties' focus to include all the issues at hand, the mediator can reduce the strategic dominance of one key issue and allow the representatives to see that compromise in a single area can be compensated for by gains in other areas. Most negotiating pairs prefer dealing with issues in subsets or in multiples, as opposed to one at a time. This explains the wide use of package offers in labor negotiations.

Applying Pressure Tactics

Pressure is an inherent part of the negotiation environment. As Simkin (1971) and Douglas (1962) have observed, the parties are under constant pressure to settle, especially in the time preceding a strike deadline. These pressures are internal to the parties, that is, independent of those initiated by the mediator. At the same time, however, these pressures are manipulable and must be perceived as crucial tools available to the mediator.

Pressure can be understood as all those issues and factors that tend to make one party or both reconsider their previous offer. For the purpose of our discussion, we will focus more on the actual tactics of applying pressure; the major exception will be directed toward understanding the mediator's manipulation of time pressures.

Toward the later stages of negotiations the mediator can often instigate a narrowing of interests or issues by suggesting that the parties' positions are within a compromise range. The hint that a settlement is possible serves to increase the pressure on the parties either to accept the mediator's proposal or to develop new positions conducive to compromise. Although by the time they have approached the strike deadline the parties may have accepted the inevitability of a strike or lockout, consistent pressure directed at the parties may provide the impetus that convinces the chief negotiators that a settlement is more beneficial to their interests.

In the final stages of negotiations the mediator often relies upon economic arguments as a means of pressuring for settlement. Although the effectiveness of economic arguments heavily depends on the mediator's ability to persuade the parties that continued conflict will be detrimental to their economic interests, there are various situations in which economic-based arguments lead to compromise. One obvious example is if either the union or the employer is economically incapable of surviving a prolonged conflict.

Additionally, inherent political elements of the bargaining relationship may serve as pressure to settle. The most obvious example is public sector bargaining, where the right to strike is invalidated by legal statute in most states. Another example is conflict in industries that contribute to ''national security,'' disputes that demand outside intervention. This is a unique case because the political pressures on the parties to settle peacefully also restrict the mediator's actions: He must honor the external time and legal pressures on his role as a third party.

This brief discussion notes only a few of the more salient and efficacious pressures involved in mediation. As the mediation process continues, new pressures appear that provide the mediator with tools by which a settlement between the parties can be achieved. Obviously, manipulating the pressures on the parties is no guarantee of a compromise solution; rather, this strategic instrument helps to establish an environment more conducive to settlement.

Initiating Proposals

Finding ways the parties can save face is a fundamental part of the mediator's role. More specifically, the mediator, as a consequence of his ''impartial'' role, can initiate proposals that neither of the parties individually could place on the table.

In every bargaining process the representatives of labor and management are confronted by the dual necessity to make concessions and yet to appear strong to the opponent (Pruitt and Johnson 1972). This dilemma makes it difficult for the parties to initiate compromise proposals because of the fear of being perceived as weak, and thus the fear of a loss of image (Pruitt 1971).

Through separate caucuses with the two chief negotiators the mediator can develop and present alternative solutions—and introduce these proposals as his own—thereby deflecting any potential loss of image. This ''trying on for size'' (Simkin 1971) is also a potent method of learning the real expectations both parties have regarding the final terms of settlement.

In addition to each party's need to save face vis-à-vis the other party, individual negotiators also need to appear strong within their own negotiating team and their larger organization. Rubin and Brown (1975) investigated in detail the pressures placed upon the negotiator by his own constituency. The authors argued that the ''mere presence of constituents (including psychological presence) motivates bargainers to seek positive evaluations (p. 44). Thus, as part of his role in helping the parties to save face, the mediator should include in his pressures for agreement an effort to help the parties convince their respective constituencies that the final document deals satisfactorily with their own strategic needs.

Mediator Strategy and Tactics

The strategies and tactics employed by mediators in carrying out these various functions have been analyzed in some detail. The bulk of the literature devoted to this topic has focused on the general actions taken by the mediator to achieve certain broad aims (Simkin 1971; Maggiolo 1971). These goals often include developing the parties' trust and confidence and developing a negotiating environment conducive to final settlement. Kochan (1980, 279–82) has equated these goals with the three key stages of the mediation process: developing acceptability and diagnosing the situation; facilitating the bargaining process; and exerting pressures for settlement.

Although the investigation of individual tactics and strategies has significant methodological difficulties, studies by Kochan and Jick (1978) and Kressel (1972) have served to focus research attention on the role played by strategies and tactics in the mediation process. In particular, these studies have shown that the existence of appropriate mediator strategies increases the likelihood of reducing conflict and achieving a settlement and well-chosen strategies by the mediator increase his prestige with the negotiators.

Strategy can be understood in general terms as an overall plan of action designed to address a specific problem. In implementing strategies, the mediator relies upon tactics, which are the ''operational element of strategies'' (Kolb 1983a). Mediator strategies and tactics have been classified along continuums from active to passive and from content (issue)-based to process-based. It is not our purpose to argue the merits of individual strategies and tactics, but rather to discuss the central tendencies in the use of different strategies and tactics.

Kressel (1972) outlined three core types of mediator strategies that appear in nearly every mediation case. These conform roughly to Kochan's three stages in the mediation process (in parentheses):

1. reflexive strategies (diagnosis and developing acceptability);
2. nondirective strategies (facilitating bargaining); and
3. directive strategies (exerting pressures for settlement).

The *reflexive strategies* are designed to elicit the negotiators' confidence in the mediator and to establish rapport between the mediator and the involved parties (Kressel 1972; Simkin 1971). Similarly, Kochan and Jick (1978) referred to these as noncontingent strategies, ones directed at establishing effective channels of communication between the mediator and the parties. Tactics the mediator employs as part of a reflexive strategy include demonstrating his concern for the dispute, his understanding of the issues, and his competence. Exhibiting that he is capable of dealing with the complexity of the existing conflict, or his expertise, in the early stages of an intervention is a prerequisite for any subsequent actions by the mediator (Kressel 1972).

Nondirective strategies are aimed at producing a climate favorable to more effective negotiations. The tactics manifested at this stage are primarily to pin down the parties' various priorities and to articulate or distinguish among the various issues. By controlling the structure of negotiating exchanges and various other administrative details, the mediator is developing his ''affect base'' (his influence upon the pattern and tone of the negotiations between the principal parties). Here the mediator concerns himself with the actual process of the negotiations.

Finally, the purpose of *directive strategies* is to move the parties toward settling the outstanding issues once, in the mediator's opinion, a contract zone has been reached. The concept of a "contract zone" refers to the point in the negotiations where both parties' final offers are within a mutually acceptable range. Directive strategies, implemented in most instances during the final stages of negotiations, involve the application of a variety of pressure tactics (Carnevale 1986). In addition, as Kressel (1972) noted, the ultimate success of the negotiations depends heavily upon the mediator's ability to symbolically reward the parties for having made concessions.

This categorization of mediator strategies is not complete, however, since the number of strategies available to the mediator is significantly smaller than the number of tactics. This is natural because tactics, although emerging out of a particular strategy, are exercised as a reaction to numerous environmental influences: the stage of the negotiations, the external pressures on the parties, and the interparty relationship. The plethora of *tactics* available to the mediator is perhaps one explanation for the view of mediation as an art. Yet, if we also consider *strategies* as a crucial part of mediation, we find that mediation exhibits a greater consistency and predictability than that view would allow. As Kolb (1983a, 249) has argued:

> Although one observes much variability in the use of tactics . . . there are patterns that can be observed. Consistent with his strategy, a mediator will tend to emphasize certain types of tactics and time their use in particular ways.

Furthermore, we can link strategies to specific groups of tactics. For example, the mediator's attempts to build the parties' trust and confidence may entail using one or more of the following tactics: clarifying the mediator's role; establishing ground rules; actively demonstrating competence; demonstrating empathy; being neutral and being seen as neutral; and being seen as sensitive to the needs of the bargaining team members. Identifying the underlying issues and the dominant negotiators constitutes another effective tactic (Ontario Education Relations Commission 1983).

A host of tactics facilitating the bargaining process are identified in the Ontario Education Relations Commission's report, *The Bargaining Process and Mediation* (1983). These include developing trust and confidence, reducing interpersonal conflict, and deflating and avoiding unrealistic expectation.

Finally, in attempting to exert pressures for settlement on the parties, the mediator can draw on another set of tactics: using delays and deadlines to build pressure; placing responsibility for settlement on the parties' shoulders; engaging in marathon bargaining; using "coercive comparisons"; reviewing the costs of a strike or lockout; making informal suggestions; making recommendations in joint conference; and making public recommendations (Ontario Education Relations Commission 1983). The tactics, though, must be consistent with the mediator's overall strategy.

Without suggesting that the relationship between strategies and tactics can be reduced to systematic cause and effect relationships—as Stevens (1963) seemed to argue—we nevertheless believe it is possible to assess the impact of strategies and tactics on the actions of negotiating parties. Thus, we can recognize fundamental connections between the appearance of a particular mediator tactic and the stage of the negotiations. Application of pressure on the parties during the later stages is but one example of the conditional relationships among the stage of the negotiations process, the mediator's strategy, and the mediator's tactics. Future research should build on our understanding of these patterns.

The Influence of Time Pressures

Studies by Vidmar (1971) and Bigoness (1976) have shown the critical impact of timing on the content of the positions advanced by the negotiating teams. In general terms, the stage of the negotiations process encourages the parties to develop compromise positions only when pressure exists to forge a compromise. This pressure usually appears only during the later stages of bargaining (Kochan and Jick 1978; Vidmar 1971).

The majority of the mediation process is devoted to establishing the range of issues to be discussed and presenting proposals and counterproposals. Under ideal conditions this narrowing of issues leads to a stage at which the mediator "precipitates the decision making process" (Douglas 1962). As noted earlier, in broad terms the mediation process is characterized by a continuous increase of pressure on the parties. The mediator, however, exerts his most serious influence—in both practical and symbolic terms—during the final hours of negotiations.

Personal Characteristics of the Mediator

A large body of the literature on mediation has focused on the characteristics of the successful mediator (Simkin 1971; Landsberger 1955; Maggiolo 1971). Yet, despite the wide variety of "effective" traits proposed in that line of research, our understanding of this topic remains extremely limited. The descriptions proffered have tended to emphasize subjectively determined or abstract characteristics rather than specific mediator behaviors (Kolb 1981).

The limitations of this research are largely the result of the methodological complexities that limit the efficacy of scientific research to isolate personal characteristics. This problem is compounded by the difficulty of replicating the pressures of the mediation process in a laboratory environment. It is well nigh impossible, for example, to reproduce the emotional environment of labor-management negotiations or to create incentives that will encourage the experimental subjects to commit themselves personally to achieving hypothetical goals (Vaughn and Bass, 1967; Brookmire and Sistrunk 1980; Chertokoff and Conley 1967). But the methodological and generalizability problems inherent in laboratory research notwithstanding, it is our view that the studies remain a source of potentially important information. The findings of several of the more notable empirical studies serve to exemplify this point.

Kochan and Jick (1978) tested a model of mediation involving the interaction between situational and personal characteristics, as well as their interrelationships with mediator strategies. The authors concluded that the two most influential factors in successful mediation were the intensity of the conflict and the assertiveness of the mediator. In particular, the more assertive the mediator, the sooner the parties reached settlement. Likewise, successful mediation was associated with the perceived intensity of the conflict. Similar conclusions were reached by Gerhart and Drotning (1980), who found that the intensity of the mediator's involvement in the negotiations was significantly related to the likelihood of early resolution. These concepts of mediator assertiveness and intensity appear to be crucial, most notably where the bargaining objectives of the parties are vague or where the parties' sophistication in bargaining is low (Kochan and Jick 1978).

A second fundamental conclusion of the Kochan and Jick study was the importance of the mediator's experience. The authors found that the amount of experience the mediator had was correlated significantly with almost all their measures of mediation effectiveness and was even correlated significantly with the probability of a settlement. It is interesting to note in this regard how experience figures in the mediator training program of the Federal Mediation and Conciliation Service; the program requires a year of apprenticeship and the gradual introduction of the junior mediator to those disputes considered to be especially difficult.

Pruitt and Johnson (1972) focused on the parties' assessment of the mediator's ability to help them save face during the process of concession making. They also examined correlations between mediator assertiveness, pressures from the mediator, and the parties' concession making. Although not directly related to the issue of mediator characteristics, their findings tend to support the conclusions of Kochan and Jick regarding mediator intensity and assertiveness.

Future study of the role played by mediator characteristics would benefit from moving beyond attempts to isolate individual traits to include discussion of mediator skills and experience. In particular, research should address the mediator's ability to analyze and interpret the problems facing the parties—an ability Chertokoff and Conley (1967) have shown to be crucial to mediator success. Thus, rather than focus on *individual characteristics*, such as humor and patience, research should consider more *general mediator qualities*. In other words, rather than attempting to isolate every single tactical manifestation of a mediator's strategy, we should search for patterns of strategies and patterns of mediator qualities that appear across a wide cross-section of cases. These steps would be consistent with our attempt to discover the systematic elements of the mediation process.

Mediation Effectiveness

The literature holds out four principal approaches to measuring the effectiveness of mediation. The first is whether, through mediation, the parties succeed in resolving their differences short of a strike. Mediation has been shown to be, in general, a very successful method of controlling labor-management hostilities and has made an important contribution to the stability of labor relations in this country (Conti 1985).

Second, in cases where the mediator arrives on the scene after a strike has commenced, mediation effectiveness is judged by how quickly thereafter the parties reach a strike settlement.

The third approach is to ask the parties themselves to assess the mediator. One technique is to ask how helpful the mediator was in aiding the parties to reach a contract settlement; another is to ask the key negotiators how willing they would be to use the mediator in the future (even though most mediation agencies assign mediators to particular cases based on factors other than the wishes of the parties).

Finally, the mediator can be assessed on his or her ability to reduce the number of issues in dispute, even if the parties reach an impasse in the negotiations. And some researchers have employed more than one of these measures of mediation effectiveness (for example, Kochan and Jick 1978).

Although at present there is little statistical information concerning the effectiveness of mediation, Kolb (1983a), in her comparative study of federal and state mediators, presented limited statistical support for the effectiveness of mediation. She found that state mediators settled an average of 70 percent of all their cases, while their federal counterparts settled almost all the disputes in which they were involved.

The effectiveness of any mediation effort is highly dependent on the characteristics of the individual labor-management relationship. At times mediation is overused; the parties involved in disputes may also attempt to draw out conflict through mediation. Similarly, mediators occasionally misinterpret the problem or fail to sublimate their views or personal interests to those of the negotiators. Nonetheless, most studies have found that labor and management hold positive atttitudes toward both individual mediators and the mediation process (Krislov and Galin 1979).

Innovations in Labor Mediation

Mediation has been most visible in resolving differences over wage issues and other crucial subjects of contract negotiations. But over the last 20 years mediation has been deployed in new areas of labor-management relations, such as grievance handling, with the belief that the successes of interest mediation can be duplicated in those areas. We will now discuss the emergence of mediation as an element of the grievance procedure, as well as the growth of preventive mediation and mediation-arbitration (med-arb).

Grievance Mediation

A well-defined and efficient grievance procedure is critical in the day-to-day dealings between workers and their supervisors. Although the grievance procedure in most labor contracts may be clearly stated, the process is often slow and cumbersome. To rectify this problem, numerous workplaces have attempted to integrate mediation in the grievance procedure (Brett and Goldberg 1983; Gregory and Rooney 1980; O'Grady 1976; Simkin 1971). Simkin proposed three potential conditions under which mediation could increase the efficiency of the grievance procedure:

1. When a large backlog of unresolved grievances has accumulated.
2. When the contractual language does not allow for a grievance procedure, or the process at the present time is ineffective.
3. As a step prior to arbitration.

Mediation as a part of the grievance process is probably most effective in dealing with a large group of issues (Brett and Goldberg 1983). It may also prove useful—as Simkin implies—in establishing a more effective grievance process. Various scholars have argued that the grievance process in most contracts today is overly centralized. As a result of this centralization, issues better resolved at the plant level are expanded into the more general area of labor-management conflict (Kuhn 1967).

Preventive Mediation

The concept of preventive mediation developed in the 1960s and was originally established as a technical assistance program within the Federal Mediation and Conciliation Service (FMCS). As in mediation within the grievance process, preventive mediation attempts to identify problems and establish objectives for improving the bargaining relationship. Through prenegotiation and continuing labor-management committees the parties attempt, with the mediator's help, to address potential problems or issues in dispute before the contract expires (Maggiolo, 1985). An offshoot of preventive mediation has been "relationships by objectives" (RBO), initiated by the FMCS in 1975. RBO is an in-depth conflict resolution process geared toward establishing common objectives for both labor and management, especially when conflict between the union and the employer has been chronic (Popular 1976).

Preventive mediation as an alternative method of conflict resolution has grown in the last decade. The attempt to confront major contractual and subsidiary issues before contract negotiations is seen by some parties as an alternative to the confrontational model of labor relations. Additionally, preventive mediation, as conceived by the FMCS, is very much an educational tool designed to train the negotiating parties in more sophisticated negotiating behavior and more accommodative means to achieve their ends.

Yet a problem remains that restricts the widespread use of preventive mediation. Both management and labor negotiators are wary of expanding the influence of the third party. They fear that any use of neutrals beyond the bargaining table will circumvent the traditional mode of labor-management relations and lessen the preeminence of labor and management as the crucial parties to the negotiations process (Simkin 1971).

Mediation-arbitration

A third relatively new form of mediation is actually a combination of mediation and arbitration. If the third party cannot, through mediation, bring the parties to agreement, they allow the same person to render a final and binding decision on the disputed issues. Med-arb has been called "persuasion with muscle" because of this dual role for the neutral (Allred 1984; Hoh 1984; Stern 1984). The rationale for this twist on mediation is that because arbitration threatens to result in a settlement less favorable than one that parties might reach themselves, they will bargain more seriously and more honestly.

As an alternative to traditional mediation, med-arb is attractive, but usually only in conflicts where a strike would have an extremely deleterious impact on the parties. For most parties med-arb is an unacceptable method, if only because the threat of arbitration upsets the traditional dominance of labor and management by placing increased strategic power in the hands of the mediator.

DISCUSSION

We can draw several conclusions from this review of the literature on mediation. First, we have found that the debate over whether mediation is an art or science is counter-productive. Neither view has garnered much support. Moreover, whatever "art" is involved in mediating, the mediation process has been shown to exhibit some systematic qualities. In particular, future research should focus on the central tendencies of mediator behavior in each of the three stages of mediation, which happen to parallel the three stages of the negotiations process.

Second, mediators can be categorized by the roles they identify for themselves in a given case based on such factors as the sector of the economy, the experience of the negotiators with collective bargaining, and the intensity of the dispute. By choosing a particular role in a given intervention, the mediator limits the number of strategies that can be used. And by choosing a particular set of strategies, the mediator further limits the number of tactical options. Thus, although the specific tactics available are greater in number than the strategies, they are by no means inexhaustible. The challenge before us is to identify the particular set of tactics that are useful in carrying out a given strategy. In so doing, we can provide a structure for more useful research on the mediation process.

Third, researchers need to develop better operational measures for many of the major factors identified in this paper. We already have several good measures for identifying characteristics of the mediator such as assertiveness, analytical skills, and experience. We also have means of determining different levels of intensity within a given dispute. Future research should focus on ways of operationalizing the factors of mediator roles, functions, strategies, and tactics.

Finally, future research should begin to test the linkage between roles, strategies, tactics, and bargaining outcomes. Much of the literature has been confined to laboratory studies, which tend to consider only a very limited number of variables. We encourage future researchers to construct models or theories of the mediation process, and then test the models or theories in the field. Tests could include participant observation, in-depth interviews, case studies, quasi-experimental treatments, or some combination of these approaches. Such testing would allow us to replace the largely atheoretical literature with predictive models.

ACKNOWLEDGMENTS

We wish to express our appreciation to George Strauss, Deborah M. Kolb, Lane Tracy, I.B. Helburn, and Nancy Napier for their comments on earlier drafts of this paper.

REFERENCES

Allred, Stephen. 1984. Med-Arb and the Resolution of the SSA-AFGE Bargaining Impasse. *Arbitration Journal* 39(2): 46–54.

Baranowski, T. A., and D. A. Summers. 1972. Perception of Response Alternatives in a Prisoner's Dilemma Game. *Journal of Personality and Social Psychology* 21(1): 35–40.

Bierman, Leonard, and Stuart A. Youngblood. 1985. Resolving Unjust Discharge Cases. *Arbitration Journal* 40(1):48–60.

Bigoness, William J. 1976. The Impact of Initial Bargaining Position and Alternative Modes of Third Party Intervention in Resolving Bargaining Impasses. *Organizational Behavior and Human Performance* 17(1):185–98.

Borah, L. E., Jr. 1963. The Effects of Threat in Bargaining: Critical and Experimental Analysis. *Journal of Abnormal and Social Psychology* 66:37–44.

Brett, Jeanne M., Rita Drieghe, and Debra L. Shapiro. 1986. Mediator Style and Mediator Effectiveness. *Negotiation Journal* 2(3):277–86.

Brett, Jeanne M., and Stephen B. Goldberg. 1983. Grievance Mediation in the Coal Industry. *Industrial and Labor Relations Review* 37(1):49–68.

Brett, Jeanne M., Stephen B. Goldberg, and Wiliam Usury. 1980. Mediation and Organizational Development: Models for Conflict Management. In *Proceedings of the Thirty-Third Annual Meeting, December 28–30, 1979*, ed. Barbara D. Dennis, 195–202. Madison, WI: Industrial Relations Research Association.

Brookmire, David A., and Frank Sistrunk. 1980. The Effects of Perceived Ability and Impartiality of Mediators and Time Pressure on Negotiation. *Journal of Conflict Resolution* 24(2):311–27.

Byrnes, J. F. 1978. Mediator-Generated Pressure Tactics. *Journal of Collective Negotiations* 7(2):103–9.

Carnevale, Peter J. D. 1986. Strategic Choice in Mediation. *Negotiation Journal* 2(1):41–56.

Chertokoff, J. M., and M. Conley. 1967. Opening Offer and Frequency of Concession as Bargaining Strategies. *Journal of Personality and Social Psychology* 7(2):181–85.

Conti, Adam J. 1985. Mediation of Work-Place Disputes: A Prescription for Organizational Health. *Employee Relations Law Journal* 11(2):291–310.

Cooley, John W. 1986. Arbitration vs. Mediation—It's Time to Settle the Differences. *Chicago Bar Record* (January-February).

Deutsch, Martin, and R. M. Krauss. 1962. Studies of International Bargaining. *Journal of Conflict Resolution* 6(8):545–52.

Douglas, Ann. 1962. *Industrial Peacemaking*. New York: Columbia University Press.

Gerhart, Paul F., and John E. Drotning. 1980. Dispute Settlement and the Intensity of Mediation. *Industrial Relations* 19(3):352–59.

Gregory, G. A., and R. E. Rooney. 1980. Grievance Mediation: A Trend in the Cost-Conscious Eighties? In *Proceedings of the Thirty-Third Annual Meeting, December 28–30, 1979*, ed. Barbara D. Dennis, 502–8. Madison, WI: Industrial Relations Research Association.

Grigsby, David W., and William J. Bigoness. 1982. Effects of Mediation and Alternative Forms of Arbitration on Bargaining Behavior: A Laboratory Study. *Journal of Applied Psychology* 67(5):549–54.

Helburn, I. B. 1984. Review of *The Mediators* by Deborah M. Kolb. *Administrative Science Quarterly* 29(3):459–61.

Hoh, Ronald, 1984. The Effectiveness of Mediation in Public Sector Arbitration Systems: The Iowa Experience. *Arbitration Journal* 39(2):30–40.

Jervis, Robert. 1976. *Perception and Misperception in International Politics*. Princeton: Princeton University Press.

Kochan, Thomas A. 1980. *Collective Bargaining and Industrial Relations*. Homewood, IL: Richard D. Irwin.

Kochan, Thomas A., and Todd Jick. 1978. Public Sector Mediation Process—Theory and Empirical Examination. *Journal of Conflict Resolution* 22(2):209–40.

Kolb, Deborah M. 1981. Roles Mediators Play: State and Federal Practice. *Industrial Relations* 20(1):1–18.

__________. 1983a. *The Mediators: Interpretive Bases of Practice*. Cambridge, MA: MIT Press.

__________. 1983b. Strategy and the Tactics of Mediation. *Human Relations* 36(3):247–68.

Kressel, Kenneth. 1972. *Labor Mediation: An Exploratory Survey*. New York: Teachers College, Columbia University.

Krislov, Joseph, and Amira Galin. 1979. Comparative Analysis of Attitudes Towards Mediation. *Labor Law Journal* 30(3):165–73.

Krislov, Joseph, John F. Mead, and J. F. B. Goodman. 1975. Attitudes Toward Mediation: U.S., Great Britain, and Ireland. *Monthly Labor Review* 98(1):55–59.

Kuhn, James W. 1967. The Grievance Process. In *Frontiers of Collective Bargaining*, ed. John T. Dunlop and Neil W. Chamberlain, 252–270. New York: Harper & Row.

Landsberger, Henry A. Interim Report of a Research Project in Mediation. *Labor Law Journal* 6(4):552–60.

Lawrence, D. B., and Ernest C. Miller. 1979. Conflict Resolution?—Or Agreement Making? . . . An Interview with Theodore Kheel. *Personnel* 56(4):28–37.

Lentz, Sidney Solberg. 1986. The Labor Model for Mediation and Its Application to the Resolution of Environmental Disputes. *Journal of Applied Behavioral Science* 22(2):127–39.

Maggiolo, Walter A. 1953. Mediation's Role on the Labor Stage. *Labor Law Journal* 4(9):632–36.

__________. 1971. *Techniques of Mediation in Labor Disputes*. Dobbs Ferry, NY: Oceana Publications.

Meyer, Arthur S. 1960. Function of the Mediator in Collective Bargaining. *Industrial and Labor Relations Review* 13(2):159–65.

O'Grady, James P. 1976. Grievance Mediation Activities by State Agencies. *Arbitration Journal* 31(2):125–30.

Ontario Education Relations Commission. 1983. *The Bargaining Process and Mediation*. Toronto: OERC.

Popular, John J. 1976. Labor-Management Relations: U.S. Mediators Try to Build Common Objectives. *World of Work Report* 1(9):1–3.

Pruitt, Dean. 1971. Indirect Communication and the Search for Agreement in Negotiation. *Journal of Applied Psychology* 1:205–39.

Pruitt, Dean G., and D. F. Johnson. 1972. Mediation as an Aid to Face Saving in Negotiation. *Journal of Personality and Social Psychology* 1(3):139–44.

Rehmus, Charles M. 1984. Review of *The Mediators* by Deborah M. Kolb. *Industrial and Labor Relations Review* 38(1):121–22.

Rodgers, Robert C. 1986. An Interesting, Bad Theory of Mediation. *Public Administration Review* 46(1):67–74.

Rubin, Jeffrey Z. 1979. *Dynamics of Third Party Intervention: Kissinger in the Middle East*. New York: Praeger.

Rubin, Jeffrey Z., and Bert R. Brown. 1975. *The Social Psychology of Bargaining and Negotiation*. New York: Academic Press.

Simkin, William. 1971. *Mediation and the Dynamics of Collective Bargaining*. Washington, DC: Bureau of National Affairs.

Stern, James L. 1984. The Mediation of Interest Disputes by Arbitration under the Wisconsin Med-Arb Law for Local Government Employees. *Arbitration Journal* 39(2):41–45.

Stevens, Carl M. 1967. Mediation and the Role of the Neutral. In *Frontiers of Collective Bargaining*, ed. John T. Dunlop and Neil W. Chamberlain, 271–90. New York: Harper & Row.

Vaughn, J. A., and B. M. Bass. 1967. Putting the Business World into the Test Tube. *Transaction* 5:50–52.

Vidmar, Neil. 1971. Effects of Representational Roles and Mediators on Negotiator Effectiveness. *Journal of Personality and Social Psychology* 17(1):48–58.

THE SKILL DISTRIBUTION AND COMPETITIVE TRADE ADVANTAGE OF HIGH-TECHNOLOGY INDUSTRIES

Ann P. Bartel and Frank R. Lichtenberg

Achieving an adequate level and rate of employment growth is among the most important objectives of economic policy. In an economy relatively open to international trade, strong growth in domestic demand is neither a necessary nor a sufficient condition for satisfactory growth in domestic employment. The higher the propensity to import foreign goods, the lower the stimulus to employment growth provided by growth in domestic demand. Conversely, if foreign demand for a country's exports is high, that country could exhibit robust employment growth even in the face of unimpressive domestic demand growth.

During the last quarter century the United States has become increasingly open to international trade. The ratio of imports to gross national product, a standard measure of openness, increased from 4.6 percent in 1960 to 12.0 percent in 1980. But the rate of growth in foreign demand for U.S. products has been significantly lower than the rate of growth in U.S. demand for foreign products. Consequently, the nation has experienced large and increasing merchandise trade deficits. In 1984 the U.S. trade deficit reached \$123 billion, more than 75 percent greater than the previous high of \$69 billion set only one year earlier; the deficit for 1985 was projected to exceed \$138 billion. Manufactured goods ac-

Advances in Industrial and Labor Relations, Volume 4, pages 161-176.

ISBN: 0-89232-909-2

count for a substantial (and growing) share of this deficit: the U.S. deficit for these goods increased from $38 billion in 1983 to $89 billion in 1984 and was expected to exceed $105 billion in 1985 (AFL-CIO 1986). The AFL-CIO estimates that a trade deficit of $138 billion results in the loss of (or failure to create) over 3 million U.S. jobs. This estimate may be slightly high (the ratio of one job per $50,000 of the trade deficit is also sometimes suggested), but it is probably of the right order of magnitude. Obviously, the ability of the U.S. economy to provide employment opportunities depends on its ability to reduce trade deficits.

Although there have been large U.S. trade deficits for manufactured goods as a whole, industries making up the "high-technology" sector of manufacturing have consistently experienced a trade surplus. As Table 1 indicates, the high-technology sector, as defined by the U.S. Department of Commerce (the issue of defining this sector is discussed in detail below), had a surplus in every year between 1970 and 1984, whereas the remainder of manufacturing had a deficit in every year except 1975. Indeed, despite the fact that the high-technology sector produced only 16 percent of the value added by manufacturing in 1977, the high-technology trade surplus was more than sufficient to offset the trade deficit generated in the other manufacturing sectors (the offset resulting in a surplus for manufactured products as a whole) in six of the fifteen years.

Our purpose in this paper is to provide and test empirically an explanation for the difference in trade performance between the high-technology sector and the other sectors of U.S. manufacturing, and to consider the implications of our explanation for macroeconomic public policy. In the next section we propose a theoretical explanation for the difference in trade performance, an explanation based on two propositions: the Heckscher-Ohlin theory of international trade, and the theory of product life cycles. The first theory implies that a country should specialize in producing (and hence tend to export) those products that make intensive use of factors in abundance in that country. The second theory implies that the United States is relatively well endowed with factors that are used extensively in the manufacture of high-technology products (that is, products at an early stage in their life cycles). Perhaps the key such factor is highly educated (and highly skilled) labor. The theory of product life cycles states that young (high-technology) industries differ from mature (other) industries in a number of important respects, such as the capital-intensity of production, the skill distribution of employment, the age of the capital stock, and the growth rate of output.

In the third section of this paper we compare the relative skill endowments of the labor force in the United States and other developed countries. The fourth section discusses our data base and the definition of the high-technology sector that we employ. The fifth presents data on real output, the capital stock, and employment in the high-technology and other manufacturing sectors in the years 1960, 1970, and 1980. This evidence provides strong support for our proposed explanation, the policy implications of which are considered in the final section.

Table 1. U.S. Trade in High-Technology and Other Manufacturing Sectors: 1970–84 (in billions of constant 1972 dollars[a])

Year	High-Technology Sector[b]			Other Manufacturing Sectors		
	Exports	*Imports*	*Balance*	*Exports*	*Imports*	*Balance*
1970[c]	$11.26	$ 4.59	$ 6.67	$20.78	$24.93	$ −4.16
1971[c]	11.87	5.10	6.77	19.79	28.54	−8.75
1972[c]	11.90	6.30	5.60	21.80	33.70	−11.90
1973[c]	15.04	7.47	7.57	27.23	37.64	−10.40
1974	18.68	8.52	10.17	36.50	43.19	−6.69
1975	18.20	7.55	10.65	38.24	36.17	2.07
1976	19.34	9.97	9.37	38.99	42.62	−3.63
1977	19.49	10.92	8.57	37.77	47.55	−9.78
1978	22.93	13.34	9.59	39.58	57.63	−18.06
1979	26.39	13.76	12.63	47.68	58.96	−11.27
1980	30.40	15.52	14.88	53.24	58.39	−5.15
1981	30.60	17.12	13.49	51.46	59.14	−7.68
1982[c]	27.75	16.45	11.31	43.31	56.19	−12.88
1983[c]	27.70	18.97	8.73	37.11	60.32	−23.21
1984[c]	29.08	26.29	2.79	38.59	77.53	−38.94

Source: National Science Board (1985).

[a]GNP implicit price deflators were used to convert current dollars to constant 1972 dollars.

[b]U.S. Department of Commerce DOC-3 definitions (see text, fourth section).

[c]Data in this row are estimates.

Government policies that tend to increase the (relative) supply of highly educated and highly skilled workers should maintain or enhance the comparative advantage in high-technology products held by the United States.

A THEORETICAL EXPLANATION

The Heckscher-Ohlin theory of international trade is rooted in the classical (Ricardian) doctrine of comparative advantage. The simplest version of the theory postulates a world in which there are two countries (1 and 2) both capable of producing two products (A and B) using two factors of production (X and Y). Each country is endowed with fixed quantities of each of the two factors. Both factors of production are assumed to be immobile between the countries, but both products are freely tradable between the countries. The two countries are assumed to have access to the same technology (that is, the production functions for each product are identical across countries). The technologies for the two products differ with respect to their relative factor intensities: Cost minimization requires that, at given relative factor prices, product A employs a greater ratio of factor X to factor Y than product B. (In other words the marginal rate of technical substitution between X and Y differs between the products when relative factor employment is the same for the two products.) Both countries face the problem of deciding how to allocate their fixed supplies of each factor between the two products or industries so that the value of the national product is maximized. The basic Heckscher-Ohlin result is that each country will specialize in (devote its resources to) the production of the product that makes intensive use of the factor with which the country is relatively well endowed. Thus, if country 1 is relatively well endowed with factor X, it will specialize in producing product A (even if consumers in country 1 tend to prefer product B). By virtue of its relative factor endowments, country 1 (2) has a comparative advantage with respect to the production of product A (B).

If we are to invoke the Heckscher-Ohlin theory as a basis for explaining why the United States has a comparative trade advantage with respect to high-technology products, we need to establish that the country is relatively well endowed with factors that are used intensively in high-technology industries. According to the theory of product life cycles this is indeed the case. As the data presented in the next section demonstrate, high-technology products tend to be at early stages in their life cycles; they tend, at least, to be produced with capital and labor of recent vintage. The life-cycle theory posits that the nature (including relative factor-intensity) of the production *process* changes in a systematic fashion as a product ages. Early in a product's life cycle no single, dominant, well-defined production technology emerges. Although the rate of output is rapidly increasing, capital equipment especially designed to produce the product has yet to be developed or diffused on a large scale. Consequently, relatively limited capital investment has occurred, and capital intensity is low. Because the technology is not yet well defined, job tasks have not been routinized or standardized. The industry's labor force is still devoting a significant amount of its energies to designing and redesigning an appropriate production technology. Relatively highly educated and highly skilled employees are required to efficiently perform such problem-solving and unstructured work activities.

As the product (or industry) matures, a dominant technology does emerge. The industry makes large-scale investment in specialized, standardized capital equipment, and the production technology is increasingly capital intensive. As the industry's cumulative output rises, the rate of (and returns to) worker learning about the technology falls. Work becomes increasingly routinized and thus can be performed by workers of lower skill. Most of the opportunities for productivity improvement and cost reduction (due in part to "learning") have already been exploited, and so output eventually begins to decelerate or even decline.

This synopsis of the theory of product life-cycles suggests that the relative factor intensities—and, in particular, the skill intensities—of young and mature industries are very different, with the young industries requiring a more highly skilled and educated labor force.

THE RELATIVE SKILL ENDOWMENTS OF THE U.S. LABOR FORCE

Before proceeding with our analysis of the skill distributions of the high-technology and other manufacturing sectors that is based on the product-life-cycle hypothesis, we need to show that the skill endowments of the U.S. labor force differ from those in other countries. UNESCO has developed a system for standardizing international educational statistics that facilitates a comparative analysis of educational attainment in different countries. In particular, we show in Table 2 the percentage of the civilian labor force that has reached the "third level" of education in each of the 15 developed countries that UNESCO has studied. According to UNESCO, "Third level refers to education which requires as a minimum condition of admission the successful completion of education at the second level (which is defined as education received in a high school, secondary school, teachers training school, vocational or technical school). It can be given in different types of institutions such as universities, teacher training institutes, technical institutes, etc."[1]

Table 2 demonstrates that the skill endowment of the U.S. labor force is sharply higher than that of the other 14 developed countries. The percentage of the U.S. labor force that has reached the third level of education is more than double any of the other percentages shown. Hence, we can conclude that the United States is relatively well endowed in highly skilled labor and should therefore have a comparative advantage in the production of those products that use

Table 2. Percentage of 1980 Civilian Labor Force with "Third Level" of Education

Country	*Percentage with Third Level*
United States	11.3
Netherlands	5.3
Spain	5.3
Belgium	4.8
Sweden	4.7
Italy	4.7
West Germany	4.5
France	4.5
Japan	4.3
Denmark	4.0
Greece	3.5
Ireland	3.4
Portugal	2.2
United Kingdom	2.0
Luxembourg	—

Source: Eurostat Review, various issues, 1974–83, Statistical Office of the European Communities.

Notes: Third level is defined as in United Nations (1984, 1047–48); See the text. Luxembourg's percentage was less than 0.05.

this factor intensively. According to the product-life-cycle hypothesis, it is the high-technology sector that will be skilled-labor-intensive.

A DEFINITION OF THE HIGH-TECHNOLOGY SECTOR AND DATA

As stated in a recent staff report of the U.S. Department of Commerce (1985, 36), "The definition of what are 'high technology' products has long been controversial. It is generally agreed that a high technology product requires 'above average' concentrations of engineering and scientific skills and/or research and development expenditures." The report indicates that the better known definitions of high technology are based on the ratio of R & D expenditures to total sales. Davis (1982) includes in the numerator not only the R & D funds spent directly by final producers, but also the funds spent by producers of intermediate products that are used in the final product; all other authors, to our knowledge, have simply included the expenditures made by final producers. If an industry equals, or is above, some threshold ratio, the industry is counted as being part of the high-technology sector of the economy.[2] We follow this approach in defining the high-technology sector of manufacturing in the United States.

We have developed a data base comprising longitudinal data for an exhaustive classification of 61 manufacturing industries during the period 1960–80; the industries are listed in the appendix. We derived the data from a number of different but consistent sources (matched on the basis of industry designation).

The Industrial Analysis and Productivity Research Program (IAPRP) of the U.S. Department of Commerce has provided us with estimates of the number of employees in each industry (coded as in the appendix), cross-classified by age, educational attainment, and occupation for the years 1960, 1970, and 1980.[3] These data are based on the Census of Population for each of those years. The IAPRP also provided data on the stock of capital and the average age of the capital stock for each of the industries in 1960, 1970, and 1980; the capital stock can be distinguished between plant and equipment. For information on industry output we used the Census/SRI/Penn Database for the same years.

Time-series data on R & D expenditures are not available for the industry classification used in our data base. Fortunately, however, Scherer (1984) constructed a technology matrix that measures each industry's R & D expenditures in 1974. Using his figures we have computed the ratio of 1974 R & D expenditures to 1974 sales (which are listed in the Census/SRI/Penn Database) for each of the industries in our classification—the ratio we employ to distinguish between the high technology industries and the rest of the manufacturing sector. Four industries had a ratio in excess of .05; the remaining 57 each had a ratio significantly less than .05, and the mean for this group was .01. The four industries and their associated R & D/sales ratios are shown in Table 3. It is these industries that we argue compose the high-technology sector. We are confident that ours is a reasonable definition of the sector because each of the four industries shown in Table 3 was classified as being in the high-technology sector according to *all* of the definitions surveyed in the U.S. Department of Commerce staff report (1985, table V-3).

OUTPUT, CAPITAL, AND EMPLOYMENT TRENDS IN THE TWO SECTORS

The data on output, capital stock, and employment in the high-technology and other manufacturing sectors are remarkably consistent with the theoretical framework presented earlier. Beginning with Tables 4 and 5 we find several results that were predicted by the theory. Table 4 shows that in all three years—1960, 1970, and 1980—the capital/labor ratio in the high-technology industries was lower than that of the other manufacturing industries; their output per worker was lower; and their capital stock (both plant and equipment) was newer. Table 5 shows that real output, the capital/labor ratio, and output per worker all grew much more rapidly in the high-technology sector between 1960 and 1980 than in the other manufacturing industries.

More specifically, all of these findings are consistent with the proposition that

Table 3. R & D/Sales Ratios in the High-Technology Sector, 1974

Industry	*R & D/Sales Ratio*
1. Office, computing, and accounting machines (SIC 357)	.090
2. Optical, ophthalmic, and photographic equipment and supplies (SIC 383, 385, 386)	.062
3. Radio, television, and communication equipment (SIC 365 and 366)	.055
4. Electronic components and accessories (SIC 367)	.051

Sources: R & D data from Scherer (1984); sales data from Census/SRI/Penn Database.

the high-technology sector is in the early stages of the product life cycle, during which no single, well-defined production technology emerges. The rate of output is rapidly increasing, but capital equipment specially designed to produce the product has not yet been developed or widely diffused. Consequently, the capital stock is of recent vintage and capital intensity is low. Since technological change is embodied in the capital stock, the relative newness of capital in the high-technology sector indicates, not surprisingly, greater technological advancement in that sector.[4] The remarkably higher rate of growth in labor productivity in the high technology sector (143 percent between 1960 and 1980) than in the rest of manufacturing (60 percent in those years) is also explained by the product-life-cycle model because the more mature sector would be expected to have already exploited most of its opportunities for productivity improvement.

The data in Table 6 confirm that highly educated labor is, indeed, employed more intensively in the young, high-technology industries than in the mature industries in the rest of manufacturing. Table 6 shows the employment shares of workers in three different educational groups: (1) those with fewer than 12 years of schooling, (2) those with 13 to 15 years of schooling, and (3) those with 16 or more years of schooling. In 1960 the high-technology sector had a substantially larger proportion of workers with 13 to 15 years of schooling (47.0 percent) than the other manufacturing industries (35.9 percent) in the latter. The high-technology sector also had a larger share of workers with 16 or more years of education than the other manufacturing industries: 10.5 percent versus 6.1 percent. Between 1960 and 1970 both sectors showed increases in the employment shares of the 13–15 and the 16+ groups, with substantial decreases in the share held by the 12− group. This, of course, is a reflection of the increase in the educational attainment of the U.S. labor force that took place during that decade.[5]

What is important to note, however, is that the high-technology industries showed a much more dramatic increase in the employment share of the 16+ group than did the other manufacturing industries. Between 1960 and 1970 the employment share of this group rose by 41 percent in the high-technology sector

Table 4. Labor, Capital, and Output in the Two Manufacturing Sectors, 1960, 1970, and 1980

Year / *Manufacturing Sector*	*Employment (in millions)* (1)	*Real Capital Stock (billions of 1972 dollars)* (2)	*Real Output (billions of 1972 dollars)* (3)	*Capital/Labor Ratio (2)/(1)* (4)	*Output Per Worker (3)/(1)* (5)	*Mean Age of Plant* (6)	*Mean Age of Equipment* (7)
1960							
High-technology industries	1.08	5.79	15.98	5.36	14.79	9.61	5.95
Other manufacturing industries	17.53	186.6	452.20	10.64	25.80	12.76	7.20
1970							
High-technology industries	1.62	13.65	39.87	8.43	24.61	9.78	5.40
Other manufacturing industries	19.50	265.21	630.38	13.60	32.33	12.93	6.90
1980							
High-technology industries	2.04	24.87	73.24	12.19	35.90	11.68	5.77
Other manufacturing industries	20.19	357.95	833.47	17.73	41.28	14.47	6.92

Table 5. Percentage Growth in Labor, Capital, and Output Measures, 1960–80

Years *Manufacturing Sector*	*Employment* *(1)*	*Real Capital Stock* *(2)*	*Real Output* *(3)*	*Capital/Labor Ratio* *(4)*	*Output Per Worker* *(5)*
1960–70					
High-technology	.50	1.36	1.49	.57	.66
Other	.11	.42	.39	.28	.25
1970–80					
High-technology	.26	.82	.84	.45	.46
Other	.035	.35	.32	.30	.27
1960–80					
High technology	.89	3.30	3.58	1.27	1.43
Other	.15	.92	.84	.67	.60

Note: The percentage growth is calculated with initial year of each period as the base.

and by only 20 percent in the rest of manufacturing, which implies that most people with college degrees or better who entered the labor force during the 1960s went to work in the high-technology sector. The picture by 1980 was one of a labor force in the high-technology sector that was substantially better educated than the labor force in the rest of manufacturing. Fully 20 percent of workers in high technology had at least a college degree in 1980, whereas only 11 percent of the workers in the rest of manufacturing did. At the other end of the spectrum only 18 percent of the high-technology workers had fewer than 12 years of

Table 6. Employment Shares by Years of Education, 1960, 1970, and 1980

	Years of Education		
Years *Manufacturing Sector*	*12 or Fewer*	*13–15*	*16 or More*
1960			
High-technology	.425	.470	.105
Other	.580	.359	.061
1970			
High-technology	.287	.565	.148
Other	.465	.461	.073
1980			
High-technology	.180	.617	.203
Other	.310	.577	.113

schooling, whereas almost one-third of the workers in the rest of manufacturing fell into this category. This is precisely what the theory of product life cycles would predict. Since technology in the younger sector is not yet well developed, the firms in the sector require relatively greater numbers of well-educated employees to design and rework the technology.

Finally Table 7 shows the employment shares of eight major occupational groups in the two manufacturing sectors. The occupational distributions in the two sectors closely mirror the educational distributions we have just discussed. Note that in each of the three years the employment share of professional and technical workers in the high-technology sector was roughly 2.5 times larger than it was in the rest of manufacturing. A very interesting fact is that the clerical occupations accounted for a larger proportion of jobs in the high-technology sector than they did in the rest of manufacturing in all three years. It appears that less educated individuals are more likely to hold clerical positions if they are in the high-technology sector than if they are in the other sector. This result is consistent with the fact that the high-technology sector has a larger proportion of female workers than the rest of manufacturing. Our data show that the proportion of jobs held by women in high technology was .31 in 1960, .34 in 1970, and .39 in 1980; the comparable figures for the other manufacturing sector are .25, .27, and .31.

PUBLIC POLICY IMPLICATIONS

Large and growing trade deficits constitute one of the most serious problems confronting the U.S. economy, representing a threat to prosperity and economic growth. Within U.S. manufacturing only the high-technology sector has managed consistently to show trade surpluses since 1970, but these have, however, declined since 1980. We have argued that comparative advantage in high-technology products held by the United States in world markets is based to an important extent on this country's being relatively well endowed with highly educated workers.

The high average educational attainment of the U.S. labor force is not entirely fortuitous, however. It is partly a consequence of governmental policies (such as support of state universities, the GI Bill, and National Defense Student Loans) to subsidize the acquisition of higher education. In the current era of budgetary austerity, governmental support for higher education is no longer as secure as it once was. Indeed, some policy makers have called for reduced public support for higher education.

The arguments and evidence presented in this paper imply that changes in public policy with respect to financial aid to education may eventually affect the competitiveness of U.S. high-technology industries. Reductions in governmental subsidies to education would increase the private cost to individuals of acquiring education and hence the relative price (wage rate) of highly educated workers.

Table 7. Employment Shares by Occupation, 1960, 1970, and 1980

Year *Manufacturing Sector*	*Professional and Technical Workers*	*Managers*	*Craft Workers*	*Operatives*	*Service Workers*	*Laborers*	*Clerical Workers*	*Sales Workers*
1960								
High-technology	.173	.050	.170	.387	.014	.018	.165	.022
Other	.072	.052	.203	.436	.018	.061	.117	.041
1970								
High-technology	.226	.060	.151	.349	.021	.020	.153	.019
Other	.088	.053	.198	.433	.024	.049	.121	.034
1980								
High-technology	.234	.093	.176	.272	.017	.025	.156	.026
Other	.093	.071	.213	.378	.023	.070	.121	.031

All industries would be affected by such a price increase to a certain extent, but because they employ a disproportionate number of highly educated workers the high-technology industries would be affected the most.

Acceptance of the notion that governmental subsidies to education tend to enhance the competitive posture of high-technology industries, and thereby U.S. export performance, does not necessarily mean we should support very large government budgets for education. The enhanced competitiveness of high-technology industries may be one of the benefits of greater educational attainment, but education is obviously a costly activity. The optimal rate of investment in education is the rate at which the marginal benefits of education (which include the greater productivity of highly educated workers) equal the marginal costs. The theories and data presented in this paper do not in themselves justify a claim that the United States is investing in education at less than the optimal rate and therefore the government should increase subsidies to education. In fact, a case could be made that most or all of the benefits of acquiring an education are appropriated by the recipient (in the form of higher wages), and therefore little or no public subsidy is required to promote an efficient rate of educational investment.

Although our analysis does not enable us to determine whether the current level of government support of education is inadequate or excessive, we think it does enable us to make predictions about the effects of changes in subsidies to education on the competitiveness of U.S. high-technology industries. Because, as we have argued, education and technological innovations are, loosely speaking, complementary, reductions in government subsidies to education are likely, in the long run, to erode the basis for the comparative advantage the United States enjoys in the production of high-technology products. We believe that policy makers engaged in debate about the size of education budgets should be aware of this linkage.

Appendix. Description of Industries, by 1972 Standard Industrial Classification Codes

	Sector Title	*1972 SIC Code*
1.	Food and kindred products	20
2.	Tobacco manufacturers	21
3.	Broad and narrow fabrics, yarn, and thread mills	221, 222, 223, 224, 226, 228
4.	Miscellaneous textile goods and floor coverings	227, 229
5.	Knitting mills	225
6.	Apparel	231, 232, 233, 234, 235, 236, 237, 238
7.	Miscellaneous fabricated textile products	239
8.	Lumber and wood products, except containers	241, 242, 243, 249
9.	Wood buildings and mobile homes	2451, 2452
10.	Wood containers	244

(*continued*)

Appendix. (*continued*)

11.	Household furniture	251
12.	Other furniture and fixtures	252, 253, 254, 259
13.	Paper and allied products, except containers, boxes, and paper mills, but including building paper	261, 263, 264, 266
14.	Paper mills, except building paper	262
15.	Paperboard containers and boxes	265
16.	Printing and publishing	27
17.	Chemicals and selected chemical products, except nitrogenous and phosphatic fertilizers, fertilizers (mixing only), and agricultural chemicals	281, 286, 289
18.	Nitrogenous and phosphatic fertilizers, fertilizers (mixing only) and agricultural chemicals not elsewhere classified	287
19.	Plastic and synthetic materials	282
20.	Drugs, cleaning and toilet preparations	283, 284
21.	Paints and allied products	285
22.	Petroleum refining	291
23.	Miscellaneous products of petroleum and coal	299
24.	Paving and roofing materials	295
25.	Rubber and miscellaneous plastics products	30
26.	Leather tanning and finishing	311
27.	Footwear and other leather products	313, 314, 315, 316, 317, 319
28.	Glass and glass products	321, 322, 323
29.	Cement, hydraulic	324
30.	Stone and clay products, except hydraulic cement	325, 326, 327, 328, 329
31.	Blast furnaces, steel works, and rolling and finishing mills	331
32.	Iron and steel foundries, forgings, and miscellaneous metal products	332, 339
33.	Primary nonferrous metals	333, 334, 335, 336
34.	Metal containers	341
35.	Heating, plumbing, and fabricated structural metal products	343, 344
36.	Screw machine products	345
37.	Metal stampings	346
38.	Other fabricated metal products	342, 347, 349
39.	Ordnance and accessories, except vehicles and guided missiles	348
40.	Engines and turbines	351
41.	Farm and garden machinery	352
42.	Constructing and mining machinery	3531, 3532, 3533, 3795
43.	Materials handling machinery and equipment	3534, 3535, 3536, 3537
44.	Metalworking machinery and equipment	354
45.	Special industry machinery and equipment	355
46.	General industrial machinery and equipment	356
47.	Miscellaneous machinery, except electrical	359
48.	Office, computing, and accounting machines	357
49.	Service industry machines	358

(*continued*)

Appendix. (*continued*)

50.	Electrical transmission and distribution equipment and industrial appliances	361, 362
51.	Household appliances	363
52.	Electrical lighting and wiring equipment	364
53.	Radio, television and communication equipment	365, 366
54.	Electronic components and accessories	367
55.	Miscellaneous electrical machinery, equipment, and supplies	369
56.	Motor vehicles and equipment	371
57.	Aircraft and parts	372, 376
58.	Other transportation equipment	373, 374, 375, 379 (exc. 3795)
59.	Professional, scientific, and controlling instruments and supplies	381, 382, 384, 387
60.	Optical, ophthalmic, and photographic equipment and supplies	383, 385, 386
61.	Miscellaneous manufacturing equipment	39

NOTES

1. This is discussed further in United Nations (1984, 1047–48).

2. Belous (1985) discusses another approach to defining the high-technology sector, namely, making qualitative judgments about the nature of the goods or services produced by the industry or about the actual production technology employed by the industry.

3. For a description of the data base created by the Industrial Analysis and Productivity Research Program, see Mohr (1980).

4. This confirms the validity of the R & D/sales ratio as the appropriate measure for distinguishing the high-technology sector from the rest of manufacturing.

5. In 1960, 50 percent of the U.S. labor force had fewer than 12 years of schooling; 40 percent had 13 to 15 years; and 9.6 percent had 16 or more years. By 1970 the distribution had changed to 34.8 percent, 52.3 percent and 12.9 percent, respectively (U.S. Department of Labor 1985, 164).

REFERENCES

American Federation of Labor–Congress of Industrial Organizations. 1986. *The National Economy and Trade: AFL-CIO Policy Recommendations for 1986*. Washington, DC: AFL-CIO.

Belous, Richard. 1985. High Technology Labor Markets: Projections and Policy Implications, paper presented at UCLA Institute of Industrial Relations Symposium, "Human Resources and Industrial Relations in High Technology Firms," June 21.

Davis, Lester A. 1982. Technology Intensity of U.S. Output and Trade, photocopy. Washington, DC: Office of Trade and Investment Analysis, International Trade Administration, U.S. Department of Commerce, July.

Kochan, Thomas A., and Thomas A. Barocci. 1985. *Human Resource Management and Industrial Relations: Text, Readings and Cases*. Boston: Little, Brown.

Mohr, Michael F. 1980. An Introduction to the Industrial Analysis and Productivity Research Program of the Bureau of Industrial Economics, BIE staff paper BIE-SP80-1. Washington, DC: U.S. Department of Commerce, November.

National Science Board. 1985. *Science Indicators: The 1985 Report*. Washington, DC: GPO.

Scherer, Frederic M. 1984. Using Linked Patent and R & D Data to Measure Interindustry Technology Flows, in Zvi Griliches (ed.) *R & D, Patents, and Productivity*. Chicago: University of Chicago Press.

Statistical Office of the European Communities, *Eurostat Review*, various issues, 1974–83.

United Nations. 1984. *1982 Statistical Yearbook*. New York: United Nations.

U.S. Department of Commerce, International Trade Administration. 1985. U.S. High Technology Trade and Competitiveness, staff report DIE-01-85. Washington, DC: GPO, February.

U.S. Department of Labor, Bureau of Labor Statistics. 1985. *Handbook of Labor Statistics*. Washington, DC: GPO.

WOMEN IN THE AUTOMATED OFFICE:

COMPUTERS, WORK, AND PROSPECTS FOR UNIONIZATION

Daniel B. Cornfield

According to the postindustrial thesis the decline in U.S. unionism since 1945 can be attributed to the aversion to unionization of women and white-collar workers and to unions' de-emphasis in targeting these groups in their organizing campaigns. Bell (1953, 1972, 1973) claimed that as white-collar workers—the majority in the labor force—have become increasingly employed in the service sector, while the declining blue-collar manufacturing sector has become saturated with union members, the percentage unionized has fallen because the labor movement is unable to organize women and white-collar workers. In accounting for these workers' aversion to unionization, the postindustrial thesis assumes the persistence of the traditional role of women in the workplace and the relatively privileged social status of white-collar workers. Female workers who harbor traditional attitudes toward their role are assumed to lack both a long-term career orientation and, consequently, an interest in unionization. White-collar workers,

Advances in Industrial and Labor Relations, Volume 4, pages 177-198.

ISBN: 0-89232-909-2

given their superior social status, are assumed to dissociate themselves from institutions, such as unions, they perceive as comprising their status inferiors.

During the 1970s and early 1980s, however, unions have made some inroads in organizing women and white-collar workers, and the percentage unionized among these groups has increased (LeGrande 1978; Gifford 1982; Kokkelenberg and Sockell 1985). Moreover, opinion research shows that nonunion, female workers are more likely than their male counterparts to favor unionization and that no gender difference in pro-union attitudes prevails among nonunion, white- or blue-collar workers when other causal variables are controlled (Kochan 1979; Freeman and Medoff 1984, 28).

These changes may suggest that the gender roles and social class of these workers, which, according to the postindustrial thesis, had impeded their unionization, have also begun to change—that new forces have begun to encourage the unionization of women and white-collar workers. It is the thesis of this chapter that these new forces include the implementation of office automation with computerized, bureaucratic managerial controls, especially among the clerical occupations that have been filled primarily by female workers. These forces also include the labor movement's growing efforts to replenish its dwindling membership by organizing female clerical workers, among others.

The purpose of this chapter is therefore to analyze the sociological conditions that influence the potential for unionization among female clerical workers. More specifically, I will discuss the conditions that motivate, facilitate, and inhibit unionization among these workers. After discussing theories of white-collar unionism and the factors that have promoted and inhibited the unionization of female clerical workers, I turn to an analysis of unionization among clerical workers in the insurance industry.

I chose to examine the insurance industry for three reasons, which are elaborated in greater detail below. First, the insurance labor force has a disproportionately large number of female clerical workers and a sufficiently high degree of occupational segregation by gender to facilitate an analysis of unionization among female clerical workers. Second, as a growing service industry that has pioneered the application of office automation, insurance may be archetypical of changing work conditions in postindustrial society—conditions that promote unionization among female clerical workers. Third, and as a result, female clerical workers in insurance, and in the financial sector as a whole, have been the objects of joint union-organizing efforts by the women's movement and the labor movement. Therefore, the unionization of women clerical workers in insurance constitutes an unusual form of unionism—one based on occupation and gender.

THEORIES OF WHITE-COLLAR UNIONISM

The postindustrial thesis rests on a decreasingly tenable assumption about white-collar workers as a social class. The thesis assumes that white-collar workers' position in the social structure is fixed and that white-collar workers' aversion to unionization stems from their relatively privileged socioeconomic standing, their identification with management, and their desire to remain apart from institutions they associate with their blue-collar inferiors in the social structure (Kassalow 1966). But theories of white-collar unionization in the United States and Great Britain, as well as theories of unionization generally, assume that social standing is not fixed but dynamic. The classical Marxian and functional theories of unionization held that industrialization and the rise of the large corporation in a market economy with a new class of tenuously employed, urban, factory wage earners simultaneously alienated these workers, shaped their common interest, and prompted them to unionize (Marx 1847; Tannenbaum 1951).

Similarly, theories of white-collar unionism suggest that white-collar unionization not only is *motivated* by decline in the socioeconomic standing of white-collar workers, but also is *facilitated* by aggressive union-organizing campaigns and *inhibited* by employer resistance to unionization (Lockwood 1958; Blackburn 1967; Kassalow 1966; Bain 1970; Adams 1975; Prandy, Stewart, and Blackburn 1983). Two forces that lower the socioeconomic standing of white-collar workers are bureaucratization and office automation. Both are common in large firms, and both deskill many white-collar jobs, especially clerical jobs, and engender centralized, impersonal managerial control of the nonsupervisory work force (Bain 1970; Whisler 1970; Braverman 1974; Hoos 1961; Glenn and Feldberg 1977; Kraft 1977; Greenbaum 1979). Numerous authors have suggested that as bureaucratization and technological change reduce the socioeconomic standing of some white-collar workers, those workers become more predisposed toward unionization (Lockwood 1958; Kassalow 1966; Bain 1970; Coleman and Rose 1975; Miller 1981-82).

The post–World War II decline in U.S. unionization, especially among the blue-collar manufacturing labor force, has turned the attention of many unions to just these workers: the growing numbers of white-collar workers in the service industries. Thus, in their recently expanded efforts to organize white-collar workers, these unions are serving to facilitate the growth of white-collar unionization. At the same time, however, organizing drives, and unionization in general, are meeting diverse forms of stepped-up employer resistance to unionization. These include employers' increasing adoption of paternalistic managerial practices, union-scale wages and benefits, and employee complaint systems that mirror union grievance systems, as well as the growing use of anti-union management consultants (Cornfield 1986).

Although the "dynamic" theories of white-collar unionism emphasize the changing social status of workers, they neglect the effects of the changing role of women in the workplace. The classical theories explained unionization in the era of the Industrial Revolution, when most wage earners were men, craft unions often denied women membership, and most class conflict occurred almost exclusively among men (Kessler-Harris 1975, 1982; Cook 1984). This is not to deny the early involvement of women in the U.S. labor movement, as exemplified, for example, by the establishment of the National Women's Trade Union League in the early twentieth century (Wertheimer 1977; Foner 1979, 1980; Dye 1980). These theories, however, *implicitly* assume that women functioned in their traditional gender role: outside of the labor force, and not directly engaged in class conflict.

By 1980, however, women had come to account for 53 percent of both white-collar workers and white-collar union members (U.S. Department of Labor 1983; Gifford 1982). Social, economic, and legal changes in the 1960s and 1970s were responsible: the renewal of the women's movement; inflation and declining real earnings in the 1970s, which compelled many women to enter the labor force on a full-time basis; and the Civil Rights Act of 1964, the Equal Employment Opportunity Act of 1972, the Comprehensive Employment and Training Act of 1973, and other legislation, which facilitated the full-time entry of women into the labor force by banning sex discrimination by employers and by providing training to disadvantaged women (Appelbaum 1981). By 1983 the labor force participation rates of married women between the ages of 20 and 44 and between the ages of 45 and 64 increased to all-time highs of about 64 percent and 48 percent, respectively (Appelbaum 1981; U.S. Department of Labor 1985).

Unionization assumes that union members have a long-term, vested interest in their jobs. In Hirschman's (1970) terms unionization allows the worker to express dissatisfaction not by "exit" from the workplace but by "voice" (Freeman and Medoff 1984).

The postindustrial thesis assumed that women, as temporary wage earners constrained by their traditional gender roles, were likely to quit employment upon marriage and therefore were unlikely to unionize (Kassalow 1966). But the increased labor force participation rate of married women, including those with small children, suggests that the same factors causing that increase may also be causing an increase in the numbers of female union members and an increasingly pro-union attitude among women (Tepperman 1976; Cook 1984; Wertheimer 1984).

Thus, changing gender roles may be increasing the pool of organizable white-collar workers, while the declining social status of some of these workers may be increasing white-collar unionization (Lockwood 1958:151-153). Let us turn now to the conditions that are motivating, facilitating, and inhibiting the unionization of female clerical workers.

CLERICAL WORKER UNIONIZATION

Motivators

Historical research on clerical work shows that office clerical work shifted from a craftlike organization toward a bureaucratic, factorylike organization beginning in the late nineteenth century (Mills 1956; Lockwood 1958; Benet 1972; Braverman 1974; Glenn and Feldberg 1977, 1979a, 1979b; McNally 1979;

Rotella 1981; Davies 1982; Fox and Hess-Biber 1984). In the small, nineteenth century office, the clerical worker was responsible for a variety of tasks. Clerks performed minor managerial and administrative functions and were often consulted on financial decisions. With industrialization and the emergence of the large corporation characterized by a salaried, managerial class (Chandler 1977), the division of labor in clerical work became more complex, the work itself became less skilled, and clerical occupations became more specialized. Furthermore, many large companies introduced scientific management techniques in the early twentieth century to rationalize office procedures as the volume of paperwork increased (Braverman 1974).

Also spurring office bureaucratization were changes in office technology. The typewriter appeared in the late 1800s, and the office computer first appeared in the private sector in the 1950s. These technological changes also increased the complexity of the division of labor in clerical work by spawning new, still lesser skilled occupations such as typists, stenographers, computer operators, and data entry operators.

Thus, the present-day clerical organization evolved from a quasi-managerial and craftlike form to one in which nonmanagerial, low-skilled clerical occupations make up a skill and status hierarchy that ranges from the executive's personal secretary to a pool of typists, file clerks, and office machine operators (Kanter 1977; Glenn and Feldberg 1977; Baker 1964; Machung 1984). As offices grew in size over the twentieth century, the chasm between managerial and clerical occupations widened; and in the post–World War II era managers have implemented increasingly impersonal techniques for controlling and monitoring clerical work and productivity, such as counting keystrokes per minute (Glenn and Feldberg 1977, 1979a, 1979b).

Two changes in the characteristics of clerical workers accompanied the bureaucratization of clerical work. First was the feminization of clerical workers. Nineteenth century clerical workers were predominantly men; women did not constitute a majority of clerical workers until 1930 (Rotella 1981, 26). Feminization resulted from cultural values that served to allocate the lowest skilled, nonmanagerial jobs to women. In the context of those values office bureaucratization led to occupational segregation by gender between the growing number of technical and managerial jobs and the growing number of new, less skilled clerical occupations in the early decades of this century (Kanter 1977).

The second change in clerical workers was in their social class origins. In the nineteenth century clerical workers were primarily sons of white-collar workers or farmers (Davies 1982). In her classic study of the intergenerational occupational mobility of Indianapolis men in 1910, Rogoff (1953) showed that 58 percent of male clerical workers were sons of white-collar or farming fathers, while the remainder were sons of fathers who held blue-collar or service jobs. In one of the few studies of intergenerational occupational mobility among female clerical workers in the 1800s, Aron (1981) showed that well over two-thirds of the women who applied for U.S. Treasury Department clerical jobs between 1862 and 1890, as well as those who were hired, were daughters of white-collar fathers. By 1962, however, a majority of clerical workers were from working-class origins. In 1962, 53 percent of married, female clerical workers were daughters of fathers who held blue-collar or service jobs (Hauser and Featherman 1977, 339); in the years 1974–77, 52 percent of female clerical workers were daughters of fathers who held blue-collar or service jobs (Roos 1985, 186).

In sum, office bureaucratization and automation, in a culture that promoted occupational segregation by gender, not only led to the feminization of clerical work but also to an increase in the proportion of clerical workers from working-class origins. The so-called proletarianization of clerical work (Glenn and Feldberg 1977)—the deskilling of clerical work—coupled with an increase in impersonal managerial control, changed the composition of clerical ranks to include women from working-class origins.

Facilitators

Clerical unionization has been facilitated by the recently expanded labor movement to organize clerical workers. Until recently, the predominantly male labor movement had neglected women and clerical workers in its organizing campaigns because it viewed both groups as unorganizable and as only temporary, or secondary, workers (Goldberg 1983; Seidman 1978; Cook 1984). But with the decline in male, blue-collar union membership, increased women's labor force participation, and the resurgence of the women's movement in the 1970s, the labor movement began to look to organizing female clerical workers as a means to replenish its sagging membership. Union organizers have made financial industries, such as insurance and banking, the particular targets of their drives; it is in these industries that clerical work has been particularly routinized by bureaucratization and office automation.

At roughly the same time the women's movement was developing organizations within and alongside the labor movement to promote the unionization of women, and female clerical workers specifically. In 1974 female trade unionists established the Coalition of Labor Union Women (CLUW) to achieve these ends as well as women's access to union leadership positions (Foner 1980). Beginning in 1972 with the founding of 9 to 5 by ten women in Boston, women's movement activists have established several working women's organizations that engage in litigation and educational activities on behalf of female workers, as well as joint organizing efforts with labor unions (Koziara and Insley 1982; Foner 1980; Goldberg 1983; Burton 1985). In 1981, 9 to 5 and the Service Employees' International Union created District 925, an autonomous local of the union, expressly for the purpose of organizing female clerical workers, especially in the financial sector (Miller 1981–82). Other unions that have organized female clerical workers include the Office and Professional Employees International Union, the

Teamsters, and the United Food and Commercial Workers (Miller 1981–82; Kilgour 1982). In 1985 the AFL-CIO launched a five-union, nationwide organizing campaign at Blue Cross and Blue Shield, targeting its efforts at clerical workers in particular (Pollock 1985).

Published time-series data on the unionization of female clerical workers are unavailable. Milkman (1980, 121) estimated, however, that 3 percent of female clerical workers were unionized in 1920. By 1980, 12.2 percent of female clerical workers were union members (Gifford 1982, 51). Recent research on clerical worker unionization has attributed that increase to women's growing participation in the labor force, the transformation of clerical work described above, and the expansion of union-organizing efforts among clerical workers (Goldberg 1983; Coleman and Rose 1975; Kilgour 1982; Miller 1981–82; Tepperman 1976).

Inhibitors

A key force inhibiting clerical unionization is the status hierarchy among clerical occupations. Typically, the higher echelon clerical workers are personal secretaries who are isolated from one another and have frequent, personal contact with their bosses. Kanter referred to this boss-subordinate relationship as bureaucratic patrimony. Patrimony, according to Kanter (1977, 74–89), consists of three elements: status contingency, principled arbitrariness, and fealty. Under patrimony, the status of the secretary is contingent on that of her boss. With no clerical job descriptions the boss arbitrarily assigns her work-related and personal tasks, expects her to maintain, in Kanter's words, his front, and evaluates her performance with particularistic criteria. Status contingency and arbitrariness engender fealty between the boss and secretary because of their mutual dependence. The secretary's status as an employee depends on her personal rapport with the boss, while the boss depends on the secretary to maintain his front. On the other hand, lower echelon clerical workers, such as file clerks and office machine operators, have infrequent, impersonal, bureaucratic relations with management, develop little fealty, and are, therefore, more likely to unionize than personal secretaries (Lockwood 1958; Kanter 1977).

Gifford's (1982, 51) unionization data for women in broadly defined clerical occupations suggest that unionization has developed unevenly in the occupational hierarchy of clerical work. Among lower echelon, female clerical workers, 13 percent of office machine operators and 16.1 percent of other clerical workers (excluding secretaries, typists, stenographers, and bookkeepers) were unionized in 1980. Among higher echelon, female clerical workers, only 8.6 percent of secretaries-typists-stenographers (about 80 percent of the women in this category were secretaries in 1980; U.S. Department of Labor 1983, 50–51), and 4.5 percent of bookkeepers were unionized. Thus, the clerical hierarchy seems to have promoted unionization among the lower echelon clerical workers who experience infrequent, impersonal contact with management (Prandy, Stewart, and Blackburn 1983), whereas it has inhibited unionization among clerical workers employed in patrimonial settings.

In sum, the transformation of clerical work and clerical workers has given rise to an exceptional form of unionism—one defined by occupation *and* gender—that has only a few rough parallels, namely, in unions of flight attendants, nurses, and the needle trades. Clerical unions, as noted earlier, have made their most extensive and publicized inroads in the finance sector, particular in insurance; and for that reason unionization in insurance is of interest as being at the frontier of clerical organizing in general.

CLERICAL WORKER UNIONIZATION IN THE INSURANCE INDUSTRY

Insurance industry unionization has historically been low. According to Kokkelenberg and Sockell (1985) approximately 4 percent to 5 percent of the insurance labor force was unionized between 1974 and 1980. Insurance unionization has mainly been concentrated among insurance sales agents in the large insurance companies. Since the late nineteenth century several unions have succeeded in organizing these primarily male agents, including the Insurance Agents International Union (AFL), the Insurance Workers of America (CIO), the Insurance Workers International Union (AFL-CIO) (which later merged with the United Food and Commercial Workers), and the Office and Professional Employees International Union (Clermont 1966). Nonetheless, wage surveys of the life insurance industry indicate that office worker unionization increased only slightly, from 2 percent to almost 5 percent, between 1961 and 1980 (U.S. Department of Labor 1962, 1967, 1973, 1978, 1981).

Motivators

Four conditions in the insurance industry have motivated unionization among female clerical workers. First, throughout the post–World War II era female and male insurance workers tended to be segregated in different occupations, as shown in Table 1. Although by 1980 women had made inroads into the professional, managerial, and agent occupations, they accounted for less than half of all professionals and less than a third of all managers and agents (see columns 1 and 2). In both 1950 and 1980 women accounted for almost 85 percent of all clerical employees in general and for almost all secretaries, typists, and stenographers. The data in columns 3 through 6 of Table 1 show that in both years, over 70 percent of all women employed in the industry were clerical workers, whereas over 75 percent of all men in the industry were employed in the professional, managerial, and insurance agent categories. By 1980 the nonclerical occupations had begun to employ a greater percentage of the women in the industry, but the clerical occupations continued to be predominantly female. For many clerical workers in insurance, therefore, mobility into higher paying positions is blocked, causing them to look to unions to help them obtain improvements in their promotion opportunities.

Second, bureaucratization and technological change in the form of office automation accompanied insurance industry growth since the end of the Second World War. According to the Bureau of Labor Statistics insurance was "a major white-collar industry which pioneered in the application of office automation" (U.S. Department of Labor 1966, iii). In the 1950s large insurance companies began to introduce computers in their offices to handle the growing volume of paperwork and to reduce clerical labor costs (U.S. Department of Labor 1960,

Table 1. The Percentage of Women and the Percentage Distribution of Female and Male Employees in Occupations in the Insurance Industry, 1950 and 1980 (raw numbers, in thousands, in parentheses)

	Women as % of All Employees in the Occupation		*Women in the Occupation as a % of All Women Employed in the Industry*		*Men in the Occupation as a % of All Men Employed in the Industry*	
Occupation	*1950 (1)*	*1980 (2)*	*1950 (3)*	*1980 (4)*	*1950 (5)*	*1980 (6)*
Professionals	21.4% (28)[a]	46.5% (158)	1.8%	6.8%	5.3%	10.3%
Managers	15.5 (73)	29.2 (197)	3.4	5.3	14.6	16.9
Insurance agents[a]	8.7 (290)	25.7 (558)	7.6	13.3	63.1	50.4
Clerical workers	84.7 (333)	84.2 (932)	85.1	72.5	12.2	17.9
Secretaries, typists, and stenographers	97.1 (140)	99.1 (292)	40.9	26.8	1.0	0.3
Other clerical	75.7 (194)	77.3 (639)	44.2	45.7	11.2	17.6
Other	25.8 (27)	37.5 (59)	2.1	2.0	4.8	4.5
Total	44.2 (751)	56.7 (1,905)	100.0 (332)	99.9[b] (1,081)	100.0 (419)	100.0 (824)

Source: U.S. Department of Commerce (1954, 1984).

[a]Includes agents, brokers, and underwriters.

[b]The total does not equal 100 because of rounding.

10). Use of the computer rapidly diffused throughout the industry to even the smaller companies by the early 1970s (Cornfield et al. 1984). The companies have applied computers to a variety of clerical and nonclerical insurance functions, including billing, actuarial research, underwriting, and premium and commission calculation (U.S. Department of Labor 1979).

Scholarly accounts suggest that three organizational changes accompanied office automation in the insurance industry. The first is centralization of managerial control over the clerical work force. In their studies of the introduction of office automation in insurance, Whisler (1970) and Helfgott (1966) documented that decision making became more centralized, supervisory jobs were enlarged, and clerical jobs became more routinized. Second, management invoked impersonal controls over clerical workers by adopting quantifiable and machine-measured indicators of clerical work quality and clerical worker productivity (Whisler 1970; Costello 1983; Working Women 1980). Other impersonal control systems, such as ''advanced office controls'' and ''analysis for improved methods,'' consist of standardized methods, predetermined in time-motion studies, for performing clerical tasks; these are widely used in the insurance industry (Wiemann 1979; Nolan 1980). Third, the computer and advanced telecommunications systems have furthered departmental consolidation and control of the home office over branch offices (U.S. Department of Labor 1966, 1979; U.S. Department of Commerce 1983). In short, office automation has increased bureaucratization, brought clerical workers under stricter, more impersonal managerial control, and reduced the amount of employee discretion in some clerical jobs. To regain discretion in their work and in setting workplace rules, clerical workers in insurance have begun to turn to unionization.

The third condition motivating clerical unionization in the industry has been the changing occupational structure of clerical work. Clerical occupations may be classified by four categories: (1) Interpersonal occupations—secretaries, information clerks (mainly receptionists), and adjusters and investigators—demand that the job holder have frequent encounters with other people, such as customers, other employees, business associates, and managers. As the terms imply, (2) computer-related occupations and (3) noncomputer office machine occupations require operators to tend machines, and (4) manual occupations require workers to perform manual clerical tasks.

As shown in Table 2 between 1970 and 1980 employment in interpersonal and computer occupations increased absolutely at a higher rate than that in nonsupervisory, clerical employment. Employment in the noncomputer office machine and manual occupations declined absolutely during the 1970s, with the exception of bookkeepers and mail and material recording, scheduling, and distributing clerks. Thus, while office automation, bureaucratization, and the industry itself grew over the 1970s, the share of interpersonal and computer occupations in the insurance labor force also grew, while the share of noncomputer office machine operators and manual clerks declined, engendering job security fears and a growing desire to unionize.

Table 2. Percentage Distribution of Employment in Nonsupervisory, Clerical Occupations in the Insurance Industry, 1970 and 1980

Occupational Category/Occupation	*1970*	*1980*	*% Change, 1970–80*
Interpersonal	43.8%	47.7%	+42.4%
Secretaries	26.0	26.2	+32.0
Information clerks	1.1	2.0	+130.0
Adjusters and investigators	16.7	19.5	+52.7
Computers	4.4	6.1	+83.1
Computer and peripheral equipment operators	1.1	2.6	+216.6
Data-entry operators	3.3	3.5	+38.7
Noncomputer office machines	1.6*	1.1	−6.9
Duplicating, mail, and other office machine operators	0.9	0.6	−9.8
Communications equipment operators	0.6	0.5	−2.7
Manual	36.8*	23.4*	−16.8
Typists and stenographers	15.4	8.2	−30.0
Statistical clerks	4.8	1.0	−72.0
Bookkeepers	7.2	6.5	+17.6
File clerks	7.0	4.3	−19.3
Mail and material recording, scheduling, and distributing clerks	2.3	3.3	+85.3
Other	13.4	21.7	+111.6
Total	100.0%	100.0%	+30.9
N	648,000	848,000	—

Source: U.S. Department of Commerce, Bureau of the Census (1972, 1984).
*Percentages of detailed occupations do not sum to the category subtotal because of rounding.

Fourth, despite the increased clerical worker productivity over that decade, which was associated with insurance office automation (Cornfield et al. 1984), the real earnings of most insurance occupations declined during the 1970s. Data on 27 nonsupervisory, clerical occupations in 1971 and 1980 wage surveys of the life insurance industry show that the real earnings of all 27 occupations declined between 1971 and 1980 (U.S. Department of Labor 1973, 1981). Thus, the desire to raise their wages is giving clerical workers yet another reason for unionizing.

Facilitators

As mentioned earlier, working women's organizations are a major force facilitating clerical unionization in the insurance industry. The issues cited by these organizations in promoting unionization and collective bargaining serve to demonstrate how the four insurance industry conditions discussed above may motivate clerical unionization. Although occupational segregation by gender effectively defines the target population of working women's organizations, bureaucratization, office automation, the changing occupational structure, and declining earnings are the workplace issues that have ostensibly created the demand for unionization.

The policy statements of 9 to 5, National Association of Working Women, the vanguard working women's organization, provide an overview of the rallying cries in clerical union organizing. In its publication *Race Against Time: Automation of the Office* (Working Women 1980) 9 to 5 presented a philosophy and critique in which technology, in both its design and its implementation, is not neutral but reflects corporate interests and managerial choices. These interests and choices are directed toward achieving lower clerical labor costs and higher worker productivity through two main strategies: a unilateral deskilling of office work with office automation, and centralized, impersonal, scientific management controls of the clerical work force. According to 9 to 5 the main consequence for female clerical workers, especially in the financial sector, is employment in degraded, low-wage, deadend, unsafe, and increasingly insecure jobs that allow the employees little discretion, restrict their physical movement, and lead to social isolation on the job. 9 to 5 opposes the spread of office piecework that has accompanied office automation, as well as the growth of shift work. The organization's critique of office automation is fairly consistent with that of the AFL-CIO and the international labor movement (see, for example, *American Labor* 1981a, 1981b; *AFL-CIO News* 1983b, 1984b, 1984c).

Given its assertion about the nonneutrality of technology in the office, 9 to 5 (Working Women 1980) maintains that office automation can and should be implemented to create fulfilling, safe jobs and that the negative human consequences of office automation must be controlled through collective bargaining. As Karen Nussbaum, one of the founders and executive director of 9 to 5 put it, "The key to improving the conditions for women lies in organizing the private sector" (Trost 1985, 1). Among the many collective bargaining goals promoted by 9 to 5 (Working Women 1980) are higher wages, job redesign, job rotation, increased break time, and limitations on working hours. Similarly, the Women Employed Institute (1979), a Chicago-based advocacy organization oriented mainly toward female clerical workers, espouses fair salary schedules, worker participation in setting office policies and procedures, employee training programs, written job descriptions, job-posting and promotion programs, grievance procedures, and equal pay for equal work.

Occupational safety and health is another chief concern in clerical worker organizing and collective bargaining and recently in the political arena as well (Andrew 1983; Apcar and Trost 1985). According to 9 to 5 (Working Women 1980) and several labor organizations, automated office work, especially typing at video display terminals (VDTs) for long hours, creates stress, eyestrain, migraine headaches, nausea, and back pain, among other problems (*AFL-CIO News* 1983b, 1984b, 1984c). The question of reproductive hazards stemming from VDT radiation emission has also been raised, though not resolved; and labor organizations are calling for "pregnancy-protection packages" that allow VDT operators to transfer out of their jobs during pregnancy without losing pay, seniority, or fringe benefits (*AFL-CIO News* 1984c). Other collective bargaining concerns about VDT, health, and safety conditions were announced at a recent 20-nation meeting of the International Confederation of Free Trade Unions, including control of radiation emission levels, rest breaks, work station lighting, facial rashes, and air contaminants (*AFL-CIO News* 1984c). 9 to 5 and the Service Employees' International Union recently launched a "Campaign for VDT Safety," targeting 18 states for the enactment of protective, "right to know" legislation and regulations (*Wall Street Journal* 1984; *AFL-CIO News* 1985a, 1985b).

District 925's widely publicized victory in organizing the Equitable Life Assurance Society of the United States, the third largest insurance company, illustrates the collective bargaining issues of female clerical workers in the insurance industry (*Wall Street Journal* 1982; Trost 1984; *AFL-CIO News* 1984a; Serrin 1984; Perl 1984; Slaughter 1984; *Service Employee* 1984–85). In February 1982 the SEIU local had won union representation among claims processors at Equitable's highly automated Syracuse, New York, office. In November 1984, after a standoff accompanied by company threats to close the office, employee picketing, and an AFL-CIO boycott of Equitable (*Wall Street Journal* 1983a, 1983b), the union signed a three-year contract, the first labor agreement with any occupational group in the company's history.

The contract provided the workers, most of whom are women, with 14 percent annual wage increases over the life of the agreement. Other economic provisions included a no-layoff clause, revised pay scales, and a commitment from the company not to close the office. The contract removed attitude and attendance criteria from performance reviews, allowed workers to challenge the computerized audits of their performances, and established a union grievance procedure with the possibility of appealing job ratings to an outside arbitrator. District 925 also gained assurances from the company that it would not stall in future union representation elections and collective bargaining and that it would not hire anti-union consultants.

The Equitable contract also addressed health and safety issues, especially for VDT operators. Among the relevant provisions were the right of pregnant VDT operators to transfer to non-VDT work, the right of VDT operators to transfer to other terminals if they believed the current terminal unsafe, extra break time for VDT work and two-hour limitations on continuous VDT use, VDT modifications to reduce stress and other physical problems, regular machine maintenance, medical vision care, and requirements for such safety equipment as glare reduction devices, detachable keyboards, and adjustable chairs.

Thus, collective bargaining for clerical workers in the insurance industry has been used to address the economic, health and safety, and discrimination problems that have accompanied bureaucratization, office automation, the changing occupational structure, and declining earnings. Collective bargaining issues, in this case, arise from the workers' perceptions that they need to gain control over the implementation of office technology in order to improve their economic livelihoods, maintain health and safety conditions at work, and limit capricious managerial decision making.

Inhibitors

Management philosophy toward the clerical work force in insurance has consisted of unilateral, centralized control, as expressed in computerized labor controls and paternalism or employee involvement initiatives, through which management attempts to instill a sense of community in the workplace. It is therefore not surprising that insurance management has opposed unionization. In line with its adherence to centralized control, insurance management has actively opposed collective bargaining, as shown in the Equitable case and in the industry's vocal opposition to the ultimate merger, in 1983, of the small Insurance Workers International Union with the United Food and Commercial Workers, which at the time was mounting an industrywide organizing campaign (*AFL-CIO News* 1983a).

In line with its paternalistic management style, the industry has also pursued greater employee involvement as a means of preventing unionization. The chief indicators of paternalism in insurance have been efforts to avoid layoffs through retraining and job reassignment, low levels of layoffs, and little technological displacement associated with office automation since the 1950s (Kassalow 1966, 359; U.S. Department of Labor 1960, 1966). This paternalism has been buttressed by relatively high rates of voluntary quits and attrition among clerical workers and rapid industry growth (Kassalow 1966; Werneke 1983; U.S. Department of Labor 1960, 1966). The beginnings of clerical worker unionization in the 1980s have hastened the extension of paternalism in the form of human relations management (*National Underwriter* 1980a, 1980b). For example, in disseminating union-avoidance advice in industry trade publications, insurance management consultant Matthew Goodfellow (1975, 1980, 1981a, 1981b) has urged the companies to improve their communications with employees and cease ''autocratic'' relations with clerical workers. Similarly, labor lawyers William Krupman and Patrick Vacarro (1981) advised the industry to address such women's issues as sexual harassment and sex discrimination in wage setting to prevent clerical worker unionization, if not litigation against sex discrimination.

Increasingly, insurance management has adopted employee involvement initiatives not only to prevent unionization, but also to overcome clerical worker resistance to office automation and raise clerical worker productivity. Of interest here are management efforts to listen carefully to employee complaints; inform employees of technological change and seek their advice on it; establish quality control circles, job enrichment programs, and flexible work schedules; and hire retirees to fill temporary vacancies (Cornfield et al. 1984).

Ironically, however, in pursuing this twofold strategy of centralization and paternalism, the insurance companies may have simultaneously retarded and promoted unions of their female clerical workers. The expression of unilateral, centralized control in the impersonal implementation of office automation became the centerpiece of the clerical union critique of employment conditions and its justification for organizing, whereas the paternalistic, human relations style of management may have staved off organizing drives in at least some insurance workplaces (Kassalow 1966; Costello 1983).

All told, then, clerical unionization in the insurance industry has been motivated by changing work conditions, facilitated by the women's and labor movements, and inhibited by employer resistance. Research on unionization suggests, however, that the forces that facilitate and inhibit unionization may differ across geographical areas and employers of different sizes. I therefore turn now to an analysis of regional and establishment variation in the percentage of unionized clerical workers in insurance.

PATTERNS OF UNIONIZATION IN LIFE INSURANCE

Theories of white-collar unionization imply that the extent of office worker unionization in life insurance will vary geographically and by establishment size. Adams (1975) maintained that the growth in union-organizing efforts by the labor movement is one factor contributing to the rise of white-collar unionization. As discussed above, the labor movement has recently paid more attention to white-collar organizing as blue-collar union membership has declined.

The results of this organizing strategy are likely to be reflected in the geographical patterns of unionization in life insurance. The largest losses in blue-collar union membership are occurring in the declining "Frostbelt" regions where industrialization and unionization had first developed; and not surprisingly, union-organizing campaigns in insurance have tended to be conducted in these same regions (Kilgour 1982). Moreover, nonunion workers in the Northeast and Great Lakes regions may be more accustomed and favorably predisposed to unionization than workers in other regions because of their relatively early industrialization and the subsequent long-standing and wide prevalence of unionization in these two regions. This proposition may especially hold true for office workers, many of whom come from the working class and, possibly, from union families.

Unionization research presents contradictory arguments about the relationship between establishment size and the likelihood of unionization. The contradiction stems from different research designs and the alternative meanings given to establishment size (measured by employment levels). One argument holds that the extent of unionization in large establishments exceeds that in small establishments because large establishments are more bureaucratically impersonal than small establishments. In other words, workers are most prone to unionization under conditions of bureaucratic impersonality. Bain's (1970) analysis of interindustry variation in the percentage unionized among white-collar workers is consistent with this argument.

Another line of research, on the determinants of union representation election outcomes in many industries, including insurance, posits and finds consistently that workers in small establishments are more likely to unionize than workers in large establishments (Kilgour 1982; Cornfield 1986). This inverse relationship between establishment size and the likelihood of unionization has been explained as arising from the relatively inferior wages and fringe benefits in small establishments and the greater capacity of large employers to resist unionization efforts by hiring anti-union management consultants.

To examine the relationship among region, establishment size, and unionization, I cross-tabulated unpublished data on the percentage unionized from a U.S. Bureau of Labor Statistics 1980 wage survey (data for earlier years are unavailable) by region and by establishment size, as shown in Table 3. As expected, the percentage unionized was greater in the Great Lakes and Northeast regions than elsewhere. In fact, no office workers were employed in unionized life insurance establishments in the other regions.

Table 3. The Percentage of Nonsupervisory Office Workers in Life Insurance Employed in Unionized Establishments,* by Region and Establishment Size, 1980

Region/Establishment Size (Number of Employees)	*Percentage*	*Number*
Northeast	1.3%	63,931
1–499	8.8	5,489
500–999	7.5	4,506
1,000+	0.0	53,936
Great Lakes	14.0	26,569
1–499	9.1	8,857
500–999	26.8	5,448
1,000+	11.9	12,264
Other Regions	0.0	46,465
U.S. Total	3.3	136,965

Source: Unpublished data from the U.S. Department of Labor, Bureau of Labor Statistics, January 1980 wage survey of the life insurance industry.

*Establishments in which a majority of the employees are covered by a collective bargaining agreement.

The relationship between establishment size and the percentage unionized is ambiguous and varies regionally. In the Northeast the percentage unionized increases with declining establishment size. In the Great Lakes region, however, the likelihood of unionization is greatest among the medium-size establishments.

That the relationship between establishment size and the percentage unionized varied across regions suggests that neither of the two arguments about establishment size is consistent with the data on the life insurance industry. This is not to deny that an impersonal bureaucracy, poor working conditions, or employers' inability to resist unions may be important determinants of unionization. Instead, establishment size may simply be an inadequate proxy for these concepts.

The regional variation in the relationship between establishment size and the percentage unionized may also reflect the nature of company-specific labor agreements in the industry, a question that must be reserved for future research because of the absence of appropriate data. The establishment size arguments discussed above implicitly assume that the industry in question consists of unilocational, single-establishment companies with establishment-specific labor agreements. This assumption excludes the possibility of master contracts between one union and many employers and of multistate, multiestablishment labor agreements between a union and a multilocational employer. The findings for establishment size in Table 3 may therefore reflect the presence of these more complex contractual arrangements. Thus, future research may need to examine the labor agreement and the parties to the agreement, rather than the establishment, as the conceptual unit of analysis.

CONCLUSION

This analysis of clerical unionization in the insurance industry illustrates some of the conditions that motivate, facilitate, or inhibit white-collar unionization. According to theories of white-collar unionization, bureaucratization and office automation lower the social status of white-collar workers and motivate unionization; aggressive union organizing facilitates unionization; and employer resistance inhibits unionization.

The case of the insurance industry suggests two reasons why the prospects for white-collar unionization are uncertain, however. First, the issues motivating nonclerical white-collar workers, such as nonsupervisory professionals, to unionize or to engage in any type of remedial collective action may not be the same as the issues motivating clerical workers. Even if they face deskilling or other changes in employment conditions that could jeopardize their social status, nonsupervisory professionals may still identify with management because they expect promotions to managerial positions. Unlike many clerical workers professionals possess educational credentials that qualify them for promotions along career tracks to join management. Indeed, blocked mobility is a major issue in clerical union organizing, as noted earlier. This implies that declining social status may be an insufficient explanation of the motivation to unionize and that worker expectations of *upward* social mobility ought to be incorporated in theories of white-collar unionization.

Second, uncertain prospects for white-collar unionization may derive from the capacity of employers to inhibit or preempt unionization. Insurance management, like managements in many industries, has become increasingly enamored of employee involvement techniques (Cornfield 1986). The purpose of these practices is to increase employee participation in decision making and, thereby, to engender a sense of community at work. While unionization has emerged to address the economic, health, and safety needs of clerical workers, management has at the same time been attempting to address employee needs for responsibility and community on the job. Thus, as noted earlier, the concepts of motivation embedded in theories of white-collar unionization ought to be broadened. The existing theories' emphasis on social class may constitute a narrow interpretation of workers' motivation to unionize, which may also include a need for community. Whether white-collar workers will act on their class interests by unionizing or accept a management-made workplace community remains an unanswered empirical question.

ACKNOWLEDGMENTS

I am grateful to Carl Barsky of the U.S. Bureau of Labor Statistics for providing me with unpublished unionization data from the 1980 wage survey of the life insurance industry; to Jo Anne Bradford, Juana M. Cain, Doris Davis, and Linda Willingham for typing the manuscript; and to Polly Phipps, Judith Gregory, and Seymour Spilerman for their helpful comments on earlier drafts.

REFERENCES

Adams, Roy. 1975. *The Growth of White-Collar Unionism in Britain and Sweden*, monograph Series, Industrial Relations Research Institute. Madison, Wis.: University of Wisconsin.

AFL-CIO News. 1983a. Insurance Union, UFCW Merger Set for October 1. 10 September, p. 1.

_________. 1983b. VDT Study Challenged on Conclusions. 20 August, p. 3.

_________. 1984a. Equitable Life Workers Win Breakthrough Pact. 17 November, p. 1.

_________. 1984b. Office Automation Conference Sees Unions Tested by Workplace Changes. 1 December, p. 2.

_________. 1984c. 20-Nation Union Conference Sets Job-Health Guidelines on VDT Use. 8 December, p. 9.

_________. 1985a. Drive Opened for Standards on VDT Safety. 5 January, p. 4.

_________. 1985b. VDT Safety Bills Spurred in Legislatures of 14 States. 23 March, p. 2.

American Labor. 1981a. An Organizing Issue for the '80s. No. 13, p. 10.

_________. 1981b. VDTs: Enough to Make You Want a Union! No. 13, p. 11.

Andrew, John. 1983. Terminal Tedium. *Wall Street Journal*, 6 May, p. 1.

Apcar, Leonard, and Cathy Trost. 1985. Labor Struggle. *Wall Street Journal*, 21 February, p. 1.

Appelbaum, Eileen. 1981. *Back to Work*. Boston: Auburn House.

Aron, Cindy. 1981. "To Barter Their Souls for Gold": Female Clerks in Federal Government Offices, 1862–1890. *Journal of American History* 67(March):835–53.

Bain, George. 1970. *The Growth of White-Collar Unionism*. London: Oxford University Press.

Baker, Elizabeth. 1964. *Technology and Woman's Work*. New York: Columbia University Press.

Bell, Daniel. 1953. The Next American Labor Mvement. *Fortune* 47(April):120 ff.

_________. 1972. Labor in the Post-Industrial Society. *Dissent* 19(Winter):163–89.

_________. 1973. *The Coming of Post-Industrial Society*. New York: Basic Books.

Benet, Mary. 1972. *The Secretarial Ghetto*. New York: McGraw-Hill.

Blackburn, R. M. 1967. *Union Character and Social Class: A Study of White-Collar Unionism*. London: B. T. Batsford.

Braverman, Harry. 1974. *Labor and Monopoly Capital*. New York: Monthly Review Press.

Burton, Joan. 1985. *Office Worker Activism: A Case Study of a Local Working Women's Organization*, Ph.D. dissertation. Nashville, TN: Department of Sociology, Vanderbilt University.

Chandler, Alfred. 1977. *The Visible Hand*. Cambridge, MA: Belknap Press.

Clermont, Harvey. 1966. *Organizing the Insurance Worker*. Washington, DC: Catholic University of America Press.

Coleman, Charles, and Jane Rose. 1975. Bank Unionization: Status and Prospects. *Monthly Labor Review* 98(October):38–41.

Cook, Alice. 1984. Introduction. In *Women and Trade Unions in Eleven Industrialized Countries*, Alice Cook, Val Lorwin, and Arlene Daniels, 3–36. Philadelphia: Temple University Press.

Cornfield, Daniel. 1986. Declining Union Membership in the Post–World War II Era: The United Furniture Workers of America, 1939–1982. *American Journal of Sociology* 91(March): 1112–53.

Cornfield, Daniel, Deborah Carter, Trudy Coker, Kathleen Kitzmiller, Diane Pejza, Polly Phipps, and Peter Wood. 1984. Office Automation, Clerical Workers and Labor Relations in the Insurance Industry, paper presented at the forty-seventh annual meeting of the Southern Sociological Society, Knoxville, TN, 11–14 April.

Costello, Cynthia. 1983. Office Workers, Collective Action, and Social Consciousness, paper presented at the annual meetings of the Society for the Study of Social Problems, Detroit.

Davies, Margery. 1982. *Woman's Place Is at the Typewriter: Office Work and Office Workers, 1870–1930*. Philadelphia: Temple University Press.

Dye, Nancy. 1980. *As Equals and As Sisters*. Columbia, MO: University of Missouri Press.

Foner, Philip. 1979. *Women and the American Labor Movement: From Colonial Times to the Eve of World War I*. New York: Free Press.

_________. 1980. *Women and the American Labor Movement: From World War I to the Present*. New York: Free Press.

Fox, Mary, and Sharlene Hesse-Biber. 1984. *Women at Work*. Palo Alto, CA: Mayfield.

Freemen, Richard B., and James L. Medoff. 1984. *What Do Unions Do*? New York: Basic Books.

Gifford, Courtney D., ed. 1982. *Directory of U.S. Labor Organizations, 1982–83 Edition*. Washington, DC: BNA Books.

Glenn, Evelyn and Roslyn Feldberg. 1977. Degraded and Deskilled: The Proletarianization of Clerical Work. *Social Problems* 25(October):52–64.

_________. 1979a. Clerical Work: The Female Occupation. In *Women: A Feminist Perspective*, ed. Jo Freeman, 313–38. Palo Alto, CA: Mayfield.

_________. 1979b. Proletarianizing Clerical Work: Technology and Organizational Control in the Office. *Case Studies on the Labor Process*, ed. Andrew Zimbalist, 51–72. New York: Monthly Review Press.

Goldberg, Roberta. 1983. *Organizing Women Office Workers*. New York: Praeger.

Goodfellow, Matthew. 1975. What's New in Union Organizing Companies? *Best's Review*, Life/Health, 76(October):10.

________. 1980. Avoiding Unions in the Insurance Clerical Field. *Best's Review*, Life/Health, 81(October):13.

________. 1981a. Is Insurance Unionization Inevitable? (Part 1). *National Underwriter*, Property/Casualty, 7 March, p. 11.

________. 1981b. Is Insurance Unionization Inevitable? (Part 2). *National Underwriter*, Property/Casualty, 13 March, p. 29.

Greenbaum, Joan. 1979. *In the Name of Efficiency*. Philadelphia: Temple University Press.

Hauser, Robert, and David Featherman. 1977. *The Process of Stratification*. New York: Academic Press.

Helfgott, Roy. 1966. EDP and the Office Work Force. *Industrial and Labor Relations Review* 19(July):503–16.

Hirschman, Albert O. 1970. *Exit, Voice, and Loyalty: Responses to Decline in Firms, Organizations, and States*. Cambridge, MA: Harvard University Press.

Hoos, Ida. 1961. *Automation in the Office*. Washington, DC: Public Affairs Press.

Kanter, Rosabeth Moss. 1977. *Men and Women of the Corporation*. New York: Basic Books.

Kassalow, Everett. 1966. White-Collar Unionism in the United States. *White-Collar Trade Unions*, ed. Adolf Sturmthall, 305–64. Urbana: University of Illinois Press.

Kessler-Harris, Alice. 1975. "Where Are the Organized Women Workers?" *Feminist Studies* 3(Fall):92–110.

________. 1982. *Out to Work*. New York. Oxford University Press.

Kilgour, John. 1982. Unionization: Is the Insurance Industry Vulnerable? *Best's Review*, Property/Casualty, 83(August):34–93.

Kochan, Thomas A. 1979. How American Workers View Labor Unions. *Monthly Labor Review* 102(April):23–31.

Kokkelenberg, Edward C., and Donna R. Sockell. 1985. Union Membership in the United States, 1973–1981. *Industrial and Labor Relations Review* 38(July):497–543.

Koziara, Karen, and Patrice Insley. 1982. Organizations of Working Women Can Pave the Way for Unions. *Monthly Labor Review* 105(June):53–54.

Kraft, Phillip. 1977. *Programmers and Managers*. New York: Springer-Verlag.

Krupman, William, and Patrick Vacarro. 1981. Labor Relations for Today's Insurers. *National Underwriter*, Property/Casualty, 8 August, p. 11.

LeGrande, Linda. 1978. Women in Labor Organizations: Their Ranks Are Increasing. *Monthly Labor Review* 101(August):8–14.

Lockwood, David. 1958. *Black-Coated Workers*. London: Allen & Unwin.

Machung, Anne. 1984. Word Processing: Forward for Business, Backward for Women. In *My Troubles Are Going to Have Trouble with Me: Everyday Trials and Triumphs of Women Workers*, ed. Karen Sacks and Dorothy Remy, 124–39. New Brunswick, NJ: Rutgers University Press.

Marx, Karl. 1847. *The Poverty of Philosophy*. New York: International Publishers, 1963.

McNally, Fiona. 1979. *Women for Hire: A Study of the Female Office Worker*. New York: St. Martin's Press.

Milkman, Ruth. 1980. Organizing the Sexual Division of Labor: Historical Perspectives on "Women's Work" and the American Labor Movement. *Socialist Review* 10(January-February): 95–150.

Miller, Ronald. 1981–82. Collective Bargaining in Financial Institutions. *Employee Relations Law Journal* 7(Winter):389–413.

Mills, C. Wright. 1956. *White Collar*. New York: Oxford University Press.

National Underwriter. 1980a. Those New Employees and Unions. Life/Health, 2 February, p. 12.

________. 1980b. Lists Causes of Unionization. Life/Health, 9 February, p. 10.

Nolan, Robert. 1980. Work Management Programs Really Work. *National Underwriter*, Property/Casualty, 15 February, p. 25.

Perl, Peter. 1984. Clerical Workers Organized at Major Insurance Firm. *Washington Post*, 10 November, p. 8.

Pollock, Michael. 1985. Labor Goes After Its Great White-Collar Hope. *Business Week*, 19 August, p. 41.

Prandy, K., A. Stewart, and R. M. Blackburn. 1983. *White-Collar Unionism*. London: Macmillan.

Rogoff, Natalie. 1953. *Recent Trends in Occupational Mobility*. Glencoe, IL: Free Press.

Roos, Patricia. 1985. *Gender and Work: A Comparative Analysis of Industrial Societies*. Albany: State University of New York Press.

Rotella, Elyce. 1981. *From Home to Office: U.S. Women at Work, 1870–1930*. Ann Arbor, MI: UMI Research Press.

Seidman, Ann ed. 1978. *Working Women: A Study of Women in Paid Jobs*. Boulder, CO: Westview Press.

Serrin, William. 1984. Upstate Office Workers Gain a Landmark Pact. *New York Times*, 10 November, p. 26.

Service Employee. 1984–85. We Win at Equitable. 44(December/January):3.

Slaughter, Jane. 1984. Clerical Workers Win First Contract at Equitable. *Labor Notes*, No. 70(November 20):1.

Tannenbaum, Frank. 1951. *A Philosophy of Labor*. New York: Alfred A. Knopf.

Tepperman, Jean. 1976. *Not Servants, Not Machines*. Boston: Beacon Press.

Trost, Cathy. 1984. Equitable Life Accord with Service Union Marks Breakthrough. *Wall Street Journal*, 13 November, p. 10.

_________. 1985. Dynamnic Trio. *Wall Street Journal*, 29 January, p. 1.

U.S. Department of Commerce, Bureau of Industrial Economics. 1983. *1983 U.S. Industrial Outlook*. Washington, DC: GPO.

U.S. Department of Commerce, Bureau of Census. 1954. *1950 Census, Vol. 4, Special Reports, Part I*, chapter C, Occupation by Industry. Washington, DC: GPO.

_________. 1972. *Census of Population: 1970*, Final Report PC(72)-7C. Washington, DC: GPO.

_________. 1984. *1980 Census of Population, Vol. 2, Special Reports*, PC(80)-2-7C. Washington, DC: GPO.

U.S. Department of Labor, Bureau of Labor Statistics. 1960. *Adjustments to the Introduction of Office Automation*, bulletin no. 1276. Washington, DC: GPO.

_________. 1962. *Industry Wage Survey, Life Insurance, May–July 1961*, bulletin no. 1324. Washington, DC: GPO.

_________. 1966. *Impact of Office Automation in the Insurance Industry*, bulletin no. 1468. Washington, DC: GPO.

_________. 1967. *Industry Wage Survey, Life Insurance, October–November 1966*, bulletin no. 1569. Washington, DC: GPO.

_________. 1973. *Industry Wage Survey, Life Insurance, December 1971*, bulletin no. 1791. Washington, DC: GPO.

_________. 1978. *Industry Wage Surveys: Banking and Life Insurance, December 1976*, bulletin no. 1988. Washington, DC: GPO.

_________. 1979. *Technology and Labor in Five Industries*, bulletin no. 2033. Washington, DC: GPO.

_________. 1981. *Industry Wage Survey: Life Insurance, February 1980*, bulletin no. 2119, microfiche. Washington, DC: GPO.

_________. 1983. *Handbook of Labor Statistics*, bulletin no. 2175. Washington, DC: GPO.

_________. 1985. *Handbook of Labor Statistics*, bulletin no. 2217. Washington, DC: GPO.

Wall Street Journal. 1982. Labor Letter. 16 February, p. 1.

_________. 1983a. Equitable Boycott. 15 March, p. 1.

_________. 1983b. Labor Letter. 4 October, p. 1.

_________. 1984. Labor Letter. 18 December, p. 1.

Werneke, Diane. 1983. *Microelectronics and Office Jobs*. Geneva: International Labour Office.

Wertheimer, Barbara. 1977. *We Were There*. New York. Pantheon.

———. 1984. The United States of America. In *Women in Trade Unions in Eleven Industrialized Countries*, ed. Alice Cook, Val Lorwin, and Arlene Daniels, 286–311. Philadelphia: Temple University Press.

Whisler, Thomas. 1970. *The Impact of Computers on Organizations*. New York: Praeger.

Wiemann, Harry. 1979. Administrative Improvement Program. *Best's Review*, Property/Casualty, 80(August):94–97.

Women Employed Institute. 1979. *The Women in the Office: The Economic Status of Clerical Workers*. Chicago: Women Employed Institute.

Working Women, National Association of Office Workers. 1980. *Race Against Time: Automation of the Office*. Cleveland: Working Women [9 to 5, National Association of Working Women].

MANAGEMENT ISSUES FACING NEW-PRODUCT TEAMS IN HIGH-TECHNOLOGY COMPANIES

Deborah Gladstein Ancona and David F. Caldwell

New products are crucial to the success of many firms. Business experts predict that the contribution new products make to sales growth will increase by one-third during the 1980s. Over this decade the portion of total company profits generated by new products is expected to increase by 50 percent (Booz, Allen and Hamilton 1982). New-product development is particularly important, if not necessary for organizational survival, in high-technology industries. For companies in highly competitive industries the issue is not solely the introduction of new products, but also how to accelerate the product development process (David 1984).

The growing importance of the development of new products can pose difficult challenges for management. As many have noted (see, for example, Drucker 1985), existing employment policies and management practices may not be adequate to ensure that the organization has the management skills and human resources necessary to guarantee that new-product ideas can be efficiently developed. Industry observers have voiced a variety of concerns about the effectiveness of organizational structure (Kanter 1983), human resource policies

Advances in Industrial and Labor Relations, Volume 4, pages 199-221.

ISBN: 0-89232-909-2

(Fombrun, Tichy, and Devanna 1984), and management techniques (Frohman 1978) in enhancing product development.

Recently, a number of strategies have been proposed to identify and improve factors that contribute to technological innovation and product development (Burgelman and Sayles 1986; Drucker 1985). Since many authors have described how the product development process can be influenced by organizational variables (for example, Baldridge amd Burnham 1975; Cohen and Mowery 1984; Damanpour and Evan 1984), it is not our intent to review or summarize these findings here. Instead, we will describe a set of management issues facing the specific work groups responsible for product development within an organization.

Within many industries the primary mechanism for product development is the new-product team. Although known by a variety of names this is the group of individuals who must cooperate to develop, design, test market, and prepare for production the new product. New-product teams differ from many other organizational groups because they are cross-functional, handle a variety of tasks, and change in composition over time. Successful new-product teams must be able to effectively obtain information and resources from others, both inside and outside the organization; process the information and resources; and use the information and resources to create and gain acceptance of a viable product (Burgelman 1983). Understanding the operation and management of these teams can be of more than practical use. Understanding the complex interactions within the team and between the team and other groups within the firm can serve as a powerful test of the generalizability of traditional research on group behavior in organizations.

The basic premise of this paper is that group processes can influence the success of new-product teams, in particular, the processes involved in managing boundary-spanning activities and group commitment. Following a discussion of the methods we used to collect data, we will describe the tasks the new-product team must accomplish. We then will discuss previous research on boundary spanning, relate this research to the new-product team's tasks, and propose some relationships between boundary spanning and team performance.

METHODS

The findings of this paper were derived from a review of the literature and from over 135 hours of interviews with new-product team managers and members at seven corporations in the computer and integrated circuit industries. We interviewed four team leaders for between three and ten hours within six weeks of completing their projects. Using a semistructured interview we asked these managers how their teams were set up, how the teams had evolved (for example, what were the key events, crises, tasks), how the teams coordinated their efforts with other groups, and how they made key decisions. Once we compiled these descriptive data, we asked the managers what they saw as important factors in the success of a new-product team. We also conducted a number of other interviews. A different team leader was interviewed every four to six weeks over a 20-month period during the project to provide some sense of the potential issues facing a product team as it develops. In addition, four managers of multiple teams, 16 new-product team leaders, and six members of teams were interviewed during the early and middle phases of product development to develop a more detailed description of team activities. The interviews were tape-recorded and transcribed; multiple raters then evaluated the transcriptions to identify transitions in the product development process and boundary-spanning behaviors.

Our research sample is obviously not representative or large enough to allow the testing of specific hypotheses. Instead, by focusing on a few team's activities, we intended to adequately represent the tasks and processes of the new-product team. By doing so we hope to augment the literature on group process with observations from the field. Hence, our approach can be loosely described as a comparative case analysis. Another reason we chose this strategy was our belief that the research on group process in organizations is at an early stage of development. Because of the paucity of formal research on interdependent groups within organizations, we believe that exploration and description, classification of phenomena, and attempting to identify observable patterns of activities must all precede thc proposition and testing of specific hypotheses on this important subject (Gladstein and Quinn 1985).

THE TASKS OF THE NEW PRODUCT TEAM

As Goodman (1986) has recently contended, understanding the tasks of a group should be an integral part of any model of group performance or group process. Without a clear understanding of a group's tasks, we are very apt to make incorrect generalizations about group behavior (Herold 1979). Before discussing the group processes within new-product teams, therefore, we must begin with an understanding of what the teams are charged with doing.

As alluded to earlier, a new-product team is a group of employees who are responsible for developing and introducing products new to the firms existing product line (Flesher, Flesher, and Skelly 1984). In general, these employees must be interdependent, see themselves as forming a group, and be viewed by others in the organization as a group (Alderfer 1976), even though the team's membership may change and increase over time. A number of different teams may form and dissolve early in the product development process. Those that survive have potential access to extensive organizational resources, and they may shape the future success of the organization itself (Kidder 1981).

The key to the success of new-product teams is to meet the separate task demands at each phase of the product development process. This requirement in turn demands that the group be able to obtain information and resources from external sources, process the information and resources, and use the information and resources to create and gain acceptance of a viable product (Burgelman 1983). Research on new-product management has identified six phases of new-product development and introduction, assuming that a new-product strategy is in place (Booz, Allen and Hamilton 1982):

1. *Idea generation.* The initial step in new-product development, this phase involves the recognition of a technical opportunity to meet a perceived need in the marketplace (Holt 1975).
2. *Screening and evaluation.* In this phase the team selects those ideas that deserve further, in-depth study. A major goal at this stage is to screen out those ideas not fitting the organization's market or technical strengths (Booz, Allen and Hamilton 1982).
3. *Business analysis.* Here the team determines how the product under consideration fits into the firm's portfolio of other products (McIntyre and Statman 1982) and whether its production is economically feasible.
4. *Development.* In this phase the team converts the original product idea into a technically feasible prototype. It is in this phase that the group does the bulk of the work involved in designing and building the initial product models.
5. *Testing.* Testing ensures that the new product can meet both technical and market goals or standards (Von Hipple 1977). This phase requires that the team monitor test data and customer complaints (Adler 1966).
6. *Commercialization.* In this final phase of product development the team decides on the production and marketing capabilities necessary to introduce the product on a large scale, including mechanisms for ongoing monitoring of the product's success (Booz, Allen and Hamilton 1982).

This typology describes the sequence of events a product must move through in order to be introduced effectively. One implication of this process is that the activities and focus of a new-product team will change over the course of product development.

Although this set of phases suggests a linear sequence of activity, in reality the process is not so straightforward (Frohman 1978). As in some forms of strategic decision making, new-product development often proceeds incrementally (Quinn 1982). Our interviews suggested that often the original product idea is very general and only slowly becomes more specific. As the team collects information and feeds it into the ongoing decision-making process, the idea gains greater specificity. And as product development continues, the team may actually cycle back through earlier phases or forward into the later phases in the model. During the screening and evaluation, or second, stage, for example, the team often develops a rough prototype to help in deciding whether to choose that product—an activity described as falling in the fourth stage. In the third phase, developing a business plan, the team also must estimate the product's commercialization costs, a task done with greater specificity in the final phase. Moreover, those responsible for commercialization need to be notified early enough in the process so that manufacturing facilities are available. If the team waits until the end of the testing phase to do this, the product may well be late to market. Research has shown that the team needs to integrate technical and economic considerations early on in its planning, or large sums of money can be wasted on a product that is technically feasible but not commercially viable (Mansfield and Wagner 1975). The process may cycle through several times, going through several hierarchical levels and numerous functional groups in the organization (Burgelman 1983).

Product development therefore seems a messy, undirected process; and indeed, it is less straightforward than the sequential phase model suggests. Nonetheless, two events serve to define or divide the process and to redirect the new-product team's activities: (1) obtaining the organization's support for the team's product idea; and (2) transferring the product to others within the organization. We refer to these two events as transition points, in that they shape and change the task demands placed on the team. As shown in Figure 1, our data suggest that these transition points divide the group's tasks or activities into three general segments. Of particular importance in understanding the group's process, our interviews indicated that each of these segments placed different internal and external demands on the team.

The first of these transition points generally seems to occur just before to the major portion of the development phase; it involves a shift from considering a *possible* project to being committed to a *definite* project. In other words, the team moves from recognizing a potentially feasible new product to being committed to one new product idea. This shift entails movement from a low-cost effort needing minimal organizational commitment to an effort requiring major capital investment and a serious commitment from top management (Pessemier 1977). By this time the team should have a fairly clear specification of the product; if not, the team cannot be clear about what it is giving in return for organizational support, which can lead to overblown or underblown expectations for the product. Moreover, without a clear product specification the team cannot structure itself internally, since it does not have specific goals and schedules in place.

The second transition usually occurs sometime during the testing phase. The team has assessed the technological problems with the product, created a prototype, and tested it. The group may very well have spent the past several months working under intense pressure trying to finish the testing by the agreed-upon date. The transition consists of moving from team ownership of the product to more general organizational ownership. At this time other organizational groups are preparing for large-scale production and distribution of the product. This corresponds to what Quinn and Mueller (1963) would call a technology transfer point, at which the emphasis moves from developing the technology to passing

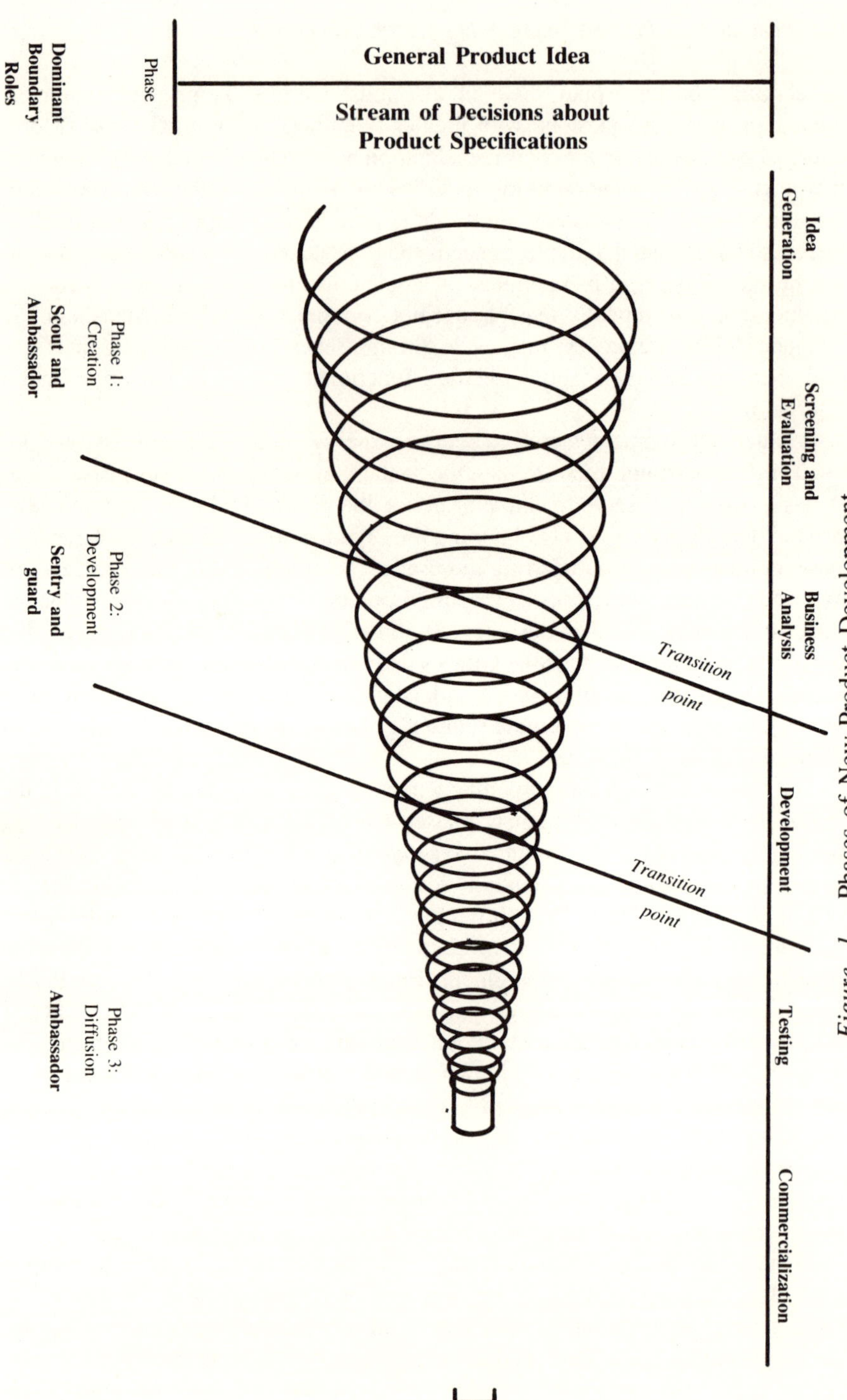

Figure 1. Phases of New-Product Development

information, enthusiasm, and authority to use that technology to other groups in the organization. The transition will not be made if the team is either unwilling to relinquish the product or unwilling to continue to work on the product when it has passed into the hands of others. As one of the managers in our sample described it: "Then we had this big fight. Manufacturing wanted to build it now and make repairs later, but engineering wanted to hold it. People were very upset. Manufacturing yanked its people off the team." Later, however, he noted: "Now we're helping to train the manufacturing people. The group isn't meeting much though, and people don't seem to know what to do now that the intensity is over."

We will label the three segments of the product development process created by these two transition points the creation, development and transfer segments. Figure 1 shows how these transitions and segments correspond with the six phases identified earlier. The spiral in the figure indicates how the team may cycle forward and backward in its activities; and its movement toward its apex indicated the narrowing specificity of the product idea. In the next section we will trace the evolution of different task demands over the course of product development. We predict that as the demands placed on the product team change across the segments of the product development process, the team's boundary-spanning processes and commitment to the product must also change.

BOUNDARY SPANNING IN NEW-PRODUCT TEAMS

Research on boundary spanning has focused primarily on the organizational and individual levels of analysis. Research at the organizational level has addressed processes by which the organization adapts to its external environment by selecting, transmitting, and interpreting information originating in the environment (see, for example, Aldrich and Herker 1977; Child 1972). Research at the individual level research has concentrated on the characteristics of boundary spanners—those who traverse organizational boundaries (see, for example, Caldwell and O'Reilly 1982a) and the role conflict these individuals experience (Kahn et al. 1964; Keller and Holland 1975; Organ and Greene 1974).

Fewer studies of boundary spanning have been done at the group level. This is surprising, because groups, like organizations, are open systems that have to manage their relationships with the external environment. But it is less surprising if we recognize that much of the research on groups has been done in the laboratory or with T-groups that work in isolation—that is, with artificial groups. For real groups the external environment consists of the organization in which they exist. Groups must interact with interdependent others to obtain resources, coordinate work, make decisions, and exchange inputs and outputs. For some groups this boundary-spanning process includes carrying out transactions beyond the organization's boundary as well (Thompson 1967).

One set of studies on boundary spanning studies that has focused on the group level examines the pattern of work-related information flow in R & D laboratories (for example, Allen 1984; Katz 1982; Tushman 1977, 1979). In general, these studies have found a relationship between the relaying of information by boundary spanners and performance in the group. For example, far greater communication with organizational colleagues outside the group occurred in high-performance R & D project teams than in low-performance teams surveyed by Allen (1984). Tushman (1979) found that communication in high-performance groups followed a two-step process, with communication "stars" first obtaining information from outside the group and then translating the information and transmitting it to the group. Although most of the group-level research on boundary spanning has been limited to studying how members bring information into the group, exchange theory would suggest that when a team is part of a system organized by an interconnecting web of relationships, a broader conceptualization of boundary spanning is needed (Bagozzi 1975).

Boundary-Spanning Decisions

Our interviews suggested that, within new-product teams, a number of decisions made by team leaders or others in positions of authority could influence the nature of the interactions the team developed with other groups. Thus, the boundary of the group could be viewed as a design variable, whereby the decisions on the boundary may determine, in part, the nature of a team's relations with other groups within or outside the organization. These boundary decisions fell into the following broad categories: the definition of the boundary; the permeability of the boundary; and the nature of the transactions across the group's boundary. The literature on groups has also addressed these properties of boundaries (see, for example, Zander 1977).

Boundary Definition

An important tool for defining the nature of the interactions the team has with other groups is the decision as to who is included in the team. Including on the team representatives from all groups with whom the team must deal is likely to lead to different boundary-spanning processes than would exist if those groups were not represented. Similarly, the decision on group membership serves to define the resources the team possesses and those that must be acquired externally. The heterogeneity of the team also has implications for the nature of the group's internal interactions (O'Reilly and Caldwell 1986) and its effectiveness in innovating (O'Reilly and Flatt 1986).

Boundary Permeability

A second tool in designing teams is the extent to which the boundary is open or closed. Groups with open boundaries are potentially less cohesive and more difficult to control than groups with more rigid boundaries (Alderfer 1976). The degree of openness of the boundary can also influence the way the group views its environment and defines the problems with which it must deal (Gladstein 1986).

Boundary Transactions

Team leaders also must make decisions about how the team will conduct transactions across its boundary. Transactions can be categorized by what is exchanged between social units as well as by the patterns of exchange. Hence, boundary-spanning activities can be categorized by whether goods and services, affect and liking, information and ideas, and influence and power flow into or out of the group, and by whether group members or outsiders initiate the exchange (Brinberg and Wood 1983; Tichy and Fombrun 1979). This broader categorization describes the set of activities involved in the social and economic exchanges necessary to accomplish interdependent tasks in environments in which resources are somewhat limited or dispersed throughout the organization. In addition, this categorization takes into account not only the boundary-spanning activities the group needs to initiate but also the reactive role that group members must play in response to external demands or requests.

Although the team's composition is often defined by the organization, at least in the short run, and hence initially fixed, boundary permeability and the nature of the boundary transactions can be influenced by the behaviors of the team members themselves. Our interviews indicated that team members often take on particular roles in their efforts to carry out transactions and change their boundary's permeability.

Boundary-Spanning Roles in New-Product Teams

As we previously noted, exchange theory would suggest that we can distinguish transactions across a boundary by whether the flow is into or out of the group and by whether the transaction is initiated within or outside the group. The data from our interviews supported this conceptualization and suggested four distinct boundary-spanning roles, as illustrated in Figure 2. One role, which we term the "scout," encompasses the activities of seeking out information or resources from other groups and attempting to bring them back into the group. The scout corresponds to the traditional conception of boundary spanning in the literature on organizations. The second role, which we label the "ambassador," encompasses the activities of transmitting information or outputs from the team to outsiders. Thus, the scout and the ambassador both carry out critical boundary-spanning transactions. The two remaining roles are those of team members who respond to requests from outsiders. The third role, the "sentry," comprises activities undertaken in response to inputs—such as new information—from outsiders. The final role encompasses activities undertaken in processing outsiders' requests for information or outputs—such as progress reports or prototypes. We term this the ''guard'' role. The sentry and guard roles help to define the permeability of the team's boundary.

This conceptualization of boundary-spanning activities is somewhat similar to Adam's (1980) typology of the activities of organizational boundary spanners. Adams outlined five classes of activities: effecting the acquisition of organizational inputs and the disposal of outputs; filtering inputs and outputs; searching for and collecting information; representing the organization to outsiders; and buffering it from external threat and pressure. At the group level these activities are likely to be more fluid than this characterization would suggest. Within a group boundary unit, as opposed to an organizational boundary unit (such as an admissions office, that is, a unit with a specialized boundary-spanning task), there is likely to be a more diverse set of external environments, a more general task and fewer formal procedures governing the criteria that determine when to accept or reject inputs and outputs from outsiders. In addition, the group must manage interactions within the organization. These observations suggest that boundary spanning is less bureaucratic in groups than in organizations and that the group must set rules as it goes along or give the boundary spanner leeway in making boundary-spanning decisions.

Given the nature of the new-product team's tasks and the dependence of the team on others within the organization, boundary-spanning activities should be important elements of the team's work. Not surprisingly, this hypothesis was supported by our interviews. All of our inteviewees noted that managing the team's relationships with other groups was critical to the product development process. Further, the boundary-spanning activities the interviewees described fit well with the theoretical distinctions outlined above. In the subsections that follow we will draw from our interviews to illustrate each of the roles and their concomitant activities in more detail.

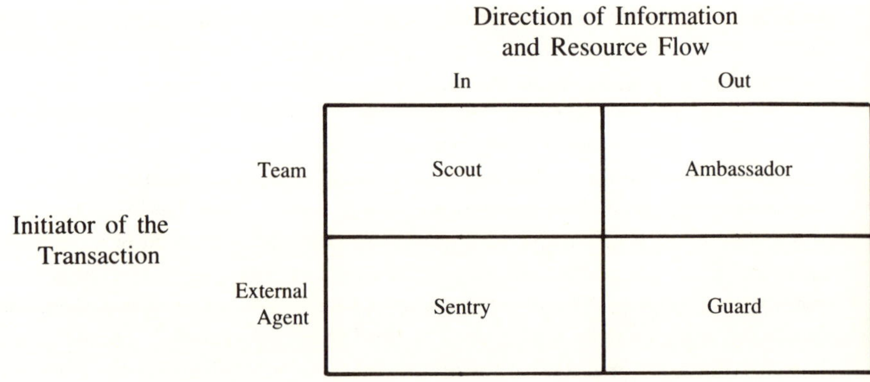

Figure 2. Boundary Roles in Teams

Scout

Recall that the activities subsumed under the scout role are to seek out and retrieve the information and resources needed by the team. In particular, the scout might collect information needed to complete tasks and resolve problems, to assess the political support for the team's activities, and to judge the demand for the team's outputs. Beyond collecting information the scout procures other resources, such as the equipment and training necessary for group functioning. If these resources are not readily provided, it is the scout who must gather intelligence so that the team can negotiate successfully to procure them. The following remarks by our interviewees illustrate some of these different functions served by the scout:

> I came back to the group once per week for a staff meeting. . . . I got the news and went back to my team with "letters from home."

> I would go around to the other groups to see what was going on. There was a great deal of coordination to take care of, and this way I could make sure that components were ordered well enough in advance so that we could get the product out on time.

> We have a kind of detector. She's very sensitive and works with the people interfaces, not the technical part. She spends time with all the groups in manufacturing to detect problems so they can be dealt with quickly.

Ambassador

The ambassador role, as noted above, involves representing the team to outsiders and relaying information, resources, or other outputs that the group chooses to transmit to others. Much of the purpose of this representation is to shape the beliefs and behaviors of outsiders (Adams 1976; 1980). The ambassador develops and maintains channels of communication in order to explain the team's activities to powerful outsiders and persuade them that the team's activities are valuable and should be supported. These functions may involve persuading others to commit themselves to, or share the goals of, the team (Kanter 1983; Kotter 1982). The following quotations from our interviews illustrate the ambassador role:

> After a few weeks we had a design review with all of R & D. We just wanted to make sure that we weren't going off in crazy directions.

> Then we started having meetings with all those people outside the group. There were representatives from purchasing, manufacturing, production planning, the diagnostics group, marketing, everyone. This was an opportunity to give information and hear about new business. Everyone was informed about progress and changes. The minutes were typed on line so that the team and those who weren't at the meeting knew what was going on. The top management group also got copies.

> I go down to where the project first hits and tell 'em what's coming down. I say that four things are coming, and this is the most critical. You can't always say rush, rush, rush. I stop

in even when there's nothing urgent, to develop a relationship with those people. I send them minutes of our meetings and when the project gets closer I send them memos explaining what's required and asking what they need from us.

I'm like a cheerleader, trying to get those guys excited about our products. But I tickle our group too; I'm not going to carry over some half-baked ideas. They'd get tired of that real quickly.

Sentry

The sentry polices the boundary by controlling the information and resources that external agents want to send into the group. Acting as a filter, the sentry decides who can give input, how much of that input will be admitted, and when the flow of input must stop. The sentry protects the group by allowing it to work with minimal distraction. Often outsiders try to communicate their priorities, interests, and demands. When the team desires these communications, the job of the sentry is to allow them entry. When they are not desired, the job of the sentry is to buffer the group from their intrusion (see, for example, Thompson 1967). The sentry also absorbs external pressures, such as political tensions, on behalf of the group. An extreme form of buffering is to separate the group physically from the rest of the organization. This buffering or sentry function is important in providing the group with the optimal amount of information necessary for effective decision making. Some evidence indicates, for example, that when action needs to be taken, increased levels of information do not improve decision making (see, for example, Gladstein and Quinn 1985; O'Reilly 1983) and that the costs of information can outweigh its benefits. Examples of the sentry role were expressed as follows:

We needed to get input from engineering at the beginning. We didn't want to come up with some kind of Dr. Seuss machine that had to be redesigned later so we let the engineering people in.

Near the end I talked to the top management group a lot. I tried to protect the group from that kind of pressure though. It's like Tom West said, we won't pass on the garbage and the politics.

Guard

Outsiders may grow curious about the team's activities or attempt to obtain resources or information from the team. The guard monitors outsiders' requests for information or resources and determines what the group will release in response to those demands. The guard role is therefore primarily reactive and requires judgment to determine if it is in the team's best interest to let information out. One outsider may request some equipment and be denied, while another's request is granted because his group has provided something of value to the team in return. Examples of the guard role can be seen in the following:

So we set up living quarters and moved the team away. That kind of intensity needed to be

> isolated. People kept coming over and saying, "How's it going? What are you up to now?" This was at best distracting, at worst like being in a pressure cooker.
>
> Near the end people started panicking. The top guys would come down and want to know if we were making progress. I told them they had to stop, that they were having a distracting and deleterious effect on the group.

Relationships among Boundary-Spanning Roles

Both conceptually and, as our interviews demonstrate, in practice these boundary-spanning roles are interrelated. The scout and sentry, for example, both deal with information that comes into the team. As such, both influence team members' perceptions of the outside world because they are likely to filter, consolidate, and interpret external inputs, thereby distorting them in some way. Scouts and sentries are also prone to other selective biases in the processing of information (see, for example, O'Reilly 1983; Zander 1977). Similarly, team members in the ambassador and guard roles influence how outsiders view the team. These roles define what is to be said and the manner in which it is to be said to those outside the team. Collectively, the activities involved in these four roles serve to define both how the team perceives the external environment and how other actors perceive the team itself.

The roles described here are complements to those that have been identified elsewhere as important to the innovation process in organizations. Roberts and Fusfeld (1983) argued that gatekeeping, idea generating, championing, project leading, and coaching are all necessary for successful innovation. The scout in our model goes beyond gatekeeping by procuring resources and bringing in political as well as technical information. The role categories we have described add detail to the championing and project-leading roles by specifying those boundary-spanning activities that promote recognition for a new-product idea (championing) and that help integrate and coordinate the diverse tasks needed to develop the product (project leading). The product champion must be a skilled ambassador, while the project leader must integrate and often simultaneously play the role of scout, ambassador, sentry, and guard. Finally, our depiction of boundary-spanning roles underscores the critical need for the team as a whole to secure and maintain support from the coach, or project leader.

In describing boundary-spanning activities in their new-product teams, our interviewees indicated that the various roles can be taken on by one team member or by many different members. Moreover, a given sequence of boundary-spanning activities may contain elements of more than one role. For example, the team leader may assume all boundary-spanning activities or assign a specific team member to interact with different outside groups. Roles may be combined, so that when in the position of ambassador, one may also do some scouting. Similarly, one individual may play a role or it may be broadly dispersed; for example, the leader may ask each team member to serve as guard by keeping certain information secret.

BOUNDARY SPANNING AND TEAM PERFORMANCE

The success of a new-product team can be defined as delivering the new product on time, within budget, and to specification; the product must also be produced and be a success in the market (Mansfield and Wagner 1975). We predict that effective boundary-spanning decisions—effectively overseeing and controlling the amount and type of boundary-spanning activity—serve as one of the critical factors contributing to a new-product team's success. Moreover, we propose that the criticality of each of the boundary-spanning roles varies across the segments of the new product development process, as shown in Figure 1. The scout and ambassador roles are more critical than the other two roles in the creation segment of the product development process because the task requires many boundary transactions. During the development segment, we would argue, the sentry and the guard roles are more critical than the others because of the team's need to reduce boundary permeability. The diffusion segment should require more ambassador activity than in the other segments because of the team's need to see the product into production. Let us examine each of these propositions in more detail.

Our interviewees suggested that it is during the creation segment of the product development process that the team (or individuals who will later form the team) must effectively collect large amounts of market, technical, and political information (see also Kanter 1983; Maquis 1969; Tushman 1977). To develop product ideas, screen them, and evaluate their economic feasibility, the team must gather information from the external environment, top management, and other functional areas in the organization. It must also elaborate an understanding of the corporate tradition and management thinking to assess whether the product will fit in the corporate strategy (Burgelman 1983). Collecting this information is the job of the scout. During the creation segment gaining top management support and the cooperation of other interdependent groups is also crucial. Burgelman (1983, 232) in his study of new ventures in corporations, described this activity as "necessary to demonstrate that what conventional corporate wisdom had classified as impossible was, in fact, possible." The scout can help in this process by informally obtaining resources to demonstrate product feasibility or creating early market interest in the product even before top management is committed to the product's development.

When the primary task of a team is to gather information, resources, or expertise from outside the group, we hypothesize that effective groups will increase those activities related to scouting. Depending on what resources the team requires, these increased scouting activities may be directed toward a variety of outside groups (Pfeffer 1985). When cooperation from others is needed for future acceptance of the team's outputs, we predict that in effective teams the scout will start early in the team's existence to identify areas of support and opposition to its efforts.

At this initial stage those activities making up the ambassador role will likely be high as well. The ambassador uses information from the scout, working to maintain the support of those who have given it and trying to persuade key individuals who oppose the group's plans to change their minds. The effective ambassador will build cooperation and support from outsiders early on and will keep those who agree to cooperate well informed of the team's progress. Once these outsiders have a stake in the team's output, they need to be updated on progress. Thus, when outside support and cooperation are necessary but not present, we predict that high-performance teams will increase the amount of selling the ambassador does. This is particularly important at the beginning of the group's existence. Once support is obtained, high-performance teams will continue to need a fair amount of ambassador activity, but its form may change.

The literature on group behavior would suggest that it is important that the ambassador role develop early in the team's existence, and data from our interviews support this contention. Friedlander and Scott (1981) found that work group activities received more legitimization and were more likely to be implemented when the group had a back-and-forth flow of ideas with top management. In addition, once a work or information channel is established, over time it tends to be used for other, unrelated purposes (March and Simon 1958), so that outsiders who are given information early in the team's development may reciprocate with assistance to the team. Our interviewees suggested that effective ambassadors were those who worked to build informal channels with other groups. Their descriptions of the actions ambassadors undertook in doing this were not unlike the requirements for voluntary coordination identified by Whetten (1986).

In the second segment of the product development process, we hypothesize that the sentry and guard roles are more critical than the other two roles. It is during this development segment, when the partial isolation of the team is most important, that the team must specify the new product design well enough to set goals and schedules for members. To achieve isolation the sentry must halt the inflow of information on outsiders' priorities and suggestions for the product design (unless market or competitive information radically changes). We would predict that the more effective teams will be those that are able to obtain the information they need (preferably during the creation segment) and then consolidate this information and move on to development. Teams that do not effectively manage this process may lose valuable time or suffer reduced effectiveness. Groups that continue to incorporate outside ideas and information have to continually change work goals and schedules; and group progress and motivation suffer. As one new-product team manager put it, "They just couldn't decide which chip they were going to use. It was debated and changed and debated until the cost and delivery got out of control. We had to scrap the whole thing and most of that team left the company." Thus, innovation and speed can be gained by having the sentry serve as a buffer against external interference and imposed organizational norms (Friedlander 1986; Galbraith 1982; Rogers 1982).

The guard also serves as a buffer. While the group is in the development phase, outsiders will want to know what the group is doing, how much progress has been made, or when the product will be finished. Our interviews suggested that if the team is to work effectively, it cannot be interrupted constantly. We therefore propose that the more important the team's product, and the more interruptions and requests for information and resources, the more the guard role is necessary. In addition, teams will often be in competition for resources and will want product information in order to compete more successfully. We hypothesize that high-performance teams will carefully define their profile in the organization and limit their exposure to others via the guard role.

It is important to note that although the sentry and guard roles are most important in the second segment of product development, the ambassador and scout roles are still necessary. Technical expertise, information about competing groups and top management support, and resource in the form of equipment and personnel may also be needed to meet the demands of this second stage. The scout addresses these needs, while the ambassador continues to garner further support and maintain the early commitments to the product idea.

In the diffusion segment of the product development process, we hypothesize that the ambassador role is more critical than the other boundary roles. It is during the transfer to actual production that teams must convey technical data as well as a sense of ownership to the groups that will manufacture and market the new product. The ambassador is critical in this endeavor. The breadth of the transition is such that it may be necessary for most team members to assume some ambassador activities. In fact, the transfer of ownership of the new product may be difficult for the team. The nature of the second segment of the development process may have caused the team to create a very impermeable boundary. Thus, although the isolation this boundary allows may be important in innovation, its existence and strength is counterproductive at this stage. We propose that the potential of this occurring makes the ambassador role critical.

Overall, we hypothesize that the criticality of the boundary roles changes depending on the particular tasks required at each phase of the product development process. General support for this hypothesis comes from a study of engineering research institutes. Ryssina and Koroleva (1984) studied the relationship between roles and team performance. Although examining slightly different roles from the ones we have specified, they reached similar conclusions about the importance of role differentiation and active management of boundary-spanning activity. In their study these two factors were associated with closer scientific contacts, better cooperation, and greater team effectiveness. In Ryssina and Koroleva's terms the "generator of ideas" and the "gatekeeper" (like our "scout") were of primary importance in early phases of research projects, and then the teams focused inward, with the burden of activity falling on the leader and the research technique specialist. Finally, in the last phase the leader, specialist, and liaison became most important.

IMPLICATIONS FOR TEAM MANAGEMENT AND FUTURE RESEARCH

An improved understanding of complex groups such as new-product teams may have implications for improving the management of work teams in general and we hope also will increase and improve research on groups.

We have identified four roles that encompass the boundary-spanning activities required in product development. The roles of scout, ambassador, sentry, and guard will not always be taken on automatically; if support for the propositions in this paper is forthcoming, we would suggest that the team leader must assign these roles to team members and evaluate the members on their performance in these roles. Role performance is also influenced by the organizational context. The team leader must work to make organizational reward and control mechanisms encourage and reward effective role behavior.

The propositions presented here have implications for research as well as management. First and foremost the paper advocates studying teams within their organizational context in order to examine boundary-spanning as well as internal processes. Also inherent in the propositions is recognition that groups should be monitored over time and that their interactions should be monitored both across levels in the hierarchy and across functional lines. This broad perspective is needed to achieve a better understanding of the group behaviors that may be required to meet the demands of complex, interdependent tasks like those involved in new-product development.

Much of the existing literature on group functioning suggests that group leaders spend their time fostering effective *internal* group processes, such as decision making and problem solving, supportiveness, and trust (for example, Argyris 1966; Dyer 1977; Zander 1977). Although these activities are definitely important in team management, this paper demonstrates that leaders may also have to foster effective processes that extend beyond the boundaries of the group. New-product team leaders, and leaders of all groups that are interdependent with external entities, must successfully manage a complex set of boundary-spanning activities if the group is to meet its goals.

Much of the existing literature on groups uses cross-sectional data. Those researchers who have taken a developmental approach have focused on the resolution of two major issues: authority (how will leadership emerge?) and intimacy (how close will group members become?) (see Hare 1973). Group development has been modeled as a sequential process; for example, (1) members become acquainted with and oriented to the task, (2) conflict develops as group members confront issues of authority, (3) members agree on norms and rules, and (4) members work to complete the task (Heinen and Jacobsen 1976). This model concentrates on the internal, interpersonal changes in behavior in groups over time. Our findings support the developmental approach, but they also indicate a need to focus on the evolution of boundary-spanning as well as internal processes. Our research also raises the question whether changes in group process follow shifts in task demands rather than a generalizable sequence of events. Future research will have to address this issue.

Beyond their usefulness in identifying boundary-spanning roles involved in the product development process, the data from our interviews lead us to speculate about an additional implication for research, that is, the effects of a group's internal processes on the nature of its boundary-spanning relations.

One topic worthy of speculation is how the *internal* processes of the group influence the permeability of the group's boundary and its transactions across the boundary (see Gladstein 1984). Our interviews suggested that at least two internal processes influenced boundary-spanning activities: the development and management of members' commitments to the team and product; and the management of the stream of decisions involved in developing the new product.

Managing Commitment

Our interviews suggested that managing the creation, maintenance, and control of the teams members' commitment to the project is important in shaping both the relations of the new product team with other groups and the overall success of the product development process. Developing new products imposes many unforeseen demands and pressures on the team; as one manager we interviewed stated, "There isn't one project that hasn't gone through a stage where the members thought they had failed—where they thought it couldn't be done." Despite this, examples abound of teams expending tremendous effort in the face of apparent failure (see, for example, Kidder 1981). Many of our interviewees recounted stories of marathon workdays, willingly forgone vacations, and intense effort toward developing the new product. It may be that becoming "fanatically committed" (Quinn 1979) to the new product is often necessary for team success in the face of perceived failure.

That very commitment may have paradoxical effects, however. Recent research (see, for example, Staw 1982) has described how individuals may become so bound to their previous actions that they remain committed to a strategy even after it has met failure. This process of escalating commitment has been termed "entrapment" (Rubin and Brockner 1975), or having "too much invested to quit" (Teger 1980). Entrapping commitment may prevent the team from abandoning poor strategies or lead the team to ignore new information. Similarly, strong commitment may lead individuals to distort or manipulate information that does not support the original plan (Caldwell and O'Reilly 1982b). All of these negative effects may serve to limit the new-product team's ability to exchange information with those other groups on which it may depend.

Thus, commitment may have implications for boundary-spanning behaviors. For example, a "fanatically committed" group may develop a less permeable boundary by exhibiting higher levels of sentry and guard activities than necessary. Similarly, the commitment may distort the boundary transactions such that the group concentrates on exporting its views without importing new information.

This then is the paradox of commitment. While fanatical commitment may be necessary to complete a project, it may also inhibit the team's work with others or ultimately inhibit the team's ability to relinquish ownership of the project to others.

Finally, research on commitment has increasingly focused on identifying how the processes by which individuals undertake an action may lead to commitment (see, for example, O'Reilly and Caldwell 1981; Salancik 1977) and how such commitment may be maintained in organizations (for example, Pfeffer 1981). One topic for future research is the management of commitment at the group level of analysis, including its implications for internal and boundary-spanning processes.

Managing the Decision-Making Process

A second internal process that is likely to influence the product team's interactions with outside groups is the nature of decision making within the team. As others have noted (for example, Janis 1982), the internal decision-making process of the group and the decisions it makes can influence external group processes. Our interviewees suggested that the way the product team made decisions had the potential to influence the way the group managed its boundary-spanning activities. For example, some teams confined collecting information to early in the decision-making process, whereas others continued collecting information well into the process.

To understand how decision making can influence boundary spanning in new-product teams, it is useful to begin with an understanding of why decisions are made. Brunsson (1982) compared two models of decision making: decision rationality and action rationality. Decision rationality corresponds to most normative models of decision making, whereby the goal of decision making is to make the "best" decision, and includes processes such as collecting all the available information, specifying complete sets of alternatives, and ranking alternatives in terms of expected values. Making "good" decisions requires avoiding such irrational processes as "group think" (Janis 1982) or rigid responses to threat (Staw, Sandelands, and Dutton 1981).

The aim in the action rationality model, on the other hand, may not be to arrive at the "best" decision, in some abstract sense, but to involve people in the decision-making process so as to gain their ideas in molding the decision and build their commitment to it. At issue here is not so much group effectiveness (whether what is being done should be done) as how the decision can best be carried out (Pfeffer and Salancik 1978). Since the building of commitment is a primary criterion for success under this model, action rationality demands that few alternatives be analyzed, a narrow range of potential consequences be considered in choosing among the alternatives, and issues of implementation be dominant throughout the entire process (Brunsson 1982; Gladstein and Quinn 1985). In contrast to decision rationality, action rationality requires that the group avoid considering all the pros and cons of multiple alternatives because doing so could evoke dysfunctional uncertainty.

Our interviews suggested that teams operating under decision rationality exhibit more permeable boundaries than those operating under action rationality. The decision rationality approach seemed to result in an openness to new information, with team members ready to move outside the boundary to seek out new alternatives and obtain information on the pros and cons of their plans. Teams operating under action rationality often wanted to accelerate the decision-making process and seemed less inclined to seek new information that might impede the decision-making process.

SUMMARY

All told these implications can be summarized as forming two general areas. First, they suggest that success in developing new products is partly a function of whether the product development team effectively manages its relationships with other groups. Second, internal team processes themselves may influence boundary-spanning activities. This relationship needs to be examined in future research. Whereas research on groups has typically looked at task and group maintenance activities, our work suggests a third area of group functioning: managing boundary-spanning activities.

ACKNOWLEDGMENTS

A Presidential Research Grant, Santa Clara University, and the Center for Innovation Management Studies at Lehigh University provided partial support for this research.

REFERENCES

Adams, J. Stacy. 1976. The Structure and Dynamics of Behavior in Organizational Boundary Roles. In *Handbook of Industrial and Organizational Psychology*, ed. Marvin D. Dunnette, 1175–99. Chicago: Rand McNally.

———. 1980. Interorganizational Processes and Organization Boundary Activities.'' In *Research in Organizational Behavior*, vol. 2, ed. L. Cummings and B. Staw. Greenwich, CT: JAI Press.

Adler, Lee. 1966. Time Lag in New Product Development. *Journal of Marketing* 30(January): 17–21.

Alderfer, Clayton P. 1976. Boundary Relations and Organizational Diagnosis. In *Humanizing Organizational Behavior*, ed. M. Meltzer and F. Wickert. Springfield, IL: Charles Thomas.

Aldrich, Howard, and Herker, Diane. 1977. Boundary Spanning Roles and Organization Structure. *Academy of Management Review* 2 (April):217–30.

Allen, Thomas J. 1984. *Managing the Flow of Technology: Technology Transfer and the Dissemination of Technological Inforamtion Within the R & D Organization*. Cambridge, MA: MIT Press.

Argyris, Chris. 1966. Interpersonal Barriers to Decision Making. *Harvard Business Review* 44(March-April):84–97.

Bagozzi, Richard P. 1975. Marketing as Exchange. *Journal of Marketing* 39(October):32–39.

Baldridge, J. Victor, and Robert A. Burnham. 1975. Organizational Innovation: Individual, Organizational, and Environmental Impacts. *Administrative Science Quarterly* 20(July): 165–76.

Booz, Allen and Hamilton, Inc. 1982. New Products Management for the 1980s. New York: Booz, Allen and Hamilton.

Brinberg, David, and Ronald Wood. 1983. A Resource Exchange Theory Analysis of Consumer Behavior. *Journal of Consumer Research* 10(December):330–38.

Brunsson, Nils. 1982. The Irrationality of Action and Action Rationality: Decisions, Ideologies and Organization Actions. *Journal of Management Studies* 19(January):29–44.

Burgelman, Robert A. 1983. A Process Model of Internal Corporate Venturing in the Diversified Major Firm. *Administrative Science Quarterly* 28(June):223–44.

Burgelman, Robert A., and Leonard Sayles. 1986. *Inside Corporate Innovation: Strategy, Structure, and Managerial Skills*. New York: Free Press.

Caldwell, David F., and Charles A. O'Reilly. 1982a. Boundary Spanning and Individual Performance: The Impact of Self Monitoring. *Journal of Applied Psychology* 67:124–27.

_________. 1982b. Responses to Failure: The Effects of Choice and Responsibility on Impression Management. *Academy of Management Journal* 25: 121–36.

Child, John. 1972. Organizational Structure, Environment, and Performance: The Role of Strategic Choice. *Sociology* 6(1):1–22.

Cohen, W., and D. Mowery. 1984. Firm Heterogeneity and R & D: An Agenda for Research. In *Strategic Management of Industrial R & D*, ed. B. Bozeman, M. Crow, and A. Link. Lexington, MA: Lexington Books.

Damanpour, Fariborz, and William M. Evan. 1984. Organizational Innovation and Performance: The Problem of "Organizational Lag." *Administrative Science Quarterly* 24(September):342–409.

David, Edward E. 1984. Trends in R & D. *Research and Development* (June):56–67.

Drucker, Peter F. 1985. The Discipline of Innovation. *Harvard Business Review* 65(May-June):67–72.

Dyer, William G. 1977. *Team Building: Issues and Alternatives*. Reading, MA: Addison-Wesley.

Flesher, D. L., T. K. Flesher, and G. U. Skelly. 1984. *The New-Product Decision*. New York: National Association of Accountants; Hamilton, Ontario: Society of Management Accountants of Canada.

Friedlander, Fred. 1986. The Ecology of Work Groups. In *The Handbook of Organizational Behavior*, ed. Jay Lorsch. New York: Prentice-Hall.

Friedlander, Fred, and B. Scott. 1981. The Use of Work Groups for Organizational Change. In *Groups at Work*, ed. C. Cooper and R. Payne. New York: John Wiley.

Frohman, Alan L. 1978. The Performance of Innovation: Managerial Roles. *California Management Review* 20(Spring):5–12.

Fombrun, Charles, Noel M. Tichy, and Mary Anne Devanra. 1984. *Strategic Human Resource Management*. New York: John Wiley.

Galbraith, Jay. 1982. Designing the Innovating Organization. *Organizational Dynamics* 10(Winter):5–26.

Gladstein, Deborah L. 1984. Groups in Context: A Model of Task Group Effectiveness. *Adminstrative Science Quarterly* 29(December):499–518.

_________. 1986. Adaptation to the External Environment: Group Development in the Organizational Context, working paper. Cambridge: Sloan School of Management, Massachusetts Institute of Technology.

Gladstein, Deborah L., and James Brian Quinn. 1985. Janis Sources of Error in Strategic Decision Making. In J. Pennings (ed.) *Strategic Decision Making*, ed. J. Pennings. San Francisco: Jossey-Bass.

Goodman, Paul. 1986. Task, Technology and Group Performance. In *Designing Effective Work Groups*, ed. Paul Goodman. San Francisco: Jossey-Bass.

Hare, Paul A. 1973. Theories of Group Development and Categories for Interaction Analysis. *Small Group Behavior* 4(August):259–303.

Heinen, J. Stephen, and Eugene Jacobson. 1976. A Model of Task Group Development in Complex Organizations and a Strategy of Implementation. *Academy of Management Review* 1(October):98–111.

Herold, David. 1979. The Effectiveness of Work Groups. In *Organizational Behavior*, ed. S. Kerr. Columbus, OH: Grid.

Holt, Knut. 1975. Information and Needs Analysis in Idea Generation. *Research Management* 18(May):24–27.

Janis, Irving. 1982. *Groupthink*, Boston: Houghton-Mifflin.

Kahn, R. L., D. M. Wolfe, R. P. Quinn, J. D. Snoek, and R. A. Rosenthal. 1964. *Organizational Stress: Studies in Role Conflict and Ambiguity*. New York: John Wiley.

Kanter, Rosabeth Moss. 1983. *The Changemasters*. New York: Simon & Schuster.

Katz, Ralph. 1982. The Effects of Group Longevity on Project Communication and Performance. *Administrative Science Quarterly* 27(March):81–104.

Keller, Robert T., and Holland, Winford E. 1975. Boundary Spanning Roles in a Research and Development Organization: An Empirical Investigation. *Academy of Management Journal* 18(June):388–93.

Kidder, Tracy. 1981. *The Soul of a New Machine*. New York: Little, Brown.

Kotter, John P. 1982. What Effective General Managers Really Do. *Harvard Business Review* 60(November-December):156–67.

McIntyre, Shelby H., and Meir Statman. 1982. Managing the Risk of New Product Development. *Business Horizons* (May-June):51–55.

Mansfield, Edwin, and Samuel Wagner. 1975. Organizational and Strategic Factors Associated with Probabilities of Success in Industrial R & D. *Journal of Business* 48:179–98.

Maquis, D. G. 1969. A Project Team Plus PERT Equals Success. Or Does It? *Innovation* 1(3):37–44.

March, James G., and Herbert A. Simon. 1958. *Organizations*. New York: John Wiley.

O'Reilly, Charles A. 1983. The Use of Information in Organization Decision Making: A Model and Some Propositions. In *Research in Organizational Behavior*, vol. 5, ed. L. Cummings and B. Staw. Greenwich, CT: JAI Press.

O'Reilly, Charles A., and David F. Caldwell. 1981. The Commitment and Job Tenure of New Employees: Some Evidence of Post-decisional Justification. *Administrative Science Quarterly* 26(December):597–616.

———. 1986. Work Group Demography, Social Integration, and Turnover, working paper. Berkeley: School of Business, University of California.

O'Reilly, Charles A., and Sylvia Flatt. 1986. Executive Team Demography, Organizational Innovation, and Firm Performance, working paper. Berkeley: School of Business, University of California.

Organ, Dennis W., and Charles N. Greene. 1974. Role Ambiguity, Locus of Control and Work Satisfaction. *Journal of Applied Psychology* 59(February):101–2.

Pessemier, Edgar A. 1977. *Product Management: Strategy and Organization*. New York: John Wiley.

Pfeffer, Jeffrey. 1981. Management as Symbolic Action: The Creation and Maintenance of Organizational Paradigms. In *Research in Organizational Behavior*, vol. 3, ed. L. Cummings and B. Staw. Greenwich, CT: JAI Press.

________. 1985. A Resource Dependence Perspective on Intercorporate relations. In *Structural Analysis of Business*, ed. M. Mizruchi and M. Schwartz. New York: Academic Press.

Quinn, James Brian. 1979. Technical Innovation, Entrepreneurship and Strategy. *Sloan Management Review* (Spring):19–30.

________. 1982. Managing Strategies Incrementally. *Omega* 10(6):613–27.

Quinn, James Brian, and James A. Mueller. 1963. Transferring Research Results to Operations. *Harvard Business Review*, 41(January-February):49–87.

Roberts, Edward B., and Allen R. Fusfeld. 1983. Staffing the Innovative Technology-Based Organization. *CHEMTECH: The Innovators' Magazine* (May):266–74.

Rogers, Everett M. 1983. *Diffusion of Innovations*. New York: Free Press.

Rubin, Jeffrey Z. and Joel Brockner. 1975. Factors Affecting Entrapment in Waiting Situations: The Rosencrantz and Guildenstern Effect. *Journal of Personality and Social Psychology* 31(June): 1054–63.

Ryssina, V. N., and G. N. Koroleva. 1984. Role Structures and Creative Potential of Working Teams. *R & D Management* 14(4):233–37.

Salancik, Gerald. 1977. Commitment and the Control of Organizational Behavior and Belief. In *New Directions in Organizational Behavior*, ed. B. Staw and G. Salancik. Chicago: St. Clair.

Staw, Barry M. 1982. Counterforces to Change: Escalation and Commitment as Sources of Administrative Inflexibility. In *Change in Organizations*, ed. P. Goodman. San Francisco: Jossey-Bass.

Staw, Barry M., Lance E. Sandelands, and Jane E. Dutton. 1981. Threat-Rigidity Effects in Organizational Behavior: A Multi-level Analysis. *Administrative Science Quarterly* 26(December):501–24.

Teger, A. 1980. *Too Much Invested to Quit*. New York: Pergamon Press.

Thompson, James D. 1967. *Organizations in Action*. New York: McGraw-Hill.

Tichy, Noel, and Charles Fombrun. 1979. Network Analysis in Organizational Settings. *Human Relations* 32(11):923–66.

Tushman, Michael L. 1977. Special Boundary Roles in the Innovation Process. *Administrative Science Quarterly* 22(December):587–605.

________. 1979. Work Characteristics and Solounit Communication Structure: A Contingency Analysis. *Administrative Science Quarterly* 24(March):82–98.

Von Hippel, Eric A. 1977. Has a Customer Already Developed Your Next Product? *Sloan Management Review* (Winter):63–74.

Whetten, D. 1986. Interorganizational Relations. In *Handbook of Organizational Behavior*, ed. J. Lorsch. New York: Prentice-Hall.

Zander, Alvin. 1977. *Groups at Work*. San Francisco: Jossey-Bass.

THE DETERMINANTS OF BARGAINING STRUCTURE:

A CASE STUDY OF AT&T

Marianne Koch, David Lewin, and Donna Sockell

Bargaining structure—the size and scope of the units engaged in collective bargaining (Hendricks and Kahn 1982) and the relationships among these units (Greenberg 1967)—is critical to an understanding of the process and outcomes of collective bargaining and the impact of bargaining on the economy. Recently, the structure of collective bargaining has undergone significant changes in many industries in the United States. Union mergers have facilitated more centralized bargaining in some industries, such as retail foods. In contrast, bargaining in the steel industry has become increasingly decentralized—a trend that is likely to continue in light of the dissolution of the industry's multiemployer bargaining arm, the Steel Companies Coordinating Committee. Bargaining has also become more decentralized in the trucking industry, and many employers and unions in the electrical products, chemical, and auto parts industries have elected to negotiate plant-by-plant labor agreements instead of more centralized agreements. In New York City, seat of the nation's largest municipal government, the formation of a union coalition comprising 80 separate bargaining units, which in 1976 and

Advances in Industrial and Labor Relations, Volume 4, pages 223-251.

ISBN: 0-89232-909-2

1980 negotiated a single master contract (Lewin and McCormick 1981), was only short lived. Some commentators have predicted that, in general, bargaining will become more decentralized in the years ahead.[1]

One major industry in which changes in bargaining structure are bound to occur is telephone service. On 1 January 1984 the American Telephone & Telegraph Company (AT&T) was required to divest itself of its Bell operating companies, the providers of local telephone service. The creation of seven regional holding companies in the wake of divestiture may eventually undermine the centralized structure of collective bargaining, reflected in the nationwide collective agreements negotiated in the industry between 1974 and 1986. If bargaining structure at the former Bell System companies becomes more decentralized, one of the significant consequences may be that regionally uniform wages and benefits will replace nationwide norms of compensation. Moreover, since the unionized portion of the telephone industry encompasses approximately 550,000 employees, changes in compensation outcomes for this industry may have a significant impact on the national economy.

Although some changes in bargaining structure in the industry have already come to pass and others may be imminent, it is less certain what the resulting structures will be. Previous research offers insight into both past and future changes in bargaining structure in the Bell System (and, indeed, other industries). This research has pointed to a number of economic, environmental, and organizational variables likely to account for bargaining structure. The purposes of this paper are (1) to examine how as well as which of these variables appear to have accounted for predivestiture bargaining structures at AT&T; (2) to use the results of that historical analysis to identify key factors likely to predict postdivestiture changes in bargaining structure; and (3) to provide additional insight into the future determination of bargaining structure by examining the concerns and preferences of the parties to collective bargaining in the industry as they prepared to enter the 1986 round of negotiations.[2]

Because of the long history of collective bargaining in the Bell System, the telephone industry provides us with an opportunity to study changes in bargaining structures as they are being decided (under new organizational arrangements). We hope that our analysis will, therefore, provide important insights into the determination of bargaining structure in other industries as well.

PREVIOUS RESEARCH ON BARGAINING STRUCTURE

Bargaining structure encompasses the level at which collective bargaining takes place and the number of groups involved in any one round of negotiations. Most definitions of bargaining structure incorporate four basis elements: (1) the informal work group, made up of employees with common interests and views of the environment, (2) the election district, or "appropriate bargaining unit," as determined by the National Labor Relations Board (NLRB), (3) the negotiations unit, or the groups making up the unit within which collective bargaining actually takes place, and (4) the unit of direct impact or any other negotiations units that are directly affected by the outcome of the particular agreement in question (Weber 1967). The bargaining structures most commonly discussed in the literature are (1) *multiemployer*, in which one contract covers the employees of multiple firms; (2) *single-employer*, in which one union and one employer negotiate a contract—that is, one contract per firm; (3) *multiplant*, in which one contract covers all plants within one company; and (4) *single-plant*, in which a contract is negotiated at each plant within a company.

To illuminate the insights and the focus of the existing research on bargaining structure (and, indeed, to understand the theoretical approach we have taken in this paper), we offer a model of its antecedents and consequences. Bargaining structure is most suitably viewed as an intervening variable, one shaped by certain environmental and organizational forces and one that, in turn, affects certain bargaining outcomes. As Weber put it, bargaining structure is "a vital element in a chain of interdependence linking together the aspirations and demands of the parties, the bargaining process and the external environment" (Weber 1967, 13).

One way to envisage these relationships is presented in Figure 1. As this figure indicates, environmental and organizational factors can be viewed as shaping both the union's and management's preferences for a particular bargaining structure. These factors also affect a party's expectations about its ability to get its opponent to agree to its preferences (that is, its own perceptions of its bargaining power[3])—another factor in forming preferences for different structures. Preferences for one structure over another, however, do not tell the full story of how structure is determined. For when the parties' preferences are dissimilar, the parties must negotiate to achieve an agreement on what the structure of bargaining will be. Finally, once the parties have agreed on a bargaining structure, it then becomes one of a number of contextual variables that ultimately influence outcomes of the collective bargaining process.[4]

It is noteworthy that most research on bargaining structure has focused on the environmental and organizational factors. These variables have been viewed as directly predicting bargaining structure or have been examined in relation to the union's and management's preferences for a bargaining structure. The inspiration for much of this research can probably be attributed to Weber (1967), who qualitatively analyzed 1,733 labor agreements that were in effect in the United States in 1961. Weber contended that bargaining structure is shaped by a number of factors. First, he cited *market factors*. To take wages out of competition, industrial unions want a bargaining structure that is coextensive with the product market. Likewise, the firm, when faced with many competitors, prefers a multiemployer structure "to impose some measure of regulation on market behavior" (Weber 1967, 16).

Second, Weber argued that the *nature of bargaining issues* affects bargaining structure. Wages, for example, have marketwide implications and are often ne-

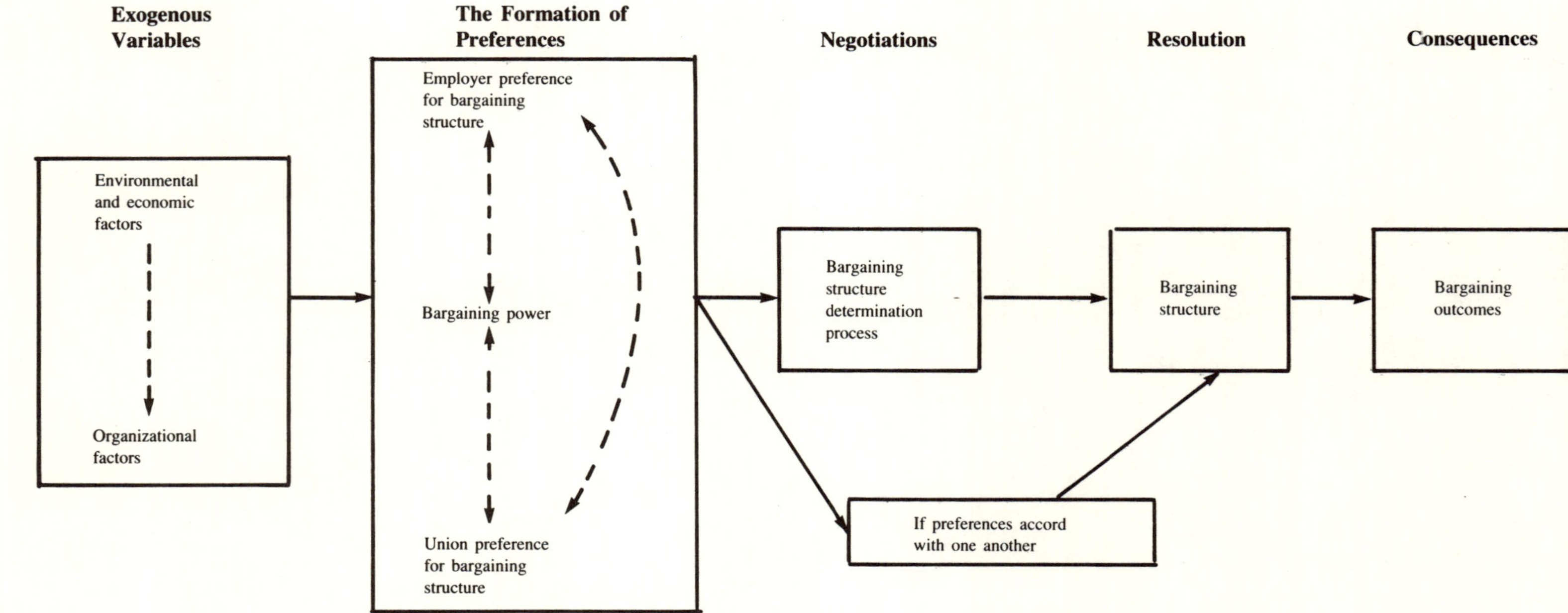

Figure 1. A Dynamic Model of Bargaining Structure

gotiated on a centralized, multiemployer basis, whereas other issues, such as work rules and safety, are local issues negotiated at the plant level.

Third, Weber stated that *representational factors* are also important because the more homogeneous the interests and outlook of members of the bargaining unit, the more centralized the bargaining structure will be.

Fourth, he cited the influence of *governmental policies*, although such policies are exogenous to the bargaining relationship. The legal requirement of exclusive representation and NLRB determination of the election district, for example, have affected the degree of centralization of many bargaining relationships in the United States.

Finally, Weber identified *tactics and power* as further determinants of bargaining structure. "Each party," he wrote, "will seek to devise a structure that will maximize its capacity for inflicting real or expected costs on the other party in the course of the bargaining process" (Weber 1967, 20). For example, management has often responded to unions' use of whipsawing by forming employer associations, while unions have sought their own alliances to counter employers' whipsawing tactics. Weber concluded that in the presence of many small employers, unions prefer a multiemployer bargaining structure, which generates economies of scale in negotiations and takes wages out of competition.

Although Weber's work was pathbreaking, it was based largely on anecdotal evidence (as were most early studies of bargaining structure; see Chamberlain 1961; Bok and Dunlop 1970). Others have relied on quantitative methods to examine bargaining structure and have extended and amplified Weber's arguments. Greenberg (1967), for example, examined the determinants of multiemployer bargaining and pattern bargaining. He hypothesized that employer concentration within an industry would be positively related to pattern following and negatively related to multiemployer bargaining. While industry pressures for labor cost uniformity could be met by either multiemployer bargaining or pattern following, according to Greenberg, those pressures on the firm would be greatest when firm concentration is lowest. Hence, employers in the least concentrated industries should be the most likely to form bargaining associations.

To test these hypotheses, Greenberg classified 52 industries according to bargaining structure by examining case studies, union periodicals, convention proceedings, officers' reports, contract settlement data, and government publications. His findings revealed a strong inverse relationship between firm concentration and pattern following. Among the variables he found to be positively associated with the incidence of multiemployer bargaining *and* pattern following were labor costs, spatial proximity (measured by the percentage of employment accounted for by each industry's top state), union involvement in the hiring process, the extent of unionization, and geographic concentration. The extent of union fragmentation (a proxy for Weber's "representational factors") and pressure from the nonunion sector were not significantly associated with multiemployer bargaining or pattern following. But these two variables, together with product market dispersion, were positively associated with single-plant bargaining.[5]

Viewing wage uniformity as a reflection of the centralization of bargaining structure, Greenberg concluded that the *degree* of uniformity of wage movements is determined by unionization, bargaining concentration (the percentage of employment accounted for by an industry's four largest bargaining units), geographic concentration, and, most important, employer concentration (the percentage of total employment accounted for by the four largest firms in the industry). But the *area* of uniformity is determined by the pressure of competition in the product market.

Deaton and Beaumont (D & B 1980), on the other hand, surveyed 970 British manufacturing firms to identify the determinants of (1) single-employer versus multiemployer bargaining structures, and (2) multiplant versus single-plant bargaining structures within individual firms. They contended that bargaining structure is shaped by the parties' desire to increase bargaining power, facilitate administrative convenience, and protect against competitive disadvantage. To examine these relationships, they identified a number of independent variables, which are listed in Table 1.

Using discriminant analysis, D & B found that regional concentration, union density, and representation by more than one union were significantly and positively correlated with multiemployer bargaining, whereas larger establishments, multiplant firms, foreign-owned firms, industry concentration, and firms with industrial relations directors or personnel departments were associated with single-employer structures. Inclusion of the industry dummy variables in the analysis showed that the paper industry was the most likely to have multiemployer bargaining, while the metal and engineering industries were most likely to have single-employer structures.

Concerning multiplant versus single-plant bargaining, D & B's analysis showed that multiplant bargaining was associated with larger plants, those with industrial relations staff, and those in the food, textile, and clothing industries. Firms with high labor costs and firms in the engineering industry were relatively more likely to bargain on a plant-by-plant basis than other firms.

Hendricks and Kahn (H & K 1982) built upon these studies of the determinants of bargaining structure. As did D & B, H & K explored the choice between multiemployer and single-employer bargaining and between multiplant and single-plant bargaining in the manufacturing sector. H & K, however, introduced to the literature on bargaining structure the notion of inducements or concessions. They pointed out that one party may (legally) induce the other party to bargain voluntarily over structure by offering concessions on other issues—although this behavior is difficult to discern unless one is present at the actual negotiations. Thus, H & K viewed bargaining structure as a distinct bargaining outcome that can be traded against other outcomes. They therefore concluded, "In analyzing the determinants of bargaining structure, one must assess union

Table 1. Deaton and Beaumont's (1980) Hypotheses about the Determinants of Bargaining Structure

	Predicted Relationship with:	
Explanatory Variables	*Multiemployer Bargaining*	*Multiplant Bargaining*
Size of establishment (number of full-time employees)	–	+
Foreign ownership*	–	+
Multiplant firm*	–	NS
Compensation based on employee performance*	–	–
Difficulty of replacing employees	–	–
Union density	?	+
Multiple unions	+	+
Industrial relations staff*	–	+
Labor costs (total wages + salaries/output)	+	–
Employer concentration (% sales by the five largest firms in an industry)	–	NS
Regional concentration (% of industry employment in the two regions with the largest number of employees)	+	NS
Seven industry dummy variables	NS	NS

NS = Not specified.
* = Operationalized as a dichotomous variable.

and management choice functions (their 'demand' for different bargaining structures) as well as each side's ability to enforce its choice (its bargaining power)'' (H & K 1982, 183).

To identify the determinants of bargaining structure, H & K followed much the same reasoning as that in the studies reviewed above. They refined some hypotheses posited by their predecessors by focusing on how environmental and organizational factors might shape the parties' preferences for a particular bargaining structure. They noted, for instance, that although both management and union representatives might prefer multiemployer bargaining because of economies of scale (for example, the savings resulting from not having to replicate preparations for different negotiations), the travel costs for representatives to attend centralized negotiations might alter that preference. H & K also proffered a firm-specific argument for single-employer contracts, namely, such negotiations allow the employer more autonomy and more room for individual strategy in bargaining.

The data base for H & K's study consisted of 3,056 agreements in effect in the United States in 1975. Using probit functions, they estimated the probability of any single contract's being a multiemployer rather than a single-employer contract and the probability of any single-employer contract's being a multiplant rather than a single-plant contract. Their results showed that worker skill and labor intensity were positively associated with multiemployer bargaining, whereas the percentage of workers in the industry who are organized, the number of unions, industry concentration, the size of the firm, and regional variables were significantly and positively associated with single-employer bargaining.

H & K also found that worker skill, industry concentration, firm size, and labor intensity were positively associated with multiplant bargaining, and that product market heterogeneity, industry concentration, and plant size were positively associated with single-employer bargaining agreements. Those findings were "consistent with the hypotheses that unions believe that spillover effects are strongest in these industries, and that firms that have the least resistance to firmwide single-employer agreements in these sectors" (H & K 1982, 194).

In a subsequent paper H & K (1984) developed separate "demand for structure" functions for the firm and the union. From H & K's perspective protection from market fluctuations in labor costs is an incentive for the firm to prefer multiemployer bargaining. As did their predecessors in the literature, H & K viewed the union as preferring multiemployer bargaining in order to take wages out of competition and to raise wage levels (see Weber 1961).

In that paper H & K envisioned the choice of bargaining structure as one made by comparing the expected utilities from single-employer and multiemployer structures, and this choice model included the costs of coalition formation. The authors hypothesized that the greater the relative benefit of a multiemployer bargaining structure, the more likely the structure is to emerge. Firms and unions must then choose between multiemployer and single-employer bargaining structures. The firm seeks to maximize its expected utility, which H & K defined as profits minus bargaining costs per worker, under each structure. Similarly, the union aims to maximize its expected utility, defined as wages minus the costs of negotiations.

Under this model bargaining structure is viewed as an outcome of binary choices by the two parties. Since public policy requires that any multiemployer structure be voluntarily established with the consent of both parties,[6] the presence of a multiemployer agreement is taken as evidence of a joint demand for that structure by the parties. Because a single-employer agreement can mean that either (1) both parties preferred this structure or (2) the parties' preferences were dissimilar (that is, one may have preferred a multiemployer bargaining structure, while the other favored a single-employer structure), the parties' actual choices cannot be inferred in this case. To address this problem, H & K estimated a partially observed bivariate model.

Employing the same data base and explanatory variables as those in their earlier study, H & K (1984) viewed the employer's demand for a multiemployer bargaining structure as a function of industry concentration, product market variables, plant size, and a proxy for the costs to the employer of joining a multiemployer association. The union's demand for multiemployer bargaining was specified as a function of the number of unions in the industry, the percentage of workers in the industry's largest union, the geographic concentration of the firms, and a proxy for the benefits to the union of a multiemployer bargaining structure. H & K's results suggested that the costs of a multiemployer contract (that is, forgone profits to the firm and forgone earnings to the union) make each party less likely to demand this type of bargaining structure than others, other things equal.

A Summary of the Literature

A primary contribution of the previous research on bargaining structure is the notion that certain variables systematically determine the structure of collective bargaining. Table 2 outlines those variables, together with signs indicating the consensus on the direction of their relationships with employer and union preferences for multiemployer bargaining. Note that the effects of some variables are uncertain. This is so because the empirical work conducted to date has neglected to consider these variables or the relevant findings have been conflicting.

As we noted earlier, most of the research on bargaining structure has concentrated on the environmental and organizational factors that account for bargaining structure or for the parties' preferences for different structures. In some of the studies bargaining power is assumed to be reflected in environmental and organizational variables. But few studies have attempted to isolate the effects of bargaining power on the formation of preferences. Moreover, most studies have relied on either industry-level or firm-level data to test models of how bargaining structure is determined. Those studies could not observe a critical phase in the determination of bargaining structure, namely, the actual negotiations process where disagreements over the appropriate structure are resolved.

Our study of bargaining structure at AT&T, on the other hand, has provided us with a glimpse into that black box. More important, however, it has provided an opportunity to attempt to explain the past developments in bargaining structure at AT&T and to predict the future (in the wake of the AT&T divestiture), since we were able to trace the effects on bargaining structure of the different exogenous factors that have been identified by our predecessors.

The research reported here is guided by the model presented in Figure 1 and by the variables listed in Table 2. We recognize the limitations of a case study and particularly the fact that such a study does not permit formal tests of hypotheses. Nonetheless, the AT&T experience offers more than a single case study and also provides an opportunity to explore systematically the potential effects on bargaining structure engendered by deregulation in a major U.S. industry.

Table 2. A Summary of Variables Affecting Preferences for Multiemployer Bargaining Structure, by Direction of Effect

Factors	*Measurement**	*Direction*	
		Union	*Firm*
Economic and Environmental Factors			
Competition in the industry (a, b)	Number of firms	+	+
Labor costs (a–e)	Labor costs/total costs in the industry	−	+
Labor supply (b–e)	Percentage of industry's labor force who are skilled	+	+
Pressure from the nonunion sector (a)	NS	?	−
Number of unions (c–e)	Number of unions representing workers	?	+
Extent of unionization (a, c–e)	Extent of industry unionized	?	?
Product market dispersion (d, e)	Dummy variable for national or local product market	+	−
Geographic concentration of firms (a, c–e)	Percentage of the industry's employment in top state(s)	?	+
Homogeneity of product (b)	NS	?	+
Governmental policy (b)	Pre- or postdivestiture, and policies of the National War Labor Board, for example	?	?
Organizational Factors			
Employer size (b–e)	Number of employees	−	−
Employer concentration (a–e)	Percentage of the industry's employment accounted for by the four largest firms	−	−
Vertical integration (a, b)	NS	?	+
Union size (c, d)	Percentage of the workers in the firm who are represented by a union	?	+

Sources: a = Greenberg (1967), b = Weber (1961), c = Deaton and Beaumont (1980), d = Hendricks and Kahn (1982), e = Hendricks and Kahn (1984).

*This column lists the common way the variable is measured in the literature on bargaining structure.

NS = The approach to measuring this variable has not been explained or specified.

ORGANIZATIONAL INFLUENCES

AT&T and its unions have faced, and still face, an array of structural options in designing their bargaining relationships. Perhaps the best way to illuminate these options is to begin with describing the main features of the union and management organizations that in large part have determined the plethora of those options. Although these descriptions may be more relevant to understanding and predicting the postdivestiture developments in bargaining structure, they will also help place our historical (predivestiture) analysis into perspective.

Management Organization

When collective bargaining began in the telephone industry in 1940, there was one company. AT&T provided all long-distance and almost all local telephone service in the United States (local service companies outside the Bell System accounted for a very small share of the market for local telephone service). Bell System operations were fourfold: (1) long-distance telephone service; (2) 22 Bell operating companies, which provided local telephone service within individual states or several contiguous states; (3) the Western Electric Company, which manufactured telephone equipment for the Bell System; and (4) Bell Laboratories, the company's research center. In essence, therefore, the telephone industry was one company, AT&T, and its only business or "product" was to provide both local and long-distance telephone service.

Because of its monopoly position in the industry, AT&T was regulated by the government. All telephone service prices were subject to the approval of state regulatory commissions, and nationwide long-distance service was subject to oversight by the Federal Communications Commission (FCC). Telephone service was vertically integrated within AT&T, which controlled the production, transmission, and distribution of virtually all telephone service in the United States.

The divestiture of AT&T on 1 January 1984 brought great changes to the telephone industry. Foremost among these was that AT&T, which had operated as one integrated company, became eight separate entities. As shown in Figure 2, the first of these, the "new" AT&T, retains the long-distance telephone service, Western Electric, and Bell Laboratories. The local telephone service portion of the Bell System was severed from AT&T and divided along geographical lines into seven distinct and independent enterprises. These seven new firms, called regional holding companies (RHCs), are Ameritech, Bell Atlantic, BellSouth, NYNEX, Pacific Telesis, Southwestern Bell Corporation, and US West. Each of the RHCs now holds, and in some cases actively manages, two or more of the 22 Bell operating companies (BOCs), that is, the suppliers of local telephone service to the individual states. The BOCs, in turn, operate a varied number of plants and facilities.

Although local telephone service within the RHCs is still regulated by the government, the new AT&T and the RHCs are free to develop new businesses and compete in industries other than telephone service, which are unregulated. For example, immediately following divestiture AT&T moved swiftly into the information industry and began to produce computers.

In light of these changes in the structure of AT&T since divestiture, four levels

Figure 2. The Bell System after Divestiture

American Telephone & Telegraph Company
- AT&T Communications, Inc. (long-distance telephone service)
- AT&T Technologies
    - AT&T Technologies, Inc. (Western Electric)
    - Bell Laboratories
    - AT&T Information Systems
    - AT&T International

*Local Telephone Service**

1. *Ameritech*
    - Illinois Bell
    - Indiana Bell
    - Missouri Bell
    - Ohio Bell
    - Wisconsin Bell
2. *Bell Atlantic*
    - Bell of Pennsylvania
    - New Jersey Bell
    - Diamond State Tel. (Delaware)
    - Chesapeake & Potomac Tel. (D.C., Maryland, Virginia, and West Virginia)
3. *BellSouth*
    - South Central Bell
    - Southern Bell
4. *NYNEX*
    - New England Telephone
    - New York Telephone
5. *Pacific Telesis*
    - Pacific Telephone
    - Nevada Bell
6. *Southwestern Bell*
    - Southwestern Bell
7. *US West*
    - Pacific Northwest Bell
    - Mountain Bell
    - Northwestern Bell

*The seven regional holding companies have all developed additional businesses beyond local telephone service.

of the management organization are conceptually relevant for collective bargaining: the national, the RHC, the BOC, and the plant or facility levels. Figure 3 identifies the potential management structures for bargaining at each of the four levels, and also shows the resulting number of contracts that would be negotiated in each case. Obviously, several levels can coexist; for instance, within the same round of negotiations some of the RHCs could bargain together at a *national level*, while others could bargain separately at the *RHC level*, and still others could engage in *BOC* or even *plant-level* negotiations. Furthermore, different issues could be taken up at different levels of bargaining.

Union Organization

The majority of employees in the telephone industry are organized by two labor unions: the CWA, which represents approximately 465,000 workers or about 85 percent of the organized work force in the industry, and the International Brotherhood of Electrical Workers (IBEW), which has about 90,000 members in the industry.[7] Although the two unions have always bargained separately, the CWA has led the way in negotiations and established contract patterns that the IBEW and other, smaller unions followed. Because of its size and dominant role

Figure 3. Potential Management Structures for Bargaining after Divestiture

Bargaining Organization Level	*Potential Structure*	*Number of Contracts with Each Union*[a]
1. National	AT&T and all RHCs together (multiemployer)	1
	AT&T separately and all RHCs together (single- and multiemployer)	2
2. Regional operating company	AT&T and each RHC separately (single-employer)	8
3. Bell operating company	Each BOC separately (single-plant)	23
4. Plant and facility	Each plant separately (single-plant), single contract	>23[b]
	Intraplant/intrafacility contracts, more than one contract per plant/facility	>23[c]

[a]This assumes that unions negotiate individually. They could bargain together, however, in a multiunion bargaining structure.

[b]The exact number of contracts depends on the number of plants or facilities within each BOC. We were unable to gather this information.

[c]In some facilities multiple bargaining units are represented by the CWA, and the CWA negotiates separate contracts on each unit's behalf (for example, one contract for production and maintenance employees and another for clerical employees).

in collective bargaining in the industry, we focus exclusively on the CWA in this paper.

The CWA's organizational structure has reflected the management organization in the industry, both before and after divestiture. After divestiture the union reorganized and consolidated its thirteen district offices into ten new ones. Historically, the district offices had been responsible for developing initial bargaining agendas as well as for negotiating supplemental, local agreements to deal with issues not taken up in national bargaining. The district organizations were not directly affected by divestiture—they were not mandated to change by the divestiture agreement per se—but the creation of the RHCs spurred their reorganization. Likewise, where there had been one Bell System Bargaining Council before divestiture, the CWA established two such councils after divestiture: one for AT&T, and the other for the RHCs (Straw 1985, 449).

METHODOLOGY

We pursue two methods in examining the determinants of bargaining structure in the telephone industry. First, using historical evidence, we examine how the generally recognized determinants of bargaining structure (listed in Table 2) help in explaining the bargaining structure adopted and changes in that structure over time. We gathered information for this analysis from several secondary sources: Brooks (1977), Craypo (1986), Shooshan (1984), and Straw (1985). We divide this history into two periods—1940 to 1974 and 1974 to 1986—reflecting the discrete change to nationwide bargaining in 1974.

Second, we conducted 31 semistructured interviews with union and management officials who were a party to the 1986 negotiations in the industry—the first bargaining round after divestiture. In those interviews, conducted in person and by telephone, we asked about how the bargaining structure was (or would be) determined and what the interviewees preferred that structure to be.[8] The interviewees included officials of the CWA (both at headquarters in Washington, D.C., and in district offices), AT&T, all seven of the RHCs, nine of the BOCs, and Bell Communications Research (the R&D division shared by the seven RHCs). The company officials interviewed included executive vice presidents, vice presidents for human resources, vice presidents for labor relations, staff researchers, and policy analysts.

The purpose of those interviews was twofold: first, to discover if there are factors that seem to matter to negotiators in choosing a particular bargaining structure (especially factors not yet identified by researchers); and second, to gain insight into the bargaining structure determination process while the structure was being shaped by the parties.

Finally, drawing on both the historical information and the interviews, we will attempt to sort out the implications of the first postdivestiture bargaining round for bargaining structure in the future, particularly as might be predicted from the existing theory.

THE EVOLUTION OF BARGAINING STRUCTURE AT AT&T

1940: Collective Bargaining Begins

On 18 July 1940 the New York Telephone Company and an affiliate of the National Federation of Telephone Workers (NFTW), which later became CWA, signed the first collective bargaining agreement in the history of AT&T. At that time the company faced little competition in the telephone industry, and the existing competition was fading. In other words, employer concentration in the industry was high. In fact, by 1934 AT&T had already come to own 80 percent of all telephones in the United States, and one BOC or another offered local telephone service to residents of virtually every major city in the nation (Shooshan 1984, 12). AT&T's monopoly power was enormous—its exclusive long-distance telephone service linked the United States from coast to coast.

Labor costs constituted a high proportion of total costs in 1940. Because all long-distance calls and about one-half of all local telephone calls required operator assistance, AT&T's demand for telephone operators had grown rapidly since the introduction of the telephone in the late 1870s. Moreover, the labor supply to

AT&T was relatively elastic.[9] Telephone operators, who made up the majority of AT&T's work force, were recruited from the ranks of young, unmarried women; and the job required little in the way of training, making the operators easily replaceable.

The market dispersion of telephone service was high in 1940, which was consistent with AT&T's goal of providing universal telephone service. To meet this goal, the size of the firm also had to increase. The geographic concentration of firms was very low in 1940; competing firms were few, and in any one municipality typically only one other local telephone company provided service. In addition, governmental regulation restricted AT&T to the provision of telephone service; that is, there was substantial product homogeneity.

Vertical integration within AT&T grew throughout the twentieth century. By virtue of owning Western Electric, the manufacturer of all equipment used in the Bell System, and Bell Laboratories, the research and development arm of AT&T, the firm increasingly controlled the means of developing, manufacturing, and marketing telephone products and services. In fact, it was the extent of this vertical integration that precipitated the federal government's antitrust suit against AT&T and Western Electric in the 1950s.

Spurred by passage of the National Labor Relations Act in 1935, 45 independent unions were representing workers at AT&T by 1940, although as noted above, none had succeeded in obtaining a labor contract with the company until July of that year. Each of these unions was small, and although 42 of them had joined together in 1939 to form the NFTW, the federation functioned as an umbrella organization and had no negotiating authority of its own. Various NFTW affiliates believed their individual interests were sufficiently unique to warrant single-unit bargaining. But NFTW leaders believed that bargaining policy and objectives were increasingly being determined by AT&T, not the individual BOCs. Consequently, some of those leaders sought—but did not achieve—centralized bargaining with the Bell System's corporatewide, or parent, organization. Later, internal disputes over bargaining structure led to the disaffiliation of some NFTW unions. As a result, NFTW membership declined by more than 4,000 workers from 1943 to 1944 (Brooks 1977, 77), although the unaffiliated and disaffiliated unions retained their membership. Overall, however, the percentage of AT&T workers who were unionized was increasing at that time. Thus, as the size of the nonunion sector was decreasing, it posed less of a threat to the bargaining relationship at AT&T.

What does this early history of AT&T's bargaining relationships suggest about union and management preferences for bargaining structure? Based on the existing theory, as summarized in Table 3, the low competition, high labor costs, large employer size, and high employer concentration in the industry in 1940 would seem to suggest that the union would have preferred decentralized bargaining. At the same time, however, the elastic supply of labor and high market dispersion would suggest a union preference for centralized bargaining. If we assign equal weights to these determinants of bargaining structure, we would predict a union preference for decentralized, or BOC-level, bargaining in the Bell System in 1940.[10]

Using this same approach to predict management preferences, however, we are unable to identify a clear management preference for centralized or decentralized bargaining. The presence of high labor costs, an elastic labor supply, little pressure from the nonunion sector, a large number of unions, considerable homogeneity of the firm's products, and substantial vertical integration in the Bell System would imply that management would have preferred centralized bargaining. But those six factors may have been offset by six others: the low competition, high product market dispersion, low geographic concentration of firms, large employer size, high employer concentration, and small union size would all suggest a management preference for decentralized, or BOC-level, bargaining. This rough analysis might tempt us to conclude that management would have been indifferent about the structure of bargaining in 1940. Yet if we build upon Hendricks and Kahn's (1982) logic that structure is a distinct bargaining outcome and recognize that management may have lacked a preference about structure, we can conclude that AT&T might have conceded to the unions' preference in return for union concessions on another outcome. In this sense, although AT&T management might not have clearly favored decentralized over centralized bargaining in 1940, it might have gained a strategic or bargaining power advantage by conceding to it.

Table 3. Bargaining Structure Determinants in 1940: Employer and Union Preferences for Bargaining Structure

	Preference	
Determinant (Measure of)	*Union*	*Firm*
Competition (low)	D	D
Labor costs (high)	D	C
Labor supply (large)	C	C
Pressure from nonunion sector (low)	?	C
Number of unions (high)	?	C
Product market dispersion (high)	C	D
Geographic concentration of firms (low)	?	D
Homogeneity of product (high)	?	C
Employer size (large)	D	D
Employer concentration (high)	D	D
Vertical integration (high)	?	C
Union size (small)	?	D
Totals	4Ds, 2Cs	6Ds, 6Cs

D = Preference for decentralized bargaining structure.
C = Preference for centralized bargaining structure.
? = Uncertain impact on the formation of preferences, based on the research to date.

In fact, collective bargaining in the Bell System initially was quite decentralized. According to Brooks (1977), AT&T bargained with the NFTW affiliates when pressured to do so, but it did not formally recognize the NFTW. And as noted above, many NFTW member unions preferred not to bargain centrally, given the diversity of interests and conditions that prevailed among the BOCs.

In short, when collective bargaining was new to the Bell System, labor had a clear preference for a decentralized bargaining structure, and that preference prevailed in the face of management ''indifference'' about bargaining structure.

1940–74: The Bargaining Structure Changes

As noted earlier, governmental policy is one of the variables that is hypothesized to affect bargaining structure. During World War II federal policy toward collective bargaining favored pattern setting and pattern following. The National War Labor Board, through its efforts to prevent and resolve labor-management disputes, succeeded in increasing the centralization of bargaining structures in all industries, including the telephone industry. The ''Little Steel'' formula of 1941 set the pattern for wage increases in manufacturing, including those of telephone workers. Indeed, to a large extent bargaining structure (and bargaining outcomes) in the telephone industry during this period were determined primarily by governmental policy rather than other factors.

In the immediate postwar years there were significant changes in the factors theory suggests account for bargaining structure preferences, especially from a union perspective. Factors likely to affect bargaining power also changed over those years. In particular, union membership grew dramatically. At that time telephone industry wages were low relative to those in other industries, which brought about scattered strikes throughout the industry. Joseph Beirne, the first president of the NFTW, recognized the discontent among the majority of the NFTW's member unions and proposed uniting all the local strikes that occurred in 1946 under the banner of one national strike against AT&T. To accomplish this, he called for the Long Lines Telephone Workers union (LLTW)—an NFTW affiliate—to lead the way in bargaining. The LLTW was obliged to bargain with AT&T, not with the BOCs, because it represented long-distance telephone workers throughout the country. According to Beirne's plan, if the LLTW were to conduct a strike, no other NFTW union would cross its picket lines and the Bell System would effectively be shut down nationwide. Beirne told the press that a national telephone strike could be averted by AT&T's considering all negotiations at one table and by applying any resulting pattern to all individual cases (Brooks 1977, 107).

Two crucial factors worked to enhance the union's bargaining power in making that threat. First, any disruption of telephone service was viewed as a threat to national security. In fact, U.S. Secretary of Labor Lewis Schwellenbach made preparations for a government takeover of the Bell System in case of a strike, and he personally took part in settling the dispute between AT&T and the NFTW

(Brooks 1977). Second, labor costs had continued to constitute a substantial proportion of total costs; more than 40 percent of all local telephone calls and all long-distance calls still required operator assistance. Consequently, the LLTW agreement reached by the AT&T vice president and the UFTW president (with the aid of the labor secretary) set terms that were then extended to all of the BOCs.

One result of that ''national''—or, more precisely, strongly pattern-setting—agreement of 1946 was the birth of the Communications Workers of America (CWA), which comprised most of the NFTW affiliates. Some NFTW affiliates split away from the CWA because of a dispute over whether the new union should affiliate with the AFL or with the CIO. This splinter group, which called itself the Telephone Workers' Organizing Committee (TWOC), included the LLTW and became affiliated with the CIO in 1947. At that time the CWA, which decided not to join either the AFL or the CIO, represented fewer than 150,000 telephone workers, or about 42 percent of all Bell System employees. The TWOC represented about 15 percent of Bell System employees; the International Brotherhood of Electrical Workers (IBEW-AFL), about 4 percent; and independent unions the remaining 39 percent. The size of the unions representing Bell System employees had grown substantially, and the vast majority of employees in the system were organized. But with the formation of the CWA, the number of unions representing Bell's workers declined dramatically. Moreover, the union's consolidation of AT&T employees became even more substantial when the CWA absorbed the TWOC in 1949.

Despite the move to centralized bargaining at AT&T in 1946 and the increases in the union's bargaining power over the previous years, management was determined to press for separate contracts for each of the BOCs in 1947 and 1948. The company held to that position throughout the 1947 bargaining round, even during a nationwide strike called on 8 April 1947. Although the strike lasted for several months, it failed to result in national-level bargaining in that round of negotiations; individual contracts between the CWA (and other Bell System unions) and the BOCs were subsequently negotiated. Union fractionalization may have contributed to AT&T's ability to withstand the strike by permitting the firm to engage in whipsawing. Further evidence of management's bargaining power lay in the telephone wage settlements of 1947, which were lower than the settlements reached in the auto and steel industries, and in the variation in contract termination dates among the BOCs, which mitigated the possibility of any future national strike.

During the 1950s collective bargaining continued on a decentralized basis between the BOCs and the CWA (and other unions). The CWA renewed its efforts to achieve national bargaining, but AT&T successfully opposed them. At that time and through the 1960s, many of the economic and environmental factors affecting bargaining structure were shifting. For example, automation in the telephone industry reduced the labor intensiveness of AT&T's operations. Many fewer operators were needed as the percentage of dial telephones increased from 75 in 1950 to 97 in 1960. Concomitantly, the number of telephone operators employed by the Bell System peaked at roughly 163,000 in 1950 and declined thereafter to 139,000 in 1960. Product market dispersion also increased as the number of telephones rose from 35,000,000 in 1950 to more than 60,000,000 ten years later. At the same time, firm size and concentration grew, and AT&T revenues and profits rose to unprecedented levels.

The CWA continued to press for national bargaining during the 1960s, but it was not until 1971 that it achieved some success. In that year the union negotiated its first contract that covered the employees of two BOCs—a contract that subsequently set the pattern for the rest of the Bell System. That event marked an important, though limited, departure from strict BOC-level bargaining. Also in 1971, at the conclusion of a seven-month strike in New York State, AT&T appeared to agree as a matter of policy to include agency-shop provisions in its labor agreements with the CWA. This arrangement provided the CWA, which then represented 85 percent of Bell System union members, with financial security, and also presaged the movement toward national level bargaining in 1974.

Beginning in that year national master agreements covering wages and fringe benefits were inaugurated. Those agreements were supplemented by separate ones at the BOC level covering hours, management rights, discipline, contracting out, work force adjustments, and grievances.[11] What the CWA had long contended was always the case behind closed doors at AT&T—namely, AT&T effectively oversaw collective bargaining in all the BOCs—became official policy and practice in 1974, at least as far as the critical, economic issues were concerned.

Interestingly, the theory would not have predicted this result. As Table 4 illustrates, seven of the twelve theoretical determinants would suggest that management preferred decentralized bargaining in 1974. Those seven are competition, low labor costs, few unions, high product market dispersion, low geographic concentration of firms, large employer size, and high employer concentration.

From the union's perspective, while low labor costs, an elastic labor supply, and high product market dispersion would suggest a preference for centralized bargaining, these factors might have been offset by low competition, large employer size, and high employer concentration. On this basis we might conclude that the union was indifferent about bargaining structure in the early 1970s. If this was the case, the union may have conceded (or agreed) to management's wishes for decentralized bargaining.

We must ask, therefore, why the theory would not have predicted the centralization of telephone industry bargaining in 1974. Perhaps the most obvious explanation is that the existing theory does not tell us which determinants are the most powerful predictors of bargaining structure; that is, our scheme of weighting each factor equally was inappropriate. It may be that certain factors contribute

Table 4. Bargaining Structure Determinants in 1974: Employer and Union Preferences for Bargaining Structure

Determinant (Measure of)	Preference: Union	Preference: Firm
Competition (low)	D	D
Labor costs (low)	C	D
Labor supply (large)	C	C
Pressure from nonunion sector (low)	?	C
Number of unions (low)	?	D
Product market dispersion (high)	C	D
Geographic concentration of firms (low)	?	D
Homogeneity of product (high)	?	C
Employer size (large)	D	D
Employer concentration (high)	D	D
Vertical integration (high)	?	C
Union size (large)	?	C
Totals	3Ds, 3Cs	7Ds, 5Cs

D = Preference for decentralized bargaining structure.
C = Preference for centralized bargaining structure.
? = Uncertain impact on the formation of preferences, based on the research to date.

disproportionately both to the strength of a party's preference for a given structure (that is, the party's willingness to make greater trade-offs to achieve its goal) and to its ability to gain concessions on structure from its opponent (that is, the party's bargaining power). For example, labor costs and union size were the only variables that changed markedly from 1940 to 1974. Both factors were likely to place the union in an advantageous bargaining position and both would imply a union preference for centralized bargaining.

1974–86: The Bell System Breaks Up

Collective bargaining in the Bell System took place at the national level from 1974 through the break up of the system on 1 January 1984. During this period there were important changes in many of the variables that theory suggests determine bargaining structure.

For example, for the first time in many decades AT&T faced competition in the long-distance telephone service market, specifically from Microwave Communications Incorporated (MCI), which began operating in 1975 and posed the largest initial threat to AT&T. But this was only the beginning of competition for AT&T in this market, and the number of long-distance service providers proliferated during the late 1970s and early 1980s. Labor costs at AT&T were higher than those at the new companies, which not only were unorganized but also had much higher capital-labor ratios than AT&T. Thus, pressure from the nonunion sector increased. In addition, with capital intensive means of providing telephone service expanding rapidly, labor supply became a less important determinant of bargaining structure. The number of unions continued to be small, with the CWA representing about 85 percent of nonsupervisory personnel at AT&T. Moreover, although the union remained large, postdivestiture layoffs have reduced its membership.

Employer size and concentration decreased after divestiture, as AT&T became eight separate companies. Vertical integration declined, as new suppliers of telephone equipment and new providers of long-distance service entered the market. Indeed, the presence of competitors in the telephone industry prompted AT&T's negotiators in the 1983 bargaining round to compare AT&T's pay and benefits rates with those of the new firms. Previously, the negotiators had made comparisons with compensation rates in other industries to demonstrate the relatively favorable position of Bell System workers (Bahr 1985; Hendricks 1987).

The last labor agreement to be negotiated before divestiture was signed in mid-1983 and expired in mid-1986. The government's consent decree, which set the terms of the divestiture, stipulated that the contract executed in 1983 continue in force until its expiration date. Thus, in 1986 the CWA had to negotiate new contracts with at least eight firms: AT&T and the seven ROCs.

The Historical Analysis: An Afterword

Given the limitations of case studies and of analyses based on secondary data, any conclusions we might draw about the usefulness of bargaining structure theory and the determination of bargaining structure at AT&T must be modest. Although the theory helped explain the bargaining structure that prevailed at AT&T in 1940, it left much to be desired in explaining the end of decentralized bargaining in 1974. This inadequacy may be attributable to the lack of consensus on the direction of influences on union preferences; that is, we do not know which structure unions will prefer when faced with pressure from the nonunion sector, union fragmentation, firm or geographic concentration, product homogeneity, vertical integration, union size, and the extent of unionization. In addition, accurate predictions may be obscured because we do not know a priori which factors are likely to be more significant determinants of preferences, for which party, and under what circumstances. In the final analysis, we were unable to evaluate many of the relationships between the theoretical determinants and the bargaining structure in the industry, because many of those variables did not vary sufficiently over the time period examined. For example, competition, employer size and concentration, product market dispersion, geographic concentration of firms, pressure from the nonunion sector, and product homogeneity all changed little over much of the period reviewed here.

Our historical analysis does seem to suggest, however, that the union's bargaining power was an important predictor of bargaining structure, particularly if we use union size and labor costs as proxies for such power. As anticipated, when labor costs were high, the union preferred decentralized bargaining so that it might take advantage of the opportunity to whipsaw the various Bell System employers. Likewise, as the CWA grew, so did its bargaining power and its ability to bring about national bargaining.

Another factor that seemed to play an important role in the evolution of bargaining structure at AT&T was public policy. During World War II and again in 1946, government officials viewed a strike by the long-distance telephone workers as a threat to national security and therefore sought to influence or override the bargaining structure preferences of both labor and management. Public policy has, of course, also been critical in the 1980s, since it was the federal government that mandated the breakup of the Bell System.

BARGAINING STRUCTURE ALTERNATIVES AFTER DIVESTITURE

The existing theories on the determination of bargaining structure and the results of our historical analysis can also be used to gain insight into the likely consequences of the AT&T divestiture for bargaining structure. To accomplish this, we apply the model of bargaining structure depicted in Figure 1 to AT&T-CWA bargaining after the 1984 divestiture. The model initially calls attention to environmental and organizational factors influencing bargaining structure. Among the key environmental influences in the telephone industry is the legal or regulatory environment that has mandated divestiture. Divestiture, in turn, has influenced the organizational configuration of both AT&T and the CWA. More specifically, the CWA has had to move its sights from the national level to the eight separate companies and alter its organizational structure accordingly. But divestiture has also had effects on other variables which we view as exogenous in the determination of bargaining structure, and these variables, in turn, affect management and union officials' preferences for bargaining structure. In this section, we will examine how preferences have been influenced by divestiture specifically and by changes in other environmental factors and what these preferences suggest about the structure of collective bargaining in the industry in the future.

As noted earlier, under divestiture AT&T continues to provide long-distance telephone service, still in a largely regulated environment, through a new entity, AT&T Communications, Inc. Another new entity, AT&T Technologies, comprises Western Electric, Bell Laboratories, and AT&T International—all of which are now eligible to compete for business with other firms in unregulated markets (see Figure 2). Before the 1986 labor negotiations, most members of

AT&T management and CWA officials expressed strong preferences for centralized or corporate-level bargaining. The parties' prebargaining proposals as well as our interview data indicated that neither party gave serious consideration to any other form of bargaining structure, such as bargaining on a decentralized or subsidiary-by-subsidiary basis. Thus, it is not surprising that on 26 June 1986 the parties reached agreement on an AT&T-wide collective bargaining contract (although not without a corporatewide strike, which lasted 26 days).

Nevertheless, it is questionable whether such centralized, corporatewide negotiations will persist in future bargaining rounds. Facing increasing economic competition from nonunion firms and firms with relatively lower labor costs, and decreasing firm concentration, geographic concentration, (new, localized competitors are forcing AT&T to pay attention to smaller markets), and vertical integration, AT&T's subsidiaries are likely to encounter more specialized product and labor markets. This, in turn, should increase management preferences for decentralized bargaining as AT&T seeks to take advantage of price and wage differences in those markets. Put differently, imminent changes in key environmental variables are likely to reshape the parties' (but especially management's) preferences for bargaining structure at AT&T, with the likely result that bargaining will become more decentralized. This possibility is consistent with our historical analysis of the variables that shaped bargaining structure in the Bell System during the predivestiture period.

The most profound realignment of bargaining structure, however, is likely to occur at the RHC level. Although the RHCs continue to operate the local telephone companies, they are now permitted to develop new, unregulated businesses. And so they have; some of their new ventures are listed in Figure 4. The new businesses and their related subsidiaries are already involving the RHCs in product and labor markets in which economic competition is greater and union concentration is lower than in the telephone business. Such forces are very likely to create pressures for more decentralized collective bargaining at the RHC level.

On the other hand, one countervailing force to decentralization is the CWA. The CWA initially sought to convince the seven RHCs to bargain as a single, national association and thus preserve a semblance of the national Bell System labor agreements that had prevailed between 1974 and mid-1986. The RHC managements not only opposed such national or coalition bargaining, but also expressed concern that they might not be able to compete with the new, nonunion telephone firms if they did bargain as a group. On a more pragmatic level and as a second countervailing force, four RHCs—BellSouth, NYNEX, Southwestern Bell, and Pacific Telesis—agreed in principle to bargain with the CWA at the regional level in 1986. Ameritech, Bell Atlantic, and US West, however, continued to insist that bargaining proceed at the operating company level, that is, more or less as it had before centralization in 1974.

Our interviews with BellSouth managers indicated that the company's intention to bargain on behalf of its two operating companies was motivated by a de-

Figure 4. Initial Diversification Efforts of the Regional Holding Companies

Regional Holding Company	*New Ventures*
1. Ameritech	Cellular radio and paging services, overseas consulting, cable television installation, teleconferencing equipment marketing, home and office security systems
2. Bell Atlantic	Cable television installation and transmission, DTS systems, office equipment financing, computer repair services, paging services
3. BellSouth	Computer software marketing
4. NYNEX	Communications terminal and office equipment, retail computer marketing
5. Pacific Telesis	Overseas ventures, real estate development and management, office equipment marketing
6. Southwestern Bell	Local packet-switching systems, national marketing of cordless phones
7. US West	Real estate development and management, national communications consulting services, cellular radio network building in Gulf of Mexico, office equipment financing

Sources: Wilke (1984, 112); Bolter (1984, 15–16).

sire to avoid whipsawing and by a belief that the two companies faced very similar product and labor market conditions. BellSouth managers also indicated that the RHC shared with its two operating companies comparable views about political relationships with the CWA. In the case of NYNEX, management officials reported that the company intended to replicate the dual-level bargaining that had evolved before divestiture, with a master agreement covering wages and benefits negotiated at the RHC level and supplemental agreements covering noneconomic items negotiated at the operating company level. The NYNEX managers did not explain the basis for that approach, however.

At Pacific Telesis the interviewees indicated that the larger of its two operating companies, Pacific Telephone, would bargain with the CWA on behalf of both operating companies. The RHC's management would not take part in the actual negotiations but would provide research and negotiating strategy support to Pacific Telephone. Thus, bargaining at Pacific Telesis was conducted on a modified regional basis. Southwestern Bell has but one operating company, so that regional bargaining occurred in effect in this RHC. Nevertheless, our interview data suggested that operating company management rather than RHC management at Southwestern Bell was to have had responsibility for negotiations with the CWA in 1986.

Among the arguments for decentralized bargaining offered by managers of Ameritech, Bell Atlantic, and US West were that (1) each constituent operating company is its own profit center possessing independent financial responsibility and, thus, should negotiate agreements specifying its own labor costs; (2) major differences in labor supplies and community wage rates exist among the operating companies; and (3) decentralized bargaining would reduce the bargaining power of the CWA. Recognize further that Ameritech, Bell Atlantic, and US West together encompass fifteen operating companies, whereas BellSouth, NYNEX, Southwestern Bell, and Pacific Telesis together hold only seven BOCs. Hence, concerns over BOC profitability, differences in labor supplies and community wage rates, and, most fundamentally, bargaining power are arguably more central to the former than to the latter group of RHCs—which helps to explain the different preferences for bargaining structure that prevailed among the managements of these two groups of regional companies.

The CWA, in contrast, remains committed to centralized bargaining. As noted earlier, the CWA has responded to divestiture and to the organizational realignment of the former Bell System by consolidating and reducing the number of its regional offices from thirteen to ten. Seven of those offices correspond to the seven RHCs, and separate regional offices will be maintained in Pennsylvania, New Jersey, and Delaware. Our interview data indicated that the union's internal organizational realignment was initiated by Morton Bahr, the CWA's new president, whose predecessor had retired early to give Bahr extra time to prepare for the 1986 negotiations. This top union leadership change was subsequently accompanied by changes in the leadership of several of the CWA's regional organizations. Together the union's organizational consolidation and leadership changes might be construed as undergirding the union's expressed preference for centralized, multiemployer bargaining with the RHCs.

Despite these recent changes in the CWA, there are several good reasons to doubt that the union will be able to reestablish centralized bargaining in the future. Many of the RHCs and some of the operating companies are reducing their work forces, technology continues to be substituted for certain types of labor, and the supply of labor to the RHCs and the BOCs continues to be relatively large and elastic. Moreover, and despite the fact that the RHC's operating companies continue to operate in regulated environments, the freedom granted to the RHCs to develop new, unregulated businesses has contributed to a stronger competitive thrust in their strategic labor relations policies and practices. Thus, in the case of Ameritech, Bell Atlantic, and US West, in particular, management preferences for decentralized bargaining, clearly reflected in our interview data, are likely to be pursued vigorously and may begin to appear in the other companies as well.

Indeed, the development of new, specialized businesses suggests that plant- and facility-level negotiations may take place in future bargaining rounds. Although management may prefer that its new businesses remain unorganized, it is precisely the development of new businesses that provides the CWA (and other unions) with opportunities to organize greater numbers of employees. If the new computing, office equipment, real estate, cable television, and home security system businesses developed by the RHCs do become unionized, the bargaining units are likely to be smaller and narrower than those now prevailing in the telephone companies. Moreover, the managements of the new businesses and of their parent RHCs can be expected to press for plant- and facility-level bargaining units and labor agreements if their employees become unionized. It is the new RHC ventures that are most likely to face highly competitive product and labor market conditions, substitutable products and services, numerous producers and sellers, and, in particular, strong pressure from nonunion firms. These factors seem to point to growing management preferences for highly decentralized bargaining—perhaps even among those RHCs whose managements still prefer centralized regional bargaining for their constituent telephone companies.

That the CWA may have organizing opportunities in the newly developed RHC businesses also raises major questions about the union's postdivestiture strategies. On the one hand, CWA leaders, who demonstrated in 1986 that they are willing to strike if necessary, may press vigorously for centralized bargaining in all of the RHCs. On the other hand, the CWA may focus its energies on organizing employees in the new businesses, and, in a sense, trade off their demand for centralized bargaining for an expanded membership base. Moreover, membership expansion may be a particularly appealing strategy to the CWA in light of the substantial work force reductions at AT&T and at somc of the RIICs and in light of the possible additional employment reductions that could occur if centralized bargaining were to result in relatively high or rigid wage levels. Thus, although the short-term strategy of the CWA may be to concentrate on achieving centralized bargaining with the RHCs, a better strategy in the long term may be to emphasize employment and membership objectives over bargaining structure and wage objectives. Put differently, over the longer term union and management preferences may converge; the parties may come to share certain objectives (more than they now realize) in adapting to the new postdivestiture industrial relations environment.

SUMMARY AND CONCLUSIONS

Questions of the determinants of bargaining structure and of changes in structure are significant for both the process and outcomes of collective bargaining. In the case of AT&T, for example, future changes in bargaining structure may yield variations in pay, benefits, and noneconomic outcomes as well as in the economic preferences of the RHCs and the operating companies. Although these are questions for future research, we have attempted in this study to use the existing research to help understand historical developments in the bargaining structure of AT&T and the CWA and to consider the likely consequences of divestiture for bargaining structure. In this process we have gained insight into the usefulness—

and limitations—of bargaining structure theory. And although we have not formally tested any hypotheses about the relationship between environmental or organizational variables and bargaining structure, our analysis suggests several conclusions.

First, key factors that appeared to account for the predivestiture bargaining structure at AT&T included public policy, labor costs, union size, and bargaining power. These factors are likely to continue to influence postdivestiture structures, but other factors, including increasing competition in the industry, pressure from the nonunion sector, product or service diversification (heterogeneity), and decreasing employer concentration, are likely to play a critical role in the future. The changing nature of these environmental variables suggests that bargaining structure at AT&T, the RHCs, and the operating companies will become increasingly decentralized.

Second, and from a research perspective, the previous studies have provided us with valuable insights into the factors likely to play a role in determining bargaining structure. Yet this literature has left us with many unanswered questions. We still do not know which environmental factors are the most salient or most important predictors of each party's preferences about structure or under what circumstances certain variables emerge as more critical than others. Future research will also have to sort out which factors play a greater role in the formation of union preferences and which play a greater role in management preferences. We also do not know which factors are likely to account for a party's ability to get its opponent to accept its proposal for the structure of bargaining (that is, its bargaining power).

Finally, and on a related note, we have found that previous research has not examined a critical phase in the determination of bargaining structure—namely, how the parties resolve their conflicting preferences. In this paper we attempted to learn more about that negotiations process by interviewing both union and management officials as they prepared to enter the first round of negotiations in the wake of divestiture. Unfortunately, the usefulness of the interviews in providing us a glimpse into that black box was only limited. Some interviewees were reticent, concerned that they might disclose facts that would jeopardize their strategy in negotiations, while others gave ambiguous answers. Nonetheless, our interviews provided partial support for hypothesizing the importance of labor costs and bargaining power in determining bargaining structure—factors that were salient in our historical analysis. In this sense these interviews have provided us with some insight into which variables may be among the critical determinants of bargaining structure in the telephone industry. To generalize these findings to other industries, however, will require that similar research—examining bargaining structure decisions as they are being made and at the level at which bargaining actually occurs—be conducted in other settings.

ACKNOWLEDGMENTS

We are grateful to Morton Bahr, Karen Boroff, John Thomas Delaney, Jeff Keefe, James W. Kuhn, and two referees for comments on an earlier version of this paper.

NOTES

1. See, for example, Fisher (1987).

2. The original version of this paper was written before the 1986 round of negotiations between the Communication Workers of America and the companies formerly part of the Bell System. Where possible, we have updated the information (but not the predictions) contained in that version to reflect the actual negotiations.

3. Using Chamberlain and Kuhn's (1986, 168–98) definition, we may view bargaining power as simply the configuration of environmental and organization factors that makes one party more or less able to get its opponent to agree to its preferences for bargaining structure (see also Kochan 1980, 306–16).

4. We do not mean to suggest here that the relationship between bargaining structure and outcomes is either simple or direct (for a theoretical treatment of how structure might affect outcomes, see, for example, Sockell 1983).

5. Greenberg (1967) did not specify how to measure several of the variables he operationalized. These variables included pressure from the nonunion sector and product market dispersion.

6. See *Kroger Co.*, 148 NLRB 569 (1964).

7. These figures reflect employment and union membership estimates for June 1986 (Straw 1985, 447; *Communications Week* 1986). It is noteworthy that employment levels and union membership have declined since that time. In addition, other, smaller unions had also represented some industry employees. Those small, independent unions formed a coalition called the Telecommunications International Union but were later absorbed by the CWA. For additional data on current employment and union membership in the industry, see Hendricks (1987).

8. A copy of the interview format is available from the authors.

9. In early research on bargaining structure a ''large'' or an ''available'' supply of workers was cited as a determinant of bargaining structure; the term elasticity was not used.

10. Although a summation of factors is a simplistic approach to determining a party's preferences for bargaining structure, previous research has not provided us with an appropriate weighting scheme.

11. Just before divestiture, the CWA had 34 labor contracts with entities embraced by the Bell System (*Daily Labor Report* 1983, 1).

REFERENCES

Bahr, Morton. 1985. Deregulation and Labor Costs in Telecommunications. Presentation at the Columbia University Seminar on Telecommunications, 23 May.

Bok, Derek, and John Dunlop. 1970. *Labor and the American Community*. New York: Simon & Schuster.

Bolter, Walter G. 1984. Restructuring in Telecommunications and Regulatory Adjustment. *Public Utilities Fortnightly*, 5 July, 15–22.

Brooks, Thomas R. 1977. *Communications Workers of America*. New York: Mason/Charter.

Chamberlain, Neil W. 1961. Determinants of Collective Bargaining Structure. In *The Structure of Collective Bargaining*, ed. Arnold R. Weber, 3–19. New York: Free Press of Glencoe.

Chamberlain, Neil W., and James W. Kuhn. 1986. *Collective Bargaining*, 3d ed. New York: McGraw-Hill.

Collective Bargaining in the Telephone Industry. 1980. Report no. 607. Washington, DC: Bureau of Labor Statistics, U.S. Department of Labor, June.

Communications Week. 1986. 10 February, p. C2.

Craypo, Charles. 1986. Bargaining in a Restructured Environment in Telecommunications. In *Proceedings of the 1986 Spring Meeting, April 17–18, 1986, Atlanta, Georgia*, ed. Barbara D. Dennis, 563–75. Madison, WI: Industrial Relations Research Association.

Daily Labor Report. 1983. No. 232, 1 December, p. 1.

Deaton, D. R., and P. B. Beaumont. 1980. The Determinants of Bargaining Structure: Some Large Scale Survey Evidence for Britain. *British Journal of Industrial Relations* 18(July):201–16.

Fisher, Ben. 1987. Changes in Labor Relations: Their Impact on Union Structure; Discussion. In *Proceedings of the Thirty-Ninth Annual Meeting, December 28–30, 1986, New Orleans*, ed. Barbara D. Dennis, 137–40. Madison, WI: Industrial Relations Research Association.

Greenberg, David H. 1967. The Structure of Collective Bargaining and Some of Its Determinants. In *Proceedings of the Nineteenth Annual Winter Meeting, December 28–29, 1966, San Francisco*, ed. Gerald G. Somers, 343–53. Madison, WI: IRRA.

Hendricks, Wallace E. 1987. Telecommunications. In *Collective Bargaining in American Industry*, ed. David B. Lipsky and Clifford B. Donn, chap. 5. Lexington, MA: Lexington Books, forthcoming.

Hendricks, Wallace E., and Lawrence M. Kahn. 1982. The Determinants of Bargaining Structure in U.S. Manufacturing Industries. *Industrial and Labor Relations Review* 35(January):181–95.

_________. 1984. The Demand for Labor Market Structure: An Economic Approach. *Journal of Labor Economics* 2(3):412–38.

Kochan, Thomas A. 1980. *Collective Bargaining and Industrial Relations*. Homewood, IL: Richard D. Irwin.

Lewin, David, and Mary McCormick. 1981. Coalition Bargaining in Municipal Government: The New York City Experience. *Industrial and Labor Relations Review* 34(January):175–90.

Mills, Daniel Quinn. 1978. *Labor Management Relations*. New York: McGraw-Hill.

Shooshan, Harry M. 1984. The Bell Breakup. *Disconnecting Bell: The Impact of the AT&T Divestiture*, ed. Harry M. Shooshan, 8–22. New York: Pergamon Press.

Sockell, Donna R. 1983. Toward a Theory of the Union's Role in an Enterprise. In *Advances in Industrial and Labor Relations*, vol. 1, ed. David B. Lipsky and Joel M. Douglas, 221–82. Greenwich, CT: JAI Press.

Straw, Ronnie J. 1985. The Effect of Divestiture on Collective Bargaining. In *Proceedings of the Thirty-Seventh Annual Meeting, December 28–30, 1984, Dallas*, ed. Barbara D. Dennis, 447–54. Madison, WI: Industrial Relations Research Association.

Weber, Arnold R., ed. 1961. *The Structure of Collective Bargaining*. New York: Free Press of Glencoe.

Weber, Arnold R. 1967. Stability and Change in the Structure of Collective Bargaining. In *Challenges to Collective Bargaining*, ed. Lloyd Ulman, 13–36. Englewood Cliffs, NJ: Prentice-Hall.

Wilke, John. 1984. Surprise! Ma Bell's Babies Are Stealing the Show. *Business Week*, 3 December, 104–16.

Research Annuals and Monographs in Series in ECONOMICS

Research Annuals

Advances in Accounting
Edited by Bill N. Schwartz, *School of Business Administration, Temple University*

Advances in Accounting Information Systems
Edited by Gary Grudnitski, *Graduate School of Business, The University of Texas at Austin*

Advances in Applied Micro-Economics
Edited by V. Kerry Smith, *Department of Economics, Vanderbilt University*

Advances in Business Marketing
Edited by Arch G. Woodside, *A.B. Freeman School, Tulane University*

Advances in Distribution Channel Research
Edited by Gary L. Frazier, *University of Southern California*

Advances in Econometrics
Edited by George F. Rhodes, Jr., *Department of Economics, Colorado State University* and Thomas Fomby, *Department of Economics, Southern Methodist University*

Advances in Financial Planning and Forecasting
Edited by Cheng F. Lee, *Department of Finance, University of Illinois*

Advances in Futures and Options Research
Edited by Frank J. Fabozzi, Visiting Professor, *Sloan School of Management, Massachusetts Institute of Technology*

Advances in Health Economics and Health Services Research
Edited by Richard M. Scheffler, *School of Public Health, University of California,* Berkeley and Louis F. Rossiter, *Department of Health Administration, Medical College of Virginia, Virginia Commonwealth University*

Advances in Industrial and Labor Relations
Edited by David B. Lipsky, *New York State School of Industrial and Labor Relations, Cornell University*

Advances in International Accounting
Edited by Kenneth S. Most, *College of Business Administration, Florida International University*

Advances in International Marketing
Edited by S. Tamer Cavusgill, *Center for Business and Economic Research, Bradley University*

Advances in Marketing and Public Policy
Edited by Paul N. Bloom, *Department of Marketing, University of North Carolina*

Advances in Mathematical Programming and Financial Planning
Edited by Kenneth D. Lawrence, *Department of Industrial and Systems Engineering, Rutgers University,* John B. Guerard, Jr. *Department of Finance, Lehigh University* and Gary R. Reeves, *Department of Management Science, University of South Carolina*

Advances in Nonprofit Marketing
Edited by Russell W. Belk, *Department of Marketing, University of Utah*

Advances in Public Interest Accounting
Edited by Marilyn Neimark, *Baruch College, The City University of New York*

Advances in Statistical Analysis and Statistical Computing
Edited by Roberto S. Mariano, *Department of Economics, University of Pennsylvania*

Research in the History of Economic Thought and Methodology
Edited by Warren J. Samuels, *Department of Economics, Michigan State University*

Research in Transportation Economics
Edited by Andrew F. Daughty, *Department of Economics, The University of Iowa* and Clifford Winston, *The Brookings Institute*

Research in Urban Economics
Edited by Robert Ebel, Director, *Economics and Finance, Corporate Competitive Strategies, Northwestern Bell, Minneapolis*

Research on Technological Innovation, Management and Policy
Edited by Richard S. Rosenbloom, *Graduate School of Business Administration, Harvard University*

Monographs in Series and Treatises

Contemporary Studies in Applied Behavioral Science
Edited by Louis A. Zurcher, *School of Social Work, The University of Texas at Austin*

Contemporary Studies in Economic and Financial Analysis
Edited by Edward I. Altman and Ingo Walter, *Graduate School of Business Administration, New York University*

Contemporary Studies in Energy Analysis and Policy
Edited by Noel D. Uri, *Division of Antitrust, Bureau of Economics Federal Trade Commission*

Decision Research: A Series of Monographs
Edited by Howard Thomas, *Department of Business Administration, University of Illinois*

Handbook of Behavioral Economics
Edited by Benjamin Gilad and Stanley Kaish, *Department of Management Studies, Rutgers University, Newark*

Industrial Development and the Social Fabric
Edited by John P. McKay, *Department of History, University of Illinois*

Political Economy and Public Policy
Edited by William Breit, *Department of Economics, Trinity University* and Kenneth G. Elzinga, *Department of Economics, University of Virginia*

Please inquire for detailed subject catalog